D1201113

HEBREWS

PREACHING THE WORD
Edited by R. Kent Hughes

Genesis | R. Kent Hughes

Exodus | Philip Graham Ryken

Leviticus | Kenneth A. Mathews

Numbers | Iain M. Duguid

Deuteronomy | Ajith Fernando

Joshua | David Jackman

Judges and Ruth | Barry G. Webb

1 Samuel | John Woodhouse

2 Samuel | John Woodhouse

1 Kings | John Woodhouse

Job | Christopher Ash

Psalms, vol. 1 | James Johnston

Proverbs | Raymond C. Ortlund Jr.

Ecclesiastes | Philip Graham Ryken

Song of Solomon | Douglas Sean O'Donnell

Isaiah | Raymond C. Ortlund Jr.

Jeremiah and Lamentations | Philip Graham Ryken

Daniel | Rodney D. Stortz

Matthew | Douglas Sean O'Donnell

Mark | R. Kent Hughes

Luke | R. Kent Hughes

John | R. Kent Hughes

Acts | R. Kent Hughes

Romans | R. Kent Hughes

1 Corinthians | Stephen T. Um

2 Corinthians | R. Kent Hughes

Galatians | Todd Wilson

Ephesians | R. Kent Hughes

Philippians, Colossians, and Philemon | R. Kent Hughes

1–2 Thessalonians | James H. Grant Jr.

1–2 Timothy and Titus | R. Kent Hughes and Bryan Chapell

Hebrews | R. Kent Hughes

James | R. Kent Hughes

1–2 Peter and Jude | David R. Helm

1–3 John | David L. Allen

Revelation | James M. Hamilton Jr.

The Sermon on the Mount | R. Kent Hughes

(((PREACHING *the* WORD)))

HEBREWS

An ANCHOR *for the* SOUL

R. KENT HUGHES

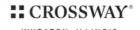
CROSSWAY®

WHEATON, ILLINOIS

Hebrews

Copyright © 2015 by R. Kent Hughes

Published by Crossway
      1300 Crescent Street
      Wheaton, Illinois 60187

Previously published as two volumes copyright © 1993 by R. Kent Hughes

Cover design: Jon McGrath, Simplicated Studio

Cover image: Adam Greene, illustrator

First printing 2015

Printed in the United States of America

Hardcover ISBN: 978-1-4335-3842-1
ePub ISBN: 978-1-4335-3845-2
PDF ISBN: 978-1-4335-3843-8
Mobipocket ISBN: 978-1-4335-3844-5

Library of Congress Cataloging-in-Publication Data

Hughes, R. Kent., 1942-
Hebrews : an anchor for the soul / R. Kent Hughes.
    pages cm. — (Preaching the word)
   Previously published as two volumes. All emphasis in Scripture quotations have been added by the author.
   Includes bibliographical references and index.
   ISBN 978-1-4335-3842-1 (hc)
1. Bible. Hebrews—Commentaries. 2. Messiah—Biblical teaching. 3. Son of God—Biblical teaching. I. Title.
BS2775.53.H83   2015
227'.8707—dc23   2014038204

Crossway is a publishing ministry of Good News Publishers.

VP		29	28	27	26	25	24	23	22	21	20	19
14	13	12	11	10	9	8	7	6	5	4	3	2

To
Dr. Charles Lee Feinberg

We have this as a sure and steadfast anchor of the soul, a hope that enters into the inner place behind the curtain, where Jesus has gone as a forerunner on our behalf, having become a high priest forever after the order of Melchizedek.

HEBREWS 6:19, 20

Contents

Acknowledgments

I must express appreciation to my wife, Barbara, for her "Hebrews 11" faith in God—and resultant faith in my calling; also to Mrs. Sharon Fritz, secretary *extraordinaire*, for her patience and care in typing the manuscripts for these studies and for making the inscrutable intelligible; to Herbert Carlburg for his cheerful, weekly proofreading and for his unfailing precision and attention to detail; to Rev. Jeff Buikema, pastor of Covenant Presbyterian Church, LaCrosse, Wisconsin, for his reading of the manuscript and helpful suggestions; and to Mr. Ted Griffin, managing editor at Crossway, for his painstaking editing. Lastly, special thanks to Dr. Lane Dennis, president of Crossway, for his vision for this undertaking and consistent encouragement.

A Word to Those Who Preach the Word

There are times when I am preaching that I have especially sensed the pleasure of God. I usually become aware of it through the unnatural silence. The ever-present coughing ceases and the pews stop creaking, bringing an almost physical quiet to the sanctuary—through which my words sail like arrows. I experience a heightened eloquence, so that the cadence and volume of my voice intensify the truth I am preaching.

There is nothing quite like it—the Holy Spirit filling one's sails, the sense of his pleasure, and the awareness that something is happening among one's hearers. This experience is, of course, not unique, for thousands of preachers have similar experiences, even greater ones.

What has happened when this takes place? How do we account for this sense of his smile? The answer for me has come from the ancient rhetorical categories of *logos*, *ethos*, and *pathos*.

The first reason for his smile is the *logos*—in terms of preaching, God's Word. This means that as we stand before God's people to proclaim his Word, we have done our homework. We have exegeted the passage, mined the significance of its words in their context, and applied sound hermeneutical principles in interpreting the text so that we understand what its words meant to its hearers. And it means that we have labored long until we can express in a sentence what the theme of the text is—so that our outline springs from the text. Then our preparation will be such that as we preach, we will not be preaching our own thoughts about God's Word, but God's actual Word, his *logos*. This is fundamental to pleasing him in preaching.

The second element in knowing God's smile in preaching is *ethos*—what you are as a person. There is a danger endemic to preaching, which is having your hands and heart cauterized by holy things. Phillips Brooks illustrated it by the analogy of a train conductor who comes to believe that he has been to the places he announces because of his long and loud heralding of them. And that is why Brooks insisted that preaching must be "the bringing of truth through personality." Though we can never *perfectly* embody the truth we preach, we must be subject to it, long for it, and make it as much a part of our ethos as possible. As the Puritan William Ames said, "Next to the Scriptures, nothing makes a sermon more to pierce, than when it comes out of the inward affection of the heart without any affectation." When a preacher's ethos backs up his *logos*, there will be the pleasure of God.

Last, there is *pathos*—personal passion and conviction. David Hume, the Scottish philosopher and skeptic, was once challenged as he was seen going to hear George Whitefield preach: "I thought you do not believe in the gospel." Hume replied, "I don't, but *he does*." Just so! When a preacher believes what he preaches, there will be passion. And this belief and requisite passion will know the smile of God.

The pleasure of God is a matter of *logos* (the Word), *ethos* (what you are), and *pathos* (your passion). As you *preach the Word* may you experience his smile—the Holy Spirit in your sails!

R. Kent Hughes
Wheaton, Illinois

Long ago, at many times and in many ways, God spoke to our fathers by the prophets, but in these last days he has spoken to us by his Son.

1:1, 2a

1

The Eloquence of God

HEBREWS 1:1, 2a

C. S. LEWIS MEMORABLY PORTRAYED the growing Christian's experience of an ever-enlarging Christ in his Chronicles of Narnia. Lucy, caught up in her spiritual quest, saw the lion Aslan—Christ—shining white and huge in the moonlight. In a burst of emotion Lucy rushed to him, burying her face in the rich silkiness of his mane, whereupon the great beast rolled over on his side so that Lucy fell, half-sitting and half-lying between his front paws. He bent forward and touched her nose with his tongue. His warm breath was all around her. She gazed up into the large, wise face.

> "Welcome, child," he said.
> "Aslan," said Lucy, "you're bigger."
> "That is because you are older, little one," answered he.
> "Not because you are?"
> "I am not. But every year you grow, you will find me bigger."[1]

Expanding souls encounter an expanding Christ! And this is why I am particularly enthused about this study volume on the book of Hebrews, for that epistle has a double dose of growth-producing power—first, because it presents the greatness of Christ as no other New Testament writing does, and, second, because it repeatedly demands a response from the reader. Seriously considered, Hebrews will make us grow and find a bigger Christ.[2]

No New Testament book has had more background research than Hebrews, and none has spawned a greater diversity of opinion. There is, of course, broad agreement about several of the most important things. Virtually all agree that the grand theme of this epistle is the supremacy and finality of Christ.

15

A consensus also exists regarding the general identity of the recipients: they were a group of Jewish Christians who had never seen Jesus in person, yet had believed. Their conversion had brought them hardship and persecution with the result that some had slipped back into Judaism. And thus the purpose for writing was to encourage them to not fall away, but to press on (cf. 2:1ff.; 3:12ff.; 6:4ff.; 10:26ff.; and 12:15ff.).[3]

There is also universal agreement, first expressed by Origen, that "Only God knows certainly" who wrote this letter. There is also agreement that the author, whoever he was, was a magnificent stylist with an immense vocabulary and a vast knowledge of the Greek Old Testament.

So there is general agreement as to the theme, the purpose, the spiritual status of the recipients, and the anonymity and ability of the author. But from here the mystery darkens, for no scholar has yet proven the exact destination or occasion of the letter—though many contemporary scholars tentatively propose that the letter was written to a small house-church of beleaguered Jewish Christians living in Rome in the mid-sixties before the destruction of the Jerusalem Temple.

The respected New Testament authority William Lane, employing this thesis, has proposed a brilliant historical reconstruction that I think accords with the internal pastoral concern of the letter and makes it come alive.[4] Hebrews, he notes, was written to a group of Jewish Christians whose world was falling apart. Their Italian locus is most probable because in the closing paragraph of Hebrews the author conveys the greetings of several Italian Christians who were with him (13:24), thus supporting the idea that the harried little church was on Italian soil—very likely in or around Rome.

Their Christianity had not been a worldly advantage. Rather, it set them up for persecution and the loss of property and privilege, and now could possibly even cost them their lives.

We know they had already paid a price for their initial commitment to Christ. As the writer recalls in 10:32–34:

> But recall the former days when, after you were enlightened, you endured a hard struggle with sufferings, sometimes being publicly exposed to reproach and affliction, and sometimes being partners with those so treated. For you had compassion on those in prison, and you joyfully accepted the plundering of your property, since you knew that you yourselves had a better possession and an abiding one.

This description of their earlier sufferings fits well into the picture of the hardships that came to Jewish Christians under Claudius in AD 49. Suetonius'

Life of the Deified Claudius records that "There were riots in the Jewish quarter at the instigation of Chrestus. As a result, Claudius expelled the Jews from Rome" (25.4). "Chrestus," historians believe, is a reference to Christ, and the riots and expulsion occurred when Jewish Christians were banished from the synagogue by the Jewish establishment.

Now, as the author of Hebrews writes, fifteen years have gone by since the Claudian persecution, and a new persecution looms. No one has been killed yet, but 12:4 raises the possibility that martyrdom may soon come—"In your struggle against sin you have *not yet* resisted to the point of shedding your blood."

Lane proposes here that the circumstances accord well with the Neronian persecution that would come with the great fire of Rome in AD 64. The historian Tacitus records that Nero made the Christians scapegoats to remove suspicion from himself (*Annals of Rome* 15:44). Lane concludes, "In the year AD 64 martyrdom became an aspect of the Christian experience in Rome. There were several house-churches in the city, and the group addressed in Hebrews had not yet been affected by the emperor's actions. But the threat of death and arrest was real."[5]

The writer of Hebrews was writing to admonish and encourage his friends, a small group of Jewish Christians who were scared stiff! Some had begun to avoid contact with outsiders. Some had even withdrawn from the worshiping community altogether (10:25). The author feared there might be those who, if arrested, would succumb to the conditions of release—a public denial of Christ (6:6; 10:29). The tiny house-church was asking some hard questions: Did God know what was going on? If so, how could this be happening to them? Did he care? Only God could protect them, but where was he? Why did he not answer? Why the silence of God?

The letter arrived, and word was sent out. The congregation gathered. Perhaps no more than fifteen or twenty were seated or standing around the house. All were quiet. The reader began what has been called "the most sonorous piece of Greek in the whole New Testament":[6] "Long ago, at many times and in many ways, God spoke to our fathers by the prophets, but in these last days he has spoken to us by his Son" (vv. 1, 2a). Through these magnificent words the beleaguered church was brought face-to-face with the God who speaks—the eloquence of God. God spoke in the past, and he speaks in the present in his Son. And this eloquence, the ultimate eloquence of the final word in God's Son, would bring them comfort in the midst of life's troubles.

God's Eloquence in the Past

Cosmic Eloquence

Even before the prophets of old, the cosmos was filled with God's eloquence. One summer one of my associate pastors and I were walking home together on a particularly clear night. We looked at the North Star, the Big Dipper, the Pleiades. My fellow-minister identified the Dog Star Canis Major (Sirius), the brightest star in both hemispheres. Then we began to joke about how all this happened "by chance." The vastness and precision of our cosmos declares the necessity of a magnificent God!

The argument from order is overwhelming. If I put ten pennies in my pocket and number them one to ten, then put my hand back in my pocket, my chances of pulling out the number one penny would be one in ten. If I place the number one penny back in my pocket and mix all the pennies again, the chances of pulling out penny number two would be one in a hundred. The chances of repeating the same procedure and coming up with penny number three would be one in a thousand. To do so with all of them (one through ten in order) would be one in ten billion! Noting the order and design of our universe, Kepler—the founder of modern astronomy, discoverer of the "Three Planetary Laws of Motion," and originator of the term *satellite*—said, "The undevout astronomer is mad." David sang:

> The heavens declare the glory of God,
>   and the sky above proclaims his handiwork.
> Day to day pours out speech,
>   and night to night reveals knowledge.
> There is no speech, nor are there words,
>   whose voice is not heard.
> Their voice goes out through all the earth,
>   and their words to the end of the world. (Psalm 19:1–4)

The cosmic eloquence of God is deafening, but many will not hear it. And even those who hear, hear partially. As Job said, "Behold, these are but the outskirts of his ways, and how small a whisper do we hear of him! But the thunder of his power who can understand?" (Job 26:14). The eloquence of God is always there for the believer willing to hear it. So often those who have heard it best have heard it when life was darkest—perhaps while persecuted or in prison. Bunyan, Rutherford, Bonhoeffer, Solzhenitsyn, Colson—

> all looked through the bars
> and saw the stars.

Prophetic Eloquence

God's people have always had more than the eloquence of the heavens, for they have had the prophets. "Long ago," says the writer, "at many times and in many ways, God spoke to our fathers by the prophets" (v. 1)—literally, "in many parts and many ways." The emphasis here is on the grand diversity of God's speech in the Old Testament. God utilized great devices to instruct his prophets. God spoke to Moses at Sinai in thunder and lightning and with the voice of a trumpet. He whispered to Elijah at Horeb in "a still small voice" (1 Kings 19:12 KJV). Ezekiel was informed by visions and Daniel through dreams. God appeared to Abram in human form and to Jacob as an angel. God declared himself by Law, by warning, by exhortation, by type, by parable.

And when God's seers prophesied, they utilized nearly every method to communicate their message. Amos gave direct oracles from God. Malachi used questions and answers. Ezekiel performed bizarre symbolic acts. Haggai preached sermons. And Zechariah employed mysterious signs.

The significance of this immensely creative and variegated communication is that it dramatically demonstrated God's loving desire to communicate with his people. It was never hackneyed, never boring, never inscrutable, never irrelevant. It was always adequate for the time. It was always progressive, revealing more of God and his ways. It was always in continuity with the previous words of God.

Through God's cosmic and prophetic eloquence men and women rose to live life on the highest plane. Abraham achieved the faith to offer his own son. Moses withstood Pharaoh through mighty miracles. David slew Goliath. Daniel achieved and maintained massive integrity in Babylon. But in all of this (its adequacy, its progressiveness, its continuity, its power), God's eloquence was never complete. As grand as it was, it was nevertheless fragmentary and lacking.

God's Eloquence in the Present

But no more! For in Christ came an astonishing eloquence, the ultimate speech of God—"but in these last days he has spoken to us by his Son" (v. 2a). Jesus is God's final word. The Greek here is simply *in huios*, "in Son"—emphasizing that the person of his Son contains everything. He is the ultimate medium of communication. God has spoken to us in his Son!

An unbeliever was once musing about what he considered to be the impossibility of knowing God. His thinking was that as Creator, God created us in the same way as a dramatist creates his characters and that the gap was so vast between God and man that men could no more know God than Hamlet could know his author-creator Shakespeare. But as the man thought further, he realized that his analogy suggested just the opposite: for Shakespeare as creator could make it possible. Extending the analogy, Shakespeare could, in principle, write himself into the play and dialogue with Hamlet. The "Shakespeare" would of course be both Shakespeare and one of Shakespeare's creatures. It is an imperfect analogy, but God the Father did write himself into life in his Son, making the ultimate communication.[7]

This amazing eloquence of God is substantially the same as that described in the chain of thought in John 1, which begins, "In the beginning was the Word, and the Word was with God, and the Word was God" (John 1:1). Jesus here, of course, is "the Word," and though much more can be said about this term because of its rich history in Greek literature, its main significance here is that *Christ has always sought to reveal himself.* An interpretative paraphrase could well read, "In the beginning was the Communication." From eternity, Christ as the Word has always longed to communicate himself.

Through the Incarnation God wrote himself into life—"The Word became flesh and dwelt among us" (John 1:14). He put on skin, so to speak. He made it possible for us to know him as we never before could. God in the flesh was the height of communication.

> God hath spoken by His prophets,
> Spoken his unchanging Word;
> Brightness of the Father's glory,
> With the Father ever one;
> Spoken by the Word Incarnate,
> God of God ere time began,
> Light of Light, to earth descending,
> Man, revealing God to man.

What is the result of all this eloquence? We meet God the Father! "No one has ever seen God," says John, but "the only God, who is at the Father's side, he has made him known" (John 1:18). Jesus exegeted God. That is some communication! The astounding eloquence of God!

Ingmar Bergman, the celebrated Swedish filmmaker, recounts that one day while he was listening to Stravinsky, he had a vision of a nineteenth-century cathedral. In the vision Bergman found himself wandering about a great building and finally coming before a picture of Christ. Realizing its importance, Bergman said to the picture, "Speak to me! I will not leave this cathedral until you speak to me!" But of course the picture did not speak. That same year he produced *The Silence*, a film about characters who despair of ever finding God.

Bergman's problem was, he was looking at the wrong picture. Rather, he needed to listen to the massive eloquence of the Christ of Scripture—"in these last days he has spoken to us by his Son." He needed to see the eloquence of Christ's character and speech and actions and, above all, the sublime eloquence of the cross, for there he speaks salvation.

The apparent silence of God in the face of imminent persecution that troubled that tiny house-church two millennia ago provides a touch-point with today, for Ingmar Bergman well-represents our troubled world that bristles at the imagined silence of God. God has eloquently spoken to us in *creation* and through his *prophets* in the Old Testament and now, most of all, through the awesome eloquence of his *Son*.

The healing method of the writer of Hebrews, as we shall see, is to lift the Son higher and higher and higher. He is sure that the eloquence of Christ's person will help his readers meet the challenges ahead. For him, holding up Christ is the most practical thing on earth. Indeed, Jesus, understood and exalted, eloquently informs every area of life.

There are only two kinds of people who hear God's Word: those who are not yet his children, and those who are. True, some are nearer than others on the road to Christ. But nevertheless there are only these two categories.

To those who are not yet true children of God, I give this challenge: Read one of the Gospels through, sincerely praying the essence of Bergman's prayer over it as you go: "Speak to me! Please speak to me!" I also challenge them to carefully study the book of Hebrews, for in it they will find life-changing thoughts that are unique to the New Testament.

I challenge those who are God's children with the thought that Hebrews is a practical book. They may be beleaguered, perhaps even wondering if they can continue on with life. Perhaps they are looking for a manual that will help them handle stress. Hebrews is the "manual" they are looking for, because the essential answer is in the supremacy and finality of Christ.

In the midst of the battle, may this be our lot:

"Lord . . . you're bigger."
"That is because you've grown my child."
"Not because you are?"
"I am not. But every year you grow, you will find me bigger."

For a time Lucy was so happy that she did not want to speak. But God has spoken. Oh, the eloquence of God!

But in these last days he has spoken to us by his Son, whom he appointed the heir of all things, through whom also he created the world. He is the radiance of the glory of God and the exact imprint of his nature, and he upholds the universe by the word of his power. After making purification for sins, he sat down at the right hand of the Majesty on high.

1:2, 3

2

The Supremacy of Christ

HEBREWS 1:2, 3

WHEN CHARLES SPURGEON opened this text to his congregation on the Lord's Day evening of May 21, 1882, he gloriously announced, "I have nothing to do to-night but to preach Jesus Christ."[1] From there he went on to show that he was following an august and hallowed train. Luke tells us that the very first Christians "kept right on teaching and *preaching Jesus* as the Christ" (Acts 5:42 NASB). When Philip went down to Samaria, he "*proclaimed to them the Christ*" (Acts 8:5). And when he climbed into the Ethiopian's chariot "he *preached Jesus* to him" (Acts 8:35 NASB). Immediately after Paul was converted, "he began to *proclaim Jesus* in the synagogues" (Acts 9:20 NASB). Regarding his preaching, Paul told the Corinthian church that he had resolved to know nothing "except Jesus Christ and him crucified" (1 Corinthians 2:2).

So as we take up our study of Hebrews 1:2, 3 we joyfully affirm that the best thing we can do is to preach Jesus Christ! This great text will allow nothing else. The Church has multiple needs, but this is the subject for which it has the greatest need. It is the theme in which the Father rejoices (Matthew 3:17). Moreover the explicit mission of the Spirit is to make Christ known (John 14:26; 16:13–15). Jesus said, "He [the Spirit] will take what is mine and declare it to you" (John 16:15). So because our text oozes with Christ, we can expect the pleasure and blessing of the Holy Trinity to be upon it as we prayerfully consider it phrase by phrase.

The grand theme of these verses is the supremacy of Christ as God's final word. Christ is held up like a great jewel to the sunlight of God's revelation, and as the light courses through it, seven facets flash with gleaming brilliance. We have given these facets names so they can be easily followed and assimilated. Christ is: *Inheritor, Creator, Sustainer, Radiator, Representor, Purifier, Ruler.*

Cosmic Supremacy

Inheritor

It is natural for the writer to first emphasize that Christ the Son is Inheritor because sons are naturally heirs. Thus the text naturally flows from sonship to heirship: "but in these last days he has spoken to us by his Son, whom he appointed the heir of all things" (v. 2a). The writer, in stating here that Jesus is "the heir of all things," is also consciously identifying him with the Lord's "Anointed" and "Son" in Psalm 2 to whom he says, "Ask of me, and I will make the nations your heritage, and the ends of the earth your possession" (Psalm 2:8). (We know that this verse is in mind because Psalm 2:7 is quoted as referring to Christ in verse 5 of our text.) Thus Jesus is specifically said to be heir to Planet Earth and its peoples. But the promise also embraces the universe and the world to come (cf. 2:5–9).[2]

The immense scope of Christ's inheritance comes from his dual functions as Creator and Redeemer. As Creator of the universe, he is its natural heir. Paul makes dramatic reference to this in Colossians 1:16b: "all things were created . . . for him." Or as some have even more graphically translated it: "All things were created . . . *toward* him."[3] Everything in the universe has its purpose and destiny in the heir, Jesus Christ. Romans 11:36 has the same idea as it tells us that everything in the work of creation is *to* him—"to him are all things." Scripture is clear: everything in the physical universe is *for* him and *to* him and will consummate *in* him as heir of a new creation.

But in addition to his natural inheritance as Creator, as Redeemer he has also earned a vast inheritance of souls renewed through his atoning work of reconciliation on the cross. We are his inheritance! This is a mind-boggling truth, to say the least. It is so stupendous that Paul prayed that the church would have its eyes opened to "the riches of his [that is, Christ's] glorious inheritance in the saints" (Ephesians 1:18).[4] The apostle was praying that his readers would understand how highly they are valued in Christ. Think of it—Jesus is heir to all the heavens and numberless worlds, but *we* are his treasures. The redeemed are worth more than the universe. We ought to be delirious with this truth.

But there is even more! In the letter to the Romans we are called "heirs— heirs of God and fellow heirs with Christ" (Romans 8:17). Because Christ and Christ alone is heir to all things, and we live in him, we are heirs of all. "All things are yours," says Paul, "whether . . . the world or life or death or the present or the future—all are yours, and you are Christ's, and Christ is God's" (1 Corinthians 3:21–23).

Creator

Having introduced the Son's superiority as Inheritor of all things, the thought naturally moves to his supremacy as the Creator of all: "through whom also he created the world" (v. 2b). The word used for "world" (*aionas*—literally "ages") is a marvelously elastic and dynamic term that fits remarkably well with what we now know of our expanding universe. Bishop Westcott defines *aionas* here as "The sum of the 'periods of time' including all that is manifested in and through them . . . an order which exists through time developed in successive stages."[5] Jesus was the agent in whom and through whom the entire universe of space and time was created.

Cambridge physicist Stephen Hawking, who has been called "the most brilliant theoretical physicist since Einstein," says in his best-selling *A Brief History of Time* that our galaxy is an average-sized spiral galaxy that looks to other galaxies like a swirl in a pastry roll and that it is over 100,000 light-years across[6]—about six hundred trillion miles. He says, "We now know that our galaxy is only one of some hundred thousand million that can be seen using modern telescopes, each galaxy itself containing some hundred thousand million stars."[7] It is commonly held that the average distance between these hundred thousand million galaxies (each six hundred trillion miles across and containing one hundred thousand million stars) is three million light-years! On top of that, the work of Edwin Hubble, based on the Doppler effect, has shown that all red-spectrumed galaxies are moving away from us—and that nearly all are red. Thus, the universe is constantly expanding.[8] Some estimates say that the most distant galaxy is eight billion light-years away—and racing away at two hundred million miles an hour. Finally, the fact of the expanding universe demands a beginning, though Hawking now doubts that a Big Bang was its beginning.[9]

We have recited all this to emphasize the stupendous creative power of Christ. He created every speck of dust in the hundred thousand million galaxies of the universe. He created every atom—the sub-microscopic solar systems with their whimsically named quarks (from James Joyce's *Three Quarks for Master Mark*) and leptons (the same Greek word used for the widow's mite) and electrons and neutrinos ("little neutral ones")—all of which have no measurable size.

This stupendous reality is richly corroborated by other cosmic statements in the New Testament.

> All things were made through him, and without him was not any thing made that was made. (John 1:3)

> Yet for us there is . . . one Lord, Jesus Christ, through whom are all things and through whom we exist. (1 Corinthians 8:6)

> For from him and through him and to him are all things. To him be glory forever. Amen. (Romans 11:36)

> For by him all things were created, in heaven and on earth, visible and invisible, whether thrones or dominions or rulers or authorities—all things were created through him and for him. (Colossians 1:16)

Everything was created by him—everything corporeal, all things incorporeal, everything substantial, all things insubstantial.

Sustainer

But not only is he Creator, he is also Sustainer—"he upholds the universe by the word of his power" (v. 3c). He is not passively upholding the universe like "Atlas sustaining the dead weight of the world."[10] Rather, he is actively holding up all things. He does it by his spoken word. The writer is very specific here. He does not use *logos* ("word"), which is used to indicate revelation, but *rhema* ("word"), the spoken word. Just as the universe was called into existence with a spoken word, so it is sustained by the utterance of the Son.[11] The Colossian hymn of creation sings of his sustaining power: "He is before all things, and in him all things hold together" (Colossians 1:17). He holds all those quarks and leptons of the microcosm together by the mysterious coulomb electrical force he made and maintains, and he likewise sustains the fleeing galaxies of the universe. Similarly, if he speaks the word, all would end, not with a Big Bang but with a Big Fizzle or Gulp!

Oh, the immense superiority of Christ as Creator and Sustainer! We cannot create the tiniest speck of dust, much less a mayfly, but he created the universe. He can do what we can never do, materially and spiritually. He can create in us clean hearts (Psalm 51:10). In fact, he can make us into new creations: "Therefore, if anyone is in Christ, he is a new creation. The old has passed away; behold, the new has come" (2 Corinthians 5:17). He can do it *ex nihilo*—out of nothing. He can take whatever you are—your "nothingness"—and create a new person. The Greek here is even more exciting: *"If anyone is in Christ, new creation!"* There is nothing in your soul that is beyond the creative power of God. You are not an exception to his creativity, no matter how unique you may imagine yourself or your problem to be. But he is also our Sustainer. He can sustain the universe, and he can sustain the struggling, harried church. Jesus is adequate for *everything*. "Not that we are adequate in ourselves to consider anything as coming from ourselves, but our adequacy is from God" (2 Corinthians 3:5 NASB).

Radiator

The fourth facet of the Son's superiority brilliantly sets forth his relation to the Father—"He is the radiance of the glory of God" (v. 3a). The ESV translation "radiance" here is proper, as against some others that use "reflection." There is a vast difference between the two, as different as the functions of our solar system's sun and moon. The moon *reflects* light, whereas the sun *radiates* light because it is its source.[12] Jesus does not simply reflect God's glory; he is part of it! This was shown on the Mount of Transfiguration when "His clothes became radiant, intensely white, as no one on earth could bleach them" (Mark 9:3). It was his own essential glory, but it was also the Father's. This is what blinded Paul on the Damascus Road (Acts 9:3; 22:6). This is why the Nicene Creed sings of Christ, "God of God, Light of Light, Very God of Very God."

Representor

The following phrase balances out his identity by emphasizing that he is also the *Representor* of God: "and the exact imprint of his nature" (v. 3b). The word translated "exact imprint" refers to the image on a coin that perfectly corresponds to the image on the die. Jesus is therefore completely the same in his being as the Father. However, there is still an important distinction—both exist separately, as do the die and its image.

Now, when you take these two facets—Radiator and Representor—together, you have a remarkable exposition of the identity of the Father in the Son. As *Radiator*—"the radiance of the glory of God"—Jesus is part of the source, one with the Father. This is what John emphasizes when he says, "the Word *was* God" (John 1:1). But also as *Representor*—"the exact imprint of his nature"—Jesus is distinct, much as John also emphasizes when he says, "the Word was *with* God." Jesus is all God, *"very God of very God."* When you see him, you see the Father. But he is also a distinct person. This is all bound in with the mystery of the holy Trinity.

Jesus is a superior revelation of God. When we see him, we know just what the God of the universe is like. We know how he thinks. We know how he talks. We know how he relates to people. God has spoken in his Son. It is his ultimate communication, his final word, his consummate eloquence. Oh, the superiority of the Son!

Priestly Supremacy

The cosmic supremacy of Christ dazzles the mind: He is *Inheritor, Creator, Sustainer, Radiator,* and *Representor.* These are beautiful, soul-expanding thoughts. But they positively vibrate with glory when we see that they introduce the priestly supremacy of Christ—he is *Purifier* and *Ruler.*

Purifier

We have been all over the universe with the cosmic Son, and then suddenly he is introduced as the priestly Purifier who paid for our sins with his own blood. The thought almost sounds like an aside—"After making purification for sins" (v. 3d). Ceaseless cosmic activity, and then *boom!* his once-and-for-all sacrifice for our sins. Actually this is a cosmic achievement because Jesus did something no man or priest could ever do: offer alone the sacrifice that paid for all sins. That had to be the work of a cosmic being!

Ruler

The immensity of his cosmic achievement is given perspective by the phrase that follows: "he sat down at the right hand of the Majesty on high" (v. 3e). He is Ruler. The overarching significance here is that priests never sat down. Levitical priests always were standing, standing, standing—because no sacrifice was complete. The borders of the high priest's garment was sewn with bells so the people could hear him moving inside the Holy of Holies—and thus know he had not been struck dead. See him enter the Holy Place trembling as he bore the sacrificial blood before the glowing mercy seat. There he entered and stood year after year, high priest after high priest, for the work was never done.

But Jesus, a high priest after the order of Melchizedek, sat down. "And every priest stands daily at his service, offering repeatedly the same sacrifices, which can never take away sins. But when Christ had offered for all time a single sacrifice for sins, he sat down at the right hand of God" (Hebrews 10:11, 12). From the cross Jesus shouted, "It is finished" (John 19:30) and then, reassured, took his seat forever.

Jesus' colossal work underlines the utter blasphemy of the thought that we can pay for our own sins with works of righteousness. There is only one way to purity, and that is the blood of Christ. The only way to justification is by faith in his blood (Romans 3:25; 5:9). Paul says, "But now the righteousness of God has been manifested apart from the law, although the Law and the Prophets bear witness to it—the righteousness of God through faith in Jesus Christ for all who believe" (Romans 3:21, 22).

Lastly, there is the *ultimate* significance of Jesus' sitting down at the right hand of the Majesty in Heaven—and that is his ruling exaltation! This was prophesied in Psalm 110:1—"The LORD says to my Lord: 'Sit at my right hand, until I make your enemies your footstool.'" While on earth our Lord applied the Psalm to himself: "But from now on the Son of Man shall be seated at the right hand of the power of God" (Luke 22:69).

"The right hand" is the place of highest honor. Paul says, "He who descended is the one who also ascended far above all the heavens, that he might fill all things" (Ephesians 4:10). And again he says, "Therefore God has highly exalted him and bestowed on him the name that is above every name, so that at the name of Jesus every knee should bow, in heaven and on earth and under the earth" (Philippians 2:9, 10).

Dare we mention anything else? We must, for our souls' sake. It is here, in this supreme exaltation at God's right hand, that Christ intercedes for us. Paul asks, "Who is to condemn?" And then he answers triumphantly, "Christ Jesus is the one who died—more than that, who was raised—who is at the *right hand* of God, who indeed is interceding for us" (Romans 8:34). The thought is utterly sublime but true—this glorious cosmic being at the apex of his splendor is praying for you and me! Can it really be? Yes! God's Word says it is so. Wonder of wonders!

Do you see why we can do no better than to preach Jesus Christ? What can be added to the eloquence of the sevenfold supremacy of the Son? He is:

Inheritor. As Creator he is heir to the universe. As Redeemer he bought our souls and so made us his personal inheritance.

Creator. He created the universe's one hundred thousand million galaxies, each with a hundred thousand million stars, each six hundred trillion miles across—and each fleeing away in never-ending expansion. Awesome!

Sustainer. He is sustaining the galloping galaxies as well as the submicroscopic universe of atoms—all by his spoken word.

Radiator. Like the sun, he is the source and radiator of divine glory—not a reflection, but part of it! He *is* God.

Representor. He is the exact representation of the Father's being. He is everything God is, yet separate. He is *with* God.

Purifier. He is the cosmic sacrifice who paid for our sins with his blood in order to purify us.

Ruler. He sits, having paid for our sins once and for all, as the supreme priest. He is at the right hand of Majesty in ineffable exaltation. And wonder of wonders, he prays for us.

Do you know this Son? Has his eloquence spoken to you? He is God's final word. There is no other!

[He became] as much superior to angels as the name he has inherited is more excellent than theirs. For to which of the angels did God ever say, "You are my Son, today I have begotten you"? Or again, "I will be to him a father, and he shall be to me a son"? And again, when he brings the firstborn into the world, he says, "Let all God's angels worship him." Of the angels he says, "He makes his angels winds, and his ministers a flame of fire." But of the Son he says, "Your throne, O God, is forever and ever, the scepter of uprightness is the scepter of your kingdom. You have loved righteousness and hated wickedness; therefore God, your God, has anointed you with the oil of gladness beyond your companions." And, "You, Lord, laid the foundation of the earth in the beginning, and the heavens are the work of your hands; they will perish, but you remain; they will all wear out like a garment, like a robe you will roll them up, like a garment they will be changed. But you are the same, and your years will have no end." And to which of the angels has he ever said, "Sit at my right hand until I make your enemies a footstool for your feet"? Are they not all ministering spirits sent out to serve for the sake of those who are to inherit salvation?

1:4–14

3

Christ's Superiority to Angels

HEBREWS 1:4–14

IN HIS PREFACE TO *Screwtape Letters* C. S. Lewis complains about the progressively distorted picture of angels that has come down to us through religious art. Says Lewis:

> Fra Angelico's angels carry in their face and gesture the peace and authority of Heaven. Later come the chubby infantile nudes of Raphael; finally the soft, slim, girlish, and consolatory angels of nineteenth century art, shapes so feminine that they avoid being voluptuous only by their total insipidity. . . . They are a pernicious symbol. In Scripture the visitation of an angel is always alarming; it has to begin by saying "Fear not." The Victorian angel looks as if it were going to say, "There, there."[1]

Later, in his imaginative best-seller *Perelandra*, Lewis created a spectacular corrective to the traditional picture when he described Dr. Ransom's encounter with planetary angels:

> . . . far off between the peaks on the other side of the little valley there came rolling wheels. There was nothing but that—concentric wheels moving with a rather sickening slowness one inside the other. There was nothing terrible about them if you could get used to their appalling size . . . suddenly two human figures stood before him on the opposite side of the lake. . . . They were perhaps thirty feet high. They were burning white like white-hot iron. The outline of their bodies when he looked at it steadily against the red landscape seemed to be faintly, swiftly undulating as though the permanence of their shape, like that of waterfalls or flames, co-existed with a rushing movement of the matter it contained. For a fraction of an inch inward from this outline the landscape was just visible through them: beyond that they were opaque. . . . Whenever he looked straight at them they appeared to be rushing towards him with enormous speed: whenever

his eyes took in their surroundings he realized that they were stationary. This may have been due in part to the fact that their long and sparkling hair stood out straight behind them as if in a great wind. But if there were a wind it was not made of air, for no petal of the flowers was shaken. . . . Their bodies, he said, were white. But a flush of diverse colours began at about the shoulders and streamed up the necks and flickered over face and head and stood out around the head like plumage or a halo.[2]

Lewis was perhaps a bit extravagant, but his portrayal was certainly in line with some of the encounters recorded in Scripture. For example, when Isaiah saw the Lord high and exalted in the temple, he also saw hovering above him two seraphim ("burning ones"). These heavenly beings were equipped, insect-like, with three pairs of wings. Two fiery wings covered their faces, two wrapped over their feet, and two glowing pinions beat the air as they intoned the *tris hagion: "qadosh, qadosh, qadosh"*—"holy, holy, holy" (Isaiah 6:1–3). Understandably, Isaiah was traumatized. Others had similar experiences with angels. For example, when Manoah and his wife, in response to an angelic visit, offered a sacrifice, "when the flame went up toward heaven from the altar, the angel of the LORD went up in the flame of the altar"—*whoosh!* (Judges 13:20).

Angels definitely can be awesome. But what are angels? What does God's Word tell us? Angels are mentioned over one hundred times in the Old Testament and more than 160 times in the New Testament. They exist in vast numbers. On one occasion they are described as assembling in a great throng "numbering myriads of myriads and thousands of thousands" (Revelation 5:11). In most cases they are invisible, as was the experience of Balaam when the Lord had to open his eyes so he could see the angel blocking his way (Numbers 22:31). Or consider Elisha's servant who had his eyes opened so he could see that he was protected by encircling chariots of fire (2 Kings 6:17).

Ordinarily when angels are visible, they have a human-like appearance and are often mistaken for men (see Genesis 18:2; 19:1, 2; Mark 16:5). Sometimes they have shined with glorious light (Matthew 28:3; Luke 2:9). Other times they have appeared as fabulous winged creatures—seraphim and cherubim (Exodus 25:20; Isaiah 6:2). The Hebrew word for angel is *malak* and the Greek *angelos*. Both mean "messenger," designating their essential functions as divine message-bearers. As God's messengers they can wield immense power—for example, staying entire armies (2 Kings 19:35) or delivering captives (Acts 12:7–11).

Regarding angels' specific function, there are at least four:

1) Angels continuously *worship and praise the God they serve* (Job 38:7; Psalm 103:20; Isaiah 6:1–3; Revelation 4:8; 5:9–12).

2) Angels *communicate God's message to man*. They assisted in bringing the Law (Acts 7:38, 53). Angels revealed the future to Daniel and to the Apostle John (Daniel 10:10–15; Revelation 17:1; 21:9; 22:16). Gabriel announced the births of both John the Baptist and Jesus (Matthew 1:19–24; Luke 1:11–28; 2:9–12).

3) Angels *minister to believers*. "The angel of the LORD encamps around those who fear him, and delivers them" (Psalm 34:7). "For he will command his angels concerning you to guard you in all your ways. On their hands they will bear you up, lest you strike your foot against a stone" (Psalm 91:11,12). Angels have dramatically delivered believers from prison (Acts 5:19; 12:6–11). Angels rejoice at the conversion of sinners (Luke 15:10). They are present within the Church (1 Corinthians 11:10). They watch the lives of believers with interest (1 Corinthians 4:9; 1 Timothy 5:21). They carry believers away at death to the place of blessedness (Luke 16:22).

4) Angels will be *God's agents in the final earthly judgments and Second Coming*. They will call forth the elect with a loud trumpet from the four winds (Matthew 24:31; 1 Thessalonians 4:16, 17) and will then separate the wheat from the chaff (Matthew 13:39–42). The book of Revelation tells us they will open the seals, blow the trumpets, and pour out the bowls of wrath. They will also execute the judgment against Satan and his servants (Revelation 19:17—20:3, 10).

What awesome beings are angels! And what terrific power they wield! But despite all their cosmic excellencies, their significance dwindles in the presence of Christ. Thus, we come to the grand theme of Hebrews 1:4–14, *Christ's superiority to angels*.

Why does the writer expound it here? Because some of the Jewish believers to whom he was writing were in danger of compromising Jesus' superiority and lapsing into Judaism. They were under pressure first from the imminent threat of Nero's persecution for being Christians, and secondly, they were pressured because of ostracism by their Jewish countrymen in the synagogue. They were being tempted to compromise. If they would simply agree that Jesus was an angel, perhaps even the greatest of angels, but not God, they would be accepted into the synagogue and escape the awful pressure. Such a prospect was tantalizing because it did not require an outright denial of Christ, but only a different affirmation of him and his greatness as an angel. And the prospect was also face-saving because it did not deny that they had had a real experience with an exalted being.[3]

It takes only a little thought to identify with this temptation, because the supremacy of Christ brings tension in everyday life. The world bristles at "Jesus only." But one does not have to deny him outright to get along. Rather we are encouraged to simply affirm that he was the very best of men to ever walk on this planet—that his ethics were exalted—that his life was heroic from beginning to end—that he is the supreme example for sacrifice. If one does this, the pressure will be off. What a temptation for the Hebrew Christian in a life-threatening context. A simple change of emphasis on the person of Christ from Son to angel and one would be spared suffering.

But the writer of Hebrews is determined that his friends not fall to this; so he creates a mosaic of Old Testament texts from the Septuagint that powerfully demonstrate the superiority of Christ over angels. The argument has many sub-surface puzzles regarding the author's use of the Old Testament Greek texts, but the argument is clear as he presents five superiorities of Christ.

A Superior Name

Christ's superiority is first adduced because he has a superior name: "[He became] as much superior to angels as the name he has inherited is more excellent than theirs. For to which of the angels did God ever say, 'You are my Son, today I have begotten you'? Or again, 'I will be to him a father, and he shall be to me a son'?" (vv. 4, 5).

According to Jewish thought, a person's name revealed his essential nature and could express rank and dignity. Jesus had the name "Son" from all eternity, and it is the name he will always keep, as the perfect tense of the phrase "the name he has inherited" indicates. No angel was ever called "Son," though sometimes they were generically referred to as sons—for example, "the sons of God" presented themselves before the Lord (Job 1:6). But no angel ever had the title "Son."

The writer establishes this through two Old Testament quotations. The first is from Psalm 2:7, "For to which of the angels did God ever say, 'You are my Son, today I have begotten you'?" (v. 5a). Psalm 2 was already a famous messianic psalm, understood to be fulfilled in a future day by a descendant of David who would be crowned king.[4] Its words were recalled at Jesus' baptism when a voice from Heaven announced, "You are my beloved Son; with you I am well pleased" (Mark 1:11).

Jesus was always God's Son, and God was his Father. But the phrase, "today I have begotten you" evidently refers to Christ's exaltation and enthronement as Son subsequent to the resurrection, because Romans 1:4

says Jesus "was declared to be the Son of God in power according to the Spirit of holiness by his resurrection from the dead." And in Acts 13:32, 33 Paul specifically proclaims that the resurrection fulfilled Psalm 2:7: "And we bring you the good news that what God promised to the fathers, this he has fulfilled to us their children by raising Jesus, as also it is written in the second Psalm, 'You are my Son, today I have begotten you'" (cf. Ephesians 1:20). "Son" is Jesus' eternal name that was given exalted declaration in his resurrection and exaltation. No angel ever had that!

Our author further grounds his argument with a second quotation, taken from 2 Samuel 7:14, "Or again [implying, to which of the angels did God ever say], 'I will be to him a father, and he shall be to me a son'?" (v. 5b). This is also a quotation from a well-known messianic passage, commonly called the Davidic Covenant, in which the prophet Nathan told David that after his death his son would build a house for God and establish a royal throne that would endure forever. God's words to the Son—Christ—were, "I will be to him a father, and he shall be to me a son."

Since Solomon failed to fulfill this, as did the following Davidic kings, the later prophets looked forward to a greater son of David who would fulfill it. The fulfillment of that ancient promise was celebrated in the angel Gabriel's annunciation to Mary: "He will be great and will be called the Son of the Most High. And the Lord God will give to him the throne of his father David, and he will reign over the house of Jacob forever, and of his kingdom there will be no end" (Luke 1:32, 33; cf. Luke 1:68; Romans 1:3).

So we see that Jesus is superior to the angels because he always was God's Son and because two Old Testament sonship prophecies were marvelously fulfilled by him at his incarnation and resurrection and exaltation. His name is "Son," while all that can be said of angels is that they are messengers. How dare anyone ever think of demoting him to the position of an archangel, much less to a perfect man!

A Superior Honor

The next point in the author's argument for Christ's superiority over angels is that he is worshiped by angels. "And again, when he brings the firstborn into the world, he says, 'Let all God's angels worship him'" (v. 6). Here he turns to the final lines of verse 43 of the Song of Moses (Deuteronomy 32:43). The Jews considered these final lines to be messianic.[5] Remarkably, the line he borrows, "Let all God's angels worship him," is not in the Hebrew original but is a Greek addition. Nevertheless, it expresses the divine mind regarding

Christ, and the Holy Spirit had the writer incorporate it into the inspired text of Hebrews.[6]

Its obvious application is to the angelic worship that had its first occurrence *on earth* at the Incarnation when all God's angels worshiped Christ as "Suddenly there was with the angel a multitude of the heavenly host praising God and saying, 'Glory to God in the highest'" (Luke 2:13, 14a). Jesus was undoubtedly worshiped by angels in eternity past; he was worshiped by angels during his thirty-three years on earth; and he is worshiped in eternity present—a worship to which we have been given a dizzy glimpse:

> Then I looked, and I heard around the throne and the living creatures and the elders the voice of many angels, numbering myriads of myriads and thousands of thousands, saying with a loud voice,
>
> > "Worthy is the Lamb who was slain,
> > to receive power and wealth and wisdom and might
> > and honor and glory and blessing!"
>
> And I heard every creature in heaven and on earth and under the earth and in the sea, and all that is in them, saying,
>
> > "To him who sits on the throne and to the Lamb
> > be blessing and honor and glory and might forever and ever!"
> > (Revelation 5:11–13)

Angels (unless they are fallen angels) do not worship other angels, for that would be angelolatry! The only one they can and do worship is God. Our job is to lift up Jesus!

A Superior Status

Next the writer demonstrates the superiority of Christ to angels by contrasting their statuses: the angels are *servants*, but the Son is *sovereign*.

Psalm 104:4 is quoted regarding the angels' being servants: "Of the angels he says, 'He makes his angels winds, and his ministers a flame of fire'" (v. 7). The Septuagint here differs slightly in emphasis from the Hebrew by emphasizing that angels become and do the work of winds and fire, whereas the Hebrew of Psalm 104:4 says, "He makes his messengers winds, his ministers a flaming fire." As to why there is this variation, we can only speculate. But the emphasis of the writer of Hebrews is clear: angels sometimes spectacularly inhabit wind and fire to do God's bidding—as when the angel shot up through the flame of Manoah's sacrifice—but in doing this they are only servants.

On the other hand, Christ, the Son, is eternally sovereign. Here the writer quotes Psalm 45:6, 7, a nuptial Psalm addressed originally to a Hebrew king, but phrased in language that could only be fulfilled by the ultimate Davidic king, the Son:[7]

But of the Son he says,

> "Your throne, O God, is forever and ever,
>   the scepter of uprightness is the scepter of your kingdom.
> You have loved righteousness and hated wickedness;
> therefore God, your God, has anointed you
>   with the oil of gladness beyond your companions." (vv. 8, 9)

His *throne*, his *scepter*, his *anointing* give us the dimensions of his brilliant sovereignty. His throne—his rule—will never end. His scepter—his authority—will be executed in his righteousness—a righteousness that he established in becoming a sacrifice for our sins. His being anointed with the oil of joy refers to the heavenly joy that was his as sovereign King of kings. It was "the joy . . . set before him" (12:2).

Angels, his servants, may at his request take on wondrous forms, become seraphim thirty feet high or men three hundred feet high, and perform feats beyond not only the capacity but the imagination of mankind. But they are still *servants*. He is the eternally enthroned, sceptered, anointed *sovereign*. It is impossible to logically think of Christ and angels as peers, any more than we could think of a sovereign and his slaves as equals.

A Superior Existence

For the fourth proof of Christ's superiority, the writer quotes Psalm 102:25–27, which contains a broken man's rising awareness and celebration of God's transcending existence (which, of course, describes Christ's existence by virtue of his creatorship: "through whom also he created the world," 1:2). Psalm 102 reads as it is recorded here in verses 10–12 of our text:

And,

> "You, Lord, laid the foundation of the earth in the beginning,
>   and the heavens are the work of your hands;
> they will perish, but you remain;
>   they will all wear out like a garment,
> like a robe you will roll them up,
>   like a garment they will be changed.

> But you are the same,
> and your years will have no end."

What stupendous thoughts! As a man during his lifetime outlives many successive suits of clothes, so Christ will see and outlive many successive material universes, yet will himself remain eternal and unchanging.[8]

In contrast, angels, because they are created, are temporal (though Christ has apparently willed to keep them immortal) and changeable and dependent. To the suffering Jewish believers who first heard these words, these sure words about Christ must have felt like refreshing rain. Their world was not only changing—it was falling apart. But their superior Christ remained the same—eternal and unchanging—"Jesus Christ is the same yesterday and today and forever" (13:8).

A Superior Vocation

The clinching argument for Christ's superiority over angels is vocation: Christ *rules*; angels *serve*. That Christ rules supreme is proven by a passage quoted more often in the New Testament than any other (fourteen times). Jesus even quoted it himself and applied it to himself at his trial (Mark 12:36). It is Psalm 110:1, which is quoted here in verse 13: "And to which of the angels has he ever said, 'Sit at my right hand until I make your enemies a footstool for your feet'?" The answer is, of course, a resounding, "None, not one, no one!"

Christ's absolute rulership is dramatically seen here in that it was the custom for a defeated king to prostrate himself and kiss his conqueror's feet (see Psalm 2:12) and for the victor to put his feet on the captive's neck so that the captive became his footstool (see Joshua 10:24). One day every knee will bow before Christ, and every tongue will confess that he is Lord (Philippians 2:10, 11; cf. 1 Corinthians 15:24, 25). And all the angels will be in that number, both good and evil, for the Son is infinitely their superior.[9]

In contrast to Christ's superior ruling vocation, the angels' vocation is that of serving. "Are [angels] not," the author writes, "all ministering spirits sent out to serve for the sake of those who are to inherit salvation?" (v. 14). This does not mean their serving is a disgraceful vocation. Far from it! It is a sublime privilege. The point here is, however, that it is inferior to the Son's vocation of ruling the universe.

So to the beleaguered Jewish believer who was being tempted to say that Christ is an angel and thus escape persecution, God's Word issues a clear call: Christ is superior to angels because he has a superior *name*—he is Son; a superior *honor*—all the angels worship him; a superior *vocation*—he is Sovereign King; a superior *existence*—he is eternal and unchangeable; a superior *status*—he rules the universe.

But there is something more here for the harried church—a double encouragement. First, this supreme Son is their God. Later the author of Hebrews would say to them:

> Since then we have a great high priest who has passed through the heavens, Jesus, the Son of God, let us hold fast our confession. For we do not have a high priest who is unable to sympathize with our weaknesses, but one who in every respect has been tempted as we are, yet without sin. Let us then with confidence draw near to the throne of grace, that we may receive mercy and find grace to help in time of need. (4:14–16)

Christ's *cosmic* superiority, *prophetic* superiority, *priestly* superiority, and *angelic* superiority were all at the believers' service in a world that was falling apart.

Second, in respect to Christ's angelic superiority, all angels had been sent by him as "ministering spirits sent out to serve for the sake of those who are to inherit salvation." The force of the original Greek is that they are perpetually being sent out to help God's people—one after another.[10]

On a dark night about a hundred years ago, a Scottish missionary couple found themselves surrounded by cannibals intent on taking their lives. That terror-filled night they fell to their knees and prayed that God would protect them. Intermittent with their prayers, the missionaries heard the cries of the savages and expected them to come through the door at any moment.

But as the sun began to rise, to their astonishment they found that the natives were retreating into the forest. The couple's hearts soared to God. It was a day of rejoicing!

The missionaries bravely continued their work. A year later the chieftain of that tribe was converted. As the missionary spoke with him, he remembered the horror of that night. He asked the chieftain why he and his men had not killed them. The chief replied, "Who were all those men who were with you?" The missionary answered, "Why, there were no men with us. There were just my wife and myself." The chieftain began to argue with him, saying, "There were hundreds of tall men in shining garments with drawn swords circling about your house, so we could not attack you."

This story, recorded in Billy Graham's book *Angels*, is one of the great tales of missionary history. The missionary was the "legendary" John G. Paton of the New Hebrides.[11]

What an astounding story! One of a kind, we might think. Actually it is just one of several similar accounts. Perhaps over the years our Lord has dispatched the same detachment of angels to protect his missionaries again and again—a special "missionary protection platoon." Possibly tall soldiers in shining clothing is the MO of angelic protectors.

Norwegian missionary Marie Monsen, who served in North China, experienced the intervention of angels on several occasions. In her autobiography *A Present Help*, published in 1960, she tells how looting soldiers had surrounded the mission compound but never entered—leaving the missionaries unharmed and happily perplexed. A few days later they learned why when a marauder explained that as they were about to enter the compound, they saw "tall soldiers with shining faces on a high roof of the compound." Miss Monsen said:

> The heathen saw them, it was a testimony to them, but they were invisible to us. It came powerfully to me and showed me how little we reckon with "the Lord, the God of Hosts," who sends forth his angels, mighty in strength "to do service for the sake of them that shall inherit salvation" (Hebrews 1:14 RV).[12]

In 1956 during the Mau Mau uprisings in East Africa, a band of roving Mau Maus came to the village of Lauri, surrounded it, and killed every inhabitant including women and children, three hundred in all. Not more than three miles away was the Rift Valley Academy, a private school where missionary children were being educated. Immediately upon leaving the carnage of Lauri the natives came with spears, bows and arrows, clubs, and torches to the school with violent intentions.

In the darkness lighted torches were seen coming toward the school. Soon there was a complete ring of terrorists around the academy, cutting off all avenues of escape. Shouts and curses could be heard coming from the Mau Maus. They began to advance on the school, tightening the circle, shouting louder and louder, coming closer. Then inexplicably, when they were close enough to throw spears, they stopped. They began retreating and soon were running into the jungle. The army was called out and fortunately captured the entire band of raiders. Later, at their trial, the leader was called to the witness stand. The judge questioned him: "On this particular night, did you kill the inhabitants of Lauri?" "Yes." "Well, then, why did you not complete the mission? Why didn't you attack the school?" The leader of the Mau Maus answered, "We were on our way to attack and destroy all the people and school . . . but as we came closer, all of a sudden, between us and the school there were many huge men, dressed in white with flaming swords and we became afraid and ran to hide!"[13]

Jim Marstaller recounts the following story, told to him by his "Uncle Clyde," Clyde Taylor, founder of the National Association of Evangelicals:

> Dr. Clyde Taylor, who married my grandfather's sister . . . and my Uncle Charlie Marstaller were missionaries in the early 1920's to a head hunting tribe in South America. They were beside a river in the forest living in a thatched hut.
>
> One day, late in the afternoon, they noticed a dugout being paddled down the river with only one man in it. Their immediate thought was that the warriors were coming to kill them that night. The dugout could hold over 40 men and they realized that the men were probably going to try to kill them that night.
>
> Uncle Clyde and Charlie had a .22 rifle in their hut and took it and some ammo out into the tall grass off to the side of their dwelling. There they stayed all night, in their own private prayer meeting, expecting that if attacked they would fire the gun into the air to frighten the head-hunters.
>
> Nothing happened that night and they had no trouble with the tribe for the rest of their term in South America.
>
> They both returned home after their term was over, and it wasn't until 9 years later that Clyde was able to visit the field. One day he encountered one of the men from the tribe who had since become a Christian; so he asked the native about what happened that night.
>
> The former head-hunter said, "I remember that night, there were 44 of us and we were coming to set fire to your hut. When we got there and surrounded the hut we realized we could not attack because there were hundreds of men, dressed in white, with swords and shields, standing all around your hut and even on the roof. That is why I am a Christian now."
>
> Uncle Clyde realized then that God had protected them with His angels and used this account to be an encouragement to many others throughout the rest of his life.[14]

In March 1980 I taped an interview with Mrs. Carol Carlson, a missionary from the church I serve as pastor, College Church in Wheaton (Illinois). Mrs. Carlson and her husband, Edwin, served in China and Tibet for over fifty years. Mrs. Carlson told of several deliverances, including this one:

> It was early in 1922 that we arrived in West China at the station called Titao, and the gatekeeper there impressed us as a man rather different from the type of Chinese we had met thus far during our first days on the field. He was bold and forward and sometimes rather brassy, not the quiet, polite Chinese we had met thus far. But he seemed to be very greatly loved by all the people on the station and we understood this when they told us he had been a professional brigand; that is, a member of a robber band that worked

the area not too far from Titao, and that the band had come one very dark night expecting to attack the mission station. They were on their way down a side street and as they drew near to the walls of the mission compound, the men were terrorized by the sight of men in white walking up and down on the wall. Of course they couldn't go any farther. But his curiosity was aroused as to what kind of people the missionaries might be and what it was they were teaching there in the church. So, little by little, he began to come and listen, which, of course, resulted in his conversion—and he was indeed a faithful, very loyal, and very useful helper for many years there on the station.

What astounding stories! And what a unified witness not only to the power of angels, but to the superiority of Christ who makes his angels "ministering spirits sent out to serve for the sake of those who are to inherit salvation" (v. 14).

The message to the harried, trembling church of the writer's day, and to the Church universal, is this: Our superior Christ has assigned his angels to minister to us. And if he wills, he can deliver us anytime and anywhere he wishes. Christ is superior to everything. He is adequate in our hour of need. We must believe it and trust him with all we are and have.

Therefore we must pay much closer attention to what we have heard, lest we drift away from it. For since the message declared by angels proved to be reliable, and every transgression or disobedience received a just retribution, how shall we escape if we neglect such a great salvation? It was declared at first by the Lord, and it was attested to us by those who heard, while God also bore witness by signs and wonders and various miracles and by gifts of the Holy Spirit distributed according to his will.

2:1–4

4

Drifting

HEBREWS 2:1-4

ONE OF THE ANCIENT SYMBOLS for the Church is a ship. The idea originated in the Gospel accounts, which tell how Jesus compelled his disciples to board a ship and sail to the other side of the Sea of Galilee (Matthew 14:22–33; John 6:16–21). That night, when they were some distance from shore, a perilous storm arose so that they tossed like a cork on the waves—until Jesus came walking across the tempest in the night. Ancient art typically pictures the Twelve crowded into a stylized, tubby little boat with their wide-eyed faces visible above the gunwales—like apprehensive children in a bathtub.

This is a most fitting picture of the Church sailing the contrary seas of this world. And it is a particularly appropriate symbol of the church to which the book of Hebrews was written, for all agree it was under stormy siege. Moreover, if our thesis is correct—that this church is a tiny house-church somewhere in Italy, possibly in or around Rome—then we can imagine the huge waves that were poised above their little boat in the imminent Neronian persecution. Some in the church were also in danger of being blown away from their moorings and drifting away from the truth of Christ and back into "the Dead Sea of Judaism."[1]

In an effort to counter this, the writer has held high the supremacy of Christ: his *prophetic* supremacy as the final word of God (1:1, 2), his *cosmic* supremacy as Creator and Sustainer of all (1:2, 3), his *Levitical* supremacy as the ultimate priest seated in Heaven (1:3), and his *angelic* supremacy in that he is superior to angels in name, honor, vocation, existence, and reign (1:4–14). This manifold superiority of Christ is meant to be an anchor to hold them to their Christian faith amidst the increasingly stormy seas of persecution. Indeed, it is meant to be the universal anchor for all imperiled souls for all time.

A Warning

So now, with the superiority of Christ ringing in their ears, the writer explicitly sounds his warning to the harried church in 2:1–4, beginning with the words: "Therefore we must pay much closer attention to what we have heard, lest we drift away from it" (v. 1). The vivid warning here uses nautical, sailing language, suggesting the image of a ship whose anchor has broken loose from the ocean floor and is dangerously drifting away.[2]

I have experienced this firsthand while fishing the tidal inlets of the California coast, when winds or surging tides have imperceptibly slipped the anchor from the seabed so that it hung suspended, and I, intent on my fishing, unknowingly moved several hundred yards and almost foundered on the rocks!

Such dangerous drifting is not intentional but comes rather from inattention and carelessness—which was precisely the problem with the pressured little church. They had become careless about their moorings in Christ. At first, in calm waters, that was not noticeable. But as the storms of opposition rose, some of them were drifting farther and farther away from Christ toward the shoals of shipwreck in their old world of Judaism.

That church's experience two thousand years ago intersects our lives in this way: *drifting is the besetting sin of our day.* And as the metaphor suggests, it is not so much intentional as from unconcern. Christians neglect their anchor—Christ—and begin to quietly drift away. There is no friction, no dramatic sense of departure. But when the winds of trouble come, the things of Christ are left far behind, even out of sight. The writer of Revelation uses different language but refers to the same thing when he quotes Jesus as saying to the ostensibly healthy Ephesian church, "I have this against you, that you have abandoned the love you had at first" (Revelation 2:4).

When our anchors begin to lift from our soul's grasp of the greatness and supremacy of life, we become susceptible to subtle tows.[3] C. S. Lewis sagely remarked: "And as a matter of fact, if you examined a hundred people who had lost their faith in Christianity, I wonder how many of them would turn out to have been reasoned out of it by honest argument? Do not most people simply drift away?"[4]

What brings such drifting? For one thing, there is the tide of *years*. You have to live for some length to observe this, but the longer you live, the more you will see it. Many who were at one time professing, fine Christians imperceptibly drifted away from their earlier, better selves. They have kept up appearances, but the years have carried them far away from their devotion.

I vividly remember the impressive public resolves of some of my college friends to follow Christ whatever would come. But today, though they have not disowned Christ, they have drifted far from their earlier faith. And their children have no understanding or interest in Christianity. This is a tragic end, an end that Robertson McQuilkin prays against for himself:

> I fear the Dark Spectre may come too soon—
> or do I mean, too late?
> That I should end before I finish
> or finish, but not well.
> That I should stain your honor, shame your
> name, grieve your loving heart.
> Few, they tell me, finish well . . .
> Lord, let me get home before dark.
>
> "Let Me Get Home Before Dark," 1981

A slow drift, given enough time, will carry you to another continent and its dark uncharted waters.

There is also the tide of *familiarity with the truth*. It is natural for us to come to regard the familiar as commonplace. Your first tour in London will leave you dazzled: Parliament, the British Museum, Covent Garden, the Savoy. But will it be so on your twentieth tour? The initial venture into the mysteries of Christ will leave us exhilarated. But with the repeated journeys, some become bored tourists. Granted, some find joy in their familiarity with the mysteries of Christ. But familiarity has both danger and reward. It depends on us.

There is the danger of *busyness* too. John Foster Dulles was a great states-man and a man of legendary busyness. He almost lived on a jet—so many were his globe-trotting responsibilities. In fact, it was once suggested that the President should tell him, "Don't just do something; stand there!"[5] I have wondered if there were some unconscious Freudian irony in Washington, DC's naming its international airport after him.

We who live in the modern era are busy people, and the multiplicity of our cares and duties can overwhelm us. A snowflake is a tiny thing, but when the air is full of them, they can bury us. Just so, the thousand cares of each day can insulate us from the stupendous excellencies of Christ, causing us to begin a deadly drift.

The drifting that comes through the combination of years, familiarity, and busyness often bares its existence when the storm of opposition comes. The anchor has long been loosed, and when the winds come, an eternal soul is suddenly on the rocks and shipwrecked. No wonder, then, that the warning is a powerfully phrased command that should be read with an exclamation point: "Therefore we must pay much closer attention to what we have heard, lest we drift away from it"!

Reasoning from the Lesser

Careful attention to what we have heard is the divinely prescribed antidote to drifting. And the writer wants to drive this point home in an even more forceful way to his wandering friends. So he uses a Hebrew argument style called *qal wa homer* (literally, "light and heavy"), which employs the reasoning that if something is true in a light or lesser thing, it is true in a heavy or greater thing.[6] He uses this argument style to frame the great question he wants to emphasize: "how shall we escape if we neglect such a great salvation?"—putting the *qal* argument before it and beginning the *homer* with it.

The *qal*, the less heavy argument from the Law, is stated in verse 2 and then flows into the great question in verse 3: "For since the message declared by angels proved to be reliable, and every transgression or disobedience received a just retribution, how shall we escape if we neglect such a great salvation?" The writer states the common teaching of contemporary Judaism and of the New Testament that the angels *mediated* the giving of the Law.[7] For example, Stephen, in his famous sermon, referred to Moses as being "with the angel who spoke to him at Mount Sinai, and with our fathers. He received living oracles to give to us" (Acts 7:38; cf. Acts 7:53; Galatians 3:19). In the midst of all the fire and lightning on Sinai, God the Father spoke through an honored angel who in turn dictated to Moses.

The point is, these words, though mediated by angels, were "reliable"— so reliable that "every transgression" and "disobedience" (unwillingness to hear and obey) "received a just retribution." Sometimes the punishment came directly from Heaven as when in one day twenty-three thousand died or on another occasion when many were killed by snakes (1 Corinthians 10:5–10). At other times the just punishment came through legal processes. For example, the Fourth Commandment demanded keeping the Sabbath. But soon after it was given, a man was found picking up sticks on the Sabbath. He was not ignorant; he knew the Law. They put him in custody and asked God what to do. The Lord answered that he must be taken out of the camp and stoned (Numbers 15:32–36). Why? Almighty God had spoken, and *though he mediated it through angels and then through Moses, it was absolutely binding.* "Every transgression or disobedience received a just retribution." This was the *qal* (the light) argument.

Reasoning from the Greater

The heavy (*homer*) argument—"how shall we escape if we neglect such a great salvation?"—gets its weight from three successive clauses in verses 3, 4.

Announced

First, it is identified as "a great salvation . . . declared at first by the Lord" (v. 3b). Jesus proclaimed it! The angels mediated the Law, but Jesus was more than a mediator of the gospel. He was the divine Son, but he was also the incarnate Son, which makes his communication infinitely superior to that of the angels. "The good news of salvation, then, derives from the Lord, whose mediatorship is absolutely other than that of angels."[8] "For there is one God, and there is one mediator between God and men, the man Christ Jesus, who gave himself as a ransom for all, which is the testimony given at the proper time" (1 Timothy 2:5, 6).

Confirmed

Next the text says that the salvation "was attested to us by those who heard" (v. 3c). This primarily refers to the apostles attesting what Jesus said and passing it along from faith to faith through the succeeding generation (cf. Luke 1:2). Eusebius, in his *Ecclesiastical History*, has preserved an autobiographical fragment from Irenaeus of Lyons that relates how the Apostle John passed along the story of the gospel to Polycarp who, before his martyrdom in AD 155 or 156, passed along the story to young Irenaeus. Irenaeus says of his experience:

> And as he [Polycarp] remembered their words, and what he heard from them concerning the Lord, and concerning his miracles and his teaching, having received them from eyewitnesses of the "Word of life" [John], Polycarp related all things in harmony with the Scriptures. These things being told me by the mercy of God, I listened to them attentively, noting them down, not on paper, but in my heart. And continually, through God's grace, I recall them faithfully. (Eusebius, *Hist. Eccl.*, V.xx.5ff., A. C. McGiffert's translation.)[9]

The church to which the book of Hebrews was written was in a far better position than we to hear confirmation from those who heard Christ because they were so close historically to the situation. Even if living in Italy as we think, they no doubt had firsthand, eyewitness confirmation.

Testified

Lastly, "God also bore witness by signs and wonders and various miracles and by gifts of the Holy Spirit distributed according to his will" (v. 4). The testimony was dynamic. "Signs" pointed beyond themselves to the mighty hand of God. "Wonders" brought awe and amazement to those who saw. "Miracles" (literally "powers") showed the power of God beyond human ability. And "gifts of the Holy Spirit" were given according to God's will. These four things bore weighty testimony to the authenticity of the word of Christ and the confirming word of those who heard him. The *homer* argument was heavy indeed.

So now we see the *qal wa homer* argument: If the word of the Law that was mediated by angels was so binding that every infraction was punished (*qal*, "light"), then how much more accountable are those who have the word of salvation direct from Christ's lips, plus the confirmation of eyewitnesses, plus the testimony of miracles, signs, wonders, and gifts (*homer*, "heavy"). Thus, the weighty question of our text, "How shall we escape if we neglect such a great salvation?"

Here the application intersects our lives again, because the writer is not concerned here about those who have never heard. The transcending concern of this warning text is for those who *have* heard. Even more, the concern is not for those who reject the gospel, but for those who "neglect" it. The concern is for one's *attitude*—the one who has let the greatness of Christ slip away—the one who no longer marvels at the atonement—the one who no longer has a desire for the Word—the one who really does not pray in his spirit—the one who is drifting back to where he came from and has little concern about his drifting.

To such the writer says there is no escape from the terrible consequences. In fact, if we think the consequences were stern for disregarding the Law, how much more catastrophic will the punishment be for ignoring the gospel? Calvin says:

> It is not only the rejecting of the Gospel, but even the neglecting of it that deserves the severest penalty in view of the greatness of the grace which is offered in it. . . . God wishes His gifts to be valued by us at their proper worth. The more precious they are, the baser is our ingratitude if they do not have their proper value for us. In accordance with the greatness of Christ, so will be the severity of God's vengeance on all despisers of the Gospel.[10]

It is more blameworthy to sin against love than against Law, to ignore God's mercy than to break his Law. There is no escape if we ignore "such a great salvation!"

The tiny storm-tossed church is not hypothetical. It was a real church of real people, in real bodies, weighing so many pounds, in a real place, with terribly real problems. And under the pressure some were going with the flow—they were drifting away. They had not rejected Christ outright, but they were, in fact, ignoring him. Their anchors were up—and they did not know how fast they were moving away on the deceptive tides.

What to do? The answer brings us full circle in the warning to where it begins: "Therefore we must pay much closer attention to what we have heard, lest we drift away from it." The force of the original is even stronger: we must pay the *"greatest attention"* to what we have heard.[11]

Two things are in view here. First, all our attention must be focused on the supremacy of Christ: *prophetic, cosmic, Levitical, and angelic.* We need to work at this—turning from Christological passage to passage, meditating on him, asking questions, memorizing, and worshiping. Lewis gave wise advice to a little girl: "If you continue to love Jesus, nothing much can go wrong with you, and I hope you always do so."[12]

Second, paying closest attention to what we have heard means living in the revelation of God's Word—and it always has. We are all familiar with the great *Shema* that calls us to lovingly make God first: "Hear, O Israel: The LORD our God, the LORD is one. You shall love the LORD your God with all your heart and with all your soul and with all your might." But we must also remember the words that follow:

> And these words that I command you today shall be on your heart. You shall teach them diligently to your children, and shall talk of them when you sit in your house, and when you walk by the way, and when you lie down, and when you rise. You shall bind them as a sign on your hand, and they shall be as frontlets between your eyes. You shall write them on the doorposts of your house and on your gates. (Deuteronomy 6:4–9)

These are crucial words and truths from which we must not drift!

For it was not to angels that God subjected the world to come, of which we are speaking. It has been testified somewhere, "What is man, that you are mindful of him, or the son of man, that you care for him? You made him for a little while lower than the angels; you have crowned him with glory and honor, putting everything in subjection under his feet." Now in putting everything in subjection to him, he left nothing outside his control. At present, we do not yet see everything in subjection to him. But we see him who for a little while was made lower than the angels, namely Jesus, crowned with glory and honor because of the suffering of death, so that by the grace of God he might taste death for everyone.

2:5–9

5

The Ultimate Intention

HEBREWS 2:5–9

THERE IS AN IRONIC LITTLE PASTORAL EPIGRAM that is often used to capsulize the task of preaching. It goes like this: The job of the preacher is to comfort the afflicted and afflict the comfortable.

That is pretty good advice, because a preacher should be given to both for a balanced ministry.

This certainly summarized the task of the writer of the letter to the Hebrews as he saw it, for his emphasis alternates between extended passages of comfort and brief sections of affliction or disturbing exhortation throughout the entire book. Thus far he has comforted the afflicted in the storm-tossed little church with a ranging summary of the superiority of Christ in chapter 1 that asserts his prophetic, cosmic, Levitical, and angelic supremacy (1:1–14). This grand vision of Christ was meant to be a firm anchor in the storms of persecution.

Correspondingly, in the beginning of chapter 2 he has afflicted the comfortable whose anchors have begun to lift from Christ, issuing a challenge that contains the ringing warning, "How shall we escape if we neglect such a great salvation?" (2:2–4).

Now, in the passage before us, the emphasis returns back to comforting the afflicted. The smallness of the tiny house-church, the immensity of the hostile sea around them, and the mounting breakers of Neronian persecution left them feeling lonely and insignificant—like a forgotten cork in the tide. This seeming insignificance is countered by the writer in verses 5–9 as he shows how Christ, through his superiority, gives them massive significance in his ultimate intention for them. The author introduces the subject of God's ultimate intention for believers with an implicit reference to the Biblical reality that angels co-minister the present world under God's direction. This is what Jacob's vision of the ladder was all about, because as he looked at the ladder he saw angels going up to Heaven and coming down (Genesis 28:10–17). The message was clear: there is angelic commerce between Heaven and earth on behalf of God's people. Apparently the administration is organized so that the angel-princes—for example, the archangel Michael—preside over ordered ranks of angels who administer God's will and combat evil spirits (cf. Daniel 10:20, 21; 12:1; Ephesians 6:12).

So amazing and significant is the angels' administration that one would expect, therefore, that they will also administer the rest of God's kingdom through the ages. But this is not the case, because verse 5 begins, "It was not to angels that God subjected the world to come, of which we are speaking. . . ." Angels are not going to rule the world to come! If God does not use the angels in the world to come, then who will he use? And the answer comes as a surprise to those who read on: *man!* God's ultimate intention is to have his kingdom ruled by redeemed men and women. Those "insignificant" people in that harried house-church, a minuscule dot in the Roman Empire, were going to rule everything!

The Original Intention

The author establishes this as the *ultimate intention* by demonstrating that it is in accord with the *original intention* of God for humanity. His proof is a quotation from the middle of Psalm 8 that celebrates God's original intention for man. He introduces and recites it in verses 6–8a of our text: "It has been testified somewhere, 'What is man, that you are mindful of him, or the son of man, that you care for him? You made him for a little while lower than the angels; you have crowned him with glory and honor, putting everything in subjection under his feet.'"

This marvelous declaration of God's intention can only be appreciated in the full context of the Psalm. The psalmist is contemplating the mighty expanse of the evening sky, studded with its orbs of light, and he is so overwhelmed with the greatness of God that he bursts into psalm—first celebrating God's majestic name, then declaring God's worthiness of praise, and next wondering at God's intention for puny little man. Says the psalmist:

> When I look at your heavens, the work of your fingers, the moon and the stars, which you have set in place, what is man that you are mindful of him, and the son of man that you care for him? Yet you have made him a little lower than the heavenly beings and crowned him with glory and honor. You

have given him dominion over the works of your hands; you have put all things under his feet. (Psalm 8:3–6)

The psalmist is completely astonished at God's intention for man. Of course the intention was not new because it was originally spelled out in Genesis:

Then God said, "Let us make man in our image, after our likeness. And let them have dominion over the fish of the sea and over the birds of the heavens and over the livestock and over all the earth and over every creeping thing that creeps on the earth." So God created man in his own image, in the image of God he created him; male and female he created them. And God blessed them. And God said to them, "Be fruitful and multiply and fill the earth and subdue it, and have dominion over the fish of the sea and over the birds of the heavens and over every living thing that moves on the earth." (Genesis 1:26–28)

God's original intention for his people is astonishing, especially with what we know today of creation. The psalmist could see only a hint of the vastness and glory of the universe. But through modern technology we "see" our planet spinning around our sun, which is only one of a hundred thousand million suns in our galaxy, which is only one of a hundred thousand million galaxies. No wonder the astonished exclamation, "What is man, that you are mindful of him, or the son of man, that you care for him?"

Think of man's astonishing *position*: "You made him for a little while lower than the angels."[1] Puny man is only lower than the angels in that man is in a corporal body and the angels are incorporeal. Man is therefore limited in a way angels are not and has lesser power. But man is not lower spiritually or in importance. What an astounding position for such temporary specks as us!

Think of man's astonishing *honor*: "you have crowned him with glory and honor." Adam and Eve were the king and queen of original creation. God set them in a glorious paradise and walked with them.

Consider man's amazing *authority*: "Putting everything in subjection under his feet." This was given to mankind through Adam (Genesis 1:28). Man was given rule over the world. Adam and Eve were God's viceroys— creature king and creature queen with the responsibility of ordering creation under the Lordship of God.[2] Poetically speaking, Adam was "an august creature with all things put in subjection to him, wearing the very sun as a diadem, treading the very stars like unconsidered dust beneath his feet."[3]

The original intention of God, to say the least, was stupendous. If the intention had been carried out, we descendants of Adam would be living with our primal parents in the same astounding position and honor and authority—a world of kings and queens. The implicit message to the beleaguered church is that we may feel ourselves insignificant, but we are not. We are in God's image, and he *cares* for each one of us.

The Intention Stalled

Grand and encouraging as God's original intention was, something has gone wrong, and the writer purposely gives it dramatic expression by using the double negative in his comment on the psalm in verse 8b—"Now in putting everything in subjection to him, he left nothing outside his control"—thus emphasizing the preceding line that God put "*everything* in subjection under his feet."[4] There is nothing, he says, in this world that is not under man's dominion—nothing—nothing!

The author intends us to take exception. He wants us to say, "Wait a moment! That's not true!"—and then he verbalizes it for us: "At present, we do not yet see everything in subjection to him" (v. 8c). You bet your life we don't!

Adam sinned, and as a consequence his God-given dominion became twisted. Man's rule over creation has through the centuries become an eco-logical disaster. His reign over the animal world is superficial. He achieves it by intimidation: "Obey me, or I'll eat you or wear you!" And sometimes he himself has been the feast. The problem is, he cannot rule over himself, let alone others. And the dictum "Power corrupts, and absolute power corrupts absolutely" is lived out before the eyes of every generation—as it was so personally being done before that storm-tossed little church. Chesterton was right: "Whatever else is true about man, this one thing is certain—man is not what he was meant to be."[5]

The Ultimate Intention

What about God's intention? Will man's alleged significance ever be achieved? The answer is a resounding "Yes!" that echoes for all eternity.

Here our text takes a great turn in the transition between verses 8 and 9: "At present, we do not yet see everything in subjection to him. But we see him [Jesus] . . ." "We do not yet see . . . we see him [Jesus]." Not only is God's *original intention* achieved, but his *ultimate intention* is achieved in Christ, the second Adam.

We must understand that Psalm 8 was not only a celebration of the sig-nificance of man in the vast cosmos—it was also a messianic psalm that had its ultimate fulfillment in Christ. We know this because while the term "son of man" originally meant nothing more than man, with the advent of Christ it came to be a messianic reference to Jesus. He repeatedly called himself "the Son of Man." He is the son of man *par excellence* and fulfills everything the psalm celebrates regarding man.

The initial phrase of verse 9, "But we see him who for a little while was made lower than the angels," was fulfilled in Jesus' incarnation. But whereas the height of *exaltation* for man is in being made a little lower than the angels, it was for Jesus the depth of his *humiliation*. Jesus stooped to reach down to the height of man's glory! Significantly, this is the first use of the name "Jesus" in the Book of Hebrews, and it is emphatic, stressing his humanity and his work of salvation.[6] It is the name given to him by Gabriel at his birth (Matthew 1:21), and it means, "the Lord is salvation."

The next phrase, "But we see him . . . crowned with glory and honor," was fulfilled, as verse 9 goes on to say, "because of the suffering of death." Paul put it this way: "He humbled himself by becoming obedient to the point of death, even death on a cross. Therefore God has highly exalted him and bestowed on him the name that is above every name, so that at the name of Jesus every knee should bow" (Philippians 2:8–10). So we see that in Christ man's glorious potential was realized. Everything was put under his feet.

As we look around we certainly see that not everything is subject to man, but we see Jesus exalted, and all creation is subject to him. And with this the possibility of man's fulfilling God's ultimate intention is made possible. Christ's glorification is our foothold in glory.

The way this happens is revealed in the final phrase of verse 9—"so that by the grace of God he might taste death for everyone." "Taste" is a Hebrew metaphor that does not mean "to sample" but "to partake fully."[7] Jesus' real death for us procured our reign, as Paul explains in Romans: "For if, because of one man's trespass, death reigned through that one man, much more will those who receive the abundance of grace and the free gift of righteousness reign in life through the one man Jesus Christ" (Romans 5:17). Ephesians expands this idea of reigning with him as it says, "And [God] raised us up with him and seated us with him in the heavenly places in Christ Jesus, so that in the coming ages he might show the immeasurable riches of his grace in kindness toward us in Christ Jesus" (Ephesians 2:6, 7).

Because we have been redeemed, our solidarity with Christ is so close that it is described as being "in" him. Paul uses that designation some 169 times in his writings.[8] The term suggests an exchange, an impartation from

Christ. Being "in Christ," the redeemed are so united with him that they share in the glory and dominion of his reign.

As we have seen, the writer is doing his best in this section to comfort the afflicted in the beleaguered little church. The illusion of insignificance has wrapped its cold fingers around many of their hearts. They feel like an unwanted speck among the millions of the Roman Empire. But that is an illusion. The reality is, they are indeed submicroscopic spots in a huge, fallen universe, but as God's children they are objects of astounding attention, for God is minutely mindful of them and cares for them in the greatest detail.

Not only that, he has an *ultimate intention* for them that no angel will ever attain—to rule the world to come! No Roman emperor in all his glory could experience a fraction of the glorious reign that is to be theirs. Moreover, the reign has already begun because they are now "in Christ." Christ on the cross is the measure of their worth. Christ on the throne is a prophecy of their significance and sure dominion.

This is meant to be our comfort today as well. You may journey into a great city such as Chicago and walk through the maze of skyscrapers with an existential sense of significance on the level of a gnat. Your workplace is perhaps within the dark recesses of a granite landmark. And your comings and goings would mean less than nothing to the city of Chicago or any other major city. But on the authority of God's Word you are important and of infinite value. You are just a little lower than the angels. You will be crowned with glory and honor. Everything will be put under your feet.

You may say, "How can this be? I don't *see* it." "But we see [Jesus], who for a little while was made a little lower than the angels, [now] crowned with glory and honor." He is our promise—he is God's ultimate intention for us!

For it was fitting that he, for whom and by whom all things exist, in bringing many sons to glory, should make the founder of their salvation perfect through suffering.

2:10

6

A God-Worthy Salvation

HEBREWS 2:10

ANYTIME ONE SITS IN JUDGMENT ON GOD, he or she is in big trouble. Leo
Tolstoy is a prime example. Many Christians have unwisely assumed he was
a believer because of his much publicized admiration of the Sermon on the
Mount and the elevated sentiments in such stories as *Where Love Is, There
God Is Also.* In actuality Tolstoy was no Christian at all, for he actually felt
himself to be Christ's older brother and thus assumed he could judge the
appropriateness of Christ's actions. Tolstoy saw himself as part of a kind of
elite apostolic succession of minds that included Moses, Isaiah, Confucius,
Socrates, and others who thought and spoke sincerely on the meaning of
life.[1] As such, he declared that to call Christ God or to pray to him was "the
greatest blasphemy." This is why the Orthodox Church properly excommunicated him in 1901.[2]

Christianity has always had its critics who, using their self-generated
ideas, have judged what a proper God should be like. The early Jewish
Christians certainly encountered such critics among fellow-countrymen who
viewed the idea of a suffering Savior-God as a completely inappropriate way
to regard the God of the universe. Paul himself evidently encountered this
thinking because he said, "we preach Christ crucified, a stumbling block to
Jews and folly to Gentiles" (1 Corinthians 1:23). To many minds a suffering
Savior was not a God-worthy concept.

Such thinking was exacting its toll on the storm-tossed little church as
it struggled amidst the rising waves of persecution. Its external critics had
aggressively asserted the absurdity of a suffering Savior, and now, in the
midst of their own suffering, some in the congregation were beginning to drift
toward agreement. "God must certainly be greater than this," they thought.

"Perhaps it would be better to return to an older, less morbid, more positive theology. It certainly would not make life any worse."

As the writer of Hebrews pens his letter to the harried little church, having reminded them of this dangerous drift in thinking as he alluded to Christ's suffering death in 2:9, in verse 10 he turns the tables on the critics with an eloquent assertion that the cross is the most fitting and the most God-worthy way of salvation. The argument crowns and controls all that follows to the end of the chapter. Moreover, its few lines contain so much that we must give them extra attention before we proceed.

Fitting Because It Corresponds to the Sovereign God of Creation

The writer begins by asserting that the work of salvation fits God's creative relationship to the universe: "It was fitting," he says, "that he, for whom and by whom all things exist [i.e., the sovereign God of creation], in bringing many sons to glory, should make the founder of their salvation perfect through suffering." In other words, the way of salvation is not arbitrary but rather befits the character of the God we know, the God "for whom and by whom all things exist."[3] God is the goal and author of all that exists, and correspondingly Jesus is the author and goal of salvation. As the *work of creation* is totally of God, so also is the *work of salvation*. Just as God poured himself into the work of creation, even so the author of salvation poured himself into it through suffering. Everything is of him!

Christ's sufferings and death are not only congruent with the character of the almighty God who did everything in creating the universe—they are an even greater demonstration of his power. Creation was done with a word. He spoke and voila!—there it was and is, ex nihilo. But his speech was not enough to effect salvation. It took not *a* word, but *the* Word—his Son incarnate who was humiliated, suffered, died, rose again, ascended, and is in session at the right hand of God—to effect a salvation that was consonant with his character.[4] From the cross come the loftiest conceptions of him "for whom and by whom all things exist." Our salvation is the greatest display of his power and character.

Thus the writer answers those who say that a suffering Savior does not fit with the idea of a sovereign, cosmic Creator. The argument is, in fact, reversed. Do you want to see the character and power of God? Look at the cosmos. Turn your face like an astronomer to the Milky Way, and as your visage is illumined, let your mind go 600 trillion miles to the edge of our galaxy and visit its neighboring galaxy, the first of some hundred thousand million more "neighbors." Then you will see something of him "for whom and by whom all things exist." Do you want to see even more of God's character and power? Then look to his final word, Christ, for in him you have an even greater display of his power and moral character.

What God did through his suffering Son fits with his eternal power. "It was fitting that he, for whom and by whom all things exist, in bringing many sons to glory, should make the founder of their salvation perfect through suffering" (v. 10).

Fitting Because of the Perfect Savior It Gave Us

Next we observe that what God did is fitting because of the kind of Savior it has given us, as is revealed in the phrase, "the founder of their salvation." The word translated "founder," *archegos*, can be rendered in various ways according to the context that surrounds it. It contains the ideas of supremacy, personal participation, originating.[5] The thought of originating is capsulized in the picture of a mountain climber who goes ahead of the others, chipping away footholds, inserting pitons, and extending the rope to his partners.

This central idea has spawned many translations for this verse: *leader* of salvation, *author* of salvation, *founder* of salvation, *hero* of salvation. But the top three renderings are *captain*, *champion*, and *pioneer*. *Captain* carries the idea of "champion of a cause." But to modern ears it has the misleading idea of the boxing ring or a great athlete. *Pioneer* is the best translation, for Christ our Savior blazed the trail of salvation that we can now follow. God has given us Jesus as the divine hero/pioneer of our salvation!

This is a title and a person to cherish. Significantly, the name bears a remarkable correspondence to the second of the four Messianic names prophesied of Christ in Isaiah 9:6—"Mighty God"—*El Gibbor*, which literally means "mighty hero God."[6] As the courageous pioneer of our salvation, Christ certainly was that!

What a gift! The Son of God is our pioneer of salvation. We might think, "That is indeed enough!" But there is something more, which pushes the borders of our credulity—he is the pioneer of our salvation made "perfect through suffering." Perhaps, like me, you have read this verse scores of times, passing through the mysteries of the opening clauses to the amazing ending— that Jesus was made perfect through sufferings—and you have sat in wonder. How could Jesus, the eternal Son of God who has always existed in perfection, who "is the radiance of the glory of God and the exact imprint of his nature" (1:3), be made perfect? How do you make the perfect more perfect? One thing is for sure: it cannot mean the addition of anything or the purging of anything from his moral nature. Christ has always been the quintessence of moral perfection in that he was absolutely sinless.

His being made "perfect through suffering" has reference to his being made a *perfect pioneer of salvation*. The idea is that he was perfectly equipped to do the job. His perfection was rooted in the Incarnation. Man was created in the image of God, the *imago Dei*, but when Christ came he took on the *imago homini*—he became man. Mike Mason beautifully states the significance of this: "In Jesus the centerpiece of the human race, the wild tangent of all the frayed and decrepit flesh of this fallen old world touches perfectly the circle of eternity."[7]

Incarnate, Christ underwent a series of perfections. Hebrews 5:8, 9 tells us, "Although he was a son, he learned obedience through what he suffered. And being made perfect, he became the source of eternal salvation to all who obey him." He was, of course, already obedient or he would never have undergone the Incarnation. But he became perfect (complete) in experiencing obedience in human flesh. Likewise, we believe that he learned such things as patience and faith. Jesus became perfect in regard to temptation by suffering temptation and putting the tempter to flight (Matthew 4:1–11). Christ's sufferings through his atoning death on the cross when "he himself bore our sins in his body on the tree" (1 Peter 2:24), taking all the sins of the world so that they were on him and in him, so that he became sin for us (2 Corinthians 5:21)—rendered him horribly perfect as our atonement.

And finally, all of this—his perfection in incarnation, temptation, and atonement—rendered in our pioneer a perfect identification with us. It was impossible for God to *fully* identify and thus *fully* sympathize with mankind apart from Christ's incarnation and human experience. But now Christ's perfection makes possible an unlimited capacity to sympathize with those exposed to troubles and temptations in this life. Lewis Bayly, one of John Bunyan's two favorite writers, eloquently portrayed Christ's willingness to embrace suffering, and his resulting ability to sympathize and lend assistance, through this imaginary dialogue between a redeemed soul and Christ:

> *Soul.* Lord, why did you let yourself be taken when you might have escaped your enemies?
> *Christ.* That your spiritual enemies should not take you, and cast you into the prison of utter darkness.
> *Soul.* Lord, why did you let yourself be bound?
> *Christ.* That I might loose the cords of your iniquities.
> *Soul.* Lord, why did you let yourself be lifted up upon a Cross?
> *Christ.* That I might lift you up with me to heaven.

Soul. Lord, why were your hands and feet nailed to the Cross?
Christ. To enlarge your hands to do the works of righteousness and to set
   your feet at liberty, to walk in the ways of peace.
Soul. Lord, why did you have your arms nailed wide?
Christ. That I might embrace you more lovingly.
Soul. Lord, why was your side opened with a spear?
Christ. That you might have a way to come near to my heart.[8]

What wonders of tenderness and sympathy Christ's incarnation and suffering have wrought!

What amazing writing has come from the pen of the author of Hebrews! In one sublime sentence he has taken the detractor's objection (that suffering is unbecoming to a Savior) and demonstrated that suffering has instead produced a perfect, pioneer Savior who can save to the uttermost because he was perfected by the sufferings engendered by his incarnation. Suffering outfitted him to be a perfect pioneer of salvation. His suffering has blazed the way for the great multitudes of his redeemed to follow. How fitting a suffering Savior is!

Fitting Because of What It Achieves for the Lost

Seeing now that suffering befitted Christ as our Savior, first, because it was congruent with God's display of power as sovereign Creator and, second, because Jesus became a perfect pioneer of salvation, we now note that it is fitting because of what it achieves for lost humanity—"in bringing many sons to glory." The picture is of a great family procession as it winds its way through this life and moves ever upward to "glory." Leading the procession is the pioneer, the captain, the champion of our salvation. He has gone before us as perfect man—living a perfect, sinless life—overcoming every temptation and hardship—dying as a perfect atonement for all our sins—resurrected to glory—and now leading us over his bloodstained path to the same glory.

There are "many," not just a few, in the procession. The sense is that of an uncountable multitude. The endless procession follows its leader until they are before the throne. "After this I looked," says John, "and behold, a great multitude that no one could number, from every nation, from all tribes and peoples and languages, standing before the throne and before the Lamb" (Revelation 7:9).

Those in the procession are not simply redeemed "units" but "sons." The great train is made up of redeemed sons and daughters who are in family relation to the Father and the Son. Their hearts' cry is, "*Abba!* Father!" They are brothers and sisters, "fellow heirs with Christ," the pioneer of their salvation (Romans 8:15–17; cf. Galatians 4:5, 6; Ephesians 1:5).

The vast train arrives in "glory." They are not only there—they are sharing in the pioneer's glory. The prophecy of Psalm 8 that the author has just quoted is thus fulfilled: "You made him for a little while lower than the angels; you have crowned him with glory and honor, putting everything in subjection under his feet" (2:7, 8). The multitude, in following their pioneer, had also themselves suffered, but it is forgotten. Paul's words, "I consider that the sufferings of this present time are not worth comparing with the glory that is to be revealed to us" (Romans 8:18), are celebrated over and over—as are these words, "For this light momentary affliction is preparing for us an eternal weight of glory beyond all comparison" (2 Corinthians 4:17).

Thinking again of that storm-tossed little church, some are drifting away because they have begun to believe the lie that Christianity's doctrine of a suffering Savior is incompatible with the majestic sovereign Creator of the universe. Rather, just the opposite is true, first of all, because a suffering Savior is perfectly consonant with the omnipotent God "for whom and by whom all things exist." Just as the work of creation is all his, so is the work of salvation. In fact, the work of salvation through his suffering Son is an even greater demonstration of his power and character than creation! Second, a suffering Savior is wonderfully fitting because of what it produces—a perfected pioneer of salvation who is able to save to the uttermost. And, third, a suffering Savior is fitting because of the salvific results—"bringing many sons to glory."

The suffering church needs to rejoice in its Savior who suffered. Why? Because suffering is a sign of their solidarity with him. Jesus himself said: "Remember the word that I said to you: 'A servant is not greater than his master.' If they persecuted me, they will also persecute you" (John 15:20). Why else? Because as they suffer, they are recipients of his perfect understanding and sympathy. He was tempted in every way just as they were, yet without sin, and so it was said to them, "Let us then with confidence draw near to the throne of grace, that we may receive mercy and find grace to help in time of need" (4:16). Lastly, their suffering meant they were on the glory train.

The message to the persecuted church was so clear: "For it was fitting that he, for whom and by whom all things exist, in bringing many sons to glory, should make the founder of their salvation perfect through suffering" (2:10). They only had to do one thing: *believe it.*

There are five ways we can avoid persecution today: (1) abandon the cosmic view of Christ taught in the Scriptures, (2) do not tell others they need Jesus, (3) accept the world's morals, (4) laugh at its jokes and smile when Christ is dishonored, and (5) ignore the sin that is around us.

It is easy to avoid persecution. However, if we espouse the supremacy of Christ, insist he is the only way, reject the world's moral consensus, weep when Christ is dishonored, and attempt to deal with sin, we will be persecuted. The Scriptures tell us in no uncertain terms, "indeed, all who desire to live a godly life in Christ Jesus will be persecuted" (2 Timothy 3:12). This is true for every believing adult, teenager, and child.

But there is also proper comfort—a God-worthy salvation wrought by Christ who suffered because he does everything in salvation, who suffered to be made a perfect Savior, and who suffered to bring us to glory.

For he who sanctifies and those who are sanctified all have one source. That is why he is not ashamed to call them brothers, saying, "I will tell of your name to my brothers; in the midst of the congregation I will sing your praise." And again, "I will put my trust in him." And again, "Behold, I and the children God has given me." Since therefore the children share in flesh and blood, he himself likewise partook of the same things, that through death he might destroy the one who has the power of death, that is, the devil, and deliver all those who through fear of death were subject to lifelong slavery. For surely it is not angels that he helps, but he helps the offspring of Abraham.

2:11–16

7

Solidarity with the Liberator

HEBREWS 2:11-16

THE FACT OF DEATH—and for most the fear of death—is a relentless real-ity. The more our minds struggle to escape it, the more it comes against us. The more we fear it, the more dreadful it becomes. Those who try to forget it have their memories filled with it. Those who try to shun it meet noth-ing else. Samuel Taylor Coleridge gave this fear chilling expression in *The Rime of the Ancient Mariner* through the image of a man being stalked on an empty road:

> Like one that on a lonesome road
> Doth walk in fear and dread,
> And having once turn'd round, walks on,
> And turns no more his head;
> Because he knows a frightful fiend
> Doth close behind him tread.[1]

Indeed, the fear of death is endemic to the human race. It keeps dogging man's steps whether he ignores it or turns and attempts to stare it down.

This fearful spectre was stalking the tiny storm-tossed first-century church as it plied the seas of persecution. No one had yet been martyred for his or her faith, but the fear of death had its icy fingers around many trembling hearts, around those people who "through [their] fear of death were subject to lifelong slavery" (v. 15). The fear was not simply following them. Rather, it rose up menacingly before them, because one word from the authorities and any one of them could be carted off to death. Such fear was immobiliz-ing—like a deadly cobra's stare upon its prey—and some in the church were experiencing the paralysis of bondage through their fear of death.

So now the writer to the Hebrews, in his ongoing attempt to encourage his friends, specifically seeks to assuage their fear in verses 11–16. His method here is to enlighten them regarding their solidarity (communion of human nature) with Christ, who both suffered and conquered the death they so feared. He does so with three emphases: first, the *fact* of solidarity (v. 11); second, the *character* of solidarity (vv. 12, 13); and third, the *liberation* of solidarity (vv. 14–16).

The Fact of Solidarity

Verse 10, which crowns and controls this section, assumes the solidarity of believers with Christ, the pioneer of their salvation. But now in verse 11 the author boldly states the fact of solidarity as he says, "For he who sanctifies and those who are sanctified all have one source. That is why he [Jesus] is not ashamed to call them brothers." The phrase "one source" is literally, "out of one" or "from one." In the present context, which emphasizes shared humanity (cf. v. 14), "one" is best understood as a reference to Adam. Both Christ and the human race come *out of one man, Adam.* (Note: Acts 17:26 uses the same words to make this same assertion.) Jesus and all humanity share the same human ancestor. Jesus Christ was 100 percent *homo sapiens*, as are all descendants of Adam. But his relationship to humanity was different than that of any other man, because he imparts holiness to those who are in him, the second Adam. Sin came to all humanity through "one man," Adam. But righteousness comes through the "one man," Christ (cf. Romans 5:12, 19).

Because Jesus shares mankind's humanity in Adam, and because as the second Adam he has redeemed his own from their sin and made them holy by giving them a transfusion of his holiness,[2] Jesus "is not ashamed to call them brothers" (v. 11b). This is a stupendous declaration in light of the cosmic greatness of Christ with which the book of Hebrews begins when it asserts, "He is the radiance of the glory of God and the exact imprint of his nature, and he upholds the universe by the word of his power" (1:3). The amazing fact is, this cosmic Son, this Jesus, is not reluctant or ashamed to call the redeemed his "brothers"! "On the contrary, he calls them brothers with all his heart, with the fervour of love, with the eloquence of earnest conviction."[3] He, in fact, rejoices to call us "brothers." He glories in the family designation, "These are my brothers and sisters!"

Now think for a moment of those in the little house-church who are so transfixed by the fear of death, who feel so alone. The healing message to them is that Jesus, the pioneer/captain of their salvation, is proudly affirming his solidarity with them. And this is not "empty religious rhetoric, or pious sentimental exaggeration."[4] He means exactly what he says: *they are his brothers and sisters, and he is proud of it!* This bold statement of the fact of solidarity, taken to heart, will begin to loosen the paralyzing grip of their fear.

The Character of Solidarity

Having established the fact of the communion of human nature shared by Christ and his suffering people, the preacher now proceeds to extend further encouragement by explaining the privilege and character of Christ's solidarity with his people. He does so by summoning three quotations from famous messianic passages in the Greek Old Testament. These passages form a subtly nuanced testimony to the profoundly deep identification of Christ with his suffering people. Significantly, all the passages feature persecution as their backdrop. They are Psalm 22:22 and Isaiah 8:17 and 8:18 respectively. These passages were, of course, far more readily understood by their hearers because they knew their Old Testaments—which is certainly *not* the case with modern-day congregations! Therefore, we must follow closely if we wish to catch the richness of meaning here.

The first quotation is from a psalm (22) that every first-century Christian knew, clearly understanding Christ to be the speaker. Almost all the first twenty-one verses were used in the early church as a *testimonium* of Christ's crucifixion.[5] Its opening words ("My God, my God, why have you forsaken me?") were quoted by Christ as he neared death on the cross (Matthew 27:46; Mark 15:34). Verses 6–8 of Psalm 22 record his experience of being mocked by the callous crowd (cf. Matthew 27:39–44). Psalm 22:14, 15 describe his agonies: "I am poured out like water, and all my bones are out of joint; my heart is like wax; it is melted within my breast; my strength is dried up like a potsherd, and my tongue sticks to my jaws; you lay me in the dust of death." Finally, verses 16–18 of the twenty-second psalm give explicit details of the crucifixion: "a company of evildoers encircles me; they have pierced my hands and feet—I can count all my bones—they stare and gloat over me" (Christ's legs were not broken by the soldiers, John 19:31–36). "They divide my garments among them, and for my clothing they cast lots" (cf. John 19:23ff.; Matthew 27:35).

Solidarity's Intimacy

Thus Christ prophetically agonizes throughout the crucifixion, interspersing his agony with prayers. But in Psalm 22:22—as the crucifixion is over and he is resurrected and exalted—Jesus cries triumphantly to God his Father, "I will tell of your name to my brothers; in the midst of the congregation I will sing your praise" (as quoted in Hebrews 2:12). Note well that it is only to his brothers or, put another way, in the presence of the congregation (which is today the church)[6] that Jesus declares and extols the Father's name. Therefore, Christians and Christians alone are the ones to whom Jesus opens God's "name"—that is, the character of God the Father! The world can get a glimpse of God in the cosmos. It can understand even more about God if its people will humbly examine the Holy Scriptures. But Christ declares and explains the character of God only to his brothers and sisters. "I will tell of your name," says Jesus, "to my brothers."

Even more, as the congregation meets, Christ joins his "brothers" (and sisters) in singing the praises of God the Father, for he says, "In the midst of the congregation I will sing your praise." John Calvin remarks here: "This teaching is the very strongest encouragement to us to bring yet more fervent zeal to the praise of God, when we hear that Christ leads our praise and is the Chief Conductor of our hymns."[7]

Jesus is proud to call his redeemed "brothers" and "sisters" and then to declare to his brothers and sisters what God is like—even leading them in singing God's praises. What privileged knowledge and intimate solidarity with him gives the Church! By recalling the amazing words of Psalm 22, the writer means for the healing salve of Christ's solidarity to further mend the struggling church's fear-infected wounds.

Solidarity's Dependence

The second Old Testament quotation—"I will put my trust in him"—is taken from Isaiah 8:17b, which is again a fragrant messianic passage (the Greek of the New Testament matches that of the Septuagint). Isaiah 8 is sandwiched between chapters of immense messianic teaching. Chapter 7 of Isaiah is decidedly messianic, containing the famous prophecy of Christ's birth: "Therefore the Lord himself will give you a sign. Behold, the virgin shall conceive and bear a son, and shall call his name Immanuel" (Isaiah 7:14). And chapter 9 is likewise messianic with its equally famous prophecy of Christ's names: "For to us a child is born, to us a son is given; and the government shall be upon his shoulder, and his name shall be called Wonderful Counselor, Mighty God, Everlasting Father, Prince of Peace" (Isaiah 9:6). But most of all, chapter 8 itself is a well-mined quarry of messianic prophecies.[8] Verse 8 with its prophecy of the name "Immanuel" (along with Isaiah 7:14) is used in Matthew 1:23. Verse 12, an exhortation to have courage, is quoted in 1 Peter 3:14ff. And verse 14, which describes "a rock of stumbling," is applied to

Christ in Romans 9:33 and 1 Peter 2:8. So the whole of Isaiah 8 (though it is by and about Isaiah) has a rich messianic aroma!

Now then, how is Isaiah's declaration "I will put my trust in him" used to describe Christ? In Isaiah 8 we see that as Isaiah realizes that his message gets no response, he seals it up (v. 16) and declares, "I will wait for the LORD, who is hiding his face from the house of Jacob, and I will hope in him" (v. 17). Isaiah would have to depend on God.

So it was with Christ as he shared the solidarity of our humanity. Isaiah's words in the mouth of Christ—"I will put my trust in him," quoted in 2:13— show that while undergoing persecution in the flesh *Jesus depended on God.* While in the frailty of human flesh, Jesus exercised faith! Even his final words on earth were words of dependence: "'Father, into your hands I commit my spirit!'" (Luke 23:46). What solidarity—what communion of nature—Jesus shares with the suffering church. They suffered? So did he! They were weak? So was he! They must depend on God—just as he did!

Solidarity's Confidence

The third and final Old Testament quotation immediately follows in Isaiah 8:18, though the author of Hebrews introduces it with the formula, "And again . . ." This is because he wants to make a further point, this time about the confidence that Christ's solidarity with his own brings. When Isaiah originally said, "Behold, I and the children whom the LORD has given me," he was referring to his own two *physical sons*, of whom he continued by saying, "[We] are signs and portents in Israel from the LORD of hosts, who dwells on Mount Zion." Both boys had been given prophetic names. One was named Maher-shalal-hash-baz, which has the meaning "the spoil speeds, the prey hastes," signifying the speedy removal of Syria and Israel as enemies of Judah (cf. Isaiah 8:1–4). The other was named Shear-jashub, which expressed the confidence, "a remnant shall return" (Isaiah 7:3).[9] Along with this, Isaiah's name means, "Yahweh is salvation."

Isaiah 8:18 gives a vivid picture of confidence. I envision Isaiah ("Yahweh is salvation") standing between his two boys. He places his hand on Maher-shalal-hash-baz, whose name predicts the removal of his oppressors—"the spoil speeds, the prey hastes." Then he places his other hand on Shear-jashub—"a remnant shall return." Now, with both hands on his prophetically named sons, he confidently says, "Behold, I and the children whom the LORD has given me are signs and portents in Israel from the LORD of hosts, who dwells on Mount Zion." His sons have given him the confidence that he and those sons (and, indeed, all God's people) have a future.

These words, applied to Christ, are a sublime statement of confidence. It is as if he places his arms around the sons and daughters of the suffering church and says, "Behold, I and the children God has given me" (v. 13)—"The fact that I have family—brothers and sisters—is a prophecy of the future. This blessed remnant will survive the onslaught, whatever comes."

Taken together these three messianic quotations provide huge comfort to the fearful little church because they reveal rich benefits coming from Christ's solidarity with his people.

First, Jesus proclaims the character of God to his brothers and sisters alone—and to no one else. He even leads them in hymns to the Father. What amazing knowledge and intimacy comes from their solidarity with Christ!

Second, as their real human brother, sharing their human frailty, he had to put his trust in God. He had to have faith in the midst of suffering, just as he calls them to do.

Finally, the fact that he is in relationship with them, that he can say, "Behold, I and the children God has given me," means they can confidently await a great future!

These wonders of solidarity with Christ would further lift the paralysis of death from the fearful church. And they ought to do the same for us, because we share the same solidarity. This is why the Holy Spirit has given us these beautifully nuanced explanations of our communion of human nature in Christ. If these truths penetrate our hearts, we will be strengthened to stand tall in life's inevitable storms.

The Liberation of Solidarity

In this world, fear of death is a real thing, though some, such as the ninety-year-old novelist Somerset Maugham, have officially denied it. In the last chapter of his memoirs, *A Traveller in Romance,* Maugham wrote:

> There are moments when I have so palpitating an eagerness for death that I could fly to it as to the arms of a lover. . . . I am drunk with the thought of it. It seems to me to offer me the final and absolute freedom. . . . There are indeed days when I feel that I have done everything too often, known too many people, read too many books, seen too many pictures, statues, churches and fine houses, and listened to too much music. I neither believe in immortality nor desire it. I should like to die quietly and painlessly, and I am content to be assured that with my last breath my soul, with its aspirations and its weaknesses, will dissolve into nothingness.[10]

That was Maugham's official self-conscious bravado. But how did

Somerset Maugham really die? In 1965, Maugham's ninety-first year, he was visited by his nephew Robin Maugham, who wrote of it in the April 9, 1978 *London Times*. According to his nephew, the visit took place at his famous uncle's Mediterranean villa shortly before he died. After his arrival, Robin spent the day viewing, among other things, the drawing room and the immensely valuable pictures and objects his uncle's success had enabled him to acquire. Somerset Maugham had eleven servants, including his cook, Annette, who was the envy of all the other millionaires on the Riviera. He dined on silver plates and was waited on by Marius, his butler, and Henri, his footman. But none of that any longer meant anything to him. His nephew writes:

> The following afternoon, I found Willie reclining on a sofa, peering through his spectacles at a Bible which had very large print. He looked horribly wizened, and his face was grim. "I've been reading the Bible you gave me . . . and I've come across the quotation: '*What shall it profit a man if he gain the whole world and lose his own soul?*' I must tell you, my dear Robin, that the text used to hang opposite my bed when I was a child. . . . Of course, it's all a lot of bunk. But the thought is quite interesting all the same." That evening, in the drawing room after dinner, Willie flung himself down onto the sofa. "Oh, Robin, I'm so tired. . . ." He gave a gulp and buried his head in his hands. . . . Willie looked up and his grip tightened on my hands. He was staring towards the floor. His face was contorted with fear, and he was trembling violently. Willie's face was ashen as he stared in horror ahead of him. Suddenly, he began to shriek. "Go away!" he cried. "I'm not ready. . . . I'm not dead yet. . . . I'm not dead yet, I tell you. . . ." His high-pitched terror-struck voice seemed to echo from wall to wall. I looked round, but the room was empty as before.

The fear of death is real and universal. All our lives are, as Mike Mason has suggested, "like the unfolding of a murder mystery in which we ourselves turn out to be the victim."

Why do we fear death? The reasons are many and of various weight: (1) the fear of pain (though most deaths are, medically speaking, not that painful); (2) the fear of separation from what we know and from the ones we love; (3) the fear of the unknown—launching one's vessel on an uncharted sea; (4) the fear of non-being—in Bertrand Russell's words, "Brief and powerless is man's life; on his and all his race the slow, sure doom falls pitiless and dark";[11] and (5) the fear of everlasting punishment.

Except for the matter of physical pain and sadness at leaving loved ones behind, Christians are not to fear death. And those in the struggling church were not to be paralyzed by death's cobra stare—not to be like "those who through fear of death were subject to lifelong slavery" (v. 15).

The reason for this is the liberation attained by Christ for his children through the profound solidarity—the real communion of nature—he shared with them. The argument is clear and compelling: "Since therefore the children share in flesh and blood, he himself likewise partook of the same things, that through death he might destroy the one who has the power of death, that is, the devil, and deliver all those who through fear of death were subject to lifelong slavery" (vv. 14, 15).

Because his incarnation was real—"blood and flesh" (Greek word order)—he was able to die for his people's sins, in their place. In Paul's language, "For our sake he made him to be sin who knew no sin, so that in him we might become the righteousness of God" (2 Corinthians 5:21), and "Christ redeemed us from the curse of the law by becoming a curse for us—for it is written, 'Cursed is everyone who is hanged on a tree'" (Galatians 3:13).

Christ's atoning death effected the destruction of Satan's power of death and thus freedom from the fear of death. Our glorified Lord commands us, "Fear not, I am the first and the last, and the living one. I died, and behold I am alive forevermore, and I have the keys of Death and Hades" (Revelation 1:17, 18).

And thus the Scriptures encourage us by saying, "'O death, where is your victory? O death, where is your sting?'. . .But thanks be to God, who gives us the victory through our Lord Jesus Christ" (1 Corinthians 15:55, 57). And, "Who shall separate us from the love of Christ? Shall tribulation, or distress, or persecution, or famine, or nakedness, or danger, or sword? . . . No, in all these things we are more than conquerors through him who loved us" (Romans 8:35, 37).

These beautiful facts about our solidarity with Christ give profound encouragement. First, the *fact* of his solidarity with us, that he delights to call us brothers and sisters, gives our souls unequalled comfort. Second, the profound *character* of his solidarity with us, with its revelations regarding our shared intimacy, dependence, and confidence, gives us great hope. And third, the *liberation* that comes from our solidarity with Christ seals our comfort as we are set free from the fear of death. Solidarity with Christ does indeed encourage us!

This is why the *Heidelberg Catechism* begins:

Question 1: What is thy only comfort in life and in death?

Answer.

That I, with body and soul, both in life and in death, am not my own, but belong to my faithful Saviour Jesus Christ, who with his precious blood has fully satisfied for all my sins, and redeemed me from all the power of the devil; and so preserves me that without the will of my Father in heaven not a hair can fall from my head; yea, that all things must work together for my salvation. Wherefore, by his Holy Spirit, he also assures me of eternal life, and makes me heartily willing and ready henceforth to live unto him.[12]

Therefore he had to be made like his brothers in every respect, so that he might become a merciful and faithful high priest in the service of God, to make propitiation for the sins of the people. For because he himself has suffered when tempted, he is able to help those who are being tempted.

2:17, 18

8

Solidarity with the High Priest

HEBREWS 2:17, 18

CHURCH HISTORIAN HENRY CHADWICK tells us that the early church appropriated symbols from the sea to express its faith. The most famous, of course, was the fish, which brought to mind the Greek word for *fish*, a five-letter acronym for "Jesus Christ God's Son Savior." Some early Christians even spoke in cryptic terms about the fish—for example, Bishop Abercius who described his experience of Communion like this: ". . . and faith everywhere led the way and served food everywhere, the Fish from the spring, immense, pure . . . with good wine, giving the cup and the loaf."[1]

Along with the fish, the other popular Christian symbol from the sea was the anchor. The inspiration for this came from 6:19, 20 where the hope produced by Jesus' ministry as eternal high priest is described as an "*anchor of the soul*"—"We have this as a sure and steadfast anchor of the soul, a hope that enters into the inner place behind the curtain, where Jesus has gone as a forerunner on our behalf, having become a high priest forever after the order of Melchizedek." So the anchor came to symbolize Christ and specifically the Christian hope emanating from the supremacy of his priesthood. The anchor became such a powerful symbol to the early church that it was found in paintings and in the design of Christians' coffins.[2] In death Christians found great comfort in the knowledge that they were anchored by Christ, the great priest, and so were not adrift for eternity.

Significantly, 2:17, 18, which expounds the church's solidarity with Christ, its high priest, anchors an extended passage that began in verse 10 regarding the comfort that comes from that solidarity with Christ. The progression of thought is like this: the *fact* of solidarity (2:10, 11), the *character* of solidarity (vv. 12, 13), the *liberation* that comes from solidarity (2:14–16), and now the *significance* of the Church's solidarity with its high priest (2:17, 18). Thus the weightiest truth, in terms of comfort for the storm-tossed church, is given last.

Specifically, verses 17, 18 tell us how Christ's perfect solidarity with the Church (his perfect communion of spirit with believers) makes him a perfect high priest and, by implication, the great anchor in the storms of life. Here, then, is the greatest of comforts—the oneness of our high priest with us and his ministry in us and for us. This, taken to heart, will give any believer a solid foundation.

The magnificent train of thought in this famous text presents Christ as a being who is at once a perfect priestly *mediator, propitiator*, and *helper*.

The writer introduces these thoughts with a memorable reference to Christ's incarnation, saying, "Therefore he had to be made like his brothers in every respect" (v. 17a; cf. 2:11). Jesus did not merely resemble humanity in *some* qualities of human nature, but "in every respect"—"in all things" (NASB). Christ's likeness to us was not simulated but absolute (Philippians 2:7)— except for sin (4:15).

Many Christians do not actually understand this, though they think they do, because nestled in their understanding of the Incarnation is the thought that though Christ had a human body, he did not have a completely human mind. Some imagine, for example, that he possessed a divine awareness as an infant, so that his smiling and cooing in his mother's arms were an accommodation of his feigned infancy, and that actually he could have been thinking, *You imagine I'm a helpless baby, but actually I created the universe!* Such thinking is a "man on the street" version of an ancient heresy called *docetism*—that Christ only *seemed* to be man.

In actuality, while it is true that the Son of God in the womb, at birth, and throughout life always retained the qualities of omniscience, omnipotence, and omnipresence, he had placed the exercise of them at the discretion of God the Father (see Philippians 2:5–11). So we must understand that Christ's awareness that he was God came when the Father willed it (at his bar mitzvah? at his baptism?), and it was a similar situation with his great acts of omnipotence and omniscience. Jesus implicitly expressed this when he said, "Truly, truly, I say to you, the Son can do nothing of his own accord, but only what he sees the Father doing. For whatever the Father does, that the Son does likewise" (John 5:19). As Leon Morris says, "It is not simply that he does not act in independence of the Father. He cannot act in independence of the Father."[3]

The point we are making is that through the infinite creative power of the Godhead, the Son remained ontologically God in the Incarnation, while at the same time being absolutely human in body, mind, and emotions. This means that Christ grew from infancy, through childhood, adolescence, young adulthood, and into maturity—in both body and mind. His body developed, as did his mind and emotions. Not only that, but both as a child and through adulthood he experienced human emotions—anger and joy and sorrow. May we reverently understand that the Incarnation meant that Christ progressively smelled like an infant, a boy, and a man—he thought like a child before he thought like a man—he knew the same range of human emotions as we did as he grew to maturity.

So it is imperative that we understand that the incarnation of Christ means that he was perfectly human in body, mind, and emotions. Even more, the language of our text that says, "Therefore he had to be made like his brothers in every respect" suggests that the writer viewed the completeness of Christ's identification with his own as a moral obligation in becoming a perfect redeemer and mediator.[4]

A Perfect Priestly Mediator

The perfections he has in mind become apparent as we read the next line: "so that he might become a merciful and faithful high priest in the service of God" (v. 17b)—namely, mercy and faithfulness.

A Merciful Mediator

Jesus' experiences in human flesh made him a mediator who is first and foremost "merciful." Mercy is more than an emotion. For example, suppose you were driving in the country and came across an accident in which a victim was lying in the road with no one to assist him. You ache for the person, you feel a surge of compassion, but you do nothing and drive on. Why? Because you are unmerciful! To be merciful, one must act to alleviate another's pain. Jesus repeatedly modeled this in the Gospels when he had *compassion* on the hungry or the ill or the grieving and then *mercy* in meeting their needs (cf. Mark 1:41; 8:2, 3; Luke 7:13).

So we understand that in being our "merciful . . . high priest" Jesus emotionally gathers up our needs to himself and then in mercy does something about them. This is a stupendous revelation—a God who has personal emotion at our miserable plight and then springs into action. Even more, our Lord's compassion and mercy are sensitized by the fact that he was really one of us and experienced like miseries; he knows how it feels.

All good husbands are compassionate and merciful when their wives give birth. But how much more merciful would they be if they first had the experience of giving birth! Made like their wives "in every respect" (in body, in hormones, in the pain of childbirth) they would be merciful indeed! Oh, the depth of Jesus' mercy, for he was made like us in every way.

A Faithful Mediator

But not only is Jesus a merciful mediator, he is also faithful—a "faithful high priest in the service of God." There is an intentional contrast here: Jesus is "*merciful*" in his priestly relationship to his people and "*faithful*" in his priestly mediation to God the Father.[5]

His faithfulness to God is seen in two ways. First, he was faithful as mankind's sin-bearer. He did everything required. Nothing deterred him from the cross. He drank the bitter cup to its dregs. "Our hell he made his, that his heaven might be ours."[6] Never has there been such faithfulness!

Second, he is faithful in representing us to the Father. At God's right hand his blood is applied to man's sins. There he faithfully prays for his own with compassion and tender mercy, honed by his human experience. This is a truth every informed heart holds dear, as did Paul when he encouraged Timothy, reminding him, "For there is one God, and there is one mediator between God and men, the man Christ Jesus, who gave himself as a ransom for all" (1 Timothy 2:5, 6).

What an anchor the author offers the storm-tossed church! God's people have a priestly mediator who, because he was made like them "in every respect" (in body, mind, and emotions), is compassionate. Christ our mediator actually feels the pangs of human existence in himself. And thus his compassion is not simulated but perfectly real. Even more, from the depth of Christ's compassion springs mercy as he acts to meet our needs. This in turn involves his faithful priestly mediation between us and God as he bears our sins and infirmities, interceding for us with tender mercy.

The knowledge of such a merciful and faithful priestly mediator, truly believed, will anchor any storm-tossed soul. It will anchor yours!

A Perfect Priestly Propitiator

The writer introduces the next major element in his thought, shifting from his emphasis on Christ's being a perfect priestly mediator to Christ's perfection as a priestly *propitiator*. We see this in the final phrase of verse 17—"to make propitiation for the sins of the people." This is literally, "that he might make propitiation with respect to the sins of the people."[7] Some recent translations render "make propitiation" as "make atonement," but this dilutes the specific meaning of the Greek texts.

Leon Morris, author of two landmark volumes on Christ's work on the cross, comments: "'Make atonement' is a curious rendering. The word *hilaskesthai* means 'to propitiate,' not 'to make atonement,' and relates to putting away the divine wrath."[8] The problem, as Morris notes, is that when translations substitute an easier word such as "atonement"[9] or "expiate,"[10] they obscure the emphasis the writer is making—namely, that Christ propitiated God's personal wrath, fully meeting it and putting it away.

When people sin, they arouse the wrath of God (Romans 1:18) and become enemies of God (Romans 5:10). The Old and New Testaments reveal an utterly holy God whose holy nature demands wrath against all sin. Wrath is the reverse side of his holiness. God cannot set aside his wrath toward our sin and remain holy.

This is where the propitiating love of God comes in. To obtain our salvation for us, God himself met the demands of his holiness in Christ, which, because of the oneness of the Trinity, means he met the demands of his holiness himself. He has, in a manner of speaking, propitiated himself in our place!

Thus we see that God, through Christ, our priestly propitiator, has done everything for us. Paul speaks of this in Romans 3:24, 25 where he describes believers as "being justified as a gift by His grace through the redemption which is in Christ Jesus; whom God displayed publicly as a propitiation in His blood . . ."(NASB).

Christ, our perfect priestly propitiator, saved us in a way that kept God's holiness (indeed Christ's holiness) intact. Revelation speaks of his righteous wrath as "the wrath of the Lamb" (Revelation 6:16). What love this perfect priest had for the storm-tossed church! They were in deep waters, but they were not under God's wrath, nor would they ever be again. Their troubled hearts rejoiced that Christ, their priest, loved them so much that he propitiated his own terrible wrath for them. Such a priest would do anything and everything consonant with his loving nature to meet their needs. We must never be fooled or disbelieve this, no matter how high the waters rise.

A Perfect Priestly Helper

The writer's comforting progression of thought has presented a being who is a perfect priestly *mediator*, then *propitiator*, and now *helper*: "For because he himself has suffered when tempted, he is able to help those who are being tempted" (v. 18).

How did Jesus suffer when he was tempted? Common sense tells us he experienced the general temptations we all know—pride, envy, hatred, self-gratification, to name a few. But there was one great difference—he was sinless. And this is exactly why he suffered. Being the sinless Son of God, temptations repulsed him far more than they could us. Many are tempted, but never *suffer* when tempted. The terrible truth is, multitudes find daily temptations to be a perverted source of pleasure. I am reminded of the story of the young boy in the kitchen who, asked by his mother, "What are you doing?" replied, "I'm just standing here with my hand in the cookie jar, resisting temptation." For many American men, Sunday afternoon is a titillating parade of beer commercials with a perpetual hand in the visual cookie jar "resisting temptation." Our Lord was saddened and suffered as he sinlessly lived out his thirty-three years assailed by everyday temptations.

But his greatest suffering occurred, as the Scriptures specifically point out, when he was tempted to forsake his calling and take an easy way out. Matthew tells us that immediately after Jesus' baptism, he was led out into the desert where he was tempted by the devil and that at the root of each of the three diabolical temptations was the lure to leave his vocation for an easier way (Matthew 4:1–11). Later, as he was establishing his ministry, Satan employed Jesus' own family to try to dissuade him through a domestic kidnapping, because they thought "He is out of his mind" (Mark 3:21). And then, at the apex of his ministry, Peter publicly rebuked Jesus for intimating that he must die on the cross. Significantly, Jesus denounced Peter's words with a statement almost identical to that with which he earlier dismissed Satan in the wilderness—"Get behind me, Satan!" (Mark 8:33; cf. Matthew 4:10). Next, in Gethsemane Jesus repeatedly cast himself to the ground, sweating great drops of blood and crying out, "Abba, Father, all things are possible for you. Remove this cup from me. Yet not what I will, but what you will" (Mark 14:36). And finally on the cross he was put to the ultimate temptation.

These famous temptations to take the easy way out were real, and they brought massive suffering to Christ's soul. He knew the horror that awaited him—he knew he would endure the unmitigated pain of sin and wrath with the full feeling and consciousness that comes from purity.

What a temptation to escape! What suffering! But he bore it all. And even more significantly, he bore it as a *man*. He was tempted and suffered and endured with a human mind, body, and emotions—and he never turned away from the cross. What is more, as a man he endured greater temptation and suffering than any other man because he never gave in to sin. As Philip Hughes explains regarding Christ: "He knows the full force of temptation in a manner that we who have not withstood it to the end cannot know."[11] Think of it this way—which bridge has undergone the greatest stress, the one that collapses under its first load of traffic, or the one that bears the same traffic morning and evening, year after year?

But what does this mean to us? Sublimely, this: "He is able to help those who are being tempted." He is able to help because he understands. A person who has always had a strong body and is physically fit has no conception of what it is like to be handicapped. Those who are mentally quick find it difficult to understand and empathize with those who find learning difficult. A person who has never grieved cannot fully identify with the grieving. I remember well when I was in seminary, one of the couples lost their little girl in a home accident, and their greatest comfort, apart from Christ himself, came from another couple who had lost their little boy years before in a domestic accident. "Comfort drops but coldly from the lips that have never uttered a sigh or a groan."[12]

Jesus never sinned, but he did suffer immense temptation. And his heart bears the blessed scars of sympathy. The people in the little church under siege were not only experiencing the temptations that are common to all, but they were being tempted to be unfaithful to God and to give up their calling. What an encouragement to know that their Savior and high priest had known similar but far greater temptations, and that he had suffered more, endured, and was victorious. He understood! He empathized! He was interceding for them! He forgave them! And he wanted to empower them to persevere in their calling, come what may.

Fellow-pilgrims of the Way, God's Word still stands true: "For because he himself has suffered when tempted, he is able to help those who are being tempted." He can help you! He can help me!

Jesus, our great high priest, is our anchor. "We have this as a sure and steadfast anchor of the soul, a hope that enters into the inner place behind the curtain, where Jesus has gone as a forerunner on our behalf, having become a high priest forever after the order of Melchizedek" (6:19, 20).

We are anchored by a perfect priestly *mediator* who, because he was made like us in every way (not simulated humanity but real humanity), is *merciful* to us and *faithful* as he ministers to the Father on our behalf. Let his priestly mercy and faithfulness anchor your soul.

We are anchored by a perfect priestly *propitiator* who propitiated his own wrath on the cross, so that we are no longer under the wrath of God. We may experience hardship, even discipline, but never the wrath of God. Because of Jesus' great propitiating work, we are ever under love. Let this be an anchor for your soul.

We are anchored by a perfect priestly *helper* whose sufferings in the course of temptation scarred his soul with sympathy. And thus "he is able to help those who are being tempted" to take the easy way out. Let this be an anchor for your soul.

Those who are experiencing high waters because of their faith and are thus tempted to look for an easy way out need an anchor. The anchor is this massive vision of Christ, our eternal high priest. This vision, seen and taken to heart, will steel the trembling soul.

What a priest we have!

Therefore, holy brothers, you who share in a heavenly calling, consider Jesus, the apostle and high priest of our confession, who was faithful to him who appointed him, just as Moses also was faithful in all God's house. For Jesus has been counted worthy of more glory than Moses—as much more glory as the builder of a house has more honor than the house itself. (For every house is built by someone, but the builder of all things is God.) Now Moses was faithful in all God's house as a servant, to testify to the things that were to be spoken later, but Christ is faithful over God's house as a son. And we are his house if indeed we hold fast our confidence and our boasting in our hope.

3:1–6

9

Superior to Moses

HEBREWS 3:1-6

IT IS DIFFICULT FOR THOSE UNFAMILIAR WITH JEWISH HISTORY to appreciate the awesome reverence accorded Moses by his people, and it is particularly difficult today amidst the revisionist, iconoclastic spirit of our century. But Moses was revered as the greatest of all Hebrews, and indeed the greatest man of history. We must understand this first if we are to get anything of the Holy Spirit's message to us in Hebrews 3.

First, we must understand that Moses was divinely *chosen* for his epic task. His life was miraculously preserved and nurtured from birth when, under the sentence of death, he was plucked from the bulrushes by Pharaoh's daughter and given a noble upbringing, with his birth mother attending him as nursemaid (Exodus 2:1–10). Then, as a man, his election as deliverer was sealed when God, the "I AM," called and ordained him at the burning bush (Exodus 3).

Second, Moses became the incomparable *deliverer* of his people through an unparalleled display of power. Exodus 7–12 tells us that the Nile turned to blood—successive plagues of frogs, gnats, and flies swarmed upon Egypt—hail and boils afflicted man and beast—and on the dark night of Passover, all the firstborn of man and beast who were not under the blood perished. With his staff Moses parted the Red Sea and the people passed through (Exodus 14, esp. vv. 21, 22), and with his staff he smote the rock and all Israel drank (Exodus 17:1–7). Delivering power radiated from Moses' life!

Third, he served as Israel's greatest *prophet*. God communicated to other prophets indirectly through various means, but he communicated directly to Moses, as God himself explained in Numbers 12:6–8:

> If there is a prophet among you, I the LORD make myself known to him in a vision; I speak with him in a dream. Not so with my servant Moses. He is faithful in all my house. With him I speak mouth to mouth, clearly, and not in riddles, and he beholds the form of the LORD.

This is, in fact, how it was when Moses received the Ten Commandments, at which time his exposure to God was so profound that his face retained a wonderful radiance (Exodus 34:29–35; cf. Deuteronomy 34:11). He was second only to unfallen Adam in intimacy. What a prophet!

Fourth, Moses was the *lawgiver*. To the Jew, the Law was the greatest thing in all the world. Moses was the conduit for the Ten Commandments, the Levitical laws, the sacrificial cultus, and the tabernacle. Everything in their religion recalled his name, for it all came from "the Law of Moses." For me, Michelangelo's *Moses*, the famous bigger-than-life statue of Moses seated, with his flowing Hebrew beard covering his great chest and his muscular right arm cradling the Law, provides an image of Moses' power as lawgiver.

Fifth, he was Israel's great *historian*. Under divine inspiration he authored the Pentateuch, the first five books of the Bible—Genesis through Deuteronomy.

Sixth, he was "very *meek*, more than all people who were on the face of the earth" (Numbers 12:3). Remarkable! He was the greatest, but it had not gone to his head. Why? Because his head had been permanently "sized" on the back side of the desert during the second forty years of his life (Exodus 2—4).

These six qualities, among others, can be summed up under one grand heading: *Moses—The Great Apostle and High Priest of the Old Testament*. *Apostle* means "one who is sent," and Moses certainly was that because he was called by God, appointed by God, and sent by God as his representative both to his people and to the court of Pharaoh.

As to his priestliness, F. F. Bruce explains: "It was his brother, Aaron, and not he who was high priest of Israel so far as title and investiture were concerned; but it was Moses and not Aaron, who was Israel's true advocate with God."[1] This was memorably illustrated as Moses' hands, held high in intercession, wrought victory over the Amalekites (Exodus 17:8–13). Significantly, his central role as priestly intercessor was emphasized by Aaron's and Hur's assistance in holding up his hands (Exodus 17:15). Also, later, after Israel's orgy surrounding the golden calf in which Aaron was shamefully implicated, it was Moses' intercession that obtained pardon for his people (Exodus 32:11ff., 31ff.; cf. Numbers 14:13ff.). In addition to his intercession, Moses as a Levite performed priestly functions such as the sprinkling of blood (Exodus 24:4–8).

Moses functioned as the greatest *apostle* and *priest* of his people, and for this he was revered. Exodus 33:8 says, "Whenever Moses went out to the tent, all the people would rise up, and each would stand at his tent door, and watch Moses until he had gone into the tent." When Moses died, the Lord himself buried him in an anonymous grave (Deuteronomy 34:5, 6)—perhaps because some would have worshiped his bones. The book of Deuteronomy closes with Moses' sublime epitaph:

> And there has not arisen a prophet since in Israel like Moses, whom the
> LORD knew face to face, none like him for all the signs and the wonders
> that the LORD sent him to do in the land of Egypt, to Pharaoh and to all
> his servants and to all his land, and for all the mighty power and all the
> great deeds of terror that Moses did in the sight of all Israel. (Deuteronomy
> 34:10–12)

To all Jews, Moses was simply the greatest. According to one early tradition, Moses was superior to the angels, having higher rank and privilege than the ministering angels.[2]

Now, seeing something of the vast regard the Jews gave to Moses, we can understand why here in Hebrews 3 the writer deems it necessary to establish the superiority of Christ over Moses. Some of his fellow-Christians/fellow-Jews, who had readily accepted Jesus' superiority to angels, perhaps do not view Christ as superior to Moses, because of their traditional overestimation of Moses and their inadequate understanding of Christ. As a result, they are in danger of drifting back into Judaism when persecution intensifies.

Focus on Jesus

To such, the writer issues a command to consider Jesus: "Therefore, holy brothers, you who share in a heavenly calling, consider Jesus, the apostle and high priest of our confession" (v. 1). The command is framed in congenial terms that reference their solidarity of experience and orientation of soul—their brotherhood, holiness, and mutual sharing. But it is unrelenting as to what it commands—namely, a focus on the man Jesus and his functions as "apostle" and "high priest." Significantly, Jesus is referred to by the terms *apostle* and *high priest* only in the Book of Hebrews: "apostle" this once and "high priest" twelve times. The words used together here are freighted with immense significance.

The titles introduce Jesus' superiority to Moses, the apostle and priest of the old economy. Jesus was and is "the apostle," "the sent one," par excellence. Jesus repeatedly describes himself (over ten times in John's writings alone) as being sent by the Father into the world. Jesus is "the first apostle, the great apostle, the source of all apostleship."[3] His apostleship is prior to all apostleship and is the foundation of all that would follow. His apostleship meant "mission accomplished."

And, of course, Jesus is also the "high priest" par excellence. Because he was perfectly human and perfectly divine, he knows both man and God. Thus he is able to speak to men for God and to intercede to God for men. He is the one person through whom man comes to God and God to man.

Understanding this, we are prepared for the full force of the command, because "consider" expresses "attention and continuous observation and regard."[4] It means to apply one's mind diligently—to fix one's attention in such a way that the significance of the thing is learned. In Luke 12:24 Jesus uses the same word when he says, "Consider the ravens"—that is, set your mind on how they are provided for and what it means in your life.[5] Here in Hebrews the word means: Think on the incarnate Son Jesus and what his being *the sent one* and *intercessor* means; keep on applying your mind to it unceasingly, and apply it to your life.

How does one "consider" in this way? It begins with *desire*. David, the psalmist, did this because he really wanted to see the Lord: "One thing have I asked of the Lord, that will I seek after: that I may dwell in the house of the Lord all the days of my life, to gaze upon the beauty of the Lord and to inquire in his temple" (Psalm 27:4). Paul poured out his desire in a passionate prayer: "I count everything as loss . . . that I may know him and the power of his resurrection, and may share his sufferings, becoming like him in his death" (Philippians 3:8–10).

Along with desire, fixing the mind calls for *concentration*. A brilliant mathematician, Norbert Wiener, was walking across the campus of MIT. He was so absorbed in thought that when a student greeted him, he failed to respond. But after a few steps he turned and said, "Pardon me, could you tell me which way I came from?" The student pointed and answered, "That way, sir!" "Thanks," said the prof. "Now I know I've had lunch!" This is extreme, to be sure, but no one's thoughts can be said to be fixed without concentration. And no one will ever learn anything about the subject being considered without it. Isaac Newton said the key to his understanding was, "I keep it before me."

Concentration, of course, requires *discipline* like that of an athlete. "Therefore, since we have so great a cloud of witnesses surrounding us, let us also lay aside every encumbrance, and the sin which so easily entangles us, and let us run with endurance the race that is set before us, fixing our eyes on

Jesus the author and perfecter of faith" (12:1, 2 NASB). Paul put it this way: "If then you have been raised with Christ, seek the things that are above, where Christ is, seated at the right hand of God. Set your minds on things that are above, not on things that are on earth" (Colossians 3:1, 2). Concentrating on Jesus requires an act of the will.

Lastly, fixing our thoughts on Jesus requires *time*, for true reflection cannot happen with a glance. No one can see the beauty of the country as he hurries through it on the interstate. It is only when we sit still and gaze that the landscape fills our souls.

What wisdom the writer was pouring on the persecuted church! He knew that its people's survival lay in turning their eyes away from their trials and fixing them upon Christ their *apostle* who accomplished his mission and their *high priest* who prays for them. This is what all of us need above everything else. Lack of this is why so many Christians are sick and useless and are falling by the way. They need to cultivate the desire, concentration, discipline, and time to fix their eyes upon Jesus.

Jesus' Superior Calling

Having challenged his friends to fix their eyes on Jesus, the ultimate apostle and high priest, the writer now explicitly addresses Jesus' superiority over Moses by showing that while both Moses and Jesus were faithful in their God-given callings, Jesus' was greater because his work was greater: "[He] was faithful to him who appointed him, just as Moses also was faithful in all God's house. For Jesus has been counted worthy of more glory than Moses—as much more glory as the builder of a house has more honor than the house itself. (For every house is built by someone, but the builder of all things is God.)" (vv. 2–4).

It was commonly held in ancient thought that an architect is greater than what he builds.[6] So the central point here is that Jesus is superior to Moses because Jesus is the builder, and Moses is part of the house/household. Bramanti and Michelangelo are greater than the great dome of their design in St. Peter's. Sir Christopher Wren is greater than St. Paul's. Frank Lloyd Wright is greater than his creations, a fact that "the master" was quick to bring up if anyone forgot!

This comparison between the builder and the house in no way minimizes Moses. His faithfulness is not in question. In fact, God highly honored him. Jesus built the spiritual house of God—Moses was a leader in the house. They are simply in different categories that are beyond comparison because

Jesus' calling is so superior. In fact, God the Father has made everything in the universe through his Son, Jesus (1:2).

Jesus, a Superior Person

The other great proof of Jesus' superiority involves looking at his person as compared to Moses. Moses was a "*servant*," but Jesus was a "*son*": "Now Moses was faithful in all God's house as a servant, to testify to the things that were to be spoken later, but Christ is faithful over God's house as a son" (vv. 5, 6a). The word used to describe Moses' servanthood is rare, being used only here in the New Testament. It denotes an honored servant who is far above a slave but is still a servant, somewhat like a squire to a great person.[7] It embodies very well Moses' honored Old Testament title "servant" of the Lord (Exodus 14:31; Numbers 11:11; 12:7; Deuteronomy 3:24; Joshua 1:2). As a servant, Moses' faithfulness was proverbial. In Exodus 35–40 there are twenty-two references to Moses' faithfulness to God.[8]

A marvelous characteristic of his faithful servanthood was his "testify[ing] to the things that were to be spoken later" (v. 5). Specifically this refers to the gospel that Jesus proclaimed as God's Son (cf. 1:1, 2). Moses' Law, the Levitical system of sacrifice, the ceremonies, the priesthood, the tabernacle were all testimony "to the things that were to be spoken later" in Christ (cf. 10:1). Jesus himself told the Jews: "If you believed Moses, you would believe me; for he wrote of me" (John 5:46). After Jesus' resurrection, while walking on the road to Emmaus, Luke tells us, Jesus conversed with two disciples: "And beginning with Moses and all the Prophets, he interpreted to them in all the Scriptures the things concerning himself" (Luke 24:27).

Moses displayed supreme human faithfulness as a servant, "to testify to the things that were to be spoken later." But he was not a son.

"But Christ," says our text, "is faithful over God's house as a *son*" (v. 6). He faithfully fulfilled every Old Testament prophecy. He faithfully and joyfully became incarnate, perfectly becoming a human in body, mind, and emotions. He faithfully submitted his "omnis"—his power, his presence, and his knowledge—to the will of the Father. He faithfully underwent temptation and suffered terribly, never giving in. He faithfully went to Gethsemane. He faithfully yielded his hands to the nails. He faithfully became sin for us, as wave after wave of the world's sin was poured over his sinless soul. Again and again during those three hours on the cross his soul recoiled and convulsed as all the lies of civilization, the murders of a thousand "Killing Fields," the whorings of the world's armies, and the noxious brew of hatreds, jealousies, and pride were poured on his purity. Finally he became a curse: "Christ redeemed us from the curse of the law by becoming a curse for us—for it is written, 'Cursed is everyone who is hanged on a tree'" (Galatians 3:13). In the darkness Jesus bore it all in silence. Not a word came from his lips. Can you see him writhing like a serpent in the gloom (see John 3:14, 15)? And, of course, he faithfully died for us—"Jesus uttered a loud cry and breathed his last" (Mark 15:37). Such was the ministry of our faithful *apostolos, the sent one.*

But now as our resurrected *high priest* he faithfully intercedes for us with a tender mercy sensitized by his apostolic faithfulness. Moses was, indeed, a faithful apostle and high priest. But Jesus is infinitely supreme! He is the great "apostle and high priest of our confession." And he is eternally faithful over God's house.

Does our faithful "apostle and high priest" require anything from us? Yes, he does!

Focus on Christ

As we have seen, we must continually "consider" him—always—perpetually. We must *desire* to gaze on him with all our heart, and then we must utilize our powers of *concentration* and must *discipline* ourselves to spend *time* doing so. By God's grace we must lift our eyes away from the troubles and distractions around us and focus on Christ.

Hold on to Christ

But in addition to this, as Jesus' faithful example would suggest, we must faithfully *persevere.* "And we are his house," concludes the writer, "if indeed we hold fast our confidence and our boasting in our hope" (v. 6b). We will find this condition again and again in Hebrews: continuance in the Christian life—holding on—is the test of real faith. "The doctrine of the final perseverance of the saints has as its corollary the salutary teaching that the saints are the people who persevere to the end."[9] The writer fears that some in the storm-tossed church will not persevere.

The Holy Spirit thus asks us, are we persevering? Or in the jostling tides of life are we drifting away? Is Christ as dear as the first day we met him—even more dear? Are we holding on to our "confidence"? Are we "boasting in our hope"? That is, are we proud of the gospel? Was there a time in our life, perhaps with the fresh glow of new faith, when we were proud and courageous for Christ, but now, with the passing of time, our proper pride, our boast, and our courage are gone? If so, God's Word says we must hold on to it.

Focus on—hold on—to Christ, your great, superior apostle and high priest.

Therefore, as the Holy Spirit says, "Today, if you hear his voice, do not harden your hearts as in the rebellion, on the day of testing in the wilderness, where your fathers put me to the test and saw my works for forty years. Therefore I was provoked with that generation, and said, 'They always go astray in their heart; they have not known my ways.' As I swore in my wrath, 'They shall not enter my rest.'" Take care, brothers, lest there be in any of you an evil, unbelieving heart, leading you to fall away from the living God. But exhort one another every day, as long as it is called "today," that none of you may be hardened by the deceitfulness of sin. For we have come to share in Christ, if indeed we hold our original confidence firm to the end. As it is said, "Today, if you hear his voice, do not harden your hearts as in the rebellion." For who were those who heard and yet rebelled? Was it not all those who left Egypt led by Moses? And with whom was he provoked for forty years? Was it not with those who sinned, whose bodies fell in the wilderness? And to whom did he swear that they would not enter his rest, but to those who were disobedient? So we see that they were unable to enter because of unbelief.

10

Finishing Well

HEBREWS 3:7–19

IN THE LONG HISTORY OF THIS EARTH, no migration of any people began so well, and with such great expectations, as Israel's exodus from Egypt. At midnight on that unforgettable night, as all Israel was snug and secure in their homes, with the pleasing aroma of roast lamb hanging protectively over them, the destroyer struck down all the firstborn of Egypt, both man and beast, and a mournful wail rose from every Egyptian house (Exodus 12:29, 30). It was the end of 430 years of bondage.

Stubborn Pharaoh summoned Moses, commanded Israel to leave, and even asked for a blessing (Exodus 12:31, 32). So as dawn broke, six hundred thousand men on foot, plus women and children (about 1,500,000 souls), and all their livestock began an orderly exodus by tribal divisions (Exodus 12:37, 41, 51). It was a proud departure, with each tribe headed by its leaders. Ephraim was particularly noticeable as it triumphantly bore the catafalque containing Joseph's bones, fulfilling his dying wish to have his bones carried back to Palestine (Exodus 13:19; cf. Genesis 50:25, 26). Israel left unexpectedly rich as well, as the Egyptians, glad to see them go, "let them have what they asked. Thus they plundered the Egyptians" (Exodus 12:36).

And then the most stupendous thing happened as they entered the wilderness—an immense pillar of cloud formed in the sky before them to lead the way. At sunset it became a pillar of fire, so that every night Israel was lighted by its swirling orange glow (Exodus 13:20–22). What a spectacle that must have been against the backdrop of the star-studded desert sky.

Then, of course, there was the ill-fated pursuit by Pharaoh that trapped Israel against the sea. But the pillar protectively moved behind Israel, shielding the people from the Egyptian armies, providing light to the Israelites and darkness to the Egyptians (Exodus 14:19, 20). Moses stretched forth his hand, and an east wind began to howl, driving a dry path through the sea for the people of Israel as they followed the pillar to safety (Exodus 14:21, 22). Pharaoh's army followed and would have caught them, but God made their chariots swerve out of control. The armies realized too late that God was fighting for Israel, and as they turned to flee at daybreak, Moses again stretched forth his hand and the sea engulfed the armies of Pharaoh (Exodus 14:23–31).

God was with them! The Song of Moses soon rose to the heavens, Aaron's sister Miriam took her tambourine in hand, and all the women followed her with tambourines and dancing:

> Sing to the LORD, for he has triumphed gloriously;
> the horse and his rider he has thrown into the sea. (Exodus 15:21)

Wild exaltation gripped the people. What a fabulous beginning! What hopes! What dreams! Soon they would be in the promised land, bury Joseph's bones, and there forever enter their rest.

It all began so well—but ended so poorly. Of the six hundred thousand men (the million-plus Israelites who began so well), only two over the age of twenty ever got to the promised land—and that was forty years later. The rest fell, disappointed corpses in the desert. The grand and terrible lesson of Israel's history is that *it is possible to begin well and end poorly*. In fact, this tragic human tendency dominates much human spiritual experience.

It is this concern that haunts the writer of the book of Hebrews, as we have repeatedly seen. His fear is that the doleful fate of the generation of the exodus will be repeated in the experience of the Jewish Christians in their storm-tossed little church. He undoubtedly personally knew this little flock. Many of their spiritual exoduses had been beautiful, even dramatic. But now that they were undergoing hardship, would they finish well? Not if they made the same errors as the Israelites did when troubles came.

A Spiritual Warning against Unbelief

To set forth his concern, the writer did what preachers often do—he appropriated a passage of Scripture that eloquently framed his thoughts—Psalm 95:7–11. Every Jew knew this passage by heart because its opening line served as a call to worship every Sabbath evening in the synagogue: "Today, if you hear his voice, do not harden your hearts" (Hebrews 3:7, 8; quoting Psalm 95:7, 8). These solemn words were intoned week after week, year after year as a call to carefully listen to the voice of God.[1] Hebrew ears perked up at their sound.

As the writer uses Psalm 95, he is convinced that the warning of the opening line and the extended warning it introduces comes directly from the Holy Spirit to his hearers, and thus he introduces it in verse 7 by saying, "Therefore, as the Holy Spirit says . . ." He understood that originally the Holy Spirit had warned the psalmist's hearers with these words, and as he uses it one thousand years later, it is still the Holy Spirit speaking. And for us today, two thousand years after the use of it in Hebrews, it remains the Holy Spirit's message. There is a timeless urgency to the message. We must listen to the Holy Spirit's message *today*, for it is God's message for the church in this troubled age. May we listen with all we have!

Psalm 95 Regarding Hardening

As we have indicated, the psalm begins with an explicit warning against hardening, as we see in our Hebrews passage:

Therefore, as the Holy Spirit says,

> "Today, if you hear his voice,
> do not harden your hearts as in the rebellion,
>   on the day of testing in the wilderness,
> where your fathers put me to the test
>   and saw my works for forty years." (vv. 7–9)

Two key words in these verses help us understand what it means to harden one's heart. They are the words "rebellion" and "testing" in verse 8. The renderings here come from the Greek Septuagint, but the original Hebrew behind the word "rebellion" is *meribah*, and behind "testing" is *massah*. Check Psalm 95:7, 8, as it is rendered in your Old Testament, and you will read: "Today, if you hear his voice, do not harden your hearts, as at Meribah, as on the day at Massah in the wilderness."

These words point us directly to Exodus 17, where early in their wilderness experience Israel was camped at Rephidim by Mount Sinai and ran out of water and began to quarrel with Moses. There *"Moses said to them, 'Why do you quarrel with me? Why do you test the Lord?'"* (Exodus 17:2). And then, following God's direction, he struck the rock, and it gave water to Israel. The account concludes with this postscript: "And he called the name of the place Massah [i.e., testing] and Meribah [i.e., quarreling], because of the *quarreling* of the people of Israel, and because they *tested* the Lord by saying, 'Is the Lord among us or not?'" (Exodus 17:7). Significantly the word *Meribah* is used in one other place, and that is forty years later at Kadesh when Israel is again out of water and threatening rebellion, and Moses tragically strikes the rock twice (Numbers 20:1–13, esp. v. 13). The point is, the mention of these words at the *beginning* and *end* of the wilderness sojourn is meant to tell us that this conduct was repeated many times during that whole period of wandering.[2]

What we deduce from these accounts in Exodus 17 and Numbers 20 is that *the hardening that took place in the wilderness was rooted in unbelief.* Many of those, perhaps most, who left in the exodus had an inadequate faith in God. At first, due to their miserable plight of 430 years of slavery, the brilliant leadership of Moses, the repeated miraculous plagues on Pharaoh, and the grand miracles of the pillars of cloud and fire and the parting of the sea, they were ready to follow God anywhere. But as soon as the initial glow wore off, they outrageously cried, "Is the LORD among us or not?" (Exodus 17:7). It was a fair-weather, herd-instinct faith—good until the first trial, when it dissolved in unbelief.

The depth of their defective belief produced one other subsidiary characteristic—*contempt/irreverence.* Hence all the railing against God and his faithful servants. Thus we understand that the pathology of a hard heart originates in *unbelief* that spawns a hardened *contempt* and, as we shall see, a hardness that works out in sinful *disobedience.*

For the psalmist who wrote Psalm 95, the apex of this hard-heartedness came in the events recorded in Numbers 13, 14: Israel's catastrophic unbelief at the border of the promised land, in Kadesh-Barnea, when the twelve spies returned from their forty-day mission with conflicting recommendations.[3] The only thing they could agree on was that the land was rich in grapes and pomegranates and figs—truly flowing with milk and honey (Numbers 13:23, 24, 27). The majority (ten out of twelve) said the land was untakable—"The land, through which we have gone to spy it out, is a land that devours its inhabitants, and all the people that we saw in it are of great height. And there we saw the Nephilim (the sons of Anak, who come from the Nephilim), and we seemed to ourselves like grasshoppers, and so we seemed to them" (Numbers 13:32, 33). That night unbelief was rampant in Israel. All the people wept. Speaker after speaker called for deposing their leaders and returning to Egypt (Numbers 14:1–4). Everyone talked about stoning Joshua and Caleb, who dared to believe God would give them the land (Numbers 14:10).

But then God answered: "But the glory of the LORD appeared at the tent of meeting to all the people of Israel. And the LORD said to Moses, 'How long will this people despise me? And how long will they not believe in me, in spite of all the signs that I have done among them?'" (Numbers 14:10b, 11). Again

God has indicted the hard hearts of Israel. They were *unbelieving*, refusing to believe. What an astounding phenomenon! They had the mutually attested miracles of the Passover and the exodus. No one could dispute the reality of those amazing supernatural events. They also still had the daily provision of the cloud by day and the fire by night. They had been regularly fed with manna and quail from Heaven—but they refused to believe God for the land. The unbelief of God's people is even more amazing than belief!

This unbelief amounted to a *contempt* for God and spawned an ugly family of behavioral stepchildren. There was *negativism*—the "grasshopper complexes"—people like Robert Fulton's detractors. When Fulton tested his steamboat, people actually stood on the shore and chanted, "It will never start, never start, never start." Then when it started and began to move, they changed the chant to "It will never stop, never stop, never stop." Faithlessness makes small mountains unclimbable and miniature seas uncrossable!

Negativism, of course, has a congenital sister in *grumbling*. The account of Israel's failure at Kadesh mentions grumbling no less than four times (Numbers 14:2, 27, 29, 36). Grousing, grumbling, grimacing come naturally to a fading faith. And, of course, this spawns *quarreling*, the daily menu at Meribah and Massah and in between. Finally, faithless children *disobey*, just as they did in trying to do it their own way at Kadesh-Barnea (Numbers 14:41–45).

So we are not left in the dark regarding the hard-heartedness that the psalmist warns against. In fact, the Scriptural description of it is mercifully clear because it even presents us with telltale behavioral signs of hard-heartedness. Hardness of heart originates in *unbelief*, which produces *contempt* for God, which in turn shows itself in distinct behavioral patterns—namely, *negativism, grumbling, quarreling,* and *disobedience.*

We owe it to ourselves to hold this practical mirror of God's Word up to our hearts, so we can take an accurate reading of our spiritual pulse. What does our behavior indicate? A hardening, unbelieving heart? Or the blessed tenderness of a faithful heart?

Psalm 95 Regarding Judgment

What was the result of Israel's hardness of heart according to Psalm 95? *Withering judgment.* Israel was debarred from the promised land, the place of God's rest. God said:

> For forty years I loathed that generation
>   and said, "They are a people who go astray in their heart,

and they have not known my ways."
Therefore I swore in my wrath,
　　"They shall not enter my rest." (Psalm 95:10, 11)

God forgave his faithless people, but the judgment remained:

> Then the LORD said, "*I have pardoned*, according to your word. But truly, as I live, and as all the earth shall be filled with the glory of the LORD, none of the men who have seen my glory and my signs that I did in Egypt and in the wilderness, and yet have put me to the test these ten times and have not obeyed my voice, *shall see the land that I swore to give to their fathers.* And none of those who despised me shall see it." (Numbers 14:20–23)

No one who was over twenty at the exodus entered the land, except for Joshua and Caleb (Numbers 14:29, 30). The rest filled a million sandy graves during the next thirty-eight years.

While God gave a general pardon to Israel for the faithless display at Kadesh, with only two exceptions they all died in the wilderness. The point the writer of Hebrews wants his readers to see is that it is possible to have a remarkable spiritual "exodus" and yet fall by the way when trouble comes. This was the Holy Spirit's message to the beleaguered little church from Psalm 95, and it is his message to us.

If we have been Christians for any length of time, we have seen this lived out. During my years as a youth pastor, I had a spectacular "convert" in my group—a classic hippie who turned overnight into a classic "Jesus person." He was intelligent, winsome, handsome, and spiritual. Just a few weeks after this "exodus," he would stand regularly to give testimony, entrancing all who heard. He even reproached the lukewarm. I was so proud!

But it all came down in one unforgettable week when a relationship he was pursuing fell through and he hurt himself in a church softball game. The result? Rejection of Christ—and a lawsuit against the church!

Jesus said of such, "As for what was sown on rocky ground, this is the one who hears the word and immediately receives it with joy, yet he has no root in himself, but endures for a while, and when tribulation or persecution arises on account of the word, immediately he falls away" (Matthew 13:20, 21). The problem today is that so many people when asked about faith point to their "exodus"—when they began with Christ. They can wax eloquent about their experience. How dare anyone question that! They went forward—they left Egypt—they were baptized and identified with God's people—they visibly drank from the same rock (Christ)—they use the same redemptive vocabulary with the same pious inflections. But troubles came, and they turned away. Their "exodus" is a convenient memory. But to trust God now? That is a problem, for their faith is dead.

A Personal Warning against Unbelief

The writer, having raised everyone's tension with the warning from Psalm 95, now proceeds to give personal exhortations meant to allay disbelief. The opening and closing verses of this section, verses 12 and 19, mention that subject.

Protect Your Heart

"Take care, brothers," says the writer, "lest there be in any of you an evil, unbelieving heart, leading you to fall away from the living God" (v. 12). "Fall away" means to willfully apostatize.

Such turning away incurs a huge penalty. Because Christ is greater than Moses, the loss incurred in rejecting Christ is greater than the loss in rejecting Moses. The rebels in Moses' day missed the promised blessing of entry into earthly Canaan, but rebellion against Christ forfeits the even greater blessings of eternal life. To turn away from "the living God" is a huge mistake, for as Hebrews later warns, "It is a fearful thing to fall into the hands of the living God" (10:31). The author of Hebrews does not think this is a remote possibility for his suffering little church, but a real and present peril. If we are wise, we will share the same regard for our souls.

Help Each Other

Having given solemn warning, the author now promotes encouragement: "But exhort one another every day, as long as it is called 'today,' that none of you may be hardened by the deceitfulness of sin" (v. 13). Think how different it might have been for Israel if they had daily encouraged one another instead of falling to negativism and grumbling and quarreling. Isolation, and particularly isolation from the mutual encouragement of the body, is a dangerous thing. In isolation we are "prone to be impressed by the specious arguments which underline worldly wisdom."[4] When you are alone and unaccountable, it is tempting to take the easy course instead of the right one.

We are to encourage each other daily, not just on the first day of the week. We need to humbly say to the drifting, "Today, brother, today, sister, listen to his voice, so that you may not be hardened by sin's deceitfulness, making tomorrow's repentance and faith more difficult."[5]

Persevere

Says the author, "We have come to share in Christ, if indeed we hold our original confidence firm to the end" (v. 14). Our translation—"our original confidence"—is excellent, as are others: "the beginning of our confidence" (KJV), "the trust with which we began" (PHILLIPS). The Israelites had no lack of confidence just after the exodus, but it faded quickly a few days into the wilderness.

New converts typically have few doubts. But years of living and learning often soften their confidence. I have heard Christians say, "I wish I didn't know so much, it would be easier to believe" as they indulge in an elite, self-congratulating agnosticism. To be sure, all Christians go through times of doubt as their faith grows. A faith that never doubts is perhaps not real, because real faith involves the fallible mind. But for Biblically literate "Christians," with some years of living under their belts, to mouth such consciously self-exculpating phrases for their unbelief is so much bunk! We had no doubts when we met Christ, and we should not have any now. Moreover, we must consciously strive to "hold our original confidence firm to the end."

I am a convinced Calvinist. I believe true Christians persevere—"the perseverance of the saints." And I believe what the Scriptures say here: "For we have come to share in Christ [perfect tense: our belief began in the past and continues], if indeed we hold our original confidence firm to the end." If we do not persevere, we are lost, just as the Apostle John has so clearly explained: "They went out from us, but they were not of us; for if they had been of us, they would have continued with us. But they went out, that it might become plain that they all are not of us" (1 John 2:19).

Even a slight lessening of confidence is a warning. We must "hold our original confidence firm to the end." Perseverance is not a foregone conclusion. So the author of Hebrews next warns us, again repeating the words of Psalm 95:7, 8, "Today, if you hear his voice, do not harden your hearts as in the rebellion" (v. 15). Brothers and sisters, if we hear his voice, we must do something now!

Six Questions

The writer closes this penetrating section of the text with six questions given in three pairs. The first question of each pair asks the question; the second question answers it. The questions are definitely phrased to raise soul-searching tensions among his hearers in the struggling church.

First set, verse 16: *Question:* "Who were those who heard and yet rebelled?" *Answering question:* "Was it not all those who left Egypt led by Moses?" *Point:* Everyone who died in the desert had begun in the glorious exodus and its great expectations.

Second set, verse 17: *Question:* "And with whom was he provoked for forty years?" *Answering question:* "Was it not with those who sinned, whose bodies fell in the wilderness?" *Point:* The men who angered God for forty years were those who did not believe he could provide for them, though they had left Egypt with great hope. This is a warning that high hopes will not suffice—there must be belief.

Third set, verse 18: *Question:* "And to whom did he swear that they would not enter his rest . . . ?" *Answering question:* Was it not "to those who were disobedient?" *Point:* Here unbelief leads to action, as it always does.

The three sets of questions present the descent of hardness of heart: from *hope* to *disbelief* to *disobedience*. Thus, the writer concludes: "So we see that they were unable to enter because of unbelief" (v. 19).

Have we experienced a spiritual exodus in Christ?

Do we claim Christ as our true passover—our lamb without blemish and without spot who gave his life for us?

Do we claim a baptism in Christ, the antitype of Israel's passage through the Red Sea (1 Corinthians 10:1ff.)?

Do we claim to spiritually feed on him by faith, as Israel was fed by manna from Heaven and water from the rock (1 Corinthians 10:3ff.)?

Do we claim to look for a heavenly rest, the ultimate spiritual counterpart of the Promised Land?

If so, we will persevere in faith and obedience, "holdi[ng] our original confidence firm to the end."

> For I do not want you to be unaware, brothers, that our fathers were all under the cloud, and all passed through the sea, and all were baptized into Moses in the cloud and in the sea, and all ate the same spiritual food, and all drank the same spiritual drink. For they drank from the spiritual Rock that followed them, and the Rock was Christ. Nevertheless, with most of them God was not pleased, for they were overthrown in the wilderness. Now these things took place as examples for us, that we might not desire evil as they did. (1 Corinthians 10:1–6)

Therefore, while the promise of entering his rest still stands, let us fear lest any of you should seem to have failed to reach it. For good news came to us just as to them, but the message they heard did not benefit them, because they were not united by faith with those who listened. For we who have believed enter that rest, as he has said, "As I swore in my wrath, 'They shall not enter my rest,'" although his works were finished from the foundation of the world. For he has somewhere spoken of the seventh day in this way: "And God rested on the seventh day from all his works." And again in this passage he said, "They shall not enter my rest." Since therefore it remains for some to enter it, and those who formerly received the good news failed to enter because of disobedience, again he appoints a certain day, "Today," saying through David so long afterward, in the words already quoted, "Today, if you hear his voice, do not harden your hearts." For if Joshua had given them rest, God would not have spoken of another day later on. So then, there remains a Sabbath rest for the people of God, for whoever has entered God's rest has also rested from his works as God did from his. Let us therefore strive to enter that rest, so that no one may fall by the same sort of disobedience.

4:1–11

11

Entering the Rest

HEBREWS 4:1-11

AS CHRISTIANS, we understand there is no rest for the soul apart from Christ. St. Augustine, in the fourth century, gave this truth its eloquent, classic expression in his *Confessions*: "Thou movest us to delight in praising Thee; for Thou hast formed us for Thyself, and our hearts are restless till they find rest in Thee" (Book I.1.1).[1] Blaise Pascal, perhaps the greatest of French minds, wrote even more explicitly in his *Pensées*:

> What is it, then, that this desire and this inability proclaim to us, but that there was once in man a true happiness of which there now remain to him only the mark and empty trace, which he in vain tries to fill from all his surroundings, seeking from things absent the help he does not obtain in things present? But these are all inadequate, because the infinite abyss can only be filled by an infinite and immutable object, that is to say, only by God Himself. (VII, para. 425)[2]

How our souls answer to the words of Augustine and Pascal! When we came to God in Christ, it was like pulling into a snug harbor from a stormy sea. There is no rest for the heart apart from Christ.

However, if we are candid we will admit that the initial rest has not always been our lot, because there is a difference between the primary experience of rest and living a life of rest on life's uneven seas. Certainly this was true of those the writer of Hebrews was addressing. Their experience of Christ was not living up to expectations. Instead of rest there was turmoil. They had given up their ancient religion but were suffering for their new faith. To some it seemed that the initial experience of rest was a cruel delusion.

It is to these endangered hearts that the writer now focuses his remarks in chapter 4 as he instructs and exhorts them on participation in the rest of God. This theme has always been contemporary and will find a responsive chord in every believer's heart—especially if he or she is sailing into the contrary winds of the world.

A Warning Regarding Rest

Chapter 4 opens with a warning based on Israel's tragic failure in the wilderness: "Therefore, while the promise of entering his rest still stands, let us fear lest any of you should seem to have failed to reach it. For good news came to us just as to them, but the message they heard did not benefit them, because they were not united by faith with those who listened" (vv. 1, 2). Israel had heard the "good news" (that is, the good news[3] brought by Caleb and Joshua that the land was theirs for the taking, the Nephilim notwithstanding).

So confident were Caleb and Joshua in heralding the good news that they said, "They are bread for us" (Numbers 14:9), or in today's language, "It's a piece of cake!" Virile chaps, these two—with a virile faith!

But Israel's response to the good news was tragically deficient: "the message they heard did not benefit them, because they were not united by faith with those who listened." Literally, "they didn't mix it with faith." As the NEB says, "They brought no admixture of faith to the hearing of it." This is amazing because they had had constant witness of God's character and provision. They had the spectacular historical examples of the plagues and the parting of the Red Sea. And there were also the ubiquitous pillars of cloud and fire and the day-in, day-out provisions of manna. But now, faced with a new challenge, they simply did not trust God and so failed to enter their rest. Many, perhaps thousands, were believers (they *believed* in God), but only two really *trusted* God and found rest.

We must keep this subtle distinction between belief and trust clear if we are to understand what kind of faith is necessary to have rest in this life. New Testament scholar Leon Morris says that "faith" here in 4:2 is "the attitude of trusting God wholeheartedly."[4] So we must understand that the opening line of verse 3, which says, "For we who have believed enter that rest," specifically means, "we who have *wholeheartedly trusted* enter that rest." Thus, it is spelled out in no uncertain terms that *faith that pleases God is belief plus trust.*

Belief, the mental acceptance of a fact as true, will simply not bring rest to any soul. Acknowledging that Jesus Christ is the Son of God and Savior of the world will not give us rest. *Trust* in him is what gives rest to our souls. "Trust brings rest," says Alexander Maclaren, "because it sweeps away, as the north wind does the banded clouds on the horizon, all the deepest causes of unrest."[5] First, trust in Christ's sacrificial death begins our rest by giving us rest from the burden of guilt for our sins and a gnawing conscience. Second, trust in his character as an almighty God and a loving Savior gives us rest as we place our burdens on him. Just as a child sleeps so well in his parents' arms, so we rest in God.

The principle is so simple: the more trust, the more rest. There is not a fretful soul in the world who is trusting. "The message they heard did not benefit them, because they were not united by faith with those who listened" (v. 2)—and so it is with us. Our belief or unbelief makes all the difference.

Few have lived as stressful and frenetic a life as Hudson Taylor, founder of China Inland Mission. But Taylor lived in God's rest, as his son beautifully attests:

> Day and night this was his secret, "just to roll the burden on the Lord." Frequently those who were wakeful in the little house at Chinkiang might hear, at two or three in the morning, the soft refrain of Mr. Taylor's favorite hymn ["Jesus, I am resting, resting in the joy of what Thou art"]. He had learned that for him, only one life was possible—just that blessed life of resting and rejoicing in the Lord under all circumstances, while He dealt with the difficulties, inward and outward, great and small.[6]

Fellow-Christians, there is a rest for you. It is not beyond your capacity. You can have it if you wish.

The Nature of the Rest

As we have noted, the writer of Hebrews is a very sophisticated man with an immense knowledge of the Greek Old Testament, and he was writing to knowledgeable Jewish Christians. So sometimes the meaning, which was obvious to the hearers, is lost on us. Here in verses 3–5 the writer describes the nature of the rest in cryptic terms that will take some decoding. He writes:

> For we who have believed enter that rest, as he has said,
>
> > "As I swore in my wrath,
> > 'They shall not enter my rest,'"
>
> although his works were finished from the foundation of the world. For he has somewhere spoken of the seventh day in this way: "And God rested on the seventh day from all his works." And again in this passage he said,
>
> > "They shall not enter my rest."

Divine Rest

We note first that he twice quotes Psalm 95:11—"They shall not enter my rest" (vv. 3, 5; cf. 3:11, 18). His purpose is not to imply that his readers will not enter the rest, but rather to show that God calls the rest being offered "my rest" because it is the rest he himself enjoys.[7] This in itself is a stupendous revelation. It means that when we are given rest by him, it is not simply a relaxation of tensions, but a rest that is qualitatively the same rest God enjoys—his personal rest that he shares with us!

To catch something of the idea here, imagine yourself invited by Prince Charles to enjoy his "rest." You are picked up by the Royal limo at Heathrow and whisked into London and through the gates of Windsor Palace where you are shown its glories. Then the two of you motor north in his 1968 Aston Martin to Balmoral Castle where you relax before a fire, scratch the ears of the royal hounds, and don a kilt and explore the royal trout streams. You are sharing what Prince Charles calls "my rest"—his personal rest.

The sublime fact that we share God's personal rest, the rest he enjoys, ought to set our hearts racing!

Cosmic Rest

In verses 3b, 4 the author further reveals the character of this rest by relating it to the rest God entered when he finished creating the universe, his cosmic rest: ". . . although his works were finished from the foundation of the world. For he has somewhere spoken of the seventh day in this way: 'And God rested on the seventh day from all his works.'" He refers in these verses to Genesis 2:2. The fact that there is no morning or evening mentioned in that verse, as there was with each of the first six days, means that the seventh day, God's Sabbath, still continues. God's rest began with the completion of the cosmos and continues on and on—and thus is available to all his children. Its fullness is available to all.

Ideal Rest

The character of God's rest is the ideal of all rests. First, it is *joyous*. Job 38:7 tells us that at creation, "the morning stars sang together and all the sons of God shouted for joy." They were, of course, echoing the joy of the Creator that he carried into his Sabbath-rest.

Second, his rest is *satisfying*. This is the repeated implication of his multiple assertions regarding creation that "it was good" (Genesis 1). When he smote his anvil the final time, sparking his final star a million million million light-years away, and put his final luminous touch on the firefly, he sat back in everlasting satisfaction.

Third, it is a *working* rest. God finished his great work and rested, but it was not a cessation from work, but rather the proper repose that comes from completing a great work. Jesus referred to his Father's ongoing work saying, "My Father is working until now, and I am working" (John 5:17). God's repose is full of active toil. God rests, and in his rest he keeps working, even now.

So we see that his rest is a *joyous, satisfying*, and *working* rest.

Fellow-Christians, God does not offer us just any rest. He offers us, in his own words, "my rest"—the repose of his soul—*divine* rest. It is *cosmic* in its origination, as old as the universe. And as such, a continuing Sabbath is available to all. It is the *ideal* rest, for it comes from a loving, almighty God.

Furthermore, it is available right now! Verse 3, which introduced this section on the nature of our rest, says, "For we who have believed enter that rest." The verb "enter" is in the present tense, which means that as believers we are in the process of entering.[8] There is a *now* and *then* to our rest. *Now*, in Christ, we have entered and are entering our rest. Our experience of rest is proportionate to our trusting in him. A wholehearted trust, for example, brings his rest into our souls in all its *divine, cosmic*, and *ideal* dimensions. But there is also a future rest in Heaven—the repose of soul in God's rest, forever *joyous, satisfied*, and *working*—"work that never becomes toil nor needs repose."[9]

What a balm the author is offering to the storm-tossed church: "You can have God's rest now, regardless of the seas you encounter. But you must trust if you are to have it."

The Availability of Rest

Some of the members of the little church had become so disheartened that they thought the rest really was not available to them. It may have been available to the Israelites in the desert, they thought, or to David's hearers when he reoffered it in Psalm 95, but rest was not really available to them in their difficult circumstances. So in verses 6–10 the author argues that the rest remains. Notice that verses 6 and 9, the opening and closing sentences of this section, assert that fact.

A Rest Remains (1)

The opening assertion in verse 6 is straightforward: "Since therefore it remains for some to enter it, and those who formerly received the good news failed to enter because of disobedience . . ." Those who formerly had the gospel (good news regarding the entry to Canaan) did not enter the land of rest because of their lack of faith, which produced shameful disobedience.[10] The point here is that nothing can prevent the promised rest from taking effect except distrust and disobedience. God's promised rest stands. Anyone can have it.

A Rest Remains (2)

Twice in chapter 3 (vv. 7, 15) the author has quoted Psalm 95:7, 8 to draw attention to the promise of rest, and here in verse 7 he does it again: "Again he appoints a certain day, 'Today,' saying through David so long afterward, in the words already quoted, 'Today, if you hear his voice, do not harden your hearts.'" In David's day the rest was offered by the Holy Spirit saying, "Today, if you hear his voice . . ." Today meant "now" in their time, and that is what it means today. The only way this rest will be missed is through a hardened heart, a disbelieving heart that shows contempt for God in disobedience. The tone here is one of urgency. *Now* is the day of salvation!

A Rest Remains (3)

In developing his point that rest remains, in verse 8 the author uses an argument that appears very subtle to modern-English readers: "For if Joshua had given them rest, God would not have spoken of another day later on." The words for "Joshua" and "Jesus" are exactly the same in the Greek—Jesus was named after Joshua.[11] The Old Testament "Jesus" (Joshua) had led his followers to the land of Canaan. But that was not the real rest but only a type. And that is why the real rest was offered by David in his "Today" and now to us in our "Today." So the great truth is, there was a "Jesus," the son of Nun, who failed to lead his people to true rest. But now there is another Jesus, the Son of God, who can. He is the pioneer and captain of our salvation—the ultimate Joshua (cf. 2:10).

> Dost ask who that may be?
> Christ Jesus it is He;
> Lord Sabaoth His name,
> From age to age the same,
> And He must win the battle.
>
> Martin Luther
> "A Mighty Fortress Is Our God," 1529

A Rest Remains (4)

Now comes the sublime statement of availability: "So then, there remains a Sabbath rest for the people of God, for whoever has entered God's rest has also rested from his works as God did from his" (vv. 9, 10). When God finished the cosmos, he rested in the Sabbath-rest that works. When Christ cried, "It is finished," he forever rested from his atoning work. But the resting Christ works, even as the working God rests. Christ is the Lord of the Sabbath! When we believed, we finished with our works-righteousness and entered God's rest. Yet we long to serve Christ.

This will all eventuate in the eternal Sabbath-rest and the beatitude of the Holy Spirit. "'Blessed are the dead who die in the Lord from now on.' 'Blessed indeed,' says the Spirit, 'that they may rest from their labors, for their deeds follow them!'" (Revelation 14:13).

The writer has used every angle to show his friends and us that we can know and experience this rest. If we learn anything from this text, we must understand that the rest is there if we want it. "So then, there remains a Sabbath rest for the people of God" (v. 9). Praise be to the Father, Son, and Holy Spirit!

The Challenge to Rest

The preacher properly closes this section with a challenge to his church: "Let us therefore strive to enter that rest, so that no one may fall by the same sort of disobedience" (v. 11). How, then, do we "strive" (or, as some translations have it, "do our utmost") "to enter that rest"?

Our passage suggests two things. First, we must do our utmost to focus on the rest. We must strive to comprehend that it is a *divine rest*—the rest that God personally enjoys—"my rest" (vv. 3, 5), as he calls it. It is a Sabbath-rest as old as the universe. It is joyous, satisfying, and productive. We must do our utmost to grasp this. There is no room for mental laziness. Think with all you have on God's rest as described by the Holy Spirit and as offered to you in this passage.

Second, we must do our utmost to combine the hearing of the good news of the offered rest with genuine faith—that is, *belief plus trust*. In the midst of life's uneven seas, we are called, as was the early church, to *believe* in the mighty God of the exodus, he who parted seas, brought forth water from the rock, and fed his people with manna. Even more, we are to believe in the Bread of Heaven who gave his life for us and rose from the dead and ascended to God in mighty power. Do we believe that our God is such a God? Do we really believe it with all our heart? We must make every effort to do so!

Finally, can we add to this belief *trust*? This was the bottom line for the wavering church. Could they trust God to take care of them? There is no rest in this life without trust.

As believers, those who have experienced the initial reality of Augustine's dictum—rest for the restless heart—what is the greatest problem we face?

Do we *believe* God can meet it?
Can we—will we—*trust* him?

If so, God's Word offers rest: "So then, there remains a Sabbath rest for the people of God" (v. 9). "For we who have believed enter that rest" (v. 3).

For the word of God is living and active, sharper than any two-edged sword, piercing to the division of soul and of spirit, of joints and of marrow, and discerning the thoughts and intentions of the heart. And no creature is hidden from his sight, but all are naked and exposed to the eyes of him to whom we must give account.

4:12, 13

12

The Double-Edged Sword

HEBREWS 4:12, 13

I WAS TWELVE YEARS OLD when I came under the knife of God's Word. The cuts went deep, deeper than blood, as they cut my soul in gracious surgery.

I was cut with the clear understanding that though I was an outward son of the church, I was not a son of God. This left me aware that I was a sinner and outside the spiritual mystery that others in the church shared. The cut hurt, and I wanted healing.

The other cut that the knife brought was the conviction that Jesus Christ was God and that he had died on the cross for my sins. This was a totally new conviction, and it throbbed with an almost sweet, unrequited pain. God's Word had surgically prepared my soul for an ultimate healing operation.

I remember everything the night it happened. My pastor directed me to read John 1:12 from my tiny India paper *King James Version*: "But as many as received him, to them gave he power to become the sons of God, even to them that believe on his name." Oh, how my heart ached, for that is what I wanted more than anything else. Then he pointed me to Romans 10:9, 10, and I read aloud, "That if thou shalt confess with thy mouth the Lord Jesus, and shalt believe in thine heart that God hath raised him from the dead, thou shalt be saved. For with the heart man believeth unto righteousness; and with the mouth confession is made unto salvation." And as I read, the lights came on. It was as if the marrow of those verses were sucked off the page and into my soul. I did believe!

How relieved I was as I wept (I can still see my tears through blurred eyes on the dusty concrete floor) and confessed my sins and received Christ as my Savior. Before I left, my pastor had me turn to another verse, Philippians

1:6—"Being confident of this very thing, that he which hath begun a good work in you will perform it until the day of Jesus Christ."

That night, by flashlight in my sleeping bag, I read those verses over and over with a welling joy. And before I went to sleep, I took a borrowed soft red pencil and underlined them. Thirty-seven years have passed, and occasionally I take out the worn little Bible and read those precious words again.

Thus began my experience with the penetrating power of God's Word. It has cut me untold numbers of times since. But each pain, responded to, has brought a fresh, satisfying healing. All Scripture is, as Paul has said, *theopneustos*, "breathed out by God" (2 Timothy 3:16). It is the very breath of divine reality. There is nothing like it. Truly, "The word of God is living and active, sharper than any two-edged sword, piercing to the division of soul and of spirit . . ." (4:12).

How I love the Word and its sweet surgery. What a privilege to open it week by week, day by day. Hebrews 4:12, 13 is the classic text on the power of God's Word. Interestingly, though the text has broad positive application, the text in its context is negative, a warning to those who disregard God's Word. An extended warning began twenty-five verses earlier in 3:7, where Psalm 95:7–11 is first quoted as the hearers are repeatedly exhorted with phrases from the psalm not to repeat the mistake Israel made at Kadesh-Barnea—disobeying God's word and missing God's rest (cf. 3:15; 4:3, 5, 7, all of which reference Psalm 95).

In fact, the warning against disobedience builds throughout this section and is summarized in 4:11, which introduces our text: "Let us therefore strive to enter that rest, so that no one may fall by the same sort of disobedience [i.e., to God's word]. For the word of God is living and active, sharper than any two-edged sword. . . ."

New Testament scholar William Lane has noted a subtle allusion to the tragedy at Kadesh-Barnea in the reference to "sword," because after Israel disobeyed God's word, God said, "None of the men . . . shall see the land" (Numbers 14:22, 23). The people then responded in essence, "We have made a tragic mistake. Let's take our weapons and enter the land. We are now prepared to believe in God" (cf. Numbers 14:39, 40). Moses warned them not to go, saying: "Do not go up, for the Lord is not among you, lest you be struck down before your enemies. For there the Amalekites and the Canaanites are facing you, and you shall fall by the sword. Because you have turned back from following the LORD, the LORD will not be with you" (Numbers 14:42, 43). But they disregarded his warning and went up without Moses and without the ark and without the blessing of God, and they did indeed fall to the swords of the Amalekites and Canaanites (Numbers 14:44, 45). So we see that the mention of a sharp, doubled-edged sword in our text is a sober warning not to disregard God's Word as Israel did in the wilderness.[1]

Hebrews 4:12, 13 therefore gives us four reasons we must not disregard God's Word. The Word of God is: (1) *living*, (2) *penetrating*, (3) *discerning*, and (4) *reckoning*. Taken positively, these are four immense reasons to celebrate God's Word.

The Living Word

As the writer begins, he directly warns that God's Word is alive, saying, "The word of God is living and active" (v. 12a). It lives because it endures forever (Psalm 119:89). Even more, it lives because it has life in itself. God is "living" (3:12), and the Word, as God's breath (2 Timothy 3:16), partakes of God's living character.[2] It is alive!

This was the experience of E. V. Rieu, the famous classics scholar when, as an unbeliever, he undertook the translation of the Gospels for the Penguin Classics series. Rieu described what happened during an exchange with J. B. Phillips on a now famous BBC interview:

> Rieu: My personal reason for doing this was my own intense desire to satisfy myself as to the authenticity and the spiritual content of the Gospels. And, if I received any new light by an intensive study of the Greek originals, to pass it on to others. I approached them in the same spirit as I would have approached them had they been presented to me as recently discovered Greek manuscripts.
>
> Phillips: Did you get the feeling that the whole material is extraordinarily alive?—I got the feeling that the whole thing was alive even while one was translating. Even though one did a dozen versions of a particular passage, it was still living. Did you get that feeling?
>
> Rieu: I got the deepest feeling that I possibly could have expected. It—changed me; my work changed me. And I came to the conclusion that these words bear the seal of—the Son of Man and God. And they're the Magna Carta of the human spirit.[3]

The character of the Word's aliveness is that it is "active," or as that word is sometimes rendered, "effective." God's Word vibrates with active, effectual power as it rushes to fulfill the purpose for which it was spoken.[4] As Isaiah 55:11 so beautifully says: "so shall my word be that goes out from my mouth; it shall not return to me empty, but it shall accomplish that which I purpose, and shall succeed in the thing for which I sent it." Indeed, the Word of God is alive and effectual!

This was the bottom line in the great Reformation. Erasmus, the brilliant Renaissance humanist, collected and collated manuscripts of the Greek New Testament, publishing a Greek New Testament that then unleashed the ineluctable power of God's Word upon the sixteenth century.

Thomas Bilney, who became one of the English Reformers, had been vigorous about his religion, all to no avail. Then he obtained a copy of Erasmus's Greek New Testament, and all changed. Says Bilney:

> I chanced upon this sentence of St. Paul (O most sweet and comfortable sentence to my soul!) in 1 Timothy 1: "It is a true saying, and worthy of all men to be embraced, that Christ Jesus came into the world to save sinners; of whom I am the chief and principal." This one sentence, through God's instruction and inward working, which I did not then perceive, did so exhilarate my heart, being before wounded with the guilt of my sins, and being almost in despair, that . . . immediately I . . . felt a marvelous comfort and quietness, insomuch that "my bruised bones leaped for joy." After this, the Scriptures began to be more pleasant to me than the honey or the honeycomb.[5]

Today when you visit Cambridge you can see Erasmus's room at Queen's College near the Mathematical Bridge, where he worked on his New Testament. And if you search the maps you can locate the site of the White Horse Inn, close to the gate to Caius and Gonville, where Bilney and his friends charted the English Reformation.

The same thing, of course, happened to Martin Luther through his study of the Scriptures, and through Luther God's Word was unleashed on the world. When Luther stood *contra mundum,* he said, "I am bound in conscience and hold fast to the Word of God." And so the power of the Word began the Reformation. As Luther later said:

> I simply taught, preached, wrote God's Word: otherwise I did nothing. And when, while I slept, or drank Wittenberg beer with my Philip and my Amsdorf, the Word so greatly weakened the papacy that never a Prince or Emperor inflicted such damage upon it, I did nothing. The Word did it all.[6]

God's Word is effectual—"living and active." It does what it promises to do. It regards neither age nor education. It can change you if you are twelve or 102. This is why I take seriously every child who sits under God's Word. If you will listen to God's Word, it will change your life. This truth is both a promise and a warning to all of us, so that "no one may fall by the same sort of disobedience [Israel's]" (4:11).

The Penetrating Word

God's Word is not only living but *penetrating*, as the next line so clearly states: "sharper than any two-edged sword, piercing to the division of soul and of spirit, of joints and of marrow" (v. 12b). Some have attempted to use this text in the dichotomist/trichotomist debate—to either prove that humans are two parts or three parts. Such attempts do harm to the practical understanding of God's Word, because all we have here is a poetic statement of the power of God's Word to pierce the human personality to its very depths. God's Word can cut through anything and bring conviction.

John Bunyan has his warrior heroes Mr. Great-heart and Mr. Valiant-for-truth converse in the respite after a battle. As I imagine the scene, these two spiritual warriors, still sweating and breathing heavily, sit down to catch their breath. After a moment, Mr. Great-heart gestures approvingly to Mr. Valiant-for-truth and says:

> "Thou has worthily behaved thyself. Let me see thy sword." So he showed it him. When he had taken it into his hand and looked thereon awhile, he said, "Ha! It is a right Jerusalem blade." Then said Mr. Valiant-for-truth, "It is so. Let a man have one of these blades, with a hand to wield it and skill to use it, and he may venture upon an angel with it. He need not fear its holding if he can but tell how to lay on. Its edges will never blunt; it will cut flesh, and bones, and soul, and spirit, and all."[7]

Tough guys! Tough weapon!

God's Word cleaves through our hard-shelled souls like a hot knife through warm butter. Certainly we Christians find this to be true in our lives. There are sections of God's Word that cut through all the pretensions and religious façade, leaving us convicted.

When God wills it, his Word will pierce *anyone*. George Whitefield, the great eighteenth-century evangelist, was hounded by a group of detractors who called themselves the "Hell-fire Club," derided his work, and mocked him. On one occasion one of them, a man named Thorpe, was mimicking Whitefield to his cronies, delivering his sermon with brilliant accuracy, perfectly imitating his tone and facial expressions, when he himself was so pierced that he sat down and was converted on the spot! Mr. Thorpe went on to become a prominent Christian leader in the city of Bristol.[8]

Thorpe was a nasty man doing a nasty deed. But in his nastiness he was far ahead of so many because he was *hearing* and *interacting* with God's Word. Nothing would have happened if he had stopped his ears and refused to listen. Nothing would have happened if he had let it all go by indifferently.

The soul safest from God's penetrating Word is never the unhappy hearer, but those who, though hearing, never *hear* and never resist. Tragically, many of these are regular church attenders. The true hearer wittingly or unwittingly invites the divine surgeon to do his gracious cutting.

The Discerning Word

Having established that God's Word is living and penetrating, the writer adds, "discerning the thoughts and intentions of the heart" (v. 12c). The root word for "discerning" is the word *kritikos*, from which we derive *critic*. So the emphasis here is on the discerning judgment of "the thoughts and intentions of the heart"—the "radical center of human selfhood," as Philip Hughes calls the heart.[9] The heart is the seat of human personality. It is hidden from all. Yet God's Word sifts through its thoughts and attitudes with unerring discrimination.

"The sword of the Spirit" (Ephesians 6:17) will tell us what is in our hearts. Fellow-believers, if we really want to understand ourselves, we must fill our souls with God's Word. God's Word—read, meditated upon, and prayerfully applied—will give us brilliant discernment and profound self-knowledge. James indicates that God's Word functions as a mirror revealing who and what we really are (cf. James 1:23, 24). This gift of self-knowledge is no small grace because when we grasp something of the serpentine ways of our hearts, we are disposed to cast ourselves even more on God's grace. And that is no small grace!

But we will also be judged by God's Word. And herein lies the warning to those who in disobedience are falling away. His judgment will be perfectly discerning. The wise Christian invites the penetrating, discerning work of God's Word in his life. As wise Christians of old prayed:

> O thou elect blade and sharpest sword who art able powerfully to penetrate the hard shell of the human heart, transfix my heart with the shaft of thy love. . . . Pierce, O Lord, pierce, I beseech thee, this most obdurate mind of mine with the holy and powerful rapier of thy grace.[10]

This is a prayer every man and woman can and ought to pray.

A Reckoning God

We have been speaking of God's Word in *its living, penetrating,* and *discerning* powers. Now in verse 13 the discussion continues, but the focus switches from God's Word to God as a *knowing* and *reckoning* God. This is very natural because God and his Word cannot be separated. Verse 13 gives us one of Scripture's great descriptions of God's knowing: "No creature is hidden from his sight, but all are naked and exposed to the eyes of him to whom we must give account."

God sees everything. This can be discomforting if we have something to hide. This was the experience of some boys who were stealing apples, because as they were in the act it so happened that the great American astronomer Samuel Alfred Mitchell was observing the sun through his telescope as it descended, and just as it set there came into view the crest of an orchard-covered hill some seven miles distant where Dr. Mitchell watched the two boys—one picking apples while the other stood guard making sure they were not seen![11]

That was a picture of what goes on under the divine gaze in both light and darkness. He sees all! "The eyes of the LORD are in every place, keeping watch on the evil and the good" (Proverbs 15:3). The psalmist likewise witnesses, "You have set our iniquities before you, our secret sins in the light of your presence" (Psalm 90:8). A. W. Tozer sums this up in lyrical cadence:

> God knows instantly and effortlessly all matter and all matters, all mind and every mind, all spirit and all spirits, all being and every being, all creaturehood and all creatures, every plurality and all pluralities, all law and every law, all relations, all causes, all thoughts, all mysteries, all enigmas, all feeling, all desires, every unuttered secret, all thrones, and dominions, all personalities, all things visible and invisible in heaven and in earth, motion, space, time, life, death, good, evil, heaven, and hell.[12]

This is sobering truth indeed. But the metaphorical language that follows makes God's knowing absolutely terrifying for those who imagine they can avoid his gaze: "All are naked and exposed to the eyes of him to whom we must give account." "All"—everything—everyone—is stark naked before him. There is nothing to hide in or behind.

Almost all commentators agree that the following Greek word means "laid bare" or "exposed." But there is no consensus as to what exactly the metaphor pictures, because "exposed" literally means "twist the neck" or "take by the throat." It can be used for bending back the neck of a sacrificial animal to administer the fatal stroke.[13] It was sometimes used to describe a wrestler's hold on the opponent's throat, rendering him helpless.[14] And sometimes it was used to describe how a man being led to execution had a knife placed beneath his chin so that he could not bow his head in shame away from the gaze of the people.[15]

Whatever the exact use of the metaphor here, its meaning is clear: all creatures are in the grip of God, totally vulnerable, helpless, and "exposed to the eyes of him to whom we must give account."

The language here forces us to imagine ourselves naked, held helpless, exposed, in God's grip, close to his omniscient eyes, and so we must give account. He cannot be fooled. Duplicity and hypocrisy will not work. Happily, this means he will miss no good thing. But to the sinning, self-righteous heart, apart from the grace of God this brings nothing but unmitigated terror.

Of course, the author means all of this to be sanctifying instruction for the tiny house-church in the welling seas of persecution. He is calling for them not to rebel against God's Word in disobedience, but to submit to it and find rest in the storms.

> For the word of God is living and active, sharper than any two-edged sword, piercing to the division of soul and of spirit, of joints and of marrow, and discerning the thoughts and intentions of the heart. And no creature is hidden from his sight, but all are naked and exposed to the eyes of him to whom we must give account. (vv. 12, 13)

How does this double-edged sword work?

First, it is the *sword of judgment*. Because it is *"living,"* it is effectually active. It accomplishes what God purposes for it to do. It is so sharp that it *penetrates*—"piercing" through everything. And then it *discerns* everything in the core of our being—leaving us "naked" and bare before our God with whom we must reckon. All of this is a gracious cutting. We see ourselves, and we see God, and we long to fly to him and be healed. That was the blessed wound I experienced as a twelve-year-old.

Second, for the believer it is the *sword of sanctification*. God's two-edged sword, his Word, is alive and effectual in our lives. Again it penetrates and discerns our hearts, exposing them to us—leaving us uncovered and laid bare, so that "naked" we flee to God for dress.

Blessed be the double-edged sword of judgment and sanctification. God cuts us deeply that we might die. God cuts us again with his Word that we might live.

Since then we have a great high priest who has passed through the heavens, Jesus, the Son of God, let us hold fast our confession. For we do not have a high priest who is unable to sympathize with our weaknesses, but one who in every respect has been tempted as we are, yet without sin. Let us then with confidence draw near to the throne of grace, that we may receive mercy and find grace to help in time of need.

4:14–16

13

Our Great High Priest

HEBREWS 4:14–16

I HAVE FOND, VIVID MEMORIES of my family's Fourth of Julys when the children were young. Mostly the memories are images of little sweaty bodies, tummies out, streaked with spilled Coke, sun-burned shoulders, sticky dirt-colored hands, and hair that at day's end looked and smelled like damp chicken feathers—a delicious aroma to a loving parent.

But the best memories for me were the fireworks—for reasons other than you might think. The reason is, early on in my fireworks lighting career, after lighting a sparkling fountain and glancing back toward the children, I discovered that the best show is not the fireworks but the children's faces. You have all seen it—the wide-eyed, joyous rapture, first white with the spangled reflection of phosphorus, and then their rapt visages changing hues—green, blue, red—finally turning amber and then disappearing as the flame goes out—only to begin all over again! The best show, by far, is the children's faces!

I imagine this was true for God's children at some of the great Biblical events—for example, Christ's ascension to Heaven. Certainly the sight of our Lord elevating to Heaven in the luminous cloud of the *Shekinah* glory was galvanizing, and no one remembered or even glanced at the apostles' glowing faces—except Heaven, which enjoyed the best show by far. The book of Acts tells us, "They were gazing into heaven as he went" (Acts 1:10). So we can reasonably imagine their raptured expression as they gazed up until the cloud began to dim with the distance and was only a reflected ember in their eyes and the angel told them to get going.

The remarkable memory of Christ's ascension was given to them as a source of comfort and a motivation to doggedly hang in there until Christ's return.

Hold on through Our Confession of Christ as Our High Priest (v. 14)

At this point the writer references the ascension as a source of encourage-ment in a section that begins in verse 14. But he goes much farther with his encouragement by presenting the great high-priestly ministry to which Christ ascended as the reason to hold on: "Since then we have a great high priest who has passed through the heavens, Jesus, the Son of God, let us hold fast our confession" (v. 14). The writer believes that Jesus' high-priestly ministry on behalf of the believers, correctly understood and implicitly believed, would be a great anchor in the coming storms.

To dramatize the greatness of Christ's priestly ministry, the author con-trasts it with the ministry of the Levitical high priest who once a year passed from the sight of the people into the Holy of Holies bearing the blood of atonement. In contrast, Jesus, our High Priest, passed once for all from the sight of his people at the ascension to the ultimate Holy of Holies, having shed his own atoning blood. Specifically the contrast becomes clear as we reflect on the temporal and circumscribed nature of the high priest's work. Once a year on the Day of Atonement (Yom Kippur) the high priest, representing all the people, entered the Holy of Holies, where he sprinkled blood on the mercy seat to symbolically atone for all the sins of the people. But even before doing this, he had to offer a sacrifice for his own sins. And then when he entered the Holy of Holies he only stayed long enough to sprinkle the atoning blood. In fact, bells were sewn to the hem of his robe so the people outside could hear him moving and thus know that God had not struck him dead.

His entrance into the Holy of Holies was through three portals. First, he bore the blood through the door into the *outer court*. Second, he entered another door into the *Holy Place*. And third, he entered through the veil of the *Holy of Holies*. Thus, the ancient high priest had a three-portaled entrance in coming before the thrice-holy God—and he had to do it year after year.

On the other hand, Jesus, our great High Priest, after his once-only sac-rifice for sins on the cross, passed "through the heavens"—going through the first heaven (the atmosphere), the second heaven (outer space), and finally into the third heaven (the most holy of all places, the presence of God, cf. 2 Corinthians 12:2–4).[1] And there he sat down (something no high priest had ever done!) because his atoning work was finished. He remains at God's right hand, making intercession for us.

The grand and great point of this for the author's Jewish hearers is the overarching *superiority* of Jesus, their great High Priest. Their preacher-writer-friend knew that amidst the rising troubles, some of them would no doubt look back through rose-colored glasses to the Levitical system, over-imagining the comfort of having priestly mediation, and some would be in danger of being sucked back into the system. To such, this strong teaching was the antidote. There is simply no contest between the Levitical system and what is provided in Christ!

Thus, we can appreciate the force of the closing command of verse 14, "Let us hold fast our confession." That confession was explicitly focused in 3:1 on "Jesus, the apostle and high priest." If you want to get through hard times, hold on to and confess Jesus "the apostle," the *sent one* of God, who did everything to procure your salvation for you. Along with this, proudly confess that he is your "high priest." Own it publicly. Make it the refrain of your soul.

Bishop Westcott, author of a great enduring commentary on Hebrews, says, "The writer everywhere insists on the duty of the public confession of the faith. The crisis claimed not simply private conviction but a clear declaration of belief openly in the face of men."[2]

Today, in our individualistic, privatistic world, we often neglect the salutary benefit of public confession of the truth we hold. When we are going through hard times, we need to confess Christ as our "apostle and high priest"—to own his magnificent ministry as our own—to clutch it close! We ought not to limit our confession to congenial company alone. There are times to confess him in unfriendly surroundings. Such confession may be just what our soul needs. Confess and embrace your High Priest!

Hold on through Understanding Christ Our High Priest (v. 15)

In order to tighten his friends' grip on their confession of Christ as "apostle and high priest," the writer seeks to enlarge and elevate their understanding of Christ in the next verse: "For we do not have a high priest who is unable to sympathize with our weaknesses, but one who in every respect has been tempted as we are, yet without sin" (v. 15). Hold tight to your confession of Jesus, he urges, because he is capable of unparalleled understanding and sympathy.

The Fact of Sympathy

This was an incredible revelation in its ancient setting. The Stoics believed that the primary attribute of God was *apatheia*, the inability to feel anything at all. They reasoned that if he could feel, he could be controlled by others and therefore would be less than God. The Epicureans believed that God dwelled in *intermudia*, the spaces between the worlds, in complete detachment. The Jews, of course, had a far more accurate picture of God. But before Jesus came it was incomplete, for he revealed the revolutionary Fatherhood of God—daring to address him as "Father" and calling his followers to do the same (Matthew 6:9).

But the assertion that God is not only a Father but has such sympathy that he enters the suffering of this world was, and is, absolutely staggering. It is impossible for us, with our heritage of Biblical revelation, to appreciate how revolutionary the idea of a sympathetic God was.

The How of Sympathy

The method for the unparalleled sympathy of God was, of course, the incarnation of his Son in human flesh. As we argued in 2:17—where it says he was "made like his brothers in every respect"—his incarnation was real. He became a real man—not an almost man or a docetic man. When he was born, he put the exercise of all-knowingness and all-powerfulness and all-presence under the direction of the Father. He did not give them up, but submitted them to the Father's discretion.

Though he was sinless, he had a real human body, mind, and emotions— with their inherent weaknesses. He was ignorant and was taught. He walked like a baby before he walked like a man. He thought and talked like a baby before he thought and talked like a man. This is why our text asserts he *is able* "to sympathize with our weaknesses." He lived with a human body, mind, and soul—with *all* their limitations, except for sin.

His instrument, so to speak, was the same as ours. It is a fact that if you have two pianos in the same room and a note is struck on one, the same note will gently respond on the other, though not touched by another's hand. This is called "sympathetic resonance."[3]

Christ's instrument was just like ours in every way. And hear this! He took that instrument, that body, to Heaven with him. It is his priestly body. And when a chord is struck in the weakness of our human instrument, it resonates in his! There is no note of human experience that does not play on Christ's exalted human instrument. "For we do not have a high priest who is unable to sympathize with our weaknesses"—praise his name!

And the reason for praise goes on: "but one who in every respect has been tempted as we are, yet without sin." This does not mean he experienced every individual temptation we do. He did not experience the specific temptations peculiar to women or married people or the elderly.[4] Neither did he experience the temptations that come from having already sinned. But he did experience the essential temptations that cover, and in his case supersede, whatever we may experience.

Even more, Jesus' experience of temptation was greater because the stakes were so high—and because he never gave in. As C. S. Lewis explained:

> A silly idea is current that good people do not know what temptation means. This is an obvious lie. Only those who try to resist temptation know how strong it is. After all, you find out the strength of the German army by fighting against it, not by giving in. You find out the strength of a wind by trying to walk against it, not by lying down. A man who gives in to temptation after five minutes simply does not know what it would have been like an hour later. That is why bad people, in one sense, know very little about badness. They have lived a sheltered life by always giving in. We never find out the strength of the evil impulse inside us until we try to fight it: and Christ, because He was the only man who never yielded to temptation, is also the only man who knows to the full what temptation means—the only complete realist.[5]

Jesus knew depths and pains we can never know, precisely because he did not sin! No human was ever tempted like Jesus was! "Because he himself has suffered when tempted, he is able to help those who are being tempted" (2:18).

The Depth of Sympathy

Jesus, our High Priest, has an unequalled capacity for sympathy. It goes far beyond the *intellectual*, because it is truly *experiential*. Jesus does not just *imagine* how we feel—he *feels* it! The word for "sympathize" here means "to share the experience of another"[6]—to sympathize through common experience.[7] The most sensitive man who ever lived feels with us.

Whatever we may be going through, there is not a note we can play, not a melody or a dirge, no minor key, no discordant note, that does not evoke a "sympathetic resonance" in Jesus. He mastered the instrument while he was here on earth, and he wears it in Heaven. Do you want sympathy? Do not go anywhere else. Dare not go to anyone but him!

Hold on through Prayers to Christ Our High Priest (v. 16)

Fittingly, the writer closes this brief section with a lyrical call to prayer in a text that is so important to the hearts of so many Christians: "Let us then with confidence draw near to the throne of grace, that we may receive mercy and find grace to help in time of need" (v. 16).

The term that the ESV renders "confidence" here has a long documented history in classical Greek and denotes "free and open speech of citizens with one another." Significantly, it was never used for prayer in pagan classical literature. Rather, it was the Jews who first began to use it in the Greek Old Testament to describe prayer. It means "bold frankness"[8]—an open outpouring of the heart.

There is no suggestion of disrespect here, but simply that we are to come to God without hesitation or tentativeness. What a contrast with the trepidation of the high priest when he entered the Holy of Holies! This is one of the grand revelations of this letter: "Come frankly and confidently to God, brothers and sisters!"

Our approach is to God's throne, but it is now called "the throne of grace"—the place from which grace flows. John Calvin marveled at this, writing:

> The basis of this confidence is that the throne of God is not marked by a naked majesty which overpowers us, but is adorned with a new name, that of *grace*. This is the name that we ought always to keep in mind when we avoid the sight of God. . . . The glory of God cannot but fill us with despair, such is the awfulness of his throne. Therefore in order to help our lack of confidence, and to free our minds of all fears, the apostle clothes it with grace and gives it a name which will encourage us by its sweetness. It is as if he were saying, Since God has fixed on His throne . . . a banner of grace and of fatherly love towards us, there is no reason why His majesty should ward us off from approaching Him.[9]

And when we come boldly, what happens? "We . . . receive mercy and find grace to help in time of need." We receive "mercy" for our *past* failures and "grace" to meet our *present* and *future* needs.[10] We receive the full heart of God as he mercifully meets us in our sins and misery—and heals us. Then we receive the full hand of God's grace, his unmerited favor and loving regard that just keeps coming and coming, so that we say with James, "He gives [us] more grace" (James 4:6)—there is always more grace. And it always comes, our verse concludes, "in time of need." That is, the help is always "appropriate to the time."[11] It is not according to *our* clock but according to Heaven's time—the perfect time.

But, of course, the condition for timely mercy and grace is confident and frank prayer. If we fail to pray, we rob ourselves of the great, timely resources God holds for us. Some in that beleaguered little house-church of the first century had allowed the mounting hardships to draw them away from God rather than closer by prayer. Their confidence was gone. What about you? Has life made you draw away from the throne of grace or draw near?

God's Word speaks to us all: "Let us then with confidence draw near to the throne of grace, that we may receive mercy and find grace to help in time of need" (v. 16).

The writer has called us to hold on in life's storms through three things: our *confession* of Christ, our *understanding* of Christ, and our *prayers* to Christ.

Confession

"Let us hold fast *our confession*" that Jesus is our apostle and great high priest—that he passed through the heavens and is at God's right hand praying for us. Let us both confess it in our hearts and to others. We confess what we truly believe.

Understanding

Next we must take to our hearts the stupendous understanding that Jesus really does sympathize with our weaknesses. He took on the same weak, human instrument that we wear. There is not a note that can be struck that does not find an answering chord in him. Believe it. Let it play in your soul. This will see you through the roughest of times.

Prayer

Finally, we can come confidently and openly in prayer to the throne of grace and so find mercy and grace that is perfectly appropriate to the time.

Hold on to your *confession* of Christ, your *understanding* of Christ, and your *prayers* to Christ and you will ride out the storm.

For every high priest chosen from among men is appointed to act on behalf of men in relation to God, to offer gifts and sacrifices for sins. He can deal gently with the ignorant and wayward, since he himself is beset with weakness. Because of this he is obligated to offer sacrifice for his own sins just as he does for those of the people. And no one takes this honor for himself, but only when called by God, just as Aaron was. So also Christ did not exalt himself to be made a high priest, but was appointed by him who said to him, "You are my Son, today I have begotten you"; as he says also in another place, "You are a priest forever, after the order of Melchizedek." In the days of his flesh, Jesus offered up prayers and supplications, with loud cries and tears, to him who was able to save him from death, and he was heard because of his reverence. Although he was a son, he learned obedience through what he suffered. And being made perfect, he became the source of eternal salvation to all who obey him, being designated by God a high priest after the order of Melchizedek.

5:1–10

14

High Priest, High Qualifications

HEBREWS 5:1–10

THE MAGNIFICENT PRIESTLY GARMENTS prescribed in Exodus 28 for Aaron and all succeeding high priests endowed the position with immense dignity and spiritual significance. The high priest first donned a linen tunic as the foundation to his priestly vestments. Over this was placed a robe of blue. Attached to the robe's hem were pomegranates artistically woven from blue, purple, and scarlet yarn and placed intermittently between small golden bells that rang musically with his every movement. A richly woven multicolored sash held the robe in place.

Next, an apron-like ephod, woven of gold threads, finely twisted linen, and blue, purple, and scarlet yarns, was worn over the robe—a priestly apron. The shoulder-pieces of the ephod each bore a large onyx stone, set in gold filigree. The names of the twelve tribes were engraved on the stones, six on one stone and six on the other, in order of birth.

Then, fastened to the front of the ephod by golden chains, was the breastplate—a nine-inch-square tapestry of gold, blue, purple, scarlet, and linen that bore four rows of three stones—first, ruby, topaz, beryl; second, turquoise, sapphire, emerald; third, jacinth, agate, amethyst; fourth, chrysolite, onyx, jasper—twelve great stones each engraved with the name of one of the twelve tribes—all twelve next to the priest's heart along with the mysterious Urim and Thummim.

Lastly, the priest was crowned with a turban of fine linen, bearing a plate of pure gold with the Hebrew inscription "Holy to the LORD" (Exodus 28:36).

What a sight the high priest must have been in the bright sunlight of Palestine as he approached the tabernacle—white linen, blue robe—the gold on his turban and chains and in the fabrics he wore, gleaming yellow in the sun—the gems on his shoulders and over his heart lit to their full colors—golden bells ringing musically with each step!

But even more, there was the profound spiritual significance of his vestments. He bore the weight of Israel on his shoulders and over his heart. The bells, says Exodus, were worn so that "its sound shall be heard when he goes into the Holy Place before the LORD, and when he comes out, so that he does not die" (Exodus 28:35), for there he was to be perpetually ministering. And, of course, the gold-etched "Holy to the LORD" was the summary of the high priest's great task.

The image of the high priest is a sanctifying picture when seriously contemplated—and it surely has served as such for pious Jews over the ages. But it is also sadly true that one could don the high priestly vestments and appear *outwardly* qualified, but fall tragically short of the *inner* qualifications so necessary to effective ministry.

It is these inner qualifications with which our text first deals in verses 1–4 before it goes on to demonstrate in verses 5–10 how Christ, our great High Priest, meets and supersedes every qualification—proving he is the priest who will get the stressed-out little church through its stormy seas. As we consider this matter of priestly qualifications, we will do well to keep the image of the Aaronic high priest before us—because Jesus is the fulfillment of everything he symbolized.

Qualifications of the Earthly High Priest (vv. 1–4)

The writer opens this section by asserting in verses 1–4 the three essential qualifications for one who would aspire to be high priest—namely, *solidarity*, *sympathy*, and *selection*.

Solidarity

Solidarity, oneness with humanity, was fundamental to priestly ministry and is explicitly stated in verse 1: "For every high priest chosen from among men is appointed to act on behalf of men in relation to God, to offer gifts and sacrifices for sins" (cf. Exodus 28:1; Numbers 8:6). No angel, no celestial being, no deceased soul could function as high priest. He had to be a living human being—a mortal like everyone else.

The reason, of course, is that his primary function was representative—"to act on behalf of men in relation to God." Thus his shared humanity, his "community of nature,"[1] was everything! To be sure, he needed to be linked to God. But what is emphasized here is that he must be well-linked to humanity.

The ideal high priest was not a man who retired to the sanctum of his priestly mansion, there to commune with God, foregoing contact with humanity except once a year when he emerged in priestly splendor to perform the atoning ritual. Rather, the ideal was a man from among men, one who related to people.

Pastorally, in terms of modern ministry, this is just as true. I recall a conversation with a young pastor who told me that for him the ideal situation would be a book-lined study connected by a tunnel to the chancel, where he could emerge once a week to preach and, having delivered his oracle, retire from the people to his books for the following week. Study is, of course, immensely important, but what deluded dreams!

It is good for the minister to be involved in life, because life is not smooth sailing. It is not smooth even when he leads an exemplary life, and it certainly is not smooth when he sins. Life's stresses and joys and misunderstandings and victories and humiliations humanize him. Raising children—busy schedules—sticky telephones—bills—these better qualify him to represent his people "in relation to God." The solidarity factor was essential to effective priestly ministry, as it is today in pastoral ministry, and the universal requirement is, as it has always been, a real man with a real link to God and a real bond to man.

Sympathy

This anticipates the next quality for the human priesthood, which is sympathy or compassion: "He can deal gently with the ignorant and wayward, since he himself is beset with weakness. Because of this he is obligated to offer sacrifice for his own sins just as he does for those of the people" (vv. 2, 3). The ideal high priest had an inner disposition that enabled him to "deal gently with the ignorant and wayward."

As to why he could be so gently disposed, our text suggests that it is because of two inner awarenesses. First he was aware that he, though high priest, was a sinner, for he had "to offer sacrifice for his own sins just as he does for those of the people" (v. 3). Specifically, on the Day of Atonement, while decked out in his spectacular priestly robes, he had to kill a bull for his *own* personal sins and his family's sins. In slaughtering the bull, he would lay his hands on its head and confess his sins. The *Mishna* records this prayer by the priest, which probably reflects something of the ancient Aaronic prayer:

> O God, I have committed iniquity and transgressed and sinned before thee,
> I and my house and the children of Aaron, thy holy people. O God, forgive,

I pray, the iniquities and transgressions and sins which I have committed and transgressed and sinned before thee, I and my house." (M *Yoma* 4:2)[2]

This was followed by the high priest taking the blood of the sacrifice into the Holy of Holies and sprinkling some *on* the mercy seat and then sprinkling more seven times *before* the seat (Leviticus 16:6–14, esp. v. 14; cf. Leviticus 4:3–12; 9:7). It was only after taking care of his own sins that he dared offer sacrifice for his people on the Day of Atonement. The ideal high priest knew he was a sinner through and through—and thus was equipped to "deal gently" with his sinful people. He did not elevate himself above them, but ministered with sympathetic grace as a priestly sinner on behalf of other sinners.

The other awareness was that he was himself "beset with weakness" (v. 2b). He shared in the universal "community of weakness"[3] of all mankind. This, of course, has primary reference to moral weakness, but it also means human weakness generally. He was subject to weakness in *body*: he sometimes became ill—he suffered trauma—he got tired—he sometimes ate too much—he was aging. He was subject to weakness of *intellect*: he sometimes felt stupid—there were things that were simply beyond him—he made mistakes. He was also subject to weakness of *emotion*: sometimes he lost control—he was sometimes depressed—the feelings of others at times controlled him. Indeed, he was part and parcel of the universal "community of weakness."

And in the ideal high priest, this awareness of weakness, coupled with his awareness of sin, produced the ability to "deal gently with the ignorant and wayward." And in this we have something most beautiful, because the word translated "deal gently" was used classically to define a course of conduct that was the middle course between *anger* and *apathy*, between being *incensed* at sin or *laissez-faire* about sin.[4] It meant "wise, gentle, patient restraint." Such a high priest was compassionate and sensitive. He dealt gently with his people.

There is a remarkable parallel between the chemistry that produces the ability to "deal gently" (*awareness of weakness* plus *sinfulness* equals *gentleness*) and the first three Beatitudes. There an awareness of *weakness*—"Blessed are the poor in spirit [those who realize there is nothing within themselves to commend them to God], for theirs is the kingdom of heaven"—is combined with an awareness of *sin*—"Blessed are those who mourn [over their sins and the sins of the world], for they shall be comforted"—to produce *gentleness*—"Blessed are the gentle, for they shall inherit the earth" (Matthew 5:3–5 NASB).

When one is truly aware that he or she is a sinner and couples this with the interior awareness of human weakness, this person will deal gently with others. Conversely, a harsh, judgmental, unsympathetic spirit is a telltale indication that one has outgrown his sense of weakness and awareness of sin. Many evangelicals fall to this syndrome after humbly coming to Christ at conversion, for their initial experience of sanctification deludes them into imagining they are better than others. Such arrogation, however, actually disqualifies them from spiritual ministry. What a beautiful priestly quality it is to "deal gently" with those falling into sin. How wonderful a priest like this would be.

Selection

The third and final qualification is straightforward—the high priestly position must spring from divine selection: "No one takes this honor for himself, but only when called by God, just as Aaron was" (v. 4). All Israel's priests were to come only through divine appointment (Exodus 28:1–3; cf. Leviticus 8:1ff.; Numbers 16:5; 20:23ff.; 25:10ff.). Attempts to do otherwise met with catastrophic judgment. Korah and his 250 followers were swallowed by the earth because they elevated themselves to the priestly office by burning unauthorized incense (Numbers 16:16–40). Saul lost his reign because he impatiently assumed Samuel's priestly function (1 Samuel 13:8ff.). And Uzziah, wrongly utilizing a priestly censer, broke out with leprosy that lasted until his dying day (2 Chronicles 26:16–21).

No genuine priest ever arrogated himself to the high priestly office. All were sovereignly chosen. Therefore, a proper priest was filled with deep humility. His work was never a career. It was a divine calling.

What an inviting picture the ideal human high priest was. He bore Israel on his shoulders and over his heart. He was crowned with holy intent for all— "Holy to the LORD." He kept the bells ringing as he worked at intercession and atonement. He was in *solidarity* with his people—he was one of them. He was a real link between them and God. He was in such *sympathy* with them that he always could "deal gently" with them. He was the product of *divine selection*—free from ego and hubris. He was selected to serve. How appealing this was to the Hebrew mind, and quite frankly to us! The ideal high priest was a man of incomparable attractiveness.

Qualifications of the Eternal High Priest (vv. 5–10)

Could anything or anyone ever exceed this ideal in attractiveness or efficacy? The answer is a resounding "Yes!"—Jesus Christ!

Selection

He too was a product of divine selection: "So also Christ did not exalt himself to be made a high priest, but was appointed by him who said to him, 'You are my Son, today I have begotten you'; as he says also in another place, 'You are a priest forever, after the order of Melchizedek'" (vv. 5, 6). Not only was Christ divinely chosen, but he was chosen for two offices—the ultimate *royal* office and the ultimate *priestly* office, as is shown by two Old Testament Scriptures.

His *royal* office was prophesied in Psalm 2:7—"You are my Son; today I have begotten you" (cf. Hebrews 1:5), which in the mind of the writer of Hebrews refers to Christ's enthronement as "both Lord and Christ" (Acts 2:36).[5] This is an implicit statement that Jesus is eternal King!

Jesus' *priestly* office was prophesied, says our writer, in Psalm 110:4— "You are a priest forever after the order of Melchizedek." This was a bombshell statement to his hearers because, while Psalm 110:1 had been applied to Christ by others (and even in Hebrews 1:13), this is the first time Jesus was ever identified with the mysterious priesthood of Melchizedek! Not only that, but Psalm 110:4 now becomes the virtual theme-text of the heart of the letter to Hebrews (that text is quoted three times, in 5:6; 7:17, 21; and there are an additional eight allusions to it in chapters 5 and 6).[6] It is especially important here to realize that Melchizedek, according to Genesis 14, was both *king* of Salem and *priest* of God Most High (Genesis 14:18; Hebrews 7:1).

So our author gives us a stupendous truth: Jesus is both eternal King and eternal priest. And it all came to him by the ordaining word of God the Father. Jesus did not seek it! Just as in eternity, he "did not count equality with God a thing to be grasped, but emptied himself, by taking the form of a servant, being born in the likeness of men" (Philippians 2:6, 7), neither did he clutch the office of king and high priest. His only goal was to glorify God the Father.

Jesus' priesthood is, therefore, far superior to that of Aaron. Aaron's was temporal, but Jesus is a priest of the same kind as Melchizedek. There was no succession of priests and hence no "order" from Melchizedek.[7] Jesus' priesthood is without ending or beginning!

Solidarity

Not only is Jesus superior as to his divine selection to be king and priest—he is also superior in his priestly solidarity with his people:

> In the days of his flesh, Jesus offered up prayers and supplications, with loud cries and tears, to him who was able to save him from death, and he

was heard because of his reverence. Although he was a son, he learned obedience through what he suffered. And being made perfect, he became the source of eternal salvation to all who obey him. (vv. 7–9)

Here we see that the prime example of Jesus' solidarity (his participating fully in the human condition) was his agony in the garden of Gethsemane where "Jesus offered up prayers and supplications, with loud cries and tears, to him who was able to save him from death" (v. 7). As we have explained in earlier studies, Jesus placed the exercise of his omniscience, omnipotence, and omnipresence under the direction of God the Father when he came to earth in the Incarnation. This explains his flashes of supernatural knowledge and power while on earth.

But it also explains how he could undergo the agony of Gethsemane with his full humanity, so that we see his authentic human agony in recoiling from the cross. Mark tells us Jesus was "greatly distressed" (Mark 14:33). The idea here is that of terrified human surprise. As he considered the cup he must drink, he was astonished with horror. Mark also tells us that Jesus said, "My soul is very sorrowful, even to death" (Mark 14:34), for his sorrow was so deep, it threatened death to his human body. Mark takes us even deeper into the terror-filled mystery, telling us: "And going a little farther, he fell on the ground and prayed that, if it were possible, the hour might pass from him. And he said, 'Abba, Father, all things are possible for you. Remove this cup from me. Yet not what I will, but what you will'" (Mark 14:35, 36). The inner circle of disciples saw Jesus' body fall prostrate to the ground. There he prayed repeatedly. Our text in Hebrews gives us even more light, for it mentions "loud cries."

Amazingly (in the light of redemptive history), he was repeatedly asking that if possible the "hour" and the "cup" (metaphors for his death) might be avoided! How could he desire something contrary to the Father's will? The answer is: Jesus was truly God and truly man. As a man he had a human will and voluntarily limited his knowledge. His prayer was not to do something other than the Father's will, but he did say in prayer that if there were a possibility of fulfilling his messianic mission without the cross, he would opt for that. As a man Christ cried for escape, but as a man he desired the Father's will even more.

John Calvin quotes Cyril of Alexandria as saying: "You see that death was not voluntary for Christ as far as the flesh was concerned, but it was voluntary, because by it, according to the will of the Father, salvation and life were given to all men."[8]

Christ asked that the cup be taken away because he was truly man. His authentic solidarity with humanity was the soil for his terrible agony.

Our text here in Hebrews tells us "he was heard because of his reverence" (v. 7b). His reverence for the Father determined that his humanity would do nothing but please the Father. His prayer was, of course, answered, for though his body died, he was saved *out of* death—and so the Father's will was done.

So authentic was Jesus' solidarity with humankind that he "learned obedience through what he suffered. And being made perfect . . ." (vv. 8, 9). This "does not mean Jesus passed from disobedience to obedience."[9] Nor does it mean that he developed from imperfection to perfection. The idea is that he became *complete* in his human experience.

Now, in his completeness, his perfection, he is "the source of eternal salvation to all who obey him" (v. 9). His solidarity with us means he can save us to the uttermost. Christ is our triumphant, eternal Savior. His superior *selection* as both eternal King and priest, coupled with his superior *solidarity* with us, makes him far superior in *sympathy* to the high priest of old.

The glorious vestments of the Aaronic high priest have always been understood as being emblematic of the ministry of the ultimate high priest, the Lord Jesus Christ. Can you see him resplendent in the glorious white light of a thousand suns in eternity? He bears our names on his shoulders and thus shows his infinite compassion for us. He has borne all our sins in his own priestly body on the tree. In his solidarity with us he bears our present burdens as well. We are always on his heart. Perhaps as he prays for us, he places a nail-pierced hand over the precious stones and presses them close. Though seated at the right hand of the Father, the golden bells constantly ring as he ministers on our behalf. And his crown, "Holy to the LORD," will be our crown because that will be the eternal outcome of his work.

Can anyone miss the message to the little church on the high seas? This was their high priest, and our high priest in life's uncertain seas today as well. Jesus persevered in submissive prayer in Gethsemane and was heard, and our prayers will be heard also if we persevere.

What motivations! We have the example of Jesus' prayers. We have Jesus, "a priest forever, after the order of Melchizedek . . . a high priest after the order of Melchizedek" (vv. 6, 10). May we avail ourselves of him day by day!

About this we have much to say, and it is hard to explain, since you have become dull of hearing. For though by this time you ought to be teachers, you need someone to teach you again the basic principles of the oracles of God. You need milk, not solid food, for everyone who lives on milk is unskilled in the word of righteousness, since he is a child. But solid food is for the mature, for those who have their powers of discernment trained by constant practice to distinguish good from evil.

5:11–14

15

Slow to Learn

HEBREWS 5:11–14

ONE THING EVERY ONE OF US had in common as children was the desire to grow up. It occurred somewhere between our second and third year with the blossoming of our new awareness that we were little people who had the potential of becoming "big." Big kids (those a year or two older than us) came to have powerful influence over us. Some became our secret heroes. We imitated the way they walked and sometimes even aped their faulty slouches. They influenced everything—the way we dressed, our likes and dislikes, the toys we wanted, the way we talked, even our habits.

In one memorable instance, our youngest child, William Carey, then two, was addicted to sucking the knuckle of his index finger. Candid family pictures from that time universally show him with knuckle in mouth. We tried everything—reason, rewards, cajoling—but to no avail. Then one day my wife overheard one of his older playmates say, "You're a baby. Babies suck their thumbs." That night as she tucked him in bed, the knuckle reflexively went in his mouth. Then he consciously withdrew it and said, "*I not a baby*"—and that was the last time we saw him with knuckle in mouth! How powerful is the desire to grow up!

Big kids get to do "big" things. A few years later, when Carey was nine, we visited Knott's Berry Farm in Southern California. The most alluring attraction for Carey was the miniature motorcycle rides. There was only one problem—all riders had to measure up to a minimum height, and he was a fraction too short. But Carey was not to be denied. He went to the restroom and neatly folded paper towels, placed them in his shoes, forced his feet back in, and returned to the concession, where he had his longed-for ride.

I am not sure we ever entirely get beyond the innate desire to grow, even in adulthood. The vestiges are subtle, but they are there. For example, when we first come into the presence of someone we have long admired, we are inwardly overcome with feelings of that old childish inadequacy.

Growth is so important to us that arrested growth is universally regarded as a tragedy, whether it be physical, as in the case of Stephen Hawking, the brilliant theoretical physicist, or mental, as comes from trauma or disease, or social, as so often occurs from the domestic and economic deprivation many have experienced.

The Problem of Spiritual Immaturity (vv. 11, 12)

But there is a massive tragedy few are aware of and with which fewer still concern themselves—namely, arrested spiritual growth, perpetual infancy, never becoming a "big person" spiritually. Set against eternity, this is a tragedy of incalculable proportions.

The writer of Hebrews has mentioned Melchizedek (5:10) and, about to compare Christ's ministry with Melchizedek's, now remembers that many of his hearers have not grown enough spiritually to grasp his explanation. Thus in verse 11 he turns aside to issue a warning to the spiritually immature, saying, "About this we have much to say [i.e., the way Melchizedek prefigures Christ], and it is hard to explain, since you have become dull of hearing" (v. 11).

This is a powerful indictment, especially when we see the form of the language in the phrase, "you have become dull of hearing." The word "dull" is only used here in the New Testament and means "sluggish" or "lethargic" (cf. Septuagint of Proverbs 22:29 and the apocryphal Sirach 4:29; 11:12). Literally, the phrase reads, "you have become sluggish in the ears." Therefore we understand that their problem was an *acquired* condition characterized by an inability to listen to spiritual truth. They were not naturally "dull," they were not intellectually deficient, but they had become spiritually lazy. They listened with the attentiveness of a slug. They had become unreceptive and closed.

When people truly come to Christ, their initial posture is one of intense listening. Though only a boy, I was "all ears" after I met Christ. I listened as best I could—and even took notes. God's Word was alive! My experience was not unique. F. R. Webber, in his massive three-volume *A History of Preaching in Britain and America*, tells us that one of the curious by-products of the Awakening was a sudden interest in shorthand. According to Webber:

> Men and women studied shorthand in order that they might take down the sermons that were stirring the English-speaking countries. This had happened once before in Scotland, and it made its appearance once more in

all countries where the influence of the Awakening was felt. It was not at all unusual to see men with a portable inkwell strapped about them, and a quill pen thrust over an ear, hastening to join the throng assembling on the village green.[1]

But as the newness of it all died down, so did the listening—just as with the Hebrews centuries before, and as with so many in the church today. To such people it is "hard to explain" the deep, needful doctrines of the faith.

The Puritan Richard Baxter, in his "Directions for Profitably Hearing the Word Preached," gives wise advice for all Christians:

> Make it your work with diligence to apply the word as you are hearing it. . . . Cast not all upon the minister, as those that will go no further than they are carried as by force. . . . You have work to do as well as the preacher, and should all the time be as busy as he . . . you must open your mouths, and digest it, for another cannot digest it for you . . . therefore be all the while at work, and abhor an idle heart in hearing, as well as an idle minister.[2]

As we hear God's Word, we ought to keep our Bible open and follow the textual argument, look up the references mentioned, take notes, identify the theme, list the subpoints and applications, and ask God to help us see exactly where he wants us to apply the Scriptures being preached. Are we "sluggish in the ears"? If so, we are self-condemned to perpetual infancy.

The writer goes on to deepen his indictment in the following sentence: "For though by this time you ought to be teachers, you need someone to teach you again the basic principles of the oracles of God" (v. 12a). Here the author is most graphic because the Greek translated "the basic principles" actually means something like, "the ABC's of the beginning of the words of God."[3] This refers to the basic truths of God's Word—what Alistair Begg has called the main things: "The plain things are the main things, and the main things are the plain things."

At first the Hebrew believers had listened attentively to the main things and had learned them, at least as well as things are learned initially. And it was real learning. However, it is sometimes well said, "use it, or lose it"—and some had lost it. Recently I heard a comedian bring the point home regarding our universal ability to forget what we have learned as he announced he was forming "The Five Minute University" where one could learn in five minutes all one will remember five years after graduation from college!

Humor aside, there was an important spiritual principle at work among the lazy minds of the Hebrew church, which is: *truth heard but not internalized and maintained will be lost to the hearer.* Jesus said regarding truth:

> For to the one who has, more will be given, and he will have an abundance, but from the one who has not, even what he has will be taken away. . . . Indeed, in their case the prophecy of Isaiah is fulfilled that says: "You will indeed hear but never understand, and you will indeed see but never perceive." For this people's heart has grown dull, and with their ears they can barely hear, and their eyes they have closed, lest they should see with their eyes and hear with their ears and understand with their heart and turn, and I would heal them. (Matthew 13:12, 14, 15)

Some in the tiny storm-tossed church should have become teachers (not necessarily preachers as such, but able to instruct others in the faith due to the progress of their own faith), but they had tragically failed. And they were losing their own grip on the truth to boot!

The church was certainly entitled to more from them than this—just as today's church is entitled to expect more from us. Paul tells us in 1 Corinthians 2:16 that as Christians "we have the mind of Christ." Thus through the Holy Spirit our minds can be constantly renewed—we can think God's thoughts, share his knowledge, relay his message. But the great scandal of today's church is *Christians without Christian minds*—those who ought to be teachers, but need someone to teach them the elementary truths of God's Word all over again.

We must each ask ourselves some frank questions: Do I know the elementary truths well enough to help others? Am I hard to teach because I have become "sluggish in the ears"? Am I a growing, learning Christian?

How aggressive the writer has been with his readers in the storm-tossed little church! The reason for this is his loving compassion for his friends, because he knows that spiritual babies will be overwhelmed by the storm.

The Cause of Spiritual Immaturity (vv. 12b, 13)

Next we observe that the author resorts to some biting, caustic sarcasm in an effort to stir his readers to spiritual growth: "You need milk, not solid food, for everyone who lives on milk is unskilled in the word of righteousness, since he is a child" (vv. 12b, 13). He assaults his friends with a grotesque image—adult infants who are still nursing. Think of the tragic absurdity of full-grown men and women in diapers who are neither capable of, nor desire solid food and who sit around sucking their thumbs. Such full-grown infants amount to a huge disgrace and drain on the Church. Obviously the writer's grotesque images are meant to shock and to motivate some of his hearers to pull out their thumbs and say, "I'm no baby."

Again the emphasis of the language warns against regression, for it literally reads, "You have become having need of milk, not solid food."[4] They had begun to eat solid food early on but were now back on the bottle. The truth is, there is simply no such thing as a static Christian. We are either moving forward or falling back. We are either climbing or falling. We are either winning or losing. Static, *status quo* Christianity is a delusion!

Helpfully, the writer has been very explicit as to who remains a spiritual infant: "Everyone who lives on milk is unskilled in the word of righteousness, since he is a child" (v. 13). "The word of righteousness" has been understood in two ways—one doctrinal and the other practical.

Those who think the emphasis is *doctrinal* argue that being "unskilled in the word of righteousness" has reference to a solid grasp of the doctrine of imputed righteousness—that is, the divine bestowing of an alien righteousness from God in effecting one's salvation as described, for example, in Romans 3:22—"the righteousness of God through faith in Jesus Christ for all who believe" (cf. Romans 1:17; Philippians 3:9).[5] Those who take this view say one must clearly understand this doctrine before it is possible to eat further food. But others understand "the word of righteousness" to be *practical*, arguing that the following context (cf. v. 14) demands that we understand this as righteous *conduct*. Thus, those who live righteous lives will be enabled to eat the solid food of God's Word.

I personally believe it is both/and. Those who would move beyond the milk stage and feed on the meat of God's Word must first have a clear *doctrinal* understanding of the radical righteousness of God. They must understand they are so radically sinful that their own works of righteousness can never save them and that their only hope is the gift of righteousness from God through Christ (2 Corinthians 5:21). However, if one is to increasingly feed on the solid Word, there must be more than this *doctrinal* understanding of righteousness— there must also be practical *righteous living*. These two together, orthodoxy and orthopraxy, enable one to feed more and more on the solid Word of God.

In respect to this truth, it is noteworthy that St. Augustine, the towering intellect of the early church, understood that the knowledge of the deep mysteries of God's Word came not just through the mind but also through holy living. At one point in his essay on the Trinity, Augustine suggests a remedial program for those who struggle with the doctrine of the Incarnation. They will gain understanding of the mystery, he says, by purging their minds, abstaining from sin, doing good works, and engaging in passionate prayer (*De Trinitate* 4:21, 31).[6]

The message is clear: if we intellectually understand the doctrine of righteousness, but are not growing in God's Word, it may well be that we need to confess our sins and ask the Holy Spirit's help in experiencing righteous living.

The Cure for Spiritual Immaturity (v. 14)

Lastly, the writer of Hebrews nails down the necessity of a profound personal righteousness as being essential to spiritual maturity by stating, "But solid food is for the mature, for those who have their powers of discernment trained by constant practice to distinguish good from evil" (v. 14). The universal fact is, a nursing baby has little or no capacity to distinguish good from evil. And while a growing child will have an increased capacity, it will necessarily be flawed. Only the mature—those who *understand* the teaching about righteousness and who *practice* it—will be able to make discerning judgment on the continual moral issues that arise in life.

Life, as we know, perpetually faces us with the problem of telling good from evil. Our spiritual perception is daily taxed. But a righteous life that feeds on the solid food of God's Word will be able to exercise mature judgment between what is good and what is evil. Precisely because the righteous are not "sluggish in the ear," they hear the voice of God. They listen with the enthusiasm they first had when they came to Christ, and as Jesus promised, more truth is then given to them. What blessings mature believers are to their families and their church. They save their loved ones from pitfalls. Their words are words of life.

The desire to grow is the most natural thing in the world. Because of it, the child forever extracts his thumb saying, "I'm no baby." The desire to grow is part of life!

When we observe someone who has had his *physical* or *mental* growth inhibited, we are properly saddened. But how much more proper and beneficial for us it would be if we could see stunted *spiritual* growth in its full-blown grotesqueness. Spiritual maturity—being full-grown—is possible if we simply take God's Word seriously:

- By listening with all we have.
- By becoming fully acquainted with its "word of righteousness" and living it out.
- By constantly applying God's Word to the decisions of life.

Away with the infant formula and on to the solid food of God's Word!

Therefore let us leave the elementary doctrine of Christ and go on to maturity, not laying again a foundation of repentance from dead works and of faith toward God, and of instruction about washings, the laying on of hands, the resurrection of the dead, and eternal judgment. And this we will do if God permits. For it is impossible, in the case of those who have once been enlightened, who have tasted the heavenly gift, and have shared in the Holy Spirit, and have tasted the goodness of the word of God and the powers of the age to come, and then have fallen away, to restore them again to repentance, since they are crucifying once again the Son of God to their own harm and holding him up to contempt. For land that has drunk the rain that often falls on it, and produces a crop useful to those for whose sake it is cultivated, receives a blessing from God. But if it bears thorns and thistles, it is worthless and near to being cursed, and its end is to be burned.

6:1–8

16

No Second Genesis

HEBREWS 6:1–8

A WELL-TRAVELED STORY that comes to us from the life of the great evangelist D. L. Moody contains wisdom every experienced pastor has come to well regard. As the account goes, Moody was once approached by a stumbling drunk on the street who slurred, "Mr. Moody, I'm one of *your* converts." To which Moody replied, "You must be, because you're certainly not one of the Lord's!"

Those of us who grew up in the fifties are quite familiar with the name Mickey Cohen because he was the most flamboyant criminal of the day. Perhaps some of us even remember Cohen's becoming a "Christian."

At the height of his career Cohen was persuaded to attend an evangelistic service at which he showed an interest in Christianity. Hearing of this, and realizing what a great influence a converted Mickey Cohen could have for Christ, many prominent Christian leaders began visiting him in an effort to convince him to accept Christ. Late one night, after repeatedly being encouraged to open the door of his life on the basis of Revelation 3:20 ("Behold, I stand at the door and knock; if any one hears My voice and opens the door, I will come in . . . ," NASB), Cohen did so.

Hopes ran high among his believing acquaintances. But with the passing of time, no one could detect any change in Cohen's life. Finally they confronted him with the fact that being a Christian meant he would have to give up his friends and his profession. The logic of his response was this: there are "Christian football players, Christian cowboys, Christian politicians; why not a Christian gangster?"[1]

Mickey certainly was not one of the Lord's converts! Down-to-earth Dwight Moody gave us an epigram that wears well because every experienced

Christian knows that the authenticity of a conversion will be revealed in time and life. As a pastor, I may witness a moving conversion. But the convert's life will reveal the ultimate reality. I have seen spectacular conversions fizzle and even produce enemies of the gospel—apostates. I have seen other conversions, both dramatic and quiet, mature into deep Christian commitment.

The same phenomenon was present in the early Hebrew church, and so the church did its best to avoid bogus conversions by catechizing converts in the basic truths, much as a responsible church does today. New Testament scholarship is in general agreement that the six facets of "the elementary doctrine of Christ" (v. 1) listed in verses 1–3 outline the primitive catechism used in Jewish churches to induct converts. Thus we get an intimate glimpse of the basics, the foundation you would have been taught before being baptized and accepted into a Jewish church two thousand years ago.

First, you would have been instructed regarding "repentance from dead works" (v. 1b)—which primarily means, in this Jewish context, turning away from the dead works of the Law and one's doomed attempt at self-salvation. But the instruction would have also included turning away from personal sin itself, which works death, just as John the Baptist and then Jesus had called for (cf. Matthew 3:2; Mark 1:4, 15; Luke 3:8). A Jewish convert, then, had to engage in the sublimely *negative* act of repentance. Conversion meant a conscious turning away from the old way of life.

Second, repentance was to be coupled with a sublimely *positive* act of faith—"and of faith toward God." Merely turning from dead works would accomplish nothing. Repentance must be joined with faith—a personal relationship of trust in God, the Father of the Lord Jesus Christ.[2] No doubt the necessity of faith was hammered home with an exposition of the faith principle from Old Testament Scriptures such as Genesis 15:6 ("And he [Abram] believed the LORD, and he counted it to him as righteousness") and Habakkuk 2:4 ("the righteous shall live by his faith"). Salvation has always been by faith—*sola fide*. Thus the first two catechetical basics provided the essentials of soteriology, the doctrine of salvation.

Third and fourth, they were given "instruction about washings, the laying on of hands . . ." (v. 2).[3] The idea here is that the Hebrew church employed the customary Jewish cleansing rites, as well as the Old Testament customs of laying on of hands, to teach the deeper, ultimate significance of Christian baptism and laying on of hands—namely, the baptism of the Holy Spirit (cf. Matthew 3:11; Acts 1:5; 1 Corinthians 12:13) and also commissioning and empowering for Christian service (cf. Acts 13:1–3). These teachings together amounted to a primary pneumatology, the doctrine of the *pneuma*, the Spirit.

Fifth and sixth, the converts were given instruction regarding "the resurrection of the dead, and eternal judgment" (v. 2). Both doctrines were known in the Old Testament (for *resurrection* cf. Job 19:23–27; Daniel 12:1–3; for *judgment* cf. Genesis 18:25; Isaiah 33:22; Daniel 7). But in the New Testament these subjects take on massive significance, with Jesus Christ at their very center. Jesus is the resurrection—"I am the resurrection and the life. Whoever believes in me, though he die, yet shall he live" (John 11:25). Jesus is the judge—"For we must all appear before the judgment seat of Christ, so that each one may receive what is due for what he has done in the body, whether good or evil" (2 Corinthians 5:10). The doctrines of resurrection and judgment served as an induction into the Christian doctrine of last things, eschatology.

So we see that the Jewish convert was catechized by the church's employing the rich fabric of his religion as a springboard for grounding him in Christ regarding *repentance* and *faith* (soteriology), *baptism* and *empowerment* (pneumatology), *resurrection* and *judgment* (eschatology). It was a brilliant catechism that provided in its foundational "elementary doctrine of Christ" an initial depth of understanding that was beyond the beginning understanding of a pagan convert, unschooled in the Old Testament. The catechism was a spiritual "Operation Head Start."

However, the excellent beginning could not avoid some problems. Some converts, despite their privilege, had calcified. They had never gone beyond "the elementary doctrine." It seemed as if they were stillborn. Others were even worse off because they were slipping back. The Hebrew Christian milieu made that especially easy, because whereas a pagan convert's apostasy was so obvious, a Jew who was sliding back to his old faith was less apparent. It was possible for Hebrew converts to yield gradually to hostile pressures from the old life and give up more and more of the distinctives of their new faith without much notice—and some were doing just that![4]

So the author issues a warning and a call to move on, a call that was clear in light of what we have said: "Therefore let us leave the elementary doctrine of Christ and go on to maturity, not laying again a foundation of repentance from dead works and of faith toward God, and of instruction about washings, the laying on of hands, the resurrection of the dead, and eternal judgment. And this we will do if God permits" (vv. 1–3). It is no pious nod to God to say they will need God's help to do this, for without God it will be impossible.[5]

This is a warning and call for all of us to make progress in our faith. The undeniable spiritual axiom is, *where there is life there is growth!* If we are not more knowledgeable in the faith now than a year ago, if we are not growing in holiness and commitment, we had better check what is going on inside. Even more, if we are sliding, losing our grasp on things that were once clear, caring less about God and holiness and the world, we had better drop everything and tend to our souls.

No Second Beginning (vv. 4–6)

The author will move on to definitely deeper things in chapter 7, with his profound exposition of Melchizedek. But first he feels compelled to deepen his warning, and he does so by giving what many consider the most terrifying warning in the New Testament—that there can be no second beginning:

> For it is impossible, in the case of those who have once been enlightened, who have tasted the heavenly gift, and have shared in the Holy Spirit, and have tasted the goodness of the word of God and the powers of the age to come, and then have fallen away, to restore them again to repentance, since they are crucifying once again the Son of God to their own harm and holding him up to contempt. (vv. 4–6)

There are three ways this passage has been understood.

Hypothetical

One view says it refers to a hypothetical situation that has never existed and therefore is a warning against a sin that is impossible to commit. The situation is presented by the writer as a warning to keep Christians from apostatizing. It is simply a sanctifying "what if" line of thought. The obvious problem with this view is that if the sin cannot be committed, it is absurd to offer it as an argument against falling to it!

Actual

Another interpretation is that those who fall away are actual, bona-fide Christians. Those who hold this view believe that God supplies grace to those who are trusting him, but the ultimate perseverance of any believer depends on the cooperation of his free will. Therefore, any Christian, whatever his state, is capable of the apostasy and condemnation here described.

Apparent

The view many, including myself, hold is that those who fall away are not true believers, but rather men and women who only appear so. They are people who have received a thorough exposure to the gospel—for example, the catechized Jewish believers of the preceding verses—and have made an ostensible profession of faith and have been received into the fellowship of God's people. However, at a later point they have abandoned their profession, even becoming opponents of Christ.[6]

The reasons I hold to this interpretation are as follows: First, the participation in spiritual realities of those who fall away, though they have been "*enlightened*" and "*shared*" and "*tasted*" the things of God, parallels the privileged experience of the children of Israel in the wilderness who fell away and died in unbelief. As part of the covenant community, the fallen Israelites had placed blood on the doorposts, eaten the Passover lamb, miraculously crossed the Red Sea, observed the pillar of cloud by day and fire by night, tasted the miraculous waters at Marah, daily ate manna, and heard the voice of God at Sinai. But their hearts were hardened in unbelief, and they fell away from the living God. True, some of those who perished in the wilderness were regenerate and some were unregenerate, but both were visible members of the covenant community and thus shared a profound mutuality of spiritual experience. Similarly, these catechized ersatz Christians of Hebrews 6 were accepted into the covenant community and likewise experienced something of the spiritual realities, but fell away.

Second, Jesus' parable of the soils teaches us there are people who at the beginning look very much like believers, but they are unregenerate. Not only do they look like Christians, but they have remarkable spiritual experiences before they fall away—just as the seed sown in rocky places "is the one who hears the word and immediately receives it with joy" (Matthew 13:20). But when trouble comes "he falls away." Significantly, in the parable of the soils only the fourth soil, the one that bears fruit, signifies true believers!

Third, I hold this view because it accords with the great Scriptural doctrine of the perseverance of the saints that is so specifically affirmed in God's Holy Word, as is evidenced by the following list compiled by Roger Nicole:

> Scripture asserts that "He who has begun a good work . . . will perfect it until the day of Christ" (Phil. 1:6; cf. Luke 14:28–32).
> Scripture asserts that "life" shall not separate believers from the love of God in Christ (Rom. 8:38, 39).
> Scripture asserts that the golden chain of God's purpose is not thinning out toward the end, but that the very people who are known, foreordained, called and justified *are also glorified* (Rom. 8:29, 30).
> Scripture asserts that believers are "kept by the power of God through faith unto final salvation and for an incorruptible inheritance" (1 Pet. 1:4, 5; cf. Jude 24, 25; 2 Tim. 1:12).

Scripture asserts that true believers are "sealed by the Spirit unto the day of redemption" (Eph. 4:30).

Scripture asserts that apostates were never true members of Christ because otherwise they would not have fallen away (1 John 2:19).

Scripture asserts again and again that the new life in Christ is "eternal" (*aionios*). What kind of eternity would that be which could be brought to an end in our own life-span?

Jesus asserts that it is impossible "to lead the elect astray" (Matt. 24:24).

Jesus asserts that "everyone who beholdeth the Son and believeth on him shall have eternal life, and he will raise him up at the last day" (John 6:40; cf. 54).

Jesus asserts, "I know my sheep, and they follow me; and I give them eternal life, and they shall never perish, and no one shall snatch them out of my hand" (John 10:27, 28).

The emphasis in this combination of statements appears to me irresistible. These passages, of course, were chosen and arranged for maximum effect. But as Nicole says, they "constitute only a fraction of scriptural support for perseverance. Is it conceivable that the author of Hebrews would contradict all this?"[7]

Fourth, the positive spiritual experiences of those who fall away, described in verses 4–6, are easily within the capacity of the unregenerate, as the successive phrases indicate.

These unregenerated "Christians" are among those "who have once been enlightened" (v. 4). They who had been catechized and admitted into the church were witness to the Light that is "the light of the world" (John 8:12). The light of Christ's presence had shone upon their recoiling souls. They had begun to see themselves, but now volitionally returned to the dark.

Next, they had "tasted the heavenly gift" (v. 4). This may refer to someone who has made a profession of faith or who has been catechized, baptized, and partaken of Communion—thus tasting the heavenly gift—an act an unbeliever is quite capable of. But this partaking is probably even more grievous. "It may indicate," says F. F. Bruce, "the whole sum of spiritual blessings which are sacramentally sealed and signified in the Eucharist."[8] This is a serious matter.

The writer also describes these ersatz Christians as those who "have shared in the Holy Spirit" (v. 4). Here Simon Magus, the sorcerer, is a prime example, because the Scriptures tell us that he "believed, and . . . [was] baptized," thus deriving the ostensible benefit of the Holy Spirit (Acts 8:13). Yet Peter said to him when he tried to buy spiritual powers:

May your silver perish with you, because you thought you could obtain the gift of God with money! You have neither part nor lot in this matter, for your heart is not right before God. Repent, therefore, of this wickedness of yours, and pray to the Lord that, if possible, the intent of your heart may be forgiven you. For I see that you are in the gall of bitterness and in the bond of iniquity. (Acts 8:20–23)

Those who apostatized also "tasted the goodness of the word of God" (v. 5). The unregenerate commonly taste and benefit from God's Word. King Herod did, for Mark 6:20 tells us he enjoyed listening to John the Baptist preach, even though John confronted him. He liked tasting God's Word, but ultimately he rejected it and reluctantly acceded to John's martyrdom.[9]

Lastly, the putative Christians experienced "the powers of the age to come" (v. 5). They experienced "signs and wonders and various miracles" (2:4), not unlike their ancestors in the wilderness. And they saw even greater miracles in the resurrections of Lazarus and Christ and the mute given voice and the blind receiving sight—yet their unbelieving hearts were never regenerated, and they fell away.

How is it possible for one to experience all of this and not be regenerated? we ask. Judas provides the answer. Very likely all the characteristics in our passage were part of his experience, yet there is no way we can imagine him as regenerate, especially since the Lord called him "a devil" (John 6:70), "the son of perdition" (John 17:12 NASB), and one for whom "it would have been better . . . if he had not been born" (Mark 14:21). Jesus knew Judas' condition from the beginning, though Judas fooled the disciples to the last![10]

Tasting the powers of the coming age proves nothing other than the fact that one has come under the blessing of the gospel! Jesus said at the conclusion of the Sermon on the Mount as he discoursed about judgment, "On that day many will say to me, 'Lord, Lord, did we not prophesy in your name, and cast out demons in your name, and do many mighty works in your name?' And then will I declare to them, 'I never knew you; depart from me, you workers of lawlessness'" (Matthew 7:22, 23).

Unpardonable!

Now the horror of the thunderous warning of this passage becomes clear: "It is impossible . . . [if they] have fallen away, to restore them again to repentance, since they are crucifying once again the Son of God to their own harm and holding him up to contempt" (vv. 4a, 6). Why is it impossible? The answer is, *they have committed the unpardonable sin!* Matthew

12, which tells us of the unpardonable sin, says that the Pharisees had just witnessed divine power in a miraculous healing, but rather than attribute the power to God's blessing in Christ and to the power of his Spirit, they ascribed the work to Satan, Beelzebub. This calculated refusal of the Spirit's witness brought their awesome, irremedial damnation: "And whoever speaks a word against the Son of Man will be forgiven, but whoever speaks against the Holy Spirit will not be forgiven, either in this age or in the age to come" (Matthew 12:32).

The Pharisees who committed this sin fit well into the experience of the apostates in Hebrews 6. They had been *"enlightened"* by their contact with Christ and his teaching (John 3:11; 9:39, 41). They had inchoately *"tasted"* of the heavenly gift in their beholding the spiritual blessings of Jesus' ministry. They had been partakers of the work of the Holy Spirit in witnessing the significant deliverance of the crippled man. They had *"tasted"* the goodness of the Word of God both in their knowledge of the Old Testament and in Christ's teaching. They had *"tasted"* the powers of the coming age in witnessing the miracles enacted before their eyes. But despite all these spiritual blessings, they attributed the miracles to Satan rather than God.

Both in the case of the Pharisees and in that of the apostates in Hebrews, the sin is the same: "man's full rejection of God under conditions of full exposure to light."[11] This amounts to "crucifying once again the Son of God to their own harm and holding him up to contempt." They stand with the crucifiers. They treat Christ, in effect, as only a man.

If those who have been catechized and baptized and have become communicants and have experienced spiritual realities reject Christ, it is all over. Repentance is impossible. The Apostle Peter says of such, "For if, after they have escaped the defilements of the world through the knowledge of our Lord and Savior Jesus Christ, they are again entangled in them and overcome, the last state has become worse for them than the first. For it would have been better for them never to have known the way of righteousness than after knowing it to turn back from the holy commandment delivered to them" (2 Peter 2:20, 21).

There could scarcely be a greater warning imaginable for church attenders who, although they have been taught and baptized and are communicants, are not true believers.

Thou a willing captive be,
Thyself thine own dark jail?

John Greenleaf Whittier

Here a word is in order to those who fear they have committed the unforgivable sin. Concern about it indicates you have not committed the unforgivable sin and that you are still capable of repentance!

A Warning with Hope

The writer ends his warning with hope, as he says to the church, "For land that has drunk the rain that often falls on it, and produces a crop useful to those for whose sake it is cultivated, receives a blessing from God. But if it bears thorns and thistles, it is worthless and near to being cursed, and its end is to be burned" (vv. 7, 8). The fact is, the life-giving rain of God's grace falls on all of us in the worshiping community, and if we allow it to bring forth fruit we will be blessed. If not, there is only a curse.

Jesus puts it this way: "As for what was sown on good soil, this is the one who hears the word and understands it. He indeed bears fruit and yields, in one case a hundredfold, in another sixty, and in another thirty" (Matthew 13:23). Christ's call here is to plow the fields of our lives and to make the soil tender to the sweet rain of divine grace—for it descends on us all.

Though we speak in this way, yet in your case, beloved, we feel sure of better things—things that belong to salvation. For God is not unjust so as to overlook your work and the love that you have shown for his name in serving the saints, as you still do. And we desire each one of you to show the same earnestness to have the full assurance of hope until the end, so that you may not be sluggish, but imitators of those who through faith and patience inherit the promises.

6:9–12

17

Make Your Hope Sure

HEBREWS 6:9–12

THE THIRTEENTH CHAPTER OF MATTHEW contains five parables universally called the Mystery Parables because they help explain the mystery of God's kingdom as it is lived out in the Church. It begins with the Parable of the Sower, who sows seed on four kinds of soil. The first three soils (the hard soil, the rocky soil, and the weed-infested soil) yielded no fruit. As Jesus explained of the infested soil, "As for what was sown among thorns, this is the one who hears the word, but the cares of the world and the deceitfulness of riches choke the word, and it proves unfruitful" (Matthew 13:22). Happily, this was not true of the fourth soil, as he further explained: "As for what was sown on good soil, this is the one who hears the word and understands it. He indeed bears fruit and yields, in one case a hundredfold, in another sixty, and in another thirty" (Matthew 13:23). Authentic, living faith produces visible fruit. Jesus says essentially the same thing at the end of the Sermon on the Mount:

> You will recognize them by their fruits. Are grapes gathered from thorn-bushes, or figs from thistles? So, every healthy tree bears good fruit, but the diseased tree bears bad fruit. A healthy tree cannot bear bad fruit, nor can a diseased tree bear good fruit. Every tree that does not bear good fruit is cut down and thrown into the fire. Thus you will recognize them by their fruits. Not everyone who says to me, "Lord, Lord," will enter the kingdom of heaven, but the one who does the will of my Father who is in heaven. (Matthew 7:16–21)

Thus Jesus helps us unravel the mystery of the Church as we are helped to understand that professions and experiences do not necessarily indicate authentic Christianity—such things must be validated by the way one lives.

This is an indispensable truth for understanding the visible church. But misapplied, it can foster far-reaching abuse by self-appointed spiritual fruit inspectors who misapply their own subjective, fallible criteria for true Christianity. Realizing this, Jesus follows up his first parable with a second Mystery Parable, that of the weeds or tares, which describes how the enemy sows bad seed among the good seed of the Sower, so that look-alike weeds grow up with the wheat. The servants asked him:

> "Then do you want us to go and gather them?" But he said, "No, lest in gathering the weeds you root up the wheat along with them. Let both grow together until the harvest, and at harvest time I will tell the reapers, Gather the weeds first and bind them in bundles to be burned, but gather the wheat into my barn." (Matthew 13:28–30)

Tragically, disregard of Jesus' advice has brought untold misery to the Church, as history sadly attests.

There is much wisdom in the first two Mystery Parables. We can generally discern the authenticity of another's faith by the way the person lives, and we ought to be discerning and, at times, confronting if another's life appears fruitless. However, we must also remember that there are copy-cat, bogus believers in the Church whose artificial fruit is very good—so good in fact that a spiritual search-and-destroy mission will uproot real believers along with the counterfeit Christians. We must therefore let God be God!

At the same time, what is to be done pastorally when, say, the preacher sees some dangerous drifts? The book of Hebrews issues terrifying warnings to the corporate church, hoping that those in the church who really need them will hear. The latest have been the thunderous warnings of 6:4–6 (discussed in our previous chapter). The chilling warnings in that passage, followed by the challenge of verses 7, 8 to lay bare the soil of one's life to the sweet rains of God's grace, no doubt made some of the more sensitive believers in the church begin to question the validity of their own faith. Such questioning can be healthy, but there is also the danger of losing one's proper confidence in salvation. So in verses 9–12 the writer works at shoring up the confidence of the believing majority in the storm-tossed little church.

Instilling Confidence (vv. 9, 10)

The author begins by tenderly expressing confidence in their faith, calling them "beloved"—"Though we speak in this way, yet in your case, beloved, we feel sure of better things—things that belong to salvation" (v. 9). He is confident that the things that characterize a real work of salvation are part of their *inner* and *outer* experience.

Inner Life

Inwardly, "things that belong to salvation" are evidenced by the witness of the Holy Spirit as he testifies with our spirits that we are God's children, as is described in Romans 8:16. We have a subjective voice within that authenticates our relationship with God. One of the primary evidences of this is the sublimely compulsive desire to address God intimately as "Father" (Romans 8:15). At the very root of this is the inner awareness that we are forgiven and reconciled. We also have an inner peace/*shalom* that is supernatural. Jesus said, "Peace I leave with you; my peace I give to you. Not as the world gives do I give to you. Let not your hearts be troubled, neither let them be afraid" (John 14:27). This is nothing less than the personal peace of Christ! These unique inward realities that characterize our experience of salvation are substantial grounds for confidence.

Outer Life

Outwardly, "things that belong to salvation" are witnessed to by the graces of character that come from truly knowing Christ: a pure life—a truthful tongue—a forgiving spirit—a generous heart. It is true that such graces may be partially produced without "salvation," but those are like artificial flowers in comparison with the real thing. They have no real life—no true fragrance. Authentic Christian life produces authentic Christian character—and such character is added ground for substantial confidence.

When we have the inner and outer evidences of "things that belong to salvation," we have reason for great confidence. When the Holy Spirit whispers that we are children of God, when the reflex of our heart cries, "dear Father," when we have a sense of the *shalom* of Christ, when our character has been spiritually altered by Christ, we can be confident of our spiritual state.

Lifestyle

The writer was confident about the church in general because he knew most of them knew the "things that belong to salvation." But his confidence was grounded even further in their past and present lifestyle, as the next verse indicates: "For God is not unjust so as to overlook your work and the love that you have shown for his name in serving the saints, as you still do" (v. 10).

The essence of their *past* lifestyle is noted in his saying, "serving the saints," a direct reference to their initial heroics when the church began, as recorded in 10:32–34.[1] There we are told that they stood tall in the face of suffering public insult, persecution, and confiscation of their property. But even more heroic is how they unselfishly committed themselves to helping their suffering brothers and sisters, for it says they were "sometimes . . . publicly exposed to reproach and affliction, and sometimes . . . partners with those so treated [i.e., insulted and persecuted]. For you had compassion on those in prison" (10:33, 34). Their Christian lifestyle was one of daring courage and compassion—giving themselves for others.

And this reaching out, this care for the Body of Christ, was not just a thing of the past but was part of their *present* lifestyle because the whole of the phrase reads, ". . . in serving the saints, *as you still do.*" Their lifestyle was an actual living out of Christ's new commandment to love each other with the sacrificial love with which he loved them (John 13:34, 35).

So we see that many in that little church lived an exalted Christian lifestyle, and if we look closer we see that it did not escape the notice of Heaven: "For God is not unjust so as to overlook your work and the love that you have shown for his name . . ." (v. 10). They will be rewarded because in helping God's people they were helping God! Jesus taught the same thing:

> Then the righteous will answer him, saying, "Lord, when did we see you hungry and feed you, or thirsty and give you drink? And when did we see you a stranger and welcome you, or naked and clothe you? And when did we see you sick or in prison and visit you?" And the King will answer them, "Truly, I say to you, as you did it to one of the least of these my brothers, you did it to me." (Matthew 25:37–40)

Their caring lifestyle for others was ultimately a caring for God!

Thus the writer has a well-grounded confidence in the spiritual authenticity of his people. A lifestyle that caught the rewarding eye of God, which, in serving others, was serving him—this lifestyle, coupled with the inner "things that belong to salvation" such as a sense of forgiveness, *shalom*, and God's Fatherhood, plus the outer character changes coming from salvation, was substance for the author's great confidence that the church would go forward.

And it is the same with us. If we have undergone an inner change through Christ that affects us outwardly in our character, producing a lifestyle that causes us to care for others, we can have the greatest confidence about our faith. Conversely, if there is no subjective inner experience of *shalom*, if our ostensible character changes are more like plastic flowers and our lifestyle is focused inward upon ourselves, we had better take careful stock of our destiny.

Insuring Confidence (vv. 11, 12)

Now, having *instilled* confidence in verses 9, 10, the writer moves on to *insure* their confidence: "And we desire each one of you to show the same earnestness to have the full assurance of hope until the end, so that you may not be sluggish, but imitators of those who through faith and patience inherit the promises" (vv. 11, 12).

Avoid Sloth

Here we see that the great enemy of perseverance is sloth or laziness—one of the seven deadly sins. The word behind "sluggish" was used earlier in 5:11 to describe those who were "dull of hearing"—literally, "sluggish in the ears." More often than not, sluggish ears go with a sluggish, lazy life. When the ear becomes dull, everything else follows suit. Spiritual sluggishness is a danger that looms over all of us if we do not work against it, for just as surely as friction will stop a train unless there is a consistent source of power, or as surely as a pendulum will settle to an inert hanging position unless the mainspring urges it on moment by moment,[2] so will each of us wind down without an assertion of the will!

The warning here is, if anything, more *apropos* to our time than for the ancients. We see this in some of our popular lingo: "Go with the flow"—"laid back"—"What's it to me?"—"I couldn't care less." Henry Fairlie, writing in his highly-regarded *The Seven Deadly Sins Today*, engages in some astute social criticism in his chapter on *acedia*, sloth:

> Children are too idle to obey. Parents are too sluggish to command. Pupils are too lazy to work. Teachers are too indolent to teach. Priests are too slack to believe. Prophets are too morbid to inspire. Men are too indifferent to be men. Women are too heedless to be women. Doctors are too careless to care well. Shoemakers are too slipshod to make good shoes. Writers are too inert to write well. Street cleaners are too bored to clean streets. Shop clerks are too uninterested to be courteous. Painters are too feckless to make pictures. Poets are too lazy to be exact. Philosophers are too fainthearted to make philosophies. Believers are too dejected to bear witness. . . .

Fairlie goes on to say that this may seem to be too sweeping a judgment, noting that there are, of course, individual exceptions to sloth. Then he adds convincingly, "But before we dismiss it as too sweeping, we must ask then why our societies have to spend so much time trying to correct us."[3]

Today's culture has come very near to making a religion of sloth. Carried to the ultimate, it separates us from God because it erases caring. Humanly speaking, apart from the mysteries of God's sovereign workings, more souls perish from sloth than from outright disbelief.

In the Parable of the Talents, the master says to the servant who did nothing with his talent, "You wicked and slothful servant!" (Matthew 25:26). Sloth is intrinsically wicked! The master goes on to pronounce a withering condemnation:

> So take the talent from him and give it to him who has the ten talents. For to everyone who has will more be given, and he will have an abundance. But from the one who has not, even what he has will be taken away. And cast the worthless servant into the outer darkness. In that place there will be weeping and gnashing of teeth. (Matthew 25:28–30)

From the lips of Jesus, then, we have a linking of laziness and damnation. A lazy life can be an indication of a graceless life. True believers persevere.

Work!

According to The Proceedings of the U.S. Naval Institute:

> The USS *Astoria* (CA-34) was the first U.S. cruiser to engage the Japanese during the Battle of Savo Island, a night action fought 8–9 August 1942. Although she scored two hits on the Imperial flagship *Chokai*, the *Astoria* was badly damaged and sank shortly after noon, 9 August.
>
> About 0200 hours a young midwesterner, Signalman 3rd Class Elgin Staples, was swept overboard by the blast when the *Astoria's* number one eight-inch gun turret exploded. Wounded in both legs by shrapnel and in semi-shock, he was kept afloat by a narrow lifebelt that he managed to activate with a simple trigger mechanism.
>
> At around 0600 hours, Staples was rescued by a passing destroyer and returned to the *Astoria*, whose captain was attempting to save the cruiser by beaching her. The effort failed, and Staples, still wearing the same lifebelt, found himself back in the water. It was lunchtime. Picked up again, this time by the USS *President Jackson* (AP-37), he was one of 500 survivors of the battle who were evacuated to Noumea.
>
> On board the transport Staples, for the first time, closely examined the lifebelt that had served him so well. It had been manufactured by Firestone Tire and Rubber Company of Akron, Ohio, and bore a registration number.
>
> Given home leave, Staples told his story and asked his mother, who worked for Firestone, about the purpose of the number on the belt. She replied that the company insisted on personal responsibility for the war effort, and that the number was unique and assigned to only one inspector. Staples remembered everything about the lifebelt, and quoted the number.

It was his mother's personal code and affixed to every item she was responsible for approving.[4]

Fifty years ago, a mother's unheralded diligence in an anonymous wartime job made sure her soon-to-be shipwrecked son's hope of survival. But how much greater are the stakes in eternal matters, and how much greater is the challenge to diligence in eternal matters! "And we desire [literally, we long for] each one of you," says the writer in verse 11, "to show the same earnestness to have the full assurance of hope until the end."

Those who work at their faith make their hope sure! The Bible is clear that no one can be saved by works, but it is also clear that saving faith works. This was the teaching given by Paul:

> But God, being rich in mercy, because of the great love with which he loved us, even when we were dead in our trespasses, made us alive together with Christ—by grace you have been saved. . . . For by grace you have been saved through faith. And this is not your own doing; it is the gift of God, not a result of works, so that no one may boast. For we are his workmanship, created in Christ Jesus for good works, which God prepared beforehand, that we should walk in them. (Ephesians 2:4–10)

Similarly he writes in Philippians, "Therefore, my beloved, as you have always obeyed, so now, not only as in my presence but much more in my absence, work out your own salvation with fear and trembling, for it is God who works in you, both to will and to work for his good pleasure" (Philippians 2:12, 13). And Paul writes of himself, "But by the grace of God I am what I am, and his grace toward me was not in vain. On the contrary, I worked harder than any of them, though it was not I, but the grace of God that is with me" (1 Corinthians 15:10). Spiritual diligence is a sign that God's grace is really at work in us!

There must be perseverance (cf. Matthew 10:22; 24:12, 13; Mark 13:13; Revelation 2:26). Perseverance in loving service is clear evidence of a sure hope!

Imitate!

The focus of this diligence involves imitation: ". . . but imitators of those who through faith and patience inherit the promises" (v. 12b). The immediate context indicates we are to put our energies into imitating the faith and patience of Abraham,[5] because it was by faith and patience that he entered the land of promise.

Here in Hebrews "faith" means the ability to take hold of the unseen and assume the promises of future blessings as our own—"Now faith is the assurance of things hoped for, the conviction of things not seen" (11:1)—and that is what the great faith chapter is all about. This idea of faith fits very well with the other dominant sense of faith in the New Testament, which is trust in Christ alone, because Christ is the revealer of the unseen things to us. But the major emphasis here in Hebrews is on imitating the posture of soul that sees the unseen and makes God's promises to us our own by anticipation.

Along with imitating the faith of Abraham, we are also to imitate his "patience"—or more accurately, his *long-suffering*. This long-suffering is not added to faith but is an integral part of it, because faith's vision will produce patient tenacity. To the storm-tossed, persecuted little church that was facing mounting waves, the message was clear: fix your eyes in faith on the great unseen heavenly realities that await you; do so with long-suffering/patience; do this diligently, thus making your hope sure.

Authentic focusing by faith on the unseen will cure all laziness. All of the great saints of chapter 11 were spurred on to legendary activism by their grasp of the unseen. Similarly, the bounding energy of the Apostle Paul came from his vision of the unseen (cf. 2 Corinthians 12:1–6). In one of his great challenges to the church, he says:

> If then you have been raised with Christ, seek the things that are above, where Christ is, seated at the right hand of God. Set your minds on things that are above, not on things that are on earth. For you have died, and your life is hidden with Christ in God. When Christ who is your life appears, then you also will appear with him in glory. (Colossians 3:1–4)

A mind set on such a blessed vision will promote a life of blessed activism!

In conclusion, the writer is confident of "better things" (v. 9) for his beloved church. He is well aware that their *inner* and *outer* life is infused with "things that belong to salvation" (v. 9) and that they have lived and are living an authentic lifestyle in caring for their spiritual brothers and sisters.

And this confidence, he says, can be insured through three logical steps: First, a conscious commitment not to be lazy. In today's world, this takes an immense act of the will, because sloth is "in" and hard work is "out"—especially in matters of the soul.

Second, they must show "earnestness to have the full assurance of hope until the end" (v. 11). The issue is not a life preserver but the preservation of the soul for eternity, for the Scriptures are clear: only "the one who endures to the end will be saved" (Matthew 24:13).

Lastly, they are to imitate the visionary faith and patience of Abraham. The writer knows that a God-dependent imitation will result in a God-aided ability to see the unseen and patiently seek the heavenly city in the sojourn below.

Confidence is the possession of all whose inner and outer lives have been changed by Christ so that their lifestyle reaches out to their brothers and sisters. This great confidence is doubly insured by a heart that is so graced that it works, persevering in sure hope to the end in imitation of the faith and patience of those who have gone before.

For when God made a promise to Abraham, since he had no one greater by whom to swear, he swore by himself, saying, "Surely I will bless you and multiply you." And thus Abraham, having patiently waited, obtained the promise. For people swear by something greater than themselves, and in all their disputes an oath is final for confirmation. So when God desired to show more convincingly to the heirs of the promise the unchangeable character of his purpose, he guaranteed it with an oath, so that by two unchangeable things, in which it is impossible for God to lie, we who have fled for refuge might have strong encouragement to hold fast to the hope set before us. We have this as a sure and steadfast anchor of the soul, a hope that enters into the inner place behind the curtain, where Jesus has gone as a forerunner on our behalf, having become a high priest forever after the order of Melchizedek.

6:13–20

18

An Anchor for the Soul

HEBREWS 6:13–20

THE BOOK OF GENESIS TELLS US that after Abram set out from the pagan city of Ur to go to the land of Canaan, he was delayed for some years in the city of Haran until the death of his father Terah (cf. Genesis 11:27–32). Genesis also records that though Abram and Sarai had been married for some years, Abram being seventy-five when he left Haran (12:4), they were still childless. So we understand that the great Abrahamic Covenant (God's promise to Abram when he departed Haran, recorded in Genesis 12:1–3, that he would make a great nation from Abram and bless all the peoples on earth) was made to a man who had no physical offspring.

We also understand that the reiterations of the covenant promise were made when he still had no children. After the tragic separation from Lot, God told him:

> Lift up your eyes and look from the place where you are, northward and southward and eastward and westward, for all the land that you see I will give to you and to your offspring forever. I will make your offspring as the dust of the earth, so that if one can count the dust of the earth, your offspring also can be counted. Arise, walk through the length and the breadth of the land, for I will give it to you. (Genesis 13:14–17)

He had no children after being in the land ten years, and on that fateful day while suffering from post-battle fatigue incurred in defending the land from four kings (Genesis 14), he drifted off to sleep, perhaps dejectedly reflecting that after all this he had no heir to carry on, when suddenly God spoke: "Fear not, Abram, I am your shield; your reward shall be very great" (Genesis 15:1). Rallying words! Nevertheless, Abram, still discouraged, voiced his fear that because he was childless his estate would go to his servant.

At this low point, the word of the Lord came to him: "'Your very own son shall be your heir.' And he brought him outside and said, 'Look toward heaven, and number the stars, if you are able to number them.' Then he said to him, 'So shall your offspring be'" (Genesis 15:4, 5).

We do not know whether Abram's response was immediate or came after some thought, or whether it was verbal or mental, but we do have this immortal record: "And he believed the LORD, and he counted it to him as righteousness" (Genesis 15:6). He believed that he would become a father, and that his offspring would have children, and that his line would go on and on like the visible stars. The aged patriarch rested everything on God's word. As a result, he was declared righteous apart from works, fourteen years before circumcision (Genesis 17) and hundreds of years before the Law!

This was one of the greatest events in the history of salvation, and the Lord commemorated it with a further sign when he ordered Abram to make sacrifices and divide them into two rows. Then, when the sun had set, God appeared in the night as "a smoking fire pot and a flaming torch [and] passed between these pieces" (Genesis 15:17) in the traditional figure-eight pattern of covenant, signifying that his promise was unconditional and that he (God) would be torn asunder like the pieces if he failed to keep his promise.

To be sure, Abram's unwavering faith displayed at this great moment (cf. Romans 4:10ff.) did suffer some future lapses, but his faith also grew to towering proportions through the hard times that were to come.

Finally, Abraham and Sarah were given their dream in baby Isaac (literally, "laughter"), and in that little boy, soon grown to manhood, they saw the promise in full bloom. Yet there was one more test and perfection awaiting the patriarch's faith. Abraham was well over one hundred years old, according to Genesis 22, when God said to him, "Take your son, your only son Isaac, whom you love, and go to the land of Moriah, and offer him there as a burnt offering on one of the mountains of which I shall tell you" (Genesis 22:2). Easily, this is the most shocking command ever given to any human being by God! We can imagine the numbing horror that must have spread over Abraham's soul. This makes his ready obedience almost as equally shocking, because with the first glow of dawn, without a word to aged Sarah, Abraham saddled his donkey, quietly called for two servants and his son Isaac, split wood for the sacrificial pyre, and began the terrible journey (Genesis 22:3).

How could he do it? we wonder. Our text gives us the answer: "On the third day Abraham lifted up his eyes and saw the place from afar. Then

Abraham said to his young men, 'Stay here with the donkey; I and the boy will go over there and worship and come again to you'" (Genesis 22:4, 5). *Abraham was confident they would return together!* This was because, as the writer of Hebrews reveals, "He [Abraham] considered that God was able even to raise him from the dead, from which, figuratively speaking, he did receive him back" (11:19; cf. vv. 17, 18). Abraham so believed that God would bless him through Isaac, giving him offspring as numerous as the stars, that he was sure God would resurrect his son!

The poignant exchange between father and son as they ascended Mt. Moriah—Isaac's dawning realization that he was the sacrifice—the construction of the altar—Isaac's voluntary submission to his aged father as he was bound—the sobbing, the kisses, the tears, the terrible blade in the father's trembling hand—the nausea, the darkness—the imminent convulsions of his only son—all this shows only the tip of Abraham's emotions as he faithfully carried out God's will.

Then with the blade poised for descent, the angel of Heaven called, "Abraham, Abraham!" and we know the rest of the story in all its tender redemptive glory. But do we remember the final pronouncement of the angel of the Lord—because it has everything to do with our text in Hebrews:

> By myself I have sworn, declares the LORD, because you have done this and have not withheld your son, your only son, I will surely bless you, and I will surely multiply your offspring as the stars of heaven and as the sand that is on the seashore. And your offspring shall possess the gate of his enemies, and in your offspring shall all the nations of the earth be blessed, because you have obeyed my voice. (Genesis 22:16–18)

The significance of this from the perspective of the writer of Hebrews is that whereas God had repeatedly *promised* Abraham he would make a great nation from him, he here *swore* an oath to do so. Hebrews 6:13, 14 tells us: "For when God made a promise to Abraham, since he had no one greater by whom to swear, he swore by himself, saying, 'Surely I will bless you and multiply you'" (quoting Genesis 22:17). God was so pleased with Abraham's supreme act of faith that he did something he had never done before—he swore that the promise would come to pass. James offers further insight into why God was pleased: "Was not Abraham our father justified by works when he offered up his son Isaac on the altar? You see that faith was active along with his works, and faith was completed by his works" (James 2:21, 22).

The pertinence of this to the little Hebrew church as it braced for the tempests ahead is expressed in the next line: "And thus Abraham, having patiently waited, obtained the promise" (v. 15). This is an implicit call to the church for a faith that is so firm it enables steadfastness through the uneven seas of life. Abraham's faith saw the unseen. He saw a living God who was sovereign in all of life—he saw his sacrificed son resurrected and living on—he saw himself fathering a sea of humanity—he saw blessing for the whole earth. And because he saw this, he was gloriously long-suffering through many years.

We Have God's Word for It (vv. 16–18)

Having introduced the subject of oaths, the writer proceeds to explain about human and divine oaths and what great encouragement the latter brings to us.

Regarding human oaths he says, "For people swear by something greater than themselves, and in all their disputes an oath is final for confirmation" (v. 16). The reason human oaths are used to end disputes is the unreliability of human speech due to sin—that is, people are naturally liars. In the context of ancient culture (when people generally feared God), swearing by a greater thing helped assure truth. And if one swore by God, it served to end an argument. This was especially true in Hebrew culture where lying while making an oath was a transgression of the Third Commandment against misusing the name of God and so deserved the punishment of God (cf. Deuteronomy 5:11). Therefore, we see that human oaths were a powerful assurance of carrying out one's word.

This is essentially why God chose to swear by an oath, as the writer explains: "So when God desired to show more convincingly to the heirs of the promise the unchangeable character of his purpose, he guaranteed it with an oath" (v. 17). God did not have to swear by an oath, but he did so as a condescension or accommodation to human weakness.

Of course, in choosing to make an oath, he could only choose to swear by himself because there was nothing or no one higher to swear by. To swear by anything lesser would have the effect of making his oath less permanent. In a different context, Rabbi Eleazar stated the principle this way:

> Lord of the world, if thou hadst sworn by heaven or by earth, I would have been able to say: As heaven and earth shall pass away, so also thine oath shall pass away. But now that thou hast sworn by thy great Name (by thyself), as thy great Name lives and abides eternally, so shall thine oath continue secure in all eternity. (Berakhot 32)[1]

The language behind our text in verse 17—"when God desired"— indicates that God's decision to make an oath in reaffirming the Abrahamic Covenant was not a whim but a passionate sovereign choice, because the

Greek word is stronger than "desired"—indicating the purposeful, deliberate exercise of his will.[2]

And why was God so premeditative about making his oath? Verse 18 answers, "[God did this] so that by two unchangeable things, in which it is impossible for God to lie, we who have fled for refuge might have strong encouragement [literally, "strong, powerful encouragement"] to hold fast to the hope set before us." Powerful encouragement indeed is here if we will address ourselves to the marrow of this text because the "two unchangeable things, in which it is impossible for God to lie" are his *word of "promise"* and his *"oath."* His *promise* to Abraham, and to us, can do nothing other than come true because God's "word is truth" (John 17:17) and because God "never lies" (Titus 1:2). He is the author of truth, the essence of truth. His *oath*, though unnecessary, is the double assurance that he cannot lie. Truth has sworn by itself that its truth shall truly be fulfilled. There is no more possibility of God's promises failing us than of God falling out of Heaven! His Word is eternally sealed with the double surety of promise and oath.

Because of this, "the hope" we have fled to and take hold of is sure. We must understand that it is an *objective* hope, and not the *subjective*, sentimental optimism the world so readily embraces. People love to boast of their optimism—for example, Sir Thomas Lipton:

> I am the world's greatest optimist. I am proud of the distinction. There is something buoyant and healthy in being an optimist. It is because of my optimism that I have gone through life smiling. I am always in good humor and good fettle. Dr. Optimist is the finest chap in any city or country. Just try a course of his treatment. It will work wonders, and this doctor charges no fees.[3]

Well, optimism is certainly better than pessimism. But blind, secular optimism flourishes best where the ground is uncritically shallow and withers with the difficulties of life. Optimism is good for the body, but it will not save you. I have seen hopeful, optimistic people die. In fact, terminal cancer victims during remission will often experience a rush of enthusiastic optimism only weeks before death. Looking at the bright side of things may seem bold and brave, but if it involves a foolish neglect of the facts that suggest the opposite, it makes failure only more bitter. Bankruptcies often visit those who insist on looking on nothing but the bright side of their finances.[4]

The hope spoken of here does not originate within us but comes from the outside. New Testament scholar William Lane says categorically, "In

Hebrews, the word 'hope' never describes a subjective attitude (i.e. 'our hope' or 'hopefulness') but always denotes the objective context of hope."[5]

Here our hope centers on the objective promises of God, which are fleshed out for us in the ultimate blessing of the world through Jesus Christ. "The hope set before us" comes from the fact that we are *in* Christ, the Son who fulfilled Abraham's covenant, and that at the last we will be *with* Christ and *like* Christ (cf. John 14:3; 1 John 3:2). Jesus is the foundation and substance of our hope.

God also swore in another place, insuring Jesus' eternal priesthood, "The LORD has sworn and will not change his mind, 'You are a priest forever after the order of Melchizedek'" (Psalm 110:4; cf. Hebrews 5:6). Jesus is the thing hoped for and the ground for eternal optimism, as we shall see.

Our hope is doubly sure! God has *promised* it and *sworn* it. Everything promised comes to us through Christ. We have God's word for it. He wants us to take hold of it!

We Have God's Anchor for It (vv. 19, 20)

Now, having God's word for it, he gives us his "anchor"—a metaphor which suggests deepest security: "We have this as a sure and steadfast anchor of the soul, a hope that enters into the inner place behind the curtain, where Jesus has gone as a forerunner on our behalf, having become a high priest forever after the order of Melchizedek" (vv. 19, 20).

To appreciate what is said here, we must remember that the curtain was a thickly woven piece of tapestry hung between the inner and outer chambers of the tabernacle. No one could see through the curtain, and the Holy of Holies was inaccessible to all but the high priest, who passed within only once a year. Outside the curtain was the Holy Place with the altar of incense, the golden candlestick, and the table of showbread—all devoted to the people's worship. It was between these two compartments of the tabernacle—the Holy Place representing the earthly worshiping life of God's people, and the Holy of Holies representing God's presence—that the curtain hung. Together these two sides of the curtain symbolize living spiritual realities—God's presence in Heaven and the storm-tossed church worshiping below (cf. Hebrews 9).

But then an anchor is hurled from the Church. But instead of falling to the depths, it rises through the blue skies and on up through deep heaven where it passes unhindered through the curtain and anchors on the throne of God in the heavenly holy of holies where Jesus is seated "at the right hand of the Majesty on high" (1:3). Our lives are accessed and anchored in Heaven!

The significance of this was immediate in the ancient world because an anchor was everything to those at sea. A firm anchorage meant security. Well-anchored, the winds could blow, but the ship would not be awash or headed for the rocks. For this reason the famous catacomb of Priscilla is decorated with no less than sixty anchors![6]

What a tremendous encouragement: "We have this as a sure and steadfast anchor of the soul, a hope that enters into the inner place behind the curtain" (v. 19). But there is something more, for there is another who has pierced the veil, one who actually tore it in two—Jesus: "Jesus has gone as a fore-runner on our behalf, having become a high priest forever after the order of Melchizedek" (v. 20; cf. Matthew 27:50, 51). We are anchored in the Father's presence for eternity—and Jesus at his right hand perpetually intercedes for his Church. His continual priestly prayer for us is the medium for our survival.

He is there as the one who "has gone as a forerunner." Just as forerun-ners were sent to explore the way for those who would follow, Christ, our *prodromos*, has gone ahead of us to prepare the way.[7] In fact, our forerunner left this message for us: "In my Father's house are many rooms. If it were not so, would I have told you that I go to prepare a place for you? And if I go and prepare a place for you, I will come again and will take you to myself, that where I am you may be also. And you know the way to where I am going" (John 14:2–4). There is no doubt that we can and will follow.

If we are true followers of Christ, the prows of our boats will always be treading heavy seas and bucking contrary winds. The disciples found this out when they obeyed Jesus and launched out in the night for the other side of Galilee. The reason they were in stormy waters was that they were doing what he said (cf. Matthew 14:22–32). It has always been that way. Abraham's ships—his camels, his desert schooners—were always facing contrary winds, "For he was looking forward to the city that has foundations, whose designer and builder is God" (11:10). "Indeed, all who desire to live a godly life in Christ Jesus will be persecuted" (2 Timothy 3:12).

But we are not flotsam on the tides. We have a hope—a hope outside ourselves.

- It is anchored in Heaven. We have continual access to God's presence, not just once a year through a fallible man, but always—at every moment—through our high priest, Jesus Christ.
- It is anchored in Christ, our *prodromos* who has gone to prepare a place for us.
- It is anchored in Christ, our Melchizedekian priest who ministers perpetu-ally and eternally.
- It is sure, for it is doubly impossible for God to lie.

So we have reason to be optimistic—we have an anchor for the soul.

> I can feel the anchor fast
> As I meet each sudden blast,
> And the cable, though unseen,
> Bears the heavenly strain between;
> Through the storm I safely ride,
> Till the turning of the tide.
> And it holds,
> my anchor holds;
> Blow your wildest, then, O gale,
> On my bark so small and frail;
> By his grace I shall not fail,
> For my anchor holds,
> my anchor holds.

Daniel B. Towner, 1902

For this Melchizedek, king of Salem, priest of the Most High God, met Abraham returning from the slaughter of the kings and blessed him, and to him Abraham apportioned a tenth part of everything. He is first, by translation of his name, king of righteousness, and then he is also king of Salem, that is, king of peace. He is without father or mother or genealogy, having neither beginning of days nor end of life, but resembling the Son of God he continues a priest forever. See how great this man was to whom Abraham the patriarch gave a tenth of the spoils! And those descendants of Levi who receive the priestly office have a commandment in the law to take tithes from the people, that is, from their brothers, though these also are descended from Abraham. But this man who does not have his descent from them received tithes from Abraham and blessed him who had the promises. It is beyond dispute that the inferior is blessed by the superior. In the one case tithes are received by mortal men, but in the other case, by one of whom it is testified that he lives. One might even say that Levi himself, who receives tithes, paid tithes through Abraham, for he was still in the loins of his ancestor when Melchizedek met him.

7:1–10

19

The Greatness of Melchizedek

HEBREWS 7:1-10

ON JUNE 27, 1976, armed operatives for the Popular Front for the Liberation of Palestine surprised the twelve crew members of an Air France jetliner and its ninety-one passengers, hijacking it to a destination unknown. The plane was tracked heading for Central Africa, where indeed it did land under the congenial auspices of Ugandan President Idi Amin. And there it remained apparently secure at Entebbe Airport where the hijackers spent the next seven days preparing for their next move. The hijackers were, by all estimations, in the driver's seat.

However, 2,500 miles away in Tel Aviv, three Israeli C-130 Hercules transports secretly boarded a deadly force of Israeli commandos, who within hours attacked Entebbe Airport under cover of darkness. In less than sixty minutes the commandos rushed the old terminal, gunned down the hijackers, and rescued 110 of the 113 hostages. The next day, July 4, Israel's Premier Yitzhak Rabin triumphantly declared the mission "will become a legend," which it surely has![1] Israel's resolve and stealth in liberating her people is admired by her friends and begrudged by her enemies.

Actually Israel's resolve is nothing new, because the same quality can be traced all the way back to the very beginning of the Hebrew nation in the prowess of their father Abraham. The kidnappers in his day were a coalition of four Canaanite kings headed by King Chedorlaomer who attacked the Transjordan, defeating the city-states of Sodom and her neighbors and carrying off a large number of hostages, including Abraham's nephew Lot (cf. Genesis 14:5–12).

Undaunted, Abraham recruited 318 trained men (Genesis 14:14)— proto-commandos!—from his own household and took off in hot pursuit until he closed in on the kidnappers somewhere close to Damascus. And there, under the cover of night, he deployed his small forces in a surprise attack. His troops, riding bawling camels and slavering horses, bore down on the hijackers and their hostages. Deadly arrows flew in the night, and bloody swords were raised gleaming in the dusty moonlight—and the four kings were put to flight.

The Genesis account gives this Entebbe-like summary of Abraham's success: "Then he brought back all the possessions, and also brought back his kinsman Lot with his possessions, and the women and the people" (Genesis 14:16). Abraham could be formidable. It was not wise to mess with father Abraham!

So when Abraham returned to his home after the slaughter of the kings he was a hero, at the pinnacle of martial success. Can you see him proudly astride his lumbering camel, smeared with the dirt and blood of battle, leading his 318 proud men plus Lot and *all* the captives and *all* the plunder through Jerusalem? If so, you have the feel necessary to begin to appreciate Abraham's strange, mystic encounter with a shadowy figure of immense grandeur—Melchizedek, the priest-king of Salem. Genesis says:

And Melchizedek king of Salem brought out bread and wine. (He was priest of God Most High.) And he blessed him and said,

"Blessed be Abram by God Most High,
    Possessor of heaven and earth;
and blessed be God Most High,
    who has delivered your enemies into your hand!"
    (Genesis 14:18–20)

So mysterious! And think of this—this is the *only* historical mention of Melchizedek in the Old Testament. What we have just read is all we know of him! Yet Abraham allowed Melchizedek to bless him and then gave him a tenth of everything.

That was around 2000 BC, and for a millennium there is no mention at all of Melchizedek, not even in retrospect. But in the tenth century BC, when the psalmist David was King of Israel, the Holy Spirit inspired him to write this prophetic word: "The LORD has sworn and will not change his mind, 'You are a priest forever after the order of Melchizedek'" (Psalm 110:4). There God declared that he was going to do something *new*. His intention was to bring into history one who would be a priest like Melchizedek. In the likeness of Melchizedek he would be both priest and king (cf. Psalm 110:1). Also, his priesthood would last forever. And, like Melchizedek, he would be appointed directly by God. It was all divinely guaranteed: "The LORD has sworn and will not change his mind." What an intriguing prophecy! God was going to establish a totally new priesthood.

Imagine for a moment that you are the writer of Hebrews writing to encourage the soon-to-be persecuted Jewish church. Also imagine yourself reflecting both on Melchizedek's *history* and this *prophecy*—and then you make the connection! Jesus Christ is the fulfillment of the prophecy! He is a priest forever, in the order of Melchizedek. Further, you are the first person in history to make the connection. You begin to muse and pray—and everything falls into place. Now in Hebrews 7 you present what you have learned as a means of encouragement to the storm-tossed church. There is no teaching like it anywhere. This is, as we sometimes say today, heavy!

The Significance of Melchizedek (vv. 1–3)

In the writer's opening statement he concisely states the significance of the historical Melchizedek as a type of the ultimate priesthood of Christ:

> For this Melchizedek, king of Salem, priest of the Most High God, met Abraham returning from the slaughter of the kings and blessed him, and to him Abraham apportioned a tenth part of everything. He is first, by translation of his name, king of righteousness, and then he is also king of Salem, that is, king of peace. He is without father or mother or genealogy, having neither beginning of days nor end of life, but resembling the Son of God he continues a priest forever. (vv. 1–3)

Foreshadowing Christ's Character

For starters, the author of Hebrews has noted that Melchizedek's titles foreshadow the character of Christ. Melchizedek bore the title of "*king*," and this is mentioned four times in verses 1, 2. Jesus is, of course, the ultimate "King of kings and Lord of lords," as will be written both on his robe and thigh when he returns (Revelation 19:16). Significantly, Melchizedek was a priest-king, something that by law no Levitical priest could ever be. But Jesus became the ultimate priest-king, fulfilling to the letter what was promised through Zechariah regarding the Messiah: "Yes, it is He who will build the temple of the LORD, and He who will bear the honor and sit and rule on His throne. Thus, He will be a priest on His throne, and the counsel of peace will be between the two offices" (Zechariah 6:13 NASB; cf. Psalm 110:1, 4).

The title Melchizedek, our author explains, means "king of righteousness," and the title "king of Salem" (i.e., Jerusalem; cf. Psalm 72) means "king of peace." Significantly here we should note that both the qualities of righteousness and peace were prophesied of the Messiah in Isaiah 9:6, 7, where his fourth title is "Prince of Peace," and he goes on to rule with "righteousness." The New Testament identifies Jesus specifically as "Jesus Christ the righteous" (1 John 2:1) and our "righteousness" (1 Corinthians 1:30). Jesus is the King of righteousness! Likewise, the New Testament says of Jesus, "For he himself is our peace" (Ephesians 2:14). Jesus is the King of peace!

So Jesus brings righteousness and peace together in his person. As the psalmist so magnificently indicates, in the Lord "righteousness and peace kiss each other" (Psalm 85:10). Righteousness and peace are the telltale kiss of his character.

He is the *King*, the sovereign, of righteousness and peace. He is the sovereign giver of the kisses of peace and righteousness. As we shall see, he is the only one in whom peace and righteousness can be found. So as we begin we see that Melchizedek foreshadowed the *character* of Christ—his kingship, his priesthood, his righteousness, and his peace.

Foreshadowing Christ's Qualifications

Going deeper, the writer also sees a distinct foreshadowing of Christ's *qualifications*, for he says Melchizedek was "without father or mother or genealogy, having neither beginning of days nor end of life, but resembling the Son of God he continues a priest forever" (v. 3). Some have inferred from these words that Melchizedek must have been an angel who took on human form for Abraham, or even a pre-incarnate appearance of Jesus himself. But such interpretations are unnecessary, because the writer is simply using a rabbinical method of interpretation from silence. His point is that the Genesis account does not mention Melchizedek's parents or genealogy or when he was born or died, thereby providing a fitting type of what would be fleshed out in the qualifications of Christ.[2]

No Genealogy

All Levitical priests had to have a priestly genealogy that could be traced all the way back to Aaron. But Melchizedek was "without father or mother or genealogy." He had no priestly genealogy through Levi or Aaron. While Jesus' royal bloodline could be traced to Judah, he had no priestly genealogy. He was, in effect, without genealogy. The point is, Jesus' priesthood, like Melchizedek's, was based solely on the call of God, not on heredity. Jesus and Melchizedek were both appointed as priests of God Most High.

No Beginning or End

Secondly, all Levitical priests served limited terms of office—no more than thirty years.[3] But with Melchizedek, there was no set beginning or end of his life. As William Lane says, "Melchizedek's sudden appearance and equally sudden disappearance from recorded history awakens within a sensitive reader the notion of eternity."[4] What was foreshadowed in Melchizedek's having no beginning or end was fully realized in Christ's eternal priesthood.

The writer caps his thoughts in the end of verse 3 by saying, "resembling the Son of God he continues a priest forever"—or more exactly, "but being *made like* the Son of God he remains a priest continuously." The silence of the Biblical record regarding Melchizedek's days suggests a continuous priesthood for Melchizedek that foreshadows what perfectly was, and is, fulfilled in Christ, who ministers continually, without interruption.[5]

The big picture the writer wants us to see is that Jesus perfectly fulfills what was foreshadowed in the Genesis account of Melchizedek. Melchizedek's *character* type regarding king, priest, righteousness, and peace was fulfilled to perfection in Christ. Melchizedek's *qualifications*, being without genealogy and without beginning or end, prefigured Jesus who had no priestly genealogy or priestly term of service but was appointed by God and ministers eternally.

No one had ever seen all of this until the writer of Hebrews presented it. His heart is full, and he expects his Jewish hearers will feel the same as they reflect on their unsure situations. Brimming over with joy, he now takes them even higher as he presents the superiority of Melchizedek over the Levitical priesthood.

The Superiority of Melchizedek

Melchizedek's superiority is presented through two occurrences in his meeting with Abraham—tithing and blessing.

Tithing and Superiority

In the ancient world, paying tithes to another was recognition of the other's superiority and a sign of subjection to that person. In the case of Abraham's rendering his title, we must remember that when Abraham returned from the slaughter of the kings, he was on a personal mountaintop. He had proven himself a man of great courage and of considerable capability. Moreover, in the eyes of succeeding generations of Jews he would be considered to be the greatest of men. He was called the "friend" of God (2 Chronicles 20:7; Isaiah

41:8; James 2:23). He was the father of the nation of Israel—*the* patriarch. But when he met Melchizedek, he recognized that personage's superior greatness and paid him "a tenth of the spoils" (7:4; literally, "the top of the heap"), the choicest spoils of war. This was a calculated recognition by Abraham that he was in the presence of one greater than himself. Our writer expresses proper astonishment: "See how great this man was to whom Abraham the patriarch gave a tenth of the spoils!" This Melchizedek was a person of transcending superiority!

The author has made a powerful point, but he realizes that some may diminish it in their minds by saying, "What's so great about that? Levitical priests collect tithes too!" So in anticipation he further argues:

> And those descendants of Levi who receive the priestly office have a commandment in the law to take tithes from the people, that is, from their brothers, though these also are descended from Abraham. But this man who does not have his descent from them received tithes from Abraham. . . . (vv. 5, 6a)

His point is that the Levites' ability to collect tithes came from the provision made by the Law, and not from any natural superiority. But Melchizedek was different. He did "not have his descent from them [Levites]," and yet, as a figure of immense superiority, he collected tithes not from the people *but from Abraham*!

The author further builds on Melchizedek's established superiority through tithing by noting that since the Scriptures do not list his end, he represents a living superior priesthood: "In the one case tithes are received by mortal men, but in the other case, by one of whom it is testified that he lives" (v. 8).

For the final expression of the superiority of Melchizedek's priesthood over the Levitical priesthood as seen in Abraham's tithing to Melchizedek, the writer appeals to the common belief that an ancestor contains all his descendants within himself. Thus he argues, "One might even say that Levi himself, who receives tithes, paid tithes through Abraham, for he was still in the loins of his ancestor when Melchizedek met him" (vv. 9, 10). Even the Levitical priesthood acknowledges the superiority of Melchizedek's priesthood—because it paid tithes to Melchizedek in advance![6]

Our writer has taken the common Hebrew understanding that tithing to another establishes the recipient's superiority and has demonstrated from every angle that Melchizedek is superior.

Blessing and Superiority

The other principle he uses to establish Melchizedek's superiority is that in a formal Biblical blessing the superior always blesses the inferior. Just as Abraham knew he should present a tithe to Melchizedek, he also knew he must bow and receive his prayer of blessing. Therefore verses 6b, 7 tell us that Melchizedek "received tithes from Abraham and blessed him who had the promises. It is beyond dispute that the inferior is blessed by the superior."

What a stupendous act on Abraham's part! Remember, God had told Abraham that "in you all the families of the earth shall be blessed" (Genesis 12:3). Abraham was the supreme blesser! All the rest of mankind were blessees! But he sees himself as inferior to Melchizedek—who towers above him with mysterious grandeur—and receives his blessing.

So we must conclude that Melchizedek's priesthood, though it has only brief mention in Scripture, is superior in every Biblical and logical way to the Old Testament Levitical priesthood. Yet, realizing that, we note that it was only a type of the ultimate superior priesthood of our Lord Jesus Christ, who is "a priest forever, after the order of Melchizedek." And as the antitype to the type, Christ supersedes it, just as living reality supersedes a photograph!

Though Melchizedek was "king of righteousness" and "king of peace," he could never make men righteous or give them peace. He was only a type. But Jesus, the grand, true, eternal Melchizedekian priest/king, gives righteousness and peace!

As to righteousness, we understand that, first, Christ *is* righteousness incarnate—"Jesus Christ the righteous" (1 John 2:1). He is intrinsically righteous, the essence of righteousness, the sum of righteousness, the source of righteousness.

Second, Jesus is the *bestower* of righteousness. "But now the righteousness of God has been manifested apart from the law, although the Law and the Prophets bear witness to it—the righteousness of God through faith in Jesus Christ for all who believe" (Romans 3:21, 22; cf. Romans 1:17; 1 Corinthians 1:30; 2 Corinthians 5:17; Philippians 3:9).

Third, he is the priestly *mediator* of righteousness. In bestowing it, he becomes our personal Melchizedekian priest who prays for the working out of his righteousness in every area of our lives. He remains forever our King and priest of righteousness!

But Christ is also the King of Peace. His peace follows the gift of righteousness—and never comes before it. The sequence is always righteousness, then peace.

We understand, first, that he *is* peace—the "Prince of Peace" (Isaiah 9:6)—that he is the essence and sum and source of all peace—that there is no peace without him.

We understand, too, that he is the *bestower* of peace. When he came to earth the angels sang, "Peace among those with whom he is pleased!" (Luke 2:14). On the eve of his death he said, "Peace I leave with you; my peace I give to you" (John 14:27). And after his glorious resurrection he came to his disciples again with the words, "Peace be with you" (John 20:19).

And finally, now as our eternal priest he *mediates* our growth in peace as he prays for us. Jesus is praying for our *shalom*—our wholeness and well-being. He is praying for it right now!

Righteousness and peace have kissed in Christ—and it is this kiss that the King repeatedly bestows on his bride.

The implications of this for the Jewish church as it bobs on the ominous tides of the first century were readily apparent—an eternal Melchizedekian king/priest has both secured their righteousness and peace and now devotes continual prayer for the working out of both qualities in their lives. This means they will survive the tides.

And there is even more (though the writer did not mention it because it was not immediately germane to the point he was making), because when the original Melchizedek greeted Abraham, he gave him bread and wine (Genesis 14:18). Now Christ, our eternal Melchizedek, offers the same to his church (Matthew 26:26–30; John 6:53–58; 1 Corinthians 11:17–34). His life—his flesh and blood—have secured our righteousness and peace. And by feeding on him as our food and drink, we receive sustenance to live as we ought and to bring his healing kiss to a broken world.

Now if perfection had been attainable through the Levitical priesthood (for under it the people received the law), what further need would there have been for another priest to arise after the order of Melchizedek, rather than one named after the order of Aaron? For when there is a change in the priesthood, there is necessarily a change in the law as well. For the one of whom these things are spoken belonged to another tribe, from which no one has ever served at the altar. For it is evident that our Lord was descended from Judah, and in connection with that tribe Moses said nothing about priests. This becomes even more evident when another priest arises in the likeness of Melchizedek, who has become a priest, not on the basis of a legal requirement concerning bodily descent, but by the power of an indestructible life. For it is witnessed of him, "You are a priest forever, after the order of Melchizedek." For on the one hand, a former commandment is set aside because of its weakness and uselessness (for the law made nothing perfect); but on the other hand, a better hope is introduced, through which we draw near to God.

7:11–19

20

The Sufficiency of Melchizedek

HEBREWS 7:11–19

IN HIS *Reflections on the Psalms*, C. S. Lewis noted a persistent connection in Jewish thinking between thoughts of the temple and thoughts of delight in God. Lewis writes:

> These poets knew far less reason than we for loving God. . . . Yet they express a longing for Him, for His mere presence, which comes only to the best Christians or to Christians in their best moments. They long to live all their days in the Temple so that they may constantly see "the fair beauty of the Lord" (27,4). Their longing to go up to Jerusalem and "appear before the presence of God" is like a physical thirst (42). From Jerusalem His presence flashes out "in perfect beauty" (50,2). Lacking that encounter with Him, their souls are parched like a waterless countryside (63,2). They crave to be "satisfied with the pleasures" of His house (65,4). Only there can they be at ease, like a bird in the nest (84,3). One day of those "pleasures" is better than a lifetime spent elsewhere (20).[1]

Though all Jews knew God's presence was everywhere, they also understood that the temple's Holy of Holies was the locus of his special earthly presence, and just the thought of being near the temple filled them with delight. Oh, to be close to his presence! Access to God was seen as the *summum bonum*, the highest good. And certainly they were right, because access presupposes a right relationship. Access would mean acceptance before God and the forgiveness of sins. And beyond that, access would also involve an exposure to the glory of his holiness. So we can see why spiritually attuned Israelites, such as the various psalmists, ached for the presence of God.

Despite their longings, all Jews lived with limited access to God, regardless of their godliness. The old covenant's Aaronic priesthood, with its sacrificial system and the veil over the Holy of Holies, institutionalized that limited access. Official access was granted only once a year to the high priest—and that was after he had first offered a sacrifice for his own sins (cf. 7:27). The problem, of course, was the radical holiness of God and the radical sinfulness of man—a dilemma that the old covenant was powerless to reconcile.

But in grand distinction the new covenant began with the rending in two of the veil at the very moment Christ offered himself as a sacrifice for sin (Matthew 27:50, 51). A new priesthood in the order of Melchizedek institutionalized access for every true believer. Unrequited longings for God's presence became a thing of the past for all Christians.

Access is the heart application with which the passage discussed in this chapter concludes (v. 19—"a better hope is introduced, through which we draw near to God"). So our study here is about access to God—a better hope. Prayerfully taken in, it will motivate and encourage our access to God.

Helpfully, the text breaks into two parts, with verses 11–14 explaining the *insufficiency* of the Aaronic priesthood and verses 15–19 the *sufficiency* of Melchizedek's priesthood. Both sections are based on the author's brilliant and original understanding of Psalm 110:4, "The LORD has sworn and will not change his mind, 'You are a priest forever after the order of Melchizedek,'" which the author saw as a solemn decree of appointment spoken by God to God the Son that would establish him as our eternal priest.

The Insufficiency of the Aaronic Priesthood (vv. 11–14)

To begin with, the author argues that the old priesthood was insufficient and was replaced because it could not bring people to perfection: "Now if perfection had been attainable through the Levitical priesthood (for under it the people received the Law), what further need would there have been for another priest to arise after the order of Melchizedek, rather than one named after the order of Aaron?" (v. 11).

Often in Scripture the word "perfection" has the meaning of "maturity" or "completeness." So some assume "perfection" here means "completeness in relation to God." But actually the meaning here is more specialized and means "to put someone in the position in which he can come, or stand, before God"[2]—*access* to God. This is also the meaning of "perfect" in verse 19, which says, "(for the Law made nothing perfect); but on the other hand, a better hope is introduced, through which we draw near to God." It is also the meaning in two other Hebrews texts—10:1, 14. So again, "perfection" here in verse 11 refers to *access to God and a right relationship to him.*

This is precisely what the old covenant Law and priesthood could not provide. The Law, of course, was not useless. After all, it came from God and was mediated by angels (cf. 2:2), and it provided important services. The Law marvelously served to enhance one's awareness of sin. Paul tells us in Romans 7:7, 8 that the Law's command not to covet made him aware that all he did was covet. The Law helped him see how spiritually dead he was (cf. 2 Corinthians 3:7ff.). The Law also programmed God's people regarding the necessity of an atonement, as seen in the repeated demand of a blood sacrifice. Sin necessitated the shedding of blood. Sin . . . blood, sin . . . blood, sin . . . blood—this developed a conditioned reflex regarding the need for atonement. Indeed, the whole system provided a type of Christ, so that John the Baptist would cry out as Jesus passed by, "Behold, the Lamb of God!" (John 1:36). The Law was, in effect, a teacher, as Paul explained in Galatians 3:24—"The Law has become our tutor to lead us to Christ, that we may be justified by faith" (NASB).

In reality, the Law was an excellent institution. The real problem was that man was sinful. "God has done what the law, weakened by the flesh, could not do . . . the mind that is set on the flesh is hostile to God, for it does not submit to God's law; indeed, it cannot" (Romans 8:3, 7).

The Old Covenant's Shortcomings

So the Law had profound limitations. It could not atone for sin. The Levitical sacrifices covered over sin, but they did not remove it. Hebrews later will tell us, "For it is impossible for the blood of bulls and goats to take away sins" (10:4), and "every priest stands daily at his service, offering repeatedly the same sacrifices, which can never take away sins" (10:11). Precisely because no dumb animal was competent to serve as a substitute for a human sinner, there was an unending repetition of sacrifices, and that repetition bore constant testimony to their impotency.

The Law could not impart spiritual life (Galatians 3:21) and could not help the conscience—"gifts and sacrifices are offered that cannot perfect the conscience of the worshiper" (9:9). Sacrifices could ease the conscience because one was doing what was required, but total clearing never took place through the system. As to the crucial matter of access, F. F. Bruce says, "The whole apparatus of worship associated with sacrifice and ritual and priesthood was calculated rather to keep men at a distance from God than to bring them near."[3] Clearly, the old covenant had profound limitations as to making *atonement*, imparting *life*, clearing the *conscience*, and providing *access*.

The New Covenant's Benefits

But the new covenant excelled the old in every way, just as Jeremiah prophesied it would when he recorded God's words six hundred years earlier.

> For this is the covenant that I will make with the house of Israel after those
> days, declares the LORD: I will put my law within them, and I will write it
> on their hearts. And I will be their God, and they shall be my people. And
> no longer shall each one teach his neighbor and each his brother, saying,
> "Know the LORD," for they shall all know me, from the least of them to
> the greatest, declares the LORD. For I will forgive their iniquity, and I will
> remember their sin no more. (Jeremiah 31:33, 34)

So now we have the great benefits of the new covenant. *Atonement*: "He
himself bore our sins in his body on the tree, that we might die to sin and live
to righteousness. By his wounds you have been healed" (1 Peter 2:24). *Life*:
Jesus said, "I am the resurrection and the life. Whoever believes in me, though
he die, yet shall he live, and everyone who lives and believes in me shall never
die" (John 11:25, 26). *Conscience*: "How much more will the blood of Christ,
who through the eternal Spirit offered himself without blemish to God, purify
our conscience from dead works to serve the living God" (9:14). *Access*: Jesus
said, "I am the way, and the truth, and the life. No one comes to the Father
except through me" (John 14:6).

Now the thrust of verse 11 becomes crystal-clear. If the Aaronic priesthood could have brought *perfection*—that is, access or nearness to God—it
would not have been replaced by a new order and a new priest, Melchizedek!
In fact, both the priesthood and the Law have been replaced because they are
inseparable—"For when there is a change in the priesthood, there is necessarily a change in the law as well" (v. 12). Christ, our Melchizedekian priest,
tells us that he did not destroy the Law but fulfilled it (Matthew 5:17). He lived
out its every requirement. And now in place of the old external principle, he
brings a new internal principle. Because of this we have perfection—access.

Think of the day this was accomplished. It was the ninth hour, about 3:00
p.m., and the darkness was beginning to lift, so that all of Jerusalem was cast
in an eerie netherland, and just then Jesus cried out in a loud voice and gave
up his spirit. At that moment the earth shook so much that rocks cracked, and
the curtain of the temple, as thick as a man's hand, tore from top to bottom.
The insufficient Levitical priesthood was over. Perfection was attained. The
new Melchizedek began his eternal ministry.

The profound inadequacy of the old priesthood was further emphasized
by the fact that the new had nothing to do with the old Aaronic priesthood:

"For the one of whom these things are spoken belonged to another tribe, from which no one has ever served at the altar. For it is evident that our Lord was descended from Judah, and in connection with that tribe Moses said nothing about priests" (vv. 13, 14).

It was no small thing to suggest, let alone categorically state, that a priest could come from any other tribe than Levi. King Uzziah had played the fool when in a moment of vanity he attempted to usurp the Levitical role, and he was confronted by the priests for it: "It is not for you, Uzziah, to burn incense to the LORD, but for the priests, the sons of Aaron, who are consecrated to burn incense. Go out of the sanctuary, for you have done wrong, and it will bring you no honor from the LORD God" (2 Chronicles 26:18). While Uzziah was raging at the priest, leprosy broke out on his forehead, and he remained a leper until his death! So the insistence that Jesus, from the tribe of Judah, was a priest was shocking to the Hebrew ear. It was, in fact, illegal (see Josephus, *Antiquities*, 20.10.1).

Distancing the Covenants

So we see that Jesus was purposely distanced from the old, inadequate priesthood. In fact, the phrase "descended from Judah" was meant to indicate that the new Melchizedekian priest was a messianic figure. The word "descended" is literally "has arisen," a term that has messianic significance in Scripture. Malachi 4:2 prophesies of the rising of one who is "the sun of righteousness." Numbers 24:17 promises the appearance of "a star . . . out of Jacob." Luke 1:78 speaks of Christ as "the sunrise . . . from on high." Second Peter 1:19 tells of the rising of "the morning star" in our hearts (cf. Revelation 2:28). The prophets also predict the raising up of a righteous Branch for David (Isaiah 11:1; Jeremiah 23:5ff.; 33:15; Zechariah 3:8; 6:12; Revelation 22:16).[4]

This careful distancing of the Melchizedekian priesthood from the Levitical system, along with showing the new priest to be messianic, was meant to be a warning to those in the beleaguered Jewish church to not turn back to Judaism and to not mix Old Testament priestly ritual with their Christianity. This may not strike us with the force that it did them, because the age of the Law is ancient history to us. But it is still relevant to evangelicals increasingly lured by the un-Biblical promises of some present-day traditions. God's Word sets the eternal standard: "For there is one God, and there is one mediator between God and men, the man Christ Jesus, who gave himself as a ransom for all" (1 Timothy 2:5, 6). Perfection—access to God—comes only through Christ.

The Sufficiency of the Melchizedekian Priesthood (vv. 15–17)

The focus naturally changes from the insufficiency of Aaron to the sufficiency of Melchizedek with the assertion that he is superior because of his unique nature—namely, his "indestructible life": "This becomes even more evident when another priest arises in the likeness of Melchizedek, who has become a priest, not on the basis of a legal requirement concerning bodily descent, but by the power of an indestructible life. For it is witnessed of him, 'You are a priest forever, after the order of Melchizedek'" (vv. 15–17).

The qualifications for the Levitical priesthood were patently *external.* A priestly candidate had to be: (1) legitimate, (2) a Levite (meaning that his mother had to be an Israelite and his father a priest before him), and (3) having no physical defects.[5] There were 142 physical blemishes listed that could disqualify him, some of which are recorded in Leviticus 21:16–23. His ordination ceremony was painstakingly external regarding how he was to be bathed, clothed, anointed with oil, and marked with blood. After his ordination he had to observe specified washings, anointings, and hair-cutting. The focus was external throughout.[6]

On the other hand, this new priest (Christ), like Melchizedek, has one grand qualification, which is not external but *internal*—"the power of an indestructible life" (v. 16b). This does not mean that he never died. It means that our priest died a death that could not hold him—a death that was followed by resurrection! Therefore, to say that Jesus is high priest on the basis of "an indestructible life" is to say that he is high priest on the basis of the Resurrection. This is implicit in the words of the Father to the Son: "You are a priest forever, after the order of Melchizedek" (v. 17).[7] Thus, the Resurrection not only declared Jesus to be the Son (Romans 1:4), but it also marks the inauguration of Christ as our high priest.

Jesus is our great high priest because of the quality of his life. He is eternal: the Alpha and Omega, the beginning and ending, the first and the last. His eternality was not suspended when for thirty-three years he took on a temporal existence. In human form he experienced all that is common to man, everything, even death—through the exercise of his own will: "I lay down my life that I may take it up again. No one takes it from me, but I lay it down of my own accord. I have authority to lay it down, and I have authority to take it up again" (John 10:17, 18). He then rose by virtue of his indestructible life—and now lives eternally as our priest.

But there is more to the quality of his priesthood than its eternality—it is *experientially* and *morally, internally* perfect—and because of that he is a perfect priest. What this means personally to us can scarcely be put into words.

What massive egocentricity on our part to imagine that he does not know how we feel or that we are somehow unique and beyond his perfect priestly ministry. May God deliver us from the self-centeredness of imagining that we are the exception to his understanding—the ego-twisted reason that thinks, "He may understand others, his empathy may be adequate for others, he may be able to meet their needs, but *not mine*! Because . . . well, I'm different." What foolishness!

What absurdity, too, to think that our problems are beyond his power, because his priesthood was established on the basis of "the power of an indestructible life." He brings to our lives the same power with which he self-resurrected.

Whatever our problem, Jesus is the answer! We must not sell our life short by looking to other places or persons for help, as contemporary evangelicalism is doing more and more. We must hold to the sufficiency of our Melchizedek with all we have!

Last, we must see his sufficiency in his bringing a better hope of access to the Father: "A former commandment is set aside because of its weakness and uselessness (for the law made nothing perfect); but on the other hand, a better hope is introduced, through which we draw near to God" (vv. 18, 19). During his student days in France, Donald Grey Barnhouse was pastor of a little Evangelical Reformed Church in the French Alps. Once a week he went to a neighboring village for an instruction class. Each time he made the trip he passed the local priest, going on a similar errand in the opposite direction. They became good friends and often chatted together for ten minutes or so before they went their separate ways.

On one occasion the priest asked him why we Protestants do not pray to the saints. "Why should we?" Barnhouse asked. The priest launched an illustration of the way one might get an interview with the president of the French Republic. One could go to the Ministry of Agriculture or to the Department of the Interior, etc.; any one of the cabinet members might succeed in opening the door of the president's office so that Barnhouse might see him. The priest's triumphant smile implied that the simplicity and clarity of the argument were such as to preclude any reply.

At that time Raymond Poincare was president of the Republic; he lived in the Palace of the Elysee in Paris—the equivalent of the White House. Barnhouse said to his friend, "But, Monsieur le Cure, suppose that I were the son of Monsieur Poincare? I am living in the Elysee with him. I get up from the breakfast table and kiss him good-bye as he goes off to his office. Then I go down to the Ministry of the Interior and ask the fourth secretary of the second assistant if it is possible for me to see the Minister of the Interior. If I succeed in reaching his office, my request is for an interview with my papa."

The absurdity of a son's having to go through a father's assistants to reach him was at once apparent. The priest was thunderstruck as Barnhouse added that he was a child of God, an heir of God and joint-heir with Christ, and that he had been saved through the death of the Savior and thus had become a son with immediate access to the Father.[8]

What "a better hope" (v. 19) is ours through the eternal priesthood of Christ. Our mild passion shames us when we think of the poets who wrote the Psalms. They knew far less than we do of the reasons for loving God. Yet they longed to live all their days in the temple, to see the beauty of the Lord. They longed with a physical thirst. Their souls were parched like the waterless countryside. They craved the pleasures of his presence. A day with him is better than a lifetime spent elsewhere. Yet they were under what is by comparison a weak and useless economy (v. 18).

Today, *perfection*—access—is ours through Jesus Christ. The veil has been sundered, inviting us to the Holy of Holies.

Let us come with joyful boldness to our constant priest and Savior and Lord!

And it was not without an oath. For those who formerly became priests were made such without an oath, but this one was made a priest with an oath by the one who said to him: "The Lord has sworn and will not change his mind, 'You are a priest forever.'" This makes Jesus the guarantor of a better covenant. The former priests were many in number, because they were prevented by death from continuing in office, but he holds his priesthood permanently, because he continues forever. Consequently, he is able to save to the uttermost those who draw near to God through him, since he always lives to make intercession for them. For it was indeed fitting that we should have such a high priest, holy, innocent, unstained, separated from sinners, and exalted above the heavens. He has no need, like those high priests, to offer sacrifices daily, first for his own sins and then for those of the people, since he did this once for all when he offered up himself. For the law appoints men in their weakness as high priests, but the word of the oath, which came later than the law, appoints a Son who has been made perfect forever.

7:20–28

21

The Superiority of Melchizedek

HEBREWS 7:20–28

WHEN I COME to the petition section of my daily devotions, it begins with a regular "ritual" of petition for my family. First, I pray a Scriptural prayer for my whole family, using texts such as Ephesians 1:18–20 or 3:14–19 or Colossians 1:9–12. My method is to pray the themes of these great prayers over and over upon my wife, my children, and my grandchildren. For example, using Ephesians 1, I pray that their spiritual eyes may be opened so that: (1) they may be enlightened regarding their eternal hope, (2) they may truly understand how Christ treasures them, and (3) they may experience his incomparable power.

Next I pray in detail for my wife, Barbara—first for her spiritual life, then for our relationship, then for her busy, busy life, and finally for the problems she may be facing. I have prayed for her like this for thirty years with the passion and attention to detail that come with a growing love.

Following this, of course, I pray for my children, from the oldest to the youngest. I make petition for my daughters and their spouses and for each of the six grandchildren, being as specific as possible, bringing to God their ongoing as well as their ever-changing needs. Lastly, my boys get the same attention as I pray through the items listed under their names—everything from their future work to their cars' specific ailments—"Lord, deliver their transmissions from bondage!"

I can say that I really do attempt to do the work of prayer over my family, and for that matter, the church. But having said this, I must admit that my prayer life is flawed and inadequate, for several reasons. For one, there is my sin, which often fogs my understanding of what my family's actual needs are. I have an intrinsic self-centeredness that regularly clouds my perceptions even regarding those I love the most.

205

There is also my limited knowledge. Try as I will, I will never fully understand my wife—nor she me! Sounding the mysteries of another's soul is one of the joys of marriage. But it also brings us face-to-face with the limitations of our knowledge. My knowledge—and my prayers—will never be adequate.

Then there is the fact that because I am human, my physical and mental limitations inhibit both the time and concentration I can give to prayer. My heart's prayers are flawed, at best.

But thank God, there is one who knows no such limitations—our high priest, Jesus, who is a priest forever in the order of Melchizedek. And praise God for the revelation of his priesthood that is given in Hebrews 7—10, and specifically for the detailed explanation of the superiority of the new covenant priesthood seen in 7:20–28.

In this section the writer gives us three consecutive reasons for the superiority of Christ's priesthood: (1) God's divine *oath*, (2) the priesthood's *permanence*, and (3) the *person* of the priest. As before, the first two reasons are firmly rooted in the prophetic words of Psalm 110:4, "The LORD has sworn and will not change his mind, 'You are a priest forever after the order of Melchizedek'"—from which the writer extracts the last drops of significance.

Superior Due to a Divine Oath (vv. 20–22)

To begin with, our attention is drawn to the fact that Jesus became our Melchizedekian priest through divine oath:

> And it was not without an oath. For those who formerly became priests were made such without an oath, but this one was made a priest with an oath by the one who said to him:
>
> > "The Lord has sworn
> > and will not change his mind,
> > 'You are a priest forever.'"
>
> This makes Jesus the guarantor of a better covenant. (vv. 20–22)

In contrast, the Aaronic priests ascended to their position, not on the basis of divine oath, but rather because of divine instruction. God said, "Then bring near to you Aaron your brother, and his sons with him, from among the people of Israel, to serve me as priests" (Exodus 28:1). This was followed by an extended ceremony, but there was no oath (cf. Exodus 28, 29; Leviticus 8, 9). Certainly God did not swear to Aaron, or any other priest, that his priesthood would be forever.

But God did swear to his Son that he would be "a priest forever after the order of Melchizedek." The only other place we know of God swearing an oath was in confirming his covenant to Abraham, as we saw in our study of 6:13–18 (cf. Genesis 22:16–18). The reason he did this was clearly stated by our writer: "So when God desired to show more convincingly to the heirs of the promise the unchangeable character of his purpose, he guaranteed it with an oath" (6:17).

An oath was not necessary, because God's word is enough. But because humanity is a race of liars, God accommodated himself within the sphere of human undependability.[1] His oath is a double-assurance to fallen, duplicitous humanity of the eternality of Jesus' Melchizedekian priesthood. Whatever "God confirms by an oath becomes something so utterly unchangeable that it is woven into the very fibre of the universe and must remain forever."[2]

The result of God's self-imposed eternally binding oath is: "This makes Jesus the guarantor of a better covenant" (v. 22b). We must understand, for two reasons, that the emphasis here is dramatically focused on *Jesus*. First, the writer places Jesus last in the Greek sentence structure, so that the full weight of verses 20–22 falls on Jesus as the guarantee. Secondly, the writer's choice of the name "Jesus" is a conscious emphasis upon the humanity and work of Jesus who "saves his people from their sins" (Matthew 1:21).

This emphatic use of Jesus' name consciously recalls his *incarnation* here on earth—that he really was human—that his human instrument was just like ours—and that, as with the piano, a chord struck in our lives will find a sympathetic resonance in his. The pain that plays in our heart plays in his! This is perfection of understanding and sympathy.

But there is more: his incarnation was terminated by his becoming the *propitiation* for our sins on the cross (2:17, Greek). Christ propitiated the Godhead's personal wrath against our sin, fully meeting it and putting it away.

Finally, after his incarnation, propitiation, and ascension, our "Jesus" is in Heaven making *intercession* for us (cf. 7:25).

The author's point here in this letter is that in Heaven "Jesus," who did all of this for us, now acts as the "guarantor" for those of us who are still on earth awaiting the full outworking of the "better covenant." For our hearts' health and steadfastness, we must understand that Jesus, our superior priest, will do anything and everything consonant with his nature to meet our needs.

We have a superior priest! We have the Father's sworn *word* for it and the Son's *guarantee*.

Superior Due to Permanence (vv. 23–25)

The Father's oath confirming the eternality of Jesus' priesthood anticipates the next reason for its superiority, which is its permanence:

> The former priests were many in number, because they were prevented by death from continuing in office, but he holds his priesthood permanently, because he continues forever. Consequently, he is able to save to the uttermost those who draw near to God through him, since he always lives to make intercession for them. (vv. 23–25)

A glance at the old Aaronic priesthood demonstrates its *impermanence.* When Aaron, the first priest, had served his term, God took him and his son Eleazar to the peak of Mount Hor. And there, the Scriptures tell us, "Moses stripped Aaron of his garments and put them on Eleazar his son. And Aaron died there on the top of the mountain. Then Moses and Eleazar came down from the mountain" (Numbers 20:28). Later, when Eleazar died, his son Phinehas succeeded him (Joshua 24:33). Aaron—Eleazar—Phinehas—the priestly succession continued on. The concluding comment for every priest was inevitably, "and he died." Josephus reckoned that some eighty-three priests served from Aaron until the destruction of the second temple in AD 70 (*Antiquities*, 20.227). But the Talmud lists even more—eighteen during the first temple and over three hundred for the second (*Yoma* 9a).[3]

In marked contrast to this, the author asserts that Jesus "holds his priesthood permanently, because he continues forever" (v. 24). The Greek word for "permanently" can have the sense of *unchangeable* or *permanent* as our translation has it, or it can mean that the priesthood is *non-transferable.* Hebrews scholar Philip Hughes thinks that "The term is enhanced by its ambivalence: the priesthood of Christ does not pass to another precisely because it is a perpetual priesthood."[4] The word may, indeed, have both senses.

But whether it is one or the other or both, the benefit of Jesus' ongoing priesthood is easily apparent. There is no unevenness in the quality of his priesthood, as there would be in a human succession of priests. We can grasp the idea here when we think of how pastors vary. One is this way, one is another. Some people relate to one, some to another. One priest was a better intercessor than the former. One did not know how to pray—he read his prayers! And so it goes on, interminably.

But the boon of Jesus' intercession is that he never changes. Think of it—you and I will never have another high priest. No young, inexperienced priest just out of seminary will succeed him! Think of all the prayers he has heard from us. And he remembers them all! He has answered every single one. Think how he knows us! Jesus is superior by virtue of his permanence.

Total Salvation

The high point for the benefits of his permanence is given in verse 25, which dramatically states his super-sufficiency for salvation: "Consequently, he is able to save to the uttermost those who draw near to God through him, since he always lives to make intercession for them." A reporter once called and asked me what I thought of Jeffrey Dahmer's professed repentance and public embrace of a relationship with Christ. (Jeffrey Dahmer was a convicted serial cannibal killer, one of the most infamous criminals in U.S. history.) I replied that I had two thoughts.

> First, I believe Mr. Dahmer may be mouthing pious conventional Christian phrases that he picked up somewhere along the way in his miserable life. Certainly he has repeatedly demonstrated an amazing ability to deceive others, along with the coldest premeditation. It is very likely, in my opinion, that he is attempting to use Christianity for his own temporal ends.
>   But, second, if he has truly turned to Christ, confessing his sins and trusting him alone for his salvation, then he has been regenerated and totally forgiven for every sin. I further explained that on the cross God "made him to be sin who knew no sin, so that in him we might become the righteousness of God" (2 Corinthians 5:21). Jesus became "a curse for us" (Galatians 3:13). Because Jesus truly took on our sins, the gospel was able to penetrate the dark alleys of ancient Rome and Corinth and to redeem murderers, prostitutes, transvestites, and even cannibals (cf. 1 Corinthians 6:9–11). And it is still the same today, from Bombay to Boston.

Amazing! You and I (and Jeffrey Dahmer if he truly believes) are as pure as Christ, shrouded with his righteousness, if we have trusted him. If we are revolted by the possibility of Jeffrey Dahmer's salvation, we do not understand the cross.

Our text argues emphatically that Jesus "is able to save to the uttermost those who draw near to God through him." The term translated "uttermost" is unusual, being used elsewhere only in Luke 13:11, and combines the idea of *completeness* with the idea of *eternality*—"for all time" (RSV). It means complete, absolute, total, eternal salvation![5] Moreover, the words here allow for no possibility of our supplementing our salvation by doing good (cf. Ephesians 2:8, 9). Salvation is all Christ's work, from beginning to end.

Whoever we are, whatever we have done, no matter how heinous our sin—whether it is murder, infidelity, perversion, betrayal, embezzlement, lying, jealousy, hateful gossip, or whatever—Christ can save us completely and eternally. We must take greatest pride in this gospel, "for it is the power of God for salvation to everyone who believes, to the Jew first and also to the Greek" (Romans 1:16).

One other observation about Christ's being "able to save to the uttermost"—the words are actually in the present tense. The reference is not just to the great initial experience of being saved. It refers to the perpetual experience of being saved (cf. 1 Corinthians 1:18). As Raymond Brown says, "He saves us, not only in the moment of initial commitment, but day by day and moment by moment"[6]—through all time! His perpetual saving work brings about our growing sanctification as we are made ever more like him.

Total Intercession

And how does he do this? Of course, as we have just said, it is through his substitutionary atonement and propitiation for our sins. But our text adds a vital and dynamic dimension: "since he always lives to make intercession for them" (v. 25b). This speaks to one of the great flaws in my human intercession for my own family and flock. My physical and mental weakness dictates intermittent intercession. I grow weary in praying, and my mind wanders. Sometimes I disobey the Spirit's call to pray. I sometimes fall asleep in the most important intercessions.

But not Christ! Later the writer will put it this way: "Christ has entered . . . into heaven itself, now to appear in the presence of God on our behalf" (9:24). Paul says, "Who is to condemn? Christ Jesus is the one who died—more than that, who was raised—who is at the right hand of God, who indeed is interceding for us" (Romans 8:34). Jesus' contact with the Father is unbroken. His intercession is never-ending. Day by day, hour by hour, year by year, millennium by millennium, Christ prays for us. How does he intercede for us? He, along with the Holy Spirit (Romans 8:26, 27) takes our feeble prayers, cleans them up, ennobles them, and presents them to the Father. St. Chrysostom, the great fourth-century preacher, provides a helpful analogy. A young boy whose father was away on a trip wanted to present his father with something that would please him. His mother sent him to the garden to gather a bouquet of flowers. The little boy gathered a sorry bouquet of weeds as well as flowers. But when his father returned home, he was presented with a beautifully arranged bouquet, for the mother had intervened, removing all the weeds.

The prayers of the church, prevailing, acceptable, and fruitful as they are, are not a thing of beauty as they leave the lips of saints. As they start their way heavenward, they are a mixed bag of weeds with a few stray flowers. When they arrive, however, thanks to the intercession of Christ they are nothing but beautiful flowers.[7] What blessed, comforting thoughts these are as we, amidst our frailties, pray.

There is a beautiful aroma from Jesus' perfect prayers, offered confidently as he sits at the right hand of God. Every prayer hits the mark and graces our lives. The reason he can save us completely is that truly "he always lives to make intercession" for us. Though we are finite, he is infinite. Though we are temporal, he is eternal. He prays with the ease of omniscience and omnipotence perfected through his own human suffering. He is praying for us right now!

Superior Due to His Person (vv. 26–28)

So far we have seen that Christ is a superior priest because of God's sworn oath and because of the permanence of Christ's priesthood. Now we see his superiority due to his person. Teodorico, the ancient Italian commentator, first identified verses 26–28 as a hymn, calling it "a hymn to the High Priest," and certainly it seems that the author stands back in awe as he celebrates the superior character of Christ the high priest. He says:

> For it was indeed fitting that we should have such a high priest, holy, innocent, unstained, separated from sinners, and exalted above the heavens. He has no need, like those high priests, to offer sacrifices daily, first for his own sins and then for those of the people, since he did this once for all when he offered up himself. For the law appoints men in their weakness as high priests, but the word of the oath, which came later than the law, appoints a Son who has been made perfect forever. (vv. 26–28)[8]

Again Christ's intercession is totally superior, whereas mine is severely flawed due to my sin that perverts my judgment and even my motives. His character is unflawed. He is "holy." He is uniquely God's Holy One. He is set apart to God. He stands accepted before God. He is "innocent"—literally, "without evil." Whereas we are intrinsically evil in our motives and deeds, there is nothing but good in him. He is "unstained." The Old Testament priests had to be externally without imperfection. But Christ is unstained within. Jesus walked through the muck and mire of this world for thirty-three years but was never stained by sin. His character rendered him immune.

Because Christ was "holy, innocent, unstained," he is "separated from sinners." He is part of humanity because he took it on for our sake, but he is separate in his character from sinful human nature. Further, he imparts his righteousness to us.

And, finally, he is "exalted above the heavens"—an allusion to the triumph of his resurrection, ascension, and glorification at the right hand of God (1:3). In contrast to my flawed intercession due to human weakness and sin, Christ in his transcendent glory is not just a figure of the past, but also of the present and the future (13:8). His intercession is just as powerful for us today as it was in the first century.[9] Christ is our contemporary and ever-present Lord and intercessor.

Human priests, because of their sin, had to offer repeated sacrifices for their own sins, and then repeatedly for the people (cf. v. 27). But Christ only had to do it once. He was and is infinite—and is infinitely pure. In his infinity he created everything—all the one hundred thousand million stars of the galaxy and the one hundred thousand million galaxies with as many or more stars. And when he hitched his infinity and infinite purity to mankind, his sacrifice was sufficient. And it follows, so is his priesthood. So our text concludes, "For the law appoints men in their weakness as high priests, but the word of the oath, which came later than the law, appoints a Son who has been made perfect forever" (v. 28).

Jesus is a superior priest because God swore his priesthood into existence, because his priesthood is permanent, and because his person is perfect.

The outcome for us is inevitable and eternal: "For it was indeed fitting that we should have such a high priest" (v. 26a). Hallelujah! Double hallelujah! How dare we go anywhere else with our need! How dare we go to others without first going to him! Either we are children or we are not. Either Christ is sufficient or he is not. *And he is!*

What is your need? Bring it to him in prayer today.

"For it was indeed fitting that we should have such a high priest. . . ."

Now the point in what we are saying is this: we have such a high priest, one who is seated at the right hand of the throne of the Majesty in heaven, a minister in the holy places, in the true tent that the Lord set up, not man. For every high priest is appointed to offer gifts and sacrifices; thus it is necessary for this priest also to have something to offer. Now if he were on earth, he would not be a priest at all, since there are priests who offer gifts according to the law. They serve a copy and shadow of the heavenly things. For when Moses was about to erect the tent, he was instructed by God, saying, "See that you make everything according to the pattern that was shown you on the mountain." But as it is, Christ has obtained a ministry that is as much more excellent than the old as the covenant he mediates is better, since it is enacted on better promises. For if that first covenant had been faultless, there would have been no occasion to look for a second. For he finds fault with them when he says: "Behold, the days are coming, declares the Lord, when I will establish a new covenant with the house of Israel and with the house of Judah, not like the covenant that I made with their fathers on the day when I took them by the hand to bring them out of the land of Egypt. For they did not continue in my covenant, and so I showed no concern for them, declares the Lord. For this is the covenant that I will make with the house of Israel after those days, declares the Lord: I will put my laws into their minds, and write them on their hearts, and I will be their God, and they shall be my people. And they shall not teach, each one his neighbor and each one his brother, saying, 'Know the Lord,' for they shall all know me, from the least of them to the greatest. For I will be merciful toward their iniquities, and I will remember their sins no more." In speaking of a new covenant, he makes the first one obsolete. And what is becoming obsolete and growing old is ready to vanish away.

22

Christ's Surpassing
Priesthood and Covenant

HEBREWS 8:1–13

THE STUDY OF THE WORD OF GOD, especially lofty passages in Revelation or Ezekiel or Hebrews, sometimes makes us feel like we are traveling on the wings of angels. For example, meditation on Revelation 4 brings to our minds a picture of angels—millions of angels—ten thousand times ten thousand—massed around the circular shore of a waveless expanse of sea that reflects our gliding images from its glass surface.

We can count twenty-four thrones set in a circle, each seating a celestial man wearing a crown. Within the ring of thrones are four magnificent seraphim. Each has a distinct visage—a lion, an ox, a man, and an eagle—and yet every inch of each of them is covered with eyes. Rather than grotesque, the effect is *gorgeous*. Fire moves back and forth among them, and the creatures speed to and fro like flashes of lightning. The sound of their whirring wings roars across the expanse, but above that rises their call:

> Holy, holy, holy,
> is the Lord God Almighty,
> who was and is and is to come! (Revelation 4:8)

Over the heads of the living creatures hangs an awesome expanse—sparkling like ice, providing a jewel-like setting for the emerald throne. On the throne sits one who has the appearance of glowing jasper and carnelian. Then appears "a Lamb standing, as though it had been slain" (Revelation 5:6). He takes the scroll from the right hand of him who sits on the throne, and all

215

fall prostrate before him—the four great angels, the twenty-four elders, and the millions around the sea—and most of all, us! And we sing with them:

> Worthy is the Lamb who was slain,
> to receive power and wealth and wisdom and might
> and honor and glory and blessing! (Revelation 5:12)

What sublime thoughts come from a collage of Revelation and Ezekiel and the imagination of everyday worship in Heaven. Certainly St. John's Revelation was given to expand our minds and quicken our heartbeats to the glories we will experience. As we continue to consider the surpassing glory of Christ's heavenly priesthood, let us imagine what it must have been like when the Lamb of God ascended to take his seat at the right hand of the Father as our eternal high priest. It is a matter of record that on the night before his crucifixion Jesus prayed, "And now, Father, glorify me in your own presence with the glory that I had with you before the world existed" (John 17:5). Imagine, then, the celestial fireworks at Jesus' homecoming and his installation as our eternal Melchizedek! Can you see him being transfigured from Lamb to priest? His hair becomes white like snow, his eyes like embers, and his face like the sun as he majestically dons a priestly robe that falls to his glowing feet and girds himself with the golden sash of a high priest.

Jesus' Priestly Superiorities (vv. 1–7)

This is what the writer of Hebrews wants us to see and take to heart at this juncture in his letter. "Now the point in what we are saying," says the writer, "is this: we have such a high priest, one who is seated at the right hand of the throne of the Majesty in heaven, a minister in the holy places, in the true tent that the Lord set up, not man" (vv. 1, 2). The precise point here is that Christ's priestly session in Heaven is transcendentally supreme and superior to the old earthly priesthood of Aaron.

Superior Session

Apart from its unspeakable glory, the supremacy of his priesthood is seen in that Jesus is *seated* at the right hand of the Father (cf. 1:3). His posture points to his completed work. It is the physical expression of his triumphant cry from the cross, "It is finished" (John 19:30). Because in his person he brought finite man and infinite God together, he could then do what no one else could—he could bear all our sins in a single cosmic sacrifice. Hence the heavenly song, "Worthy are you to take the scroll and to open its seals, for you were slain, and by your blood you ransomed people for God from every tribe and language and people and nation" (Revelation 5:9). In contrast, no earthly Levitical priest ever sat down. "And every priest stands daily at his service, offering repeatedly the same sacrifices, which can never take away sins" (10:11).

The fact that Christ is seated must not be interpreted to suggest priestly inactivity, because as we observed in verse 2, he also serves as "a minister in the holy places, in the true tent that the Lord set up, not man." This willingness to serve others runs counter to the natural grain of humanity, because those in exalted positions characteristically view their role otherwise.

Charles Colson had a glimpse of this in his White House days when on a Sunday evening he accompanied the President from the Oval Office in the West Wing of the White House to the Residence. The President was musing about what people wanted in their leaders. He slowed a moment, looking into the distance across the South Lawn, and said, "The people really want a leader a little bigger than themselves, don't they, Chuck?" Colson agreed. "I mean someone like de Gaulle," he continued. "There's a certain aloofness, a power that's exuded by great men that people feel and want to follow."

Colson comments in retrospect, "Jesus Christ exhibited none of this self-conscious aloofness. He served others first; He spoke to those to whom no one spoke; He dined with the lowest members of society; He touched the untouchables."[1]

Jesus' footwashing service here on earth was not an aberration of the Incarnation. Serving is part of his divine being. Think of it! Jesus, our eternal priest who *sits* at the Father's right hand in ineffable glory enthroned on emerald atop a crystal sea amongst the adoration of millions, *serves* in our behalf! "God serves me!" It is a ludicrous expression but *true*. Take a deep breath, swallow your incredulity, and humbly believe it. Jesus' prayers are placed in your service and mine. There are no lapses, no disaffections, no uneven devotion—only a loving constancy of intercession—serving, serving, serving . . .

Superior Reality

The writer goes on to further demonstrate the surpassing nature of Christ's priesthood by pointing to its superior reality and substance:

> For every high priest is appointed to offer gifts and sacrifices; thus it is necessary for this priest also to have something to offer. Now if he were on earth, he would not be a priest at all, since there are priests who offer gifts according to the law. They serve a copy and shadow of the heavenly things. For when Moses was about to erect the tent, he was instructed by God, say-

ing, "See that you make everything according to the pattern that was shown you on the mountain." (vv. 3–5)

The warning to follow "the pattern" (quoted from Exodus 25:40) was given in the midst of minute instructions about the ark, the table, the lampstand, and the size, shape, and materials specified to build the tabernacle (Exodus 25—31; cf. 25:9; 26:30; 27:8). The word "pattern" meant something more than verbal instruction. Very likely it denoted a model along with verbal explanation.[2] Moses may have been privileged to view a model on Sinai, then was given personal instruction.

This produced inventive rabbinical speculation. For example, the Talmud says, "An ark of fire and a table of fire and a candlestick of fire came down from heaven; and these Moses saw and reproduced" (*TB Menahoth* 29a).[3] Some rabbis held that the angel Gabriel descended in a workman's apron from Heaven with models of the tabernacle furniture, which he showed Moses how to build.[4]

All this is, of course, groundless speculation. But the tabernacle does, indeed, have massive symbolic significance in its major features, and we must understand this, as long as we do not try "to look for some sublime mystery in every nail and other minutiae" (John Calvin).[5] For example, the mercy seat is nothing less than a symbol of Christ and his work as our propitiation (cf. Romans 3:25).

It can truly be said of the Aaronic priesthood, as verse 5a avers, "They serve a copy and shadow of the heavenly things." The substance, the ultimate reality, of the tabernacle is where Jesus is—at the right hand of God. This being so—and coupled with the dizzying glory of the Lamb surrounded by the four living creatures and the twenty-four elders amidst rainbows of praise—what must the real sanctuary and his priestly ministry be like? Imagine the multi-faceted shadow of the glorious tabernacle, and then imagine the ultimate heavenly reality! Remember that the heavenly counterpart is free from the spatial and material limitations of the earthly tabernacle and temple. If such was the shadow, what must be the substance? Do not fail to employ your imagination, because however grand and wondrous your imagining is, it will not exceed the reality of Christ's heavenly tabernacle and priesthood!

To possess the benefits of a perfect sacrifice, administered by a perfect priest serving in perfect session, in the perfect substantiality of the ultimate real sanctuary built not by man but by God, was, and is, a grace that came for the first time through the new covenant in Christ. It is no mere shadow. It is the real thing—"the true tent that the Lord set up" (v. 2)—eternally substantial. And it is ours!

Superior Covenant

Our author's logic moves from Christ's superior *session*, through his superior *reality*, and now to his superior *covenant* and ministry. He introduces the subject of the new covenant by pronouncing the old covenant flawed:

> But as it is, Christ has obtained a ministry that is as much more excellent than the old as the covenant he mediates is better, since it is enacted on better promises. For if that first covenant had been faultless, there would have been no occasion to look for a second. For he finds fault with them. . . . (vv. 6–8a)

The old covenant was flawed, not in what was spelled out in the Law's requirements, for the Law was good (cf. Romans 7:12), but in that it was "weakened by the flesh" of the people (Romans 8:3), because "the mind that is set on the flesh is hostile to God, for it does not submit to God's law; indeed, it cannot" (Romans 8:7, 8). Because of this, it could not deliver on its wonderful promises. But the new covenant was founded on "better promises," both because of their extent and because of the covenant's ability to bring them to fulfillment in the lives of sinful humanity. The new covenant could deliver!

From here on (vv. 8–12) the writer quotes at length from Jeremiah 31:31–34, which is a direct quotation from God in the first person—"I," "me," "my." The quotation dates back over six hundred years to Josiah's reign, when after the rediscovery of the Law, a national time of repentance, and a public covenant to keep the Law Israel again failed. In the midst of this dark failure, God promised a new covenant—not conditional like the old, but unconditional—totally dependent upon the work of God:

> Behold, the days are coming, declares the Lord, when I will establish a new covenant with the house of Israel and with the house of Judah, not like the covenant that I made with their fathers on the day when I took them by the hand to bring them out of the land of Egypt. For they did not continue in my covenant, and so I showed no concern for them, declares the Lord. (vv. 8, 9)

The New Covenant's Superiorities (vv. 10–12)

This new covenant was to prove superior in every way, because it was founded on "better promises" (v. 6), which now crown our exposition of this magnificent section. And though the new covenant was made with Israel, it is shared today by the Church (those who share the continuity of faith with believing Israel). So the "better promises" are for Jew and Gentile alike.

Superior Inwardness

First of all, the new covenant promises superior inwardness: "For this is the covenant that I will make with the house of Israel after those days, declares the Lord: I will put my laws into their minds, and write them on their hearts" (v. 10a). The problem with the old covenant was, it was patently external. Its laws were written on stone (Exodus 32:15, 16). They provided no internal power to live them out. To be sure, there was great benefit in memorizing God's Word. Those who obeyed the wisdom of Deuteronomy 6:6–9 and tied God's Word on their hands and foreheads and wrote them on the doorframes in their homes and impressed them on their children surely benefitted in their minds and hearts (cf. Deuteronomy 6:6). Psalms 1 and 119 eloquently testify to the benefit of knowing the Law, for it could guide and influence the heart. But the writing on the heart was beyond the power of unaided man. Something far more radical was needed—a spiritual heart operation.

On one occasion Dr. Christian Barnard, the first surgeon ever to do a heart transplant, impulsively asked one of his patients, Dr. Philip Blaiberg, "Would you like to see your old heart?" At 8 p.m. on a subsequent evening, "the men stood in a room of the Groote Schuur Hospital, in Cape Town, South Africa. Dr. Barnard went up to a cupboard, took down a glass container and handed it to Dr. Blaiberg. Inside that container was Blaiberg's old heart. For a moment he stood there stunned into silence—the first man in history ever to hold his own heart in his hands. Finally he spoke and for ten minutes plied Dr. Barnard with technical questions. Then he turned to take a final look at the contents of the glass container, and said, 'So this is my old heart that caused me so much trouble.' He handed it back, turned away and left it forever."[6]

This, in essence, is what Christ does. We still have the same heart, but it is radically new. God has written his laws within us. He has made his people partakers of the divine nature (2 Peter 1:4). True, we still battle with our fleshly nature, but through baptism into Christ's Body God's laws suddenly became perfectly suited to our own spiritual inclinations (cf. John 14:15–17; 16:12, 13; 1 Corinthians 12:13). They are no longer external and foreign but internal. "Therefore, if anyone is in Christ, he is a new creation. The old has passed away; behold, the new has come" (2 Corinthians 5:17). What a better promise!

Superior Relationship

Next, the new covenant promises a superior relationship: "I will be their God, and they shall be my people" (v. 10b). This was one of the formula expressions of the goal of the old covenant. God's word to Israel through Moses was, "I will take you to be my people, and I will be your God" (Exodus 6:7). The Old Testament echoes this repeatedly, though it was only fulfilled in some of the hearers. But this is perfectly fulfilled in all who partake of the new covenant, in which believers actually become God's possession and possess God.

In a transcendent sense, God is God "to every star that burns, and to every worm that creeps, and to every gnat that dances for a moment. . . . He is a God to every man that lives lavishing upon him manifestations of divinity, and sustaining him in life."[7] But there is also a tender, truer relationship of heart to heart, spirit to spirit—so that "I will be their God, and they shall be my people" is true in a deeper, more soul-satisfying way than those on the outside can imagine. "I will be their God" means he *gives* himself to us. And "they shall be my people" means he *takes* us to himself! When this happens, everything my complex nature can require is found in him!

Superior Knowledge

Superior inwardness and superior relationship are followed by a superior knowledge: "And they shall not teach, each one his neighbor and each one his brother, saying, 'Know the Lord,' for they shall all know me, from the least of them to the greatest" (v. 11). The old covenant of Sinai was corporately entered into by a nation, including many who did not know God personally. But those who experience the new covenant come one by one as they are born into a relationship with God. Jesus defined eternal life by saying, "And this is eternal life, that they know you the only true God, and Jesus Christ whom you have sent" (John 17:3). So those who are partakers of the new covenant all know God, "from the least of them to the greatest." No one needs to say, "Know the Lord" to such persons, though at the same time this is a command and invitation to a lost world. For those on the outside, God's command is, "Know the Lord!" That command is meant to allure men and women, boys and girls toward life. For those on the inside, personal knowledge will make them ache for more—"For his sake I have suffered the loss of all things . . . that I may know him and the power of his resurrection, and may share his sufferings, becoming like him in his death" (Philippians 3:8, 10).

Superior Forgiveness

Finally, there is the promise of superior forgiveness in the new covenant: "For I will be merciful toward their iniquities, and I will remember their sins no more" (v. 12). This is precisely what the old covenant could not do. Under the old covenant, sins were never completely forgiven because they were never truly forgotten. They were covered, awaiting and pointing to the true forgiveness through Christ's death.

Forgiveness is the most important of the qualities we have discussed, for it is the basis of the other three. Here forgiveness is tied to memory. Some of our race have had phenomenal memories. It was said that the elder Seneca (c. 55 BC–AD 37) would impress his students by asking "each member of a class of two hundred to recite a line of poetry, and then he would recite all the lines they had quoted—in reverse order, from last to first. Saint Augustine, who also had begun life as a teacher of rhetoric, reported his admiration of a friend who could recite the whole text of Virgil—backwards!"[8]

But God beats everyone! He never forgets anything. In fact, he cannot forget *unless* he wills to do so. Any sin he remembers must be punished because he is holy. And when sins are not remembered, "it is because His grace has determined to forgive them—not in spite of his holiness, but in harmony with it" (F. F. Bruce).[9]

The new covenant brings total forgiveness! God does not just forget our sins. It is impossible for God to remember them!

Now let us put it all together. Approaching on the wings of angels we observed a *superior priesthood*. Jesus is *seated* in session at the right hand of the Father. The heartbeat of the universe pulses with radiant light on his emerald throne beside the Father and the Spirit. He is surrounded closely by the four fiery living creatures and the thrones of the twenty-four elders. Around the crystal sea are myriads singing his praise. Yet there, seated amidst his glory, he *serves us* as he prays for you and me. Can we believe it?

The tabernacle on earth was only a shadowy copy of the glory of his eternal priesthood. Oh, the surpassing greatness of it all! A perfect sacrifice—a perfect priest—a perfect sanctuary—perfect substance—superior to anything ever thought or dreamed about our intercessor!

Then we descend toward earth on the wings of angels, leaving the third heaven, speeding through deep space and on to the visited planet where we see the superior new covenant at work. Its heartbeat is Jesus' surpassing Melchizedekian priesthood.

Its glories are these:

- A sublime *inwardness*—God's Law written in the minds and hearts of his people.
- A sublime *relationship*—he has given himself to us—"I will be their God," and he has taken us to himself—"and they shall be my people."
- A sublime *knowledge*—they all know him. There is no need to say, "Know the Lord."
- A sublime *forgiveness*—he cannot remember their sins. Total forgiveness!

The covenant is *new* and eternally fresh, whereas the old covenant's permanently sundered curtain dramatizes its obsolescence. "In speaking of a new covenant," says the author, "he makes the first one obsolete. And what is becoming obsolete and growing old is ready to vanish away" (v. 13). This gives the lie to the view of some that the sacrifices will start again in the Millennial Kingdom. Jesus Christ's once-and-for-all sacrifice has provided the believing with direct access to God for all eternity.

A superior covenant! A superior hope!

Then I looked, and I heard around the throne and the living creatures and the elders the voice of many angels, numbering myriads of myriads and thousands of thousands, saying with a loud voice,

"Worthy is the Lamb who was slain,
to receive power and wealth and wisdom and might
and honor and glory and blessing!"

And I heard every creature in heaven and on earth and under the earth and in the sea, and all that is in them, saying,

"To him who sits on the throne and to the Lamb
be blessing and honor and glory and might forever and ever!"
(Revelation 5:11–13)

Now even the first covenant had regulations for worship and an earthly place of holiness. For a tent was prepared, the first section, in which were the lampstand and the table and the bread of the Presence. It is called the Holy Place. Behind the second curtain was a second section called the Most Holy Place, having the golden altar of incense and the ark of the covenant covered on all sides with gold, in which was a golden urn holding the manna, and Aaron's staff that budded, and the tablets of the covenant. Above it were the cherubim of glory overshadowing the mercy seat. Of these things we cannot now speak in detail. These preparations having thus been made, the priests go regularly into the first section, performing their ritual duties, but into the second only the high priest goes, and he but once a year, and not without taking blood, which he offers for himself and for the unintentional sins of the people. By this the Holy Spirit indicates that the way into the holy places is not yet opened as long as the first section is still standing (which is symbolic for the present age). According to this arrangement, gifts and sacrifices are offered that cannot perfect the conscience of the worshiper, but deal only with food and drink and various washings, regulations for the body imposed until the time of reformation. But when Christ appeared as a high priest of the good things that have come, then through the greater and more perfect tent (not made with hands, that is, not of this creation) he entered once for all into the holy places, not by means of the blood of goats and calves but by means of his own blood, thus securing an eternal redemption. For if the blood of goats and bulls, and the sprinkling of defiled persons with the ashes of a heifer, sanctify for the purification of the flesh, how much more will the blood of Christ, who through the eternal Spirit offered himself without blemish to God, purify our conscience from dead works to serve the living God.

9:1–14

23

Covenant and Conscience

HEBREWS 9:1–14

THE WRITER OF HEBREWS begins his telling comparison between the saving powers of the old and new covenants with a brief summary in verses 1–5 of the layout and furnishings of the wilderness tabernacle, which he concludes by saying, "Of these things we cannot now speak in detail" (v. 5). And, indeed, there was no real need to discuss them in detail because his Jewish readers were well acquainted with the desert sanctuary and its regulations for worship. But we are not. And so some detail is in order before we launch into the comparison of the covenantal systems.

The Tabernacle

Israel's tabernacle was a portable tent-shrine that was always situated at the geographical heart of Israel, with all the tribes camped around it in designated orderly formation. Approaching the tabernacle, one first would see the white linen walls of the court of the tabernacle, which formed an enclosure 150 feet long and seventy-five feet wide. The uniform whiteness of the enclosure's walls broadcast the holiness of its function.

When a worshiper entered the courtyard, he was immediately in front of the altar of burnt offering, a large bronze altar with a horn at each of its four corners to which offerings could be tied. This was as far as the layman could come, and it is the place where he laid his hands on the head of the sin offering (Leviticus 1:4). Behind the altar and a little to the right stood the bronze laver, a washbasin for the exclusive use of the priests, which, if neglected, imperiled their lives (Exodus 30:20, 21).

Directly behind the laver was the tabernacle, a flat-roofed, oblong tent fifteen feet in height and width and forty-five feet long. It was covered with three layers. The first consisted of gorgeous woven tapestries of blue, purple, and scarlet yarns and linen, which was then overlaid with two layers of animal skins. Inside, the tabernacle was divided into two rooms by an ornate veil woven of the same colors along with gold and embroidered with cherubim. The veil was supported by four golden columns set on silver bases. The first outer room was called the *Holy Place*, and the second inner compartment the *Most Holy Place* or *Holy of Holies*.

Our writer briefly describes these rooms. Of the first room he says, "For a tent was prepared, the first section, in which were the lampstand and the table and the bread of the Presence. It is called the Holy Place" (v. 2). The lampstand was made of solid gold, with three branches springing from either side and each of its seven branches supporting a flower-shaped lampholder (cf. Exodus 25:31ff.; 37:17ff.). The table, called "the table of the bread of the Presence" (Numbers 4:7), contained twelve loaves of bread, one for each tribe. These furnishings were all profoundly prophetic of Christ. The seven-branched candlestick of pure gold speaks of the Divine Son who left Heaven's glory to become the light of the world and make his people to shine as such (cf. Matthew 5:14–16; John 1:4, 5; 8:12). The consecrated bread anticipates Christ's words, "I am the bread of life" (John 6:35ff.). He is the true spiritual sustenance of his people, and apart from him there is no life.

Next, the author is equally brief about the contents of the Holy of Holies. "Behind the second curtain," he says, "was a second section called the Most Holy Place, having the golden altar of incense and the ark of the covenant covered on all sides with gold, in which was a golden urn holding the manna, and Aaron's staff that budded, and the tablets of the covenant. Above it were the cherubim of glory overshadowing the mercy seat" (vv. 3–5).

Scholars have been puzzled because elsewhere the Scriptures place the golden altar of incense not inside the Holy of Holies, but in the outer room "in front of the veil" before the Holy of Holies (Exodus 30:6). In fact, it had to be outside the Holy of Holies because it was used daily by other priests (Exodus 30:7, 8). So why does the author of Hebrews present the altar of incense as part of the Most Holy Place? Most likely, as Leon Morris explains, "The author has in mind the intimate connection of the incense altar with the Most Holy Place. So it 'belonged to the inner sanctuary' (1 Kings 6:22), as is shown by its situation 'in front of the curtain that is before the ark of testimony—before the atonement cover [mercy seat] that is over the Testimony (Exodus 30:6)."[1] While the location of the incense altar is puzzling to some, its prophetic significance is not, for the incense prophesies of the ultimate prayers offered by Christ, our high priest, in the presence of God.

Finally, the cover of the ark of the covenant is even more redolent with Christ. It was at the mercy seat, the gold plate covering the ark upon which the blood of the atonement was sprinkled, that the sins of Israel were propitiated. Romans 3:25 tells us Christ was "displayed publicly as a propitiation in His blood" (NASB). Likewise, 1 John 2:2 proclaims, "and he Himself is the propitiation for our sins" (NASB). The mercy seat symbolized Christ's work. Moreover, Jesus fleshed out the contents of the ark. He perfectly fulfilled the stone tablets of the Law (Deuteronomy 10:5; Matthew 5:17). Aaron's staff that budded when it confirmed him as high priest (Numbers 17:1–11) is fully flowered in Christ's priesthood. And the manna again speaks of him who is the ultimate Bread of Life (cf. Exodus 16:33, 34; John 6:35ff.).

It was all so glorious! "The cherubim of glory" (9:5) perpetually looked down in wonder as they knelt at the mercy seat with their wings arched and touching overhead. "Glory" here is a synonym for God.[2] Everything says, "Glory!"

Tabernacle Worship

When you have a feel for the tabernacle, you can begin to appreciate its worship. Its daily worship was continual. Worshipers brought their sacrifices to the great bronze altar in the outer courtyard one after another. Week by week priests were chosen by lot for the high honor of their career to serve in the first room, the Holy Place (cf. Luke 1:8ff.). There they tended to the seven lamps morning and evening, keeping them full-flamed (Exodus 27:20ff.) and stoked the coals on the altar of incense, upon which they dropped handfuls of incense, filling the room with a delicious cloud. Weekly they exchanged the bread with fresh and then were privileged to partake of the sacred loaves. But none even dared to glance into the Most Holy Place on pain of death (Numbers 18:3–7). They had no access whatsoever.

Ministry in the Holy of Holies was the domain of the high priest *once* a year. And what a day it was (cf. Leviticus 16)! During New Testament times, the high priest underwent rigorous preparation for that day. Seven days before the Day of Atonement, the priest left home and stayed day and night in the temple (*Yoma* 1.1).[3] During the week he practiced what he would do on that great day, so he would make no mistake (*Yoma* 2.2). He was especially cautious not to come close to anything that would make him ceremonially unclean.

Then on the morning of the Day of Atonement, the high priest offered a burnt offering (Numbers 29:8–11). Following this, he ritually bathed his entire body and then, instead of putting on his traditional gorgeous robes, donned a sacred white linen tunic along with white undergarments and a white sash and white turban (Leviticus 16:4)—thus symbolizing that he was free from defilement (*Yoma* 3.4–6).

Next he placed his hands on the head of a bull, selected as a sacrifice for his own sins and those of his family, praying:

> O God, I have committed iniquity, transgressed and sinned before thee, I and my house, as it is written in the Law of thy servant Moses, *"For on this day shall atonement be made for you to cleanse you; from all your sins shall ye be clean before the Lord."* And they answered after him, "Blessed be the name of the glory of his kingdom for ever and ever!" (*Yoma* 3.8)

Then, leaving the bull for a few moments, he turned to two goats nearby and chose lots over them. One was designated for *Jehovah* and the other for *Azazel*, the scapegoat (Leviticus 16:8, 10, 26; *Yoma* 4.1). A piece of crimson wool was tied to the horns of the scapegoat, and a thread was bound around the goat to be slaughtered (*Yoma* 4.2). Then the goats were left standing together.

The high priest now turned to the bull and sacrificed it (*Yoma* 4.3). Next he filled a censer with burning coals from the altar of burnt offerings and entered the Holy of Holies, where he poured two handfuls of incense on the coals so that a cloud of incense covered the mercy seat (Leviticus 16:12, 13; *Yoma* 5.1). This done, he exited, obtaining some of the bull's blood, which he then sprinkled on the mercy seat and then seven times on the ground before the cover (Leviticus 16:14; *Yoma* 5.3).

After this, he sacrificed the goat designated for Jehovah and performed the same ritual in the Holy of Holies. Upon emerging, he mixed the blood of the bull and the goat, put it on the horns of the altar, and sprinkled the altar seven times to consecrate it from the uncleanness of the Israelites (Leviticus 16:18,19; *Yoma* 5.4–6).

Then came the patently joyous part of the day's ceremonies. The priest laid both hands on the head of the live goat and confessed "all the iniquities of the people of Israel, and all their transgressions, all their sins. And he shall put them on the head of the goat" (Leviticus 16:21). The goat was then led away into the desert amidst the jeering of the people—"Bear [our sins] and be gone!" (*Yoma* 6.4).

After this, the high priest put off his white garments, bathed again, arrayed himself in his gorgeous robes, and completed the burnt offerings of the bull and goat, plus other offerings. The remains were carried outside the camp and burned (Leviticus 16:23–28).

The Mishnah says that whenever the high priest pronounced the divine name (YHWH), all the congregation prostrated themselves and cried, "Blessed be the name of the glory of His kingdom forever and ever" (*Yoma* 6.2). At the conclusion of the day, so great was the relief of the people that they accompanied the high priest to his home where he entertained them at a feast. Then the people gave themselves to rejoicing, and the daughters of Jerusalem danced in the vineyards (cf. *Taanith* 4.8).[4]

What sumptuous ritual! This was the old covenant at its apex. Everything was there—the tabernacle so rich in ornament and meaning, which bore in its *sanctus sanctorum* God's presence—and a ritual that taught both the holiness of God and the depth of man's sin, in that no one could enter God's presence without the shedding of blood. It was *sui generis*, one of a kind. It stood alone in the world's religions. There has been nothing that comes close.

But with all of this, it was nevertheless inadequate. And this is what the friends of the writer of Hebrews must see.

The Inadequacy of the Old Covenant (vv. 6–10)

The old system was inadequate for two encompassing reasons—its limited access and its limited efficacy.

Limited Access

Just how restricted the access was is seen in the experience of the official, hereditary priesthood as verse 6 describes it: "These preparations having thus been made [i.e., the two rooms of the tabernacle], the priests go regularly into the first section, performing their ritual duties." If they were fortunate, they got into the outer room once in their priestly lives—for a week. The Israelite layperson's access was even less—the front of the courtyard, and that's all! If one was fortunate enough to attain to high priest (and in later years "fortunate" meant "politicized"), one could have access for a few blessed (and tense!) minutes at best. On the Day of Atonement, when the high priest took his censer in to first burn incense in God's presence, it was prescribed that he must not stay too long "lest he put Israel in terror." The people waited with bated breath, so that when he came out from the Presence alive, there went up a sigh of relief "like a gust of wind."[5] The writer is explicit here:

> But into the second [room] only the high priest goes, and he but once a year, and not without taking blood, which he offers for himself and for the unintentional sins of the people. By this the Holy Spirit indicates that the way into the holy places is not yet opened as long as the first section is still standing. (vv. 7, 8)

His point is crystal-clear: throughout the ages of the old covenant, there was no direct access to God, period!

Limited Efficacy

But as inadequate as the access to God under the old system was, it was exceeded by its limited efficacy. The blood sacrifice that the high priest offered only covered sins of *ignorance*: "But into the second [room] only the high priest goes, and he but once a year, and not without taking blood, which he offers for himself and for the unintentional sins of the people" (v. 7). There was no provision in the old covenant's sacrificial system for forgiveness of premeditated sins! Premeditated, willful sins were called sins of the "high hand," and for such there was no remedy. Numbers 15:30, 31 is unequivocal: "But the person who does anything with a high hand, whether he is native or a sojourner, reviles the LORD, and that person shall be cut off from among his people. Because he has despised the word of the LORD and has broken his commandment, that person shall be utterly cut off; his iniquity shall be on him."

The premeditated sinner was in a huge dilemma! Consider, for example, King David after his premeditated sin with Bathsheba and the cold-blooded murder of Uriah. The system simply did not provide a remedy. This is what Psalm 51 is all about. David knew he was a sinner and confessed it: "For I know my transgressions, and my sin is ever before me. Against you, you only, have I sinned and done what is evil in your sight, so that you may be justified in your words and blameless in your judgment. Behold, I was brought forth in iniquity, and in sin did my mother conceive me" (Psalm 51:3–5). And he knew there was no sacrifice he could bring: "For you will not delight in sacrifice, or I would give it; you will not be pleased with a burnt offering" (Psalm 51:16). What could he do? Only one thing—come to God with a contrite heart and throw himself on God's mercy: "The sacrifices of God are a broken spirit; a broken and contrite heart, O God, you will not despise" (Psalm 51:17). This is how David was forgiven and was saved. Thus, we see that the spiritually informed in the Old Testament came to understand that their only hope was a repentant heart and God's grace. Ultimately salvation rested on the blood of Christ.

The spiritual limitations of the old system went even deeper, because since only sins of ignorance were forgiven (even on the Day of Atonement), no one could have a completely clear conscience: ". . . (which is symbolic for the present age). According to this arrangement, gifts and sacrifices are offered that cannot perfect the conscience of the worshiper, but deal only with food and drink and various washings, regulations for the body imposed until the time of reformation" (vv. 9, 10). This does not mean all Old Testament believers were afflicted with inflamed consciences. If they were faithful in utilizing the old sacrificial system, they were forgiven for their sins of ignorance—which was no small thing.[6] Moreover, some people had fewer premeditated sins to their credit than others, and less real guilt. But, nevertheless, a clear conscience in the *absolute* sense of the word was beyond their reach. The old system was deficient. It was external and superficial.

So the limitations of the old covenant were profound—*limited access* and *limited efficacy*. Average Joes were several ecclesiastical layers removed from access to God's presence—and their consciences never rested easy.

The Adequacy of the New Covenant (vv. 11–14)

Unlimited Access

Christ's untrammeled access is dramatically stated in verses 11, 12:

> But when Christ appeared as a high priest of the good things that have come, then through the greater and more perfect tent (not made with hands, that is, not of this creation) he entered once for all into the holy places, not by means of the blood of goats and calves but by means of his own blood, thus securing an eternal redemption.

Jesus did not just slip into the Most Holy Place amidst a protective cloud of incense to breathlessly perform a ritual sprinkling and then exit until next year. Instead he came having given his own precious blood once and for all, and there he sat down at the right hand of the Father—never more to leave. Everything foreshadowed by the earthly tabernacle—the altar, the laver, the candlestick, the altar of incense, the ark of the covenant, and the tabernacle itself—is fulfilled in his new priesthood in ways beyond description. To catch the idea, we must think of seraphim and emerald thrones and lightning and wheels within wheels and our priest radiant with stars in his right hand gliding among flickering candlesticks!

Unlimited Efficacy

But there is even more, for the unlimited access is crowned with unlimited efficacy as Christ makes consciences clean. To make this point, the author reiterates the limited nature of the old system: "For if the blood of goats and bulls, and the sprinkling of defiled persons with the ashes of a heifer, sanctify for the purification of the flesh . . ." (v. 13). The limited efficacy of the old covenant could make people ceremonially clean as well as atone for sins of ignorance. For example, if an Israelite became ceremonially defiled by touching a dead body, the remedy was ready. All he had to do was go to a priest who had in his possession the ashes of a red heifer that had been ritually sacrificed and burned with a mixture of cedar, hyssop, and scarlet wool. These ashes, mixed in water and ritually sprinkled on the defiled, would bring him external cleansing (cf. Numbers 19:1–13).

Considering that the blood of bulls and goats and the ashes of a heifer had that much effect, "how much more will the blood of Christ, who through the eternal Spirit offered himself without blemish to God, purify our conscience from dead works to serve the living God" (v. 14). There is deep, glorious forgiveness in the new covenant, and it is available to all.

Albert Speer was once interviewed about his last book on ABC's "Good Morning, America." Speer was the Hitler confidant whose technological genius was credited with keeping Nazi factories humming throughout World War II. In another era he might have been one of the world's industrial giants. He was the only one of twenty-four war criminals tried in Nuremburg who admitted his guilt. Speer spent twenty years in Spandau prison.

The interviewer referred to a passage in one of Speer's earlier writings: "You have said the guilt can never be forgiven, or shouldn't be. Do you still feel that way?" The look of pathos on Speer's face was wrenching as he responded, "I served a sentence of twenty years, and I could say, 'I'm a free man, my conscience has been cleared by serving the whole time as punishment.' But I can't do that. I still carry the burden of what happened to millions of people during Hitler's lifetime, and I can't get rid of it. This new book is part of my atoning, of clearing my conscience." The interviewer pressed the point. "You really don't think you'll be able to clear it totally?" Speer shook his head. "I don't think it will be possible."

For thirty-five years Speer had accepted complete responsibility for his crime. His writings were filled with contrition and warnings to others to avoid his moral sin. He desperately sought expiation. All to no avail.[7]

How pitifully sad, for forgiveness was available in the blood of Jesus Christ. Coming to Christ would truly have been like being born again. He literally could have had a new conscience—without the slightest sense of lingering guilt.

You can have a clear conscience if you want one, and the offer is for anyone. If you have not yet come to Christ, the offer stands, as it always has. If you are wondering how to come, perhaps the following story will help.

Charles Simeon, one of the greatest preachers of the Church of England, explained his coming to Christ like this:

> As I was reading Bishop Wilson on the Lord's supper, I met with an expression to this effect—"That the Jews knew what they did, when they transferred their sin to the head of their offering." The thought came into my mind, "What, may I transfer all my guilt to another? Has God provided an Offering for me, that I may lay my sins on His head? Then, God willing, I will not bear them on my own soul one moment longer." Accordingly I sought to lay my sins upon the sacred head of Jesus.[8]

If you want access to Christ and forgiveness of your sins and a new conscience, prayerfully imagine Christ standing before you. Now extend your hands humbly and lay your sins on the head of Jesus.

> I lay my sins on Jesus
> The spotless Lamb of God;
> He bears them all, and frees us
> From the accursed load:
> I bring my guilt to Jesus.
> To wash my crimson stains
> White in His blood most precious,
> Till not a stain remains.
>
> Horatius Bonar, 1843

What glorious benefits come from the new covenant. We have *unlimited access*, hinted at so beautifully by the elegance of the tabernacle and its liturgy. Think of the old shadow, and now the substance. Think of Jesus' access. Think of ours! "[God] raised us up with him and seated us with him in the heavenly places in Christ Jesus, so that in the coming ages he might show the immeasurable riches of his grace in kindness toward us in Christ Jesus" (Ephesians 2:6, 7).

Then there is the *unlimited efficacy* of Christ. What more could we ask for than forgiveness of our sins and a clear conscience? And we have exactly that in Christ!

Therefore he is the mediator of a new covenant, so that those who are called may receive the promised eternal inheritance, since a death has occurred that redeems them from the transgressions committed under the first covenant. For where a will is involved, the death of the one who made it must be established. For a will takes effect only at death, since it is not in force as long as the one who made it is alive. Therefore not even the first covenant was inaugurated without blood. For when every commandment of the law had been declared by Moses to all the people, he took the blood of calves and goats, with water and scarlet wool and hyssop, and sprinkled both the book itself and all the people, saying, "This is the blood of the covenant that God commanded for you." And in the same way he sprinkled with the blood both the tent and all the vessels used in worship. Indeed, under the law almost everything is purified with blood, and without the shedding of blood there is no forgiveness of sins. Thus it was necessary for the copies of the heavenly things to be purified with these rites, but the heavenly things themselves with better sacrifices than these. For Christ has entered, not into holy places made with hands, which are copies of the true things, but into heaven itself, now to appear in the presence of God on our behalf. Nor was it to offer himself repeatedly, as the high priest enters the holy places every year with blood not his own, for then he would have had to suffer repeatedly since the foundation of the world. But as it is, he has appeared once for all at the end of the ages to put away sin by the sacrifice of himself. And just as it is appointed for man to die once, and after that comes judgment, so Christ, having been offered once to bear the sins of many, will appear a second time, not to deal with sin but to save those who are eagerly waiting for him.

24

Covenant and Blood

HEBREWS 9:15-28

FROM MY STUDENT DAYS I can recall with uncommon vividness my English professor expressing amused horror at the lines of William Cowper's great hymn:

> There is a fountain filled with blood
> Drawn from Immanuel's veins;
> And sinners, plunged beneath that flood,
> Lose all their guilty stains:
> Lose all their guilty stains,
> Lose all their guilty stains;
> And sinners, plunged beneath that flood,
> Lose all their guilty stains.

Then for a few minutes my professor condescendingly reflected on these primitive sentiments (swimming in a fountain of blood, dog-paddling among the clots!) which were still so prevalent in Restoration and Augustan English. The prof used such phrases as "slaughterhouse religion" and "Bible thumpers." I could feel myself flushing as crimson as the despised fountain. But as an outsider (and the professor was definitely on the outside!) he did have a point, because the Old Testament sacrificial system, which provides the prefigurement for Christ's sacrifice, was a gory affair indeed! During the thousand-plus years of the old covenant, there were more than a million animal sacrifices. So considering that each bull's sacrifice spilled a gallon or two of blood, and each goat a quart, the old covenant truly rested on a sea of blood. During the Passover, for example, a trough was constructed from the temple down into the Kidron Valley for the disposal of blood—a sacrificial plumbing system!

Why the perpetual sea of blood? For one main reason—to teach that sin demands the shedding of blood. This in no way suggests that blood itself atones for sins *ex opere operato* (otherwise sacrifices would have been bled rather than killed), but it does demonstrate that sin both brings and demands death. Steaming blood provided the sign—even the smell—of the old covenant.

Sin brings death . . . sin brings death . . . sin brings death.

Thus, the devout worshiper of the old covenant came with a definite awareness, first, that sin requires death—second, that such a sacrifice required a spirit of repentance—third, that he was pleading the mercy of God—and, fourth, in some cases, that a great sin-bearer was coming (cf. Psalm 22; Isaiah 53).

Of course, the old covenant system was flawed in that, by design, it could only deal with sins of ignorance (9:7) and could never completely clear one's conscience (9:9). But then came Jesus with the new covenant in his own blood—a superior blood sacrifice that completely atoned for sins (9:12) and completely cleared the conscience (9:14). Jesus was no uncomprehending, unwilling animal, but rather a perfect God-man who consciously set his will to atone for our sins. He is therefore a superior Savior and priest. The old priesthood was the shadow—he is the substance—cleansing both *sin* and *conscience*.

This understood, the logic of verse 15 and following becomes clear: "Therefore he [Jesus] is the mediator of a new covenant, so that those who are called may receive the promised eternal inheritance, since a death has occurred that redeems them from the transgressions committed under the first covenant."

Mediator

The job of a mediator is to arbitrate in order to bring two parties together—here, the holy God and sinful humanity. As the Father's mediator, it is Christ's job to bridge the vast gulf and obtain entrance for us into God's holy presence. His sacrifice is the medium of arbitration, because his shed blood is both retroactive and proactive in bringing forgiveness for sins.

Our text is specific about the *retroactive* power of his blood: "a death has occurred that redeems them from the transgressions committed under the first covenant" (v. 15b). Significantly, the annual sacrifice on the Day of Atonement (which prefigured Christ's ultimate sacrifice) was also retroactive, atoning for the sins of ignorance committed over the past year (9:7). But Christ's death was surpassingly retroactive, reaching all the way back to the Garden of Eden. Paul expounds the same truth in Romans: "whom God displayed publicly as a propitiation in His blood through faith. This was to demonstrate His righteousness, because in the forbearance of God He passed over the sins previously committed" (Romans 3:25 NASB). Because of this, we understand that believers were saved under the old covenant through their obedient faith in God—demonstrated by their sacrifices as they humbly acknowledged that sin required death and as they placed their souls under the mercy of God. Their sacrifices were not a means of salvation, but they were evidence of believing, faithful hearts. To these, Christ's blood extended its retroactive power.

Those of us who are new covenant believers are beneficiaries of the *proactive* power of Christ's death, for he has paid for our sins. When he gave us the grace to believe, he activated his saving power in our lives—paying for our sins past, present, and future.

Testator

As the writer further develops his argument, he does something that our English text cannot show. The word "covenant" (*diatheke*), which he uses twice in verse 15, is also used twice in verses 16, 17, where it is translated "will" ("covenant" and "will" are the same Greek word). But the reason for the two different translations is that the word is used *religiously* in verse 15 (hence "covenant") and *legally* in verses 16, 17 (meaning "will").[1]

So we read, "For where a will is involved, the death of the one who made it must be established. For a will takes effect only at death, since it is not in force as long as the one who made it is alive" (vv. 16, 17). This is true in every culture. A will is activated by the death of the one who made the will, the testator. You may be the stated recipient of a fabulous will that includes millions of dollars, a luxurious apartment, season tickets to the hottest team in town and the Lyric Opera, a villa in Majorca, and a quiver full of Orvis fly rods, but it will do you no good unless the testator dies! Such a fact has provided endless grist for writers from William Shakespeare to Neil Simon.

The writer's point is that Christ's death activated his incredibly rich will—a fact alluded to by Paul in 2 Corinthians: "For you know the grace of our Lord Jesus Christ, that though he was rich, yet for your sake he became poor, so that you by his poverty might become rich" (2 Corinthians 8:9). Think of the benefits we enjoy because of Christ's death: forgiveness, a clear conscience, peace (*shalom*—well-being, wholeness), purpose, and ultimately eternal life in Heaven! All this is impossible apart from his death. And it is all activated by his death!

Jesus has become both *testator* and *mediator* of the new covenant—dual functions impossible for any being except one who rose from the dead. Jesus died, leaving the greatest inheritance ever. But he also lives to mediate his will.

The Old Covenant: Activated by Blood/Death (vv. 18–22)

Law Initiated with Blood

The writer wants his readers to understand that old covenant law was initiated with a pronounced spilling of sacrificial blood that prefigured Christ's blood in initiating the new covenant. The noun "blood" is used six times in verses 18–22. He says:

> Therefore not even the first covenant was inaugurated without blood. For when every commandment of the law had been declared by Moses to all the people, he took the blood of calves and goats, with water and scarlet wool and hyssop, and sprinkled both the book itself and all the people, saying, "This is the blood of the covenant that God commanded for you." (vv. 18–20)

Exodus 24 gives the full account of this. The Ten Commandments had already been delivered (Exodus 19, 20), and then the Book of the Covenant was read (Exodus 20:18—23:33), to which the people responded with one voice, "'All the words that the LORD has spoken we will do.' And Moses wrote down all the words of the LORD" (Exodus 24:3, 4). The next few verses complete the picture:

> And he sent young men of the people of Israel, who offered burnt offerings and sacrificed peace offerings of oxen to the LORD. And Moses took half of the blood and put it in basins, and half of the blood he threw against the altar. Then he took the Book of the Covenant and read it in the hearing of the people. And they said, "All that the LORD has spoken we will do, and we will be obedient." And Moses took the blood and threw it on the people and said, "Behold the blood of the covenant that the LORD has made with you in accordance with all these words." (Exodus 24:5–8)

From Exodus and Hebrews we understand that everything of significance was doused with blood—half on the altar and the other half on the people and the scroll.[2] It was not a pretty sight, except in its supreme symbolism. The altar, people, and book dripped with blood.

This done, the Exodus account records that Moses, his lieutenants, and seventy elders ascended Mt. Sinai, where they all saw, from a distance, God standing on a pavement of sapphire. Moses then left them, going on to the pinnacle where he spent forty days amidst God's glory, which "was like a devouring fire on the top of the mountain" (Exodus 24:9–18).

The Tabernacle Initiated with Blood

The inauguration of the covenant was at once a glorious and bloody affair. So was the subsequent beginning of tabernacle worship some time later: "And in the same way he sprinkled with the blood both the tent and all the vessels used in worship" (v. 21). On its inauguration day, the gorgeous tabernacle as well as its tapestries, golden appointments, and priestly vestments all dripped with blood.[3]

From this lavish use of blood in the inauguration of the two great institutions of the old covenant, we are given this principle: "Under the law almost everything is purified with blood, and without the shedding of blood there is no forgiveness of sins" (v. 22). This text says, "almost everything" because exceptions were made—for example, in the case of the poor. If an impoverished Israelite could not afford a lamb or the next best thing, a pair of turtle doves or pigeons, he was permitted to bring a cereal offering for a *sin* offering (Leviticus 5:11ff.).[4] This is because it was understood that blood was a symbol, and if the symbol was beyond one's reach, a secondary, ersatz symbol would suffice.

But the principle remains—"without the shedding of blood there is no forgiveness." This saying was proverbial in Biblical culture (TB *Yoma* A and TB *Zebahim* 6a)[5]—and was based on Leviticus 17:11—"For the life of the flesh is in the blood, and I have given it for you on the altar to make atonement for your souls, for it is the blood that makes atonement by the life." Sin must bring the forfeiting of life. Sin demands death.

The old covenant sailed on a sea of blood, for two vast reasons. First, to emphasize the seriousness of sin. The Bible takes sin seriously, more than any other religious scripture. Sin alienates one from God. Sin is rooted in the hearts of humanity. Sin cannot be vindicated by any self-help program. Sin leads to death—and it will not be denied. The second reason is the costliness of forgiveness. Death is the payment. It will either be Christ's life or ours!

The New Covenant: Benefits Initiated by the Blood/Death of Christ (vv. 23–28)

Having demonstrated the importance of blood/death in inaugurating the old covenant, the writer now describes the surpassing effect of Christ's sacrifice in establishing the new covenant.

Better Purity

He begins by stating that the better sacrifice of Christ brings better purity: "Thus it was necessary for the copies of the heavenly things to be purified with these rites, but the heavenly things themselves with better sacrifices than these" (v. 23). What are the "heavenly things" that are purified? Nothing less than *us*! Just as the tabernacle had to be anointed and purified so that God might show his presence there, even so the people of God must be cleansed and sanctified so as to become "a dwelling place for God by the Spirit" (Ephesians 2:22).[6]

Peter says the same thing: "You yourselves like living stones are being built up as a spiritual house, to be a holy priesthood, to offer spiritual sacrifices acceptable to God through Jesus Christ" (1 Peter 2:5). To be this "spiritual house," it is necessary to be cleansed through "sprinkling with his blood" (1 Peter 1:2), "with the precious blood of Christ, like that of a lamb without blemish or spot" (1 Peter 1:19). The blood of Christ makes us acceptable to God and makes our presence and praise more acceptable than that of the angels! No angel can call God his Father. To address God as "Abba, Father" is the believer's privilege alone. No angel was ever purchased by the blood of God's Son either, but we were!

Better Representation

Next, Jesus' blood grants us a better representation before the Father: "For Christ has entered, not into holy places made with hands, which are copies of the true things, but into heaven itself, now to appear in the presence of God on our behalf" (v. 24). As soon as he took his seat at the Father's right hand, he began his intercession for us. What is more, he was in his newly acquired human body, perfectly sensitized to our humanity by his life and death.

As such, he is our constant attorney. As our writer earlier said, ". . . since he always lives to make intercession for them" (7:25). To this Paul agrees: "Who is to condemn? Christ Jesus is the one who died—more than that, who was raised—who is at the right hand of God, who indeed is interceding for us" (Romans 8:34).

And there is the testimony of St. John as well: "My little children, I am writing these things to you so that you may not sin. But if anyone does sin, we have an advocate with the Father, Jesus Christ the righteous" (1 John 2:1). This incredible representation brings the greatest comfort to our hearts.

> I know not where his islands lift
> Their fronded palms in air.

I only know I cannot drift
Beyond his love and care.[7]

Better Sacrifice/Efficacy

A further evidence of the superiority of Jesus' shed blood is its efficacy:

> Nor was it to offer himself repeatedly, as the high priest enters the holy
> places every year with blood not his own, for then he would have had to
> suffer repeatedly since the foundation of the world. But as it is, he has ap-
> peared once for all at the end of the ages to put away sin by the sacrifice
> of himself. And just as it is appointed for man to die once, and after that
> comes judgment, so Christ, having been offered once to bear the sins of
> many . . . (vv. 25–28a)

Christ's sacrifice was sufficient and thus needed no repeating. He is
our constant priest, but this in no way suggests that he is perpetually offering himself. Some have ignored the truth of Scripture and have instituted in
the celebration of the Eucharist a repeated reenactment here on earth. How
utterly contradictory to our text—and misleading. The sacrifice was so monumental and efficacious that it could only be once-for-all. His blood is totally
sufficient.

In a rural village lived a doctor who was noted both for his professional
skill and his devotion to Christ. After his death, his books were examined.
Several entries had written across them in red ink: "Forgiven—too poor to
pay." Unfortunately, his wife was of a different disposition. Insisting that
these debts be settled, she filed a suit before the proper court. When the case
was being heard, the judge asked her, "Is this your husband's handwriting in
red?" She replied that it was. "Then," said the judge, "not a court in the land
can touch those whom he has forgiven."

Jesus writes in bold crimson letters across our lives, "Forgiven!" "Who
shall bring any charge against God's elect? It is God who justifies. Who is
to condemn? Christ Jesus is the one who died—more than that, who was
raised—who is at the right hand of God, who indeed is interceding for us"
(Romans 8:33, 34).

The sufficiency of Christ's atoning death is the centerpiece of our salvation. Believing this, how our souls resonate with these words from the last
will and testament of the father of Allan C. Emery, one of the founders of The
ServiceMaster Company:

> I commit my Soul into the Hands of my Savior in full confidence that, hav-
> ing redeemed it and washed it in his Most Precious Blood, He will present

it faultless before the Presence of my Heavenly Father; and I entreat my children to maintain and defend at all hazards and at any cost of personal sacrifice the blessed doctrine of complete atonement for sin through the Blood of Jesus Christ once offered and through that alone.[8]

Better Hope

Finally Christ's blood gives us a better hope that he "will appear a second time, not to deal with sin but to save those who are eagerly waiting for him" (v. 28b). Here we have a brilliant and fresh perspective on the return of Christ. The force of the perspective comes from the analogy of the sequence of events in the Day of Atonement. On that great day the congregation watched the high priest enter the sanctuary with a basin of sacrificial blood and then waited breathlessly outside until he emerged, at which time they breathed a corporate sigh of relief. His emergence told them that his offering on their behalf had been accepted by God. The sense of excitement that greeted the high priest's reappearance was given by Joshua ben Sira, who was present in Jerusalem when Simon II the Just (a priest 219–196 BC) officiated at the Day of Atonement:[9]

> How glorious he was when the people gathered round him
> as he came out of the inner sanctuary!
> Like the morning star among the clouds,
> like the moon when it is full;
> like the sun shining upon the temple of the Most High,
> and like the rainbow gleaming in glorious clouds;
> like roses in the days of the first fruits,
> like lilies by a spring of water,
> like a green shoot on Lebanon on a summer day;
> like fire and incense in the censer,
> like a vessel of hammered gold adorned
> with all kinds of precious stones;
> like an olive tree putting forth its fruit,
> and like a cypress towering in the clouds
>
> Sirach 50:6–10

Our Lord Jesus entered the heavenly sanctuary "to appear in the presence of God on our behalf" (v. 24), and he "will appear a second time, not to deal with sin but to save those who are eagerly waiting for him" (v. 28). Hallelujah!—he is coming again as both King and priest.

> Coming! In the opening east
> Herald brightness slowly swells;

Coming! O my glorious Priest,
Hear we not thy golden bells?

                                    Francis Ridley Havergal

The blood of Christ may be a stumbling-block to a lost world. The gruesome metaphor may prove grist for ignorant humor—crimson hands backstroking in a sea of blood. But for the heart that knows the depth of its sin and its lostness, the metaphor is sweet because it means Jesus gave his life for us.

There is a fountain filled with blood
Drawn from Immanuel's veins;
And sinners, plunged beneath that flood,
Lose all their guilty stains.
The dying thief rejoiced to see
That fountain in his day;
And there may I, though vile as he,
Wash all my sins away.

For since the law has but a shadow of the good things to come instead of the true form of these realities, it can never, by the same sacrifices that are continually offered every year, make perfect those who draw near. Otherwise, would they not have ceased to be offered, since the worshipers, having once been cleansed, would no longer have any consciousness of sins? But in these sacrifices there is a reminder of sins every year. For it is impossible for the blood of bulls and goats to take away sins. Consequently, when Christ came into the world, he said, "Sacrifices and offerings you have not desired, but a body have you prepared for me; in burnt offerings and sin offerings you have taken no pleasure. Then I said, 'Behold, I have come to do your will, O God, as it is written of me in the scroll of the book.'" When he said above, "You have neither desired nor taken pleasure in sacrifices and offerings and burnt offerings and sin offerings" (these are offered according to the law), then he added, "Behold, I have come to do your will." He does away with the first in order to establish the second. And by that will we have been sanctified through the offering of the body of Jesus Christ once for all. And every priest stands daily at his service, offering repeatedly the same sacrifices, which can never take away sins. But when Christ had offered for all time a single sacrifice for sins, he sat down at the right hand of God, waiting from that time until his enemies should be made a footstool for his feet. For by a single offering he has perfected for all time those who are being sanctified. And the Holy Spirit also bears witness to us; for after saying, "This is the covenant that I will make with them after those days, declares the Lord: I will put my laws on their hearts, and write them on their minds," then he adds, "I will remember their sins and their lawless deeds no more." Where there is forgiveness of these, there is no longer any offering for sin.

25

Covenant and Perfection

HEBREWS 10:1-18

AS WE SAID EARLIER, no New Testament book has had more background research than Hebrews, and none has spawned a greater diversity of opinion, though there is broad agreement that the grand theme of this epistle is the supremacy and finality of Jesus Christ.

A consensus also exists regarding the general identity of the recipients: they were a group of Jewish Christians who had never seen Jesus in person, yet had believed. Their conversion had brought them hardship and persecution with the result that some had slipped back into Judaism. And, thus, the purpose for the letter was to encourage them to not fall away, but to press on (cf. 2:1ff.; 3:12ff.; 6:4ff.; 10:26ff.; and 12:15ff.).

There is also universal agreement, first expressed by Origen, that "only God knows certainly" who wrote this letter. There is also agreement that the author, whoever he was, was a magnificent stylist with an immense vocabulary and a vast knowledge of the Greek Old Testament.

Despite general agreement on these matters, no scholar has yet proven the exact destination or occasion of the letter—though many contemporary scholars tentatively propose that the letter was written to a small house-church of beleaguered Jewish Christians in the mid-sixties before the destruction of the Jerusalem temple. Hebrews was evidently written to a group of Jewish Christians whose world was falling apart. The author's conveying the greetings of several Italian Christians who were with him (13:24) supports the idea that the harried little church was on Italian soil—very likely in or around Rome.

Their Christianity had not been a worldly advantage. Rather, it set them up for persecution and the loss of property and privilege, and now could possibly even cost them their lives.

We know they had already paid a price for their initial commitment to Christ. As the writer recalls in 10:32–34:

> But recall the former days when, after you were enlightened, you endured a hard struggle with sufferings, sometimes being publicly exposed to reproach and affliction, and sometimes being partners with those so treated. For you had compassion on those in prison, and you joyfully accepted the plundering of your property, since you knew that you yourselves had a better possession and an abiding one.

This description of their earlier sufferings fits well into the picture of the hardships that came to Jewish Christians under Claudius in AD 49. Suetonius' *Life of the Deified Claudius* records that "there were riots in the Jewish quarter at the instigation of Chrestus. As a result, Claudius expelled the Jews from Rome" (25.4). "Chrestus," historians believe, is a reference to Christ, and the riots and expulsion occurred when Jewish Christians were banished from the synagogue by the Jewish establishment.

Now, as the author of Hebrews writes, fifteen years have gone by since the Claudian persecution, and a new persecution looms. No one has been killed yet, but 12:4 raises the possibility that martyrdom may soon come—"In your struggle against sin you have *not yet* resisted to the point of shedding your blood."

The writer of Hebrews was writing to admonish and encourage his friends, a small group of Jewish Christians who were scared stiff! Some had begun to avoid contact with outsiders. Some had even withdrawn from the worshiping community altogether (10:25). The author feared there might be those who, if arrested, would succumb to the conditions of release—a public denial of Christ (6:6; 10:29). The tiny home-church was asking some hard questions: Did God know what was going on? If so, how could this be happening to them? Did he care? Only God could protect them, but where was he? Why did he not answer? Why the silence of God?

The letter arrived, and word was sent out. The congregation gathered. Perhaps no more than fifteen or twenty were seated or standing around the house. All were quiet. Through these magnificent words the beleaguered church was brought face-to-face with the God who speaks, and this God—through his superior Son, Jesus Christ—would bring them comfort in the midst of life's troubles.

Soon after I began to date my future wife, Barbara, I obtained her picture—a beautiful black-and-white 8 x 10 photograph taken the year before we met—and it immediately became an item of pre-nuptial "worship." It was one of those bare-shouldered, sorority-style pictures so popular at the time. She looked like an angel floating in the clouds. It became my portable hope, most often sitting on my desk, sometimes in my car, at other times propped in front of my plate and my love-struck eyes.

However, the day came when we stood before God and our families and friends and pledged our lives to each other as she became mine. Suddenly I had gone from the possession of a one-dimensional portrait to the possession of the real thing, who smiled, talked, and laughed—a real, three-dimensional wife—a living, life-loving soul! And the picture? It remained just as beautiful, but from then on it received relatively scant attention.

But imagine that one day I appear before my wife holding the black-and-white photograph, and I say, "My dear, I've missed your picture, and I'm going back to it. I really am attached to the silhouette and the monochrome shading and the matte finish." Then I passionately kiss the glass protecting the photograph, clutch it to my chest, and exit mumbling my devotion to the picture—"I love you, O photograph of my wife. You're everything to me."

People's suspicions that pastors are weird would be confirmed. Time to call for the men in the white jackets!

How absurd for anyone, once having the substance, to go back to the shadow. Yet, some in the early church were forsaking the covenant of grace for the old covenant of the Law. And this is what the author of Hebrews wants to steel his people against as he concludes his comparison of the old and new covenants in 10:1–18.

The Problem of Imperfection (vv. 1–4)

The author/pastor begins with a forthright statement of the facts: "For since the law has but a shadow of the good things to come instead of the true form of these realities . . ." (v. 1a). As "a shadow," the Law is only a pale reflection, a mere outline or silhouette, and is thus unsubstantial.[1] The Ten Commandments, the Book of the Covenant, and the tabernacle cultus only foreshadow the reality of Christ. And as a shadow, the Law had substantial imperfections that the writer proceeds to spell out:

> It can never, by the same sacrifices that are continually offered every year, make perfect those who draw near. Otherwise, would they not have ceased to be offered, since the worshipers, having once been cleansed, would no longer have any consciousness of sins? But in these sacrifices there is a reminder of sins every year. For it is impossible for the blood of bulls and goats to take away sins. (vv. 1b–4)

Imperfect Cleansing

Of course, the author of Hebrews was not the first to understand that animal blood would not atone for sins. Scriptural writers had been alert to this for hundreds of years. David's repentant words head the list: "You will not delight in sacrifice, or I would give it; you will not be pleased with a burnt offering. The sacrifices of God are a broken spirit; a broken and contrite heart, O God, you will not despise" (Psalm 51:16, 17). Consider also Samuel's words to King Saul: "Has the LORD as great delight in burnt offerings and sacrifices, as in obeying the voice of the LORD? Behold, to obey is better than sacrifice, and to listen than the fat of rams" (1 Samuel 15:22). And Isaiah said:

> What to me is the multitude of your sacrifices?
>   says the LORD;
> I have had enough of burnt offerings of rams
>   and the fat of well-fed beasts;
> I do not delight in the blood of bulls,
>   or of lambs, or of goats.
>
> When you come to appear before me,
>   who has required of you
>   this trampling of my courts?
> Bring no more vain offerings. (Isaiah 1:11–13a)

Later Isaiah expressed God's displeasure at offerings when one's heart is not right:

> He who slaughters an ox is like one who kills a man;
>   he who sacrifices a lamb, like one who breaks a dog's neck;
> he who presents a grain offering, like one who offers pig's blood;
>   he who makes a memorial offering of frankincense, like one who
>   blesses an idol.
> These have chosen their own ways . . .
> because when I called, no one answered,
>   when I spoke, they did not listen. (Isaiah 66:3, 4)

Similarly, Jeremiah inveighed against sacrifices presented without an obedient heart:

> Thus says the LORD of hosts, the God of Israel: "Add your burnt offerings
> to your sacrifices, and eat the flesh. For in the day that I brought them out
> of the land of Egypt, I did not speak to your fathers or command them
> concerning burnt offerings and sacrifices. But this command I gave them:

'Obey my voice, and I will be your God, and you shall be my people.'"
(Jeremiah 7:21–23)

God said through Hosea, "For I desire steadfast love and not sacrifice, the knowledge of God rather than burnt offerings" (Hosea 6:6). And Amos shared God's thoughts about wrong-hearted sacrifices:

I hate, I despise your feasts,
   and I take no delight in your solemn assemblies.
Even though you offer me your burnt offerings and grain offerings,
   I will not accept them;
and the peace offerings of your fattened animals,
   I will not look upon them.
Take away from me the noise of your songs;
   to the melody of your harps I will not listen.
But let justice roll down like waters,
   and righteousness like an ever-flowing stream. (Amos 5:21–24)

Lastly, we include the famous words of Micah:

"With what shall I come before the LORD,
   and bow myself before God on high?
Shall I come before him with burnt offerings,
   with calves a year old?
Will the LORD be pleased with thousands of rams,
   with ten thousands of rivers of oil?
Shall I give my firstborn for my transgression,
   the fruit of my body for the sin of my soul?"
He has told you, O man, what is good;
   and what does the LORD require of you
but to do justice, and to love kindness,
   and to walk humbly with your God? (Micah 6:6–8)

It is a fact that at the time of Christ many pious Jews honored the sacrificial system and even offered sacrifices, but realized that those sacrifices could not remove sin. This is why, when the temple was destroyed and the sacrifices ended, the people so easily adapted. They understood that animal sacrifice was insufficient to obtain forgiveness.[2]

An Imperfect Conscience

Because the old system could not take away their sin, it produced a second imperfection—a guilty conscience (cf. v. 2). Of course one's conscience can be seared or defaced, as C. S. Lewis noted in joking with a friend when he wrote:

We were talking about cats and dogs the other day and decided that both have consciences but the dog being an honest, humble person, always has a bad one, but the cat is a Pharisee and always has a good one. When he sits and stares you out of countenance he is thanking God that he is not as these dogs, or these humans, or even as these other cats![3]

But assuming that one didn't have a cat's non-conscience, one's conscience under the old covenant always had a pervasive sense of disease. One's inner moral discernment[4] always registered a floating guilt, and in some, this was a raging, unquenchable guilt.

Not all the blood of beasts
On Jewish altars slain,
Could give the guilty conscience rest
Or wash away one stain.

Memorialized Imperfection

The result was, as verse 3 points out, that the sacrifices remained as "a reminder of sins every year." As a matter of fact, the Day of Atonement increased the burden of those with sensitive hearts. The Day's well-defined ritual was constructed to aggravate one's conscience. The shadow of the old covenant law and sacrifice inflamed the unrequited need for *forgiveness* and a *clear conscience*. The photograph, so to speak, pictured what could be and activated an ache for the reality.

The old covenant simply could not "make perfect those who draw near" (v. 1). It was good, as far as it went. But it was frustratingly inadequate.

The Solution for Imperfection (vv. 5–9)

Of course, the Godhead was not unaware of this, and beginning in verse 5 we have a brief synopsis of the conversation that took place there when Jesus elected to come into the world as a man.

The Divine Dialogue

"Consequently, when Christ came into the world, he said [Christ's preincarnate words], 'Sacrifices and offerings you have not desired, but a body have you prepared for me; in burnt offerings and sin offerings you have taken no pleasure. Then I said, "Behold, I have come to do your will, O God, as it is written of me in the scroll of the book"'" (vv. 5–7). Actually Christ's words here were a quotation from King David taken from a paraphrased Greek version of Psalm 40:6–8 (LXX, Psalm 39:7–9). David had spoken it one thousand years earlier, but Christ in Heaven took it and reapplied it, so as to describe his own inner thinking and dialogue with the Father when he came into the world.

What a high place this gives Scripture! Our pre-incarnate Savior quoted Psalm 40 as being prophetic of his thoughts at his human birth. Interestingly, the Hebrew of Psalm 40:6 literally reads, "ears you have dug for me," but the Greek paraphrase of it that Christ and the author quoted in Hebrews is, "a body have you prepared for me." This may be because the Greek translator regarded the creation of ears as part of fashioning a whole human body.[5]

Whatever the explanation may be, Christ said in essence, "My Father, the Old Testament sacrifices have proven unsatisfactory, so you have prepared a body for me, that I might become a pleasing sacrifice." (The author reiterates this idea in verse 8, noting that the Father was not pleased with the old sacrifices although they were "offered according to the law.") The fact was, though God had instituted blood animal sacrifices (Exodus 24), he had never been pleased with them and did not see them as ends. He had established them as object lessons to instruct his people about the sinfulness of their hearts, his hatred of sin, the fact that sin leads to death, the need of an atonement, and his delight in those whose hearts were clean and obedient and faithful. But there was nothing appealing to him in the sight of a dying animal. God had no pleasure in the moans and death-throes of lambs or bulls. What he did find pleasure in was those who offered a sacrifice with a contrite, obedient heart.

The Divine Disposition

Having verbalized what the Father wanted—Jesus Christ's sacrificial death—our Lord now states his joyous resolve: "Then I said, 'Behold, I have come to do your will, O God, as it is written of me in the scroll of the book'" (v. 7). On the verge of the Incarnation, the Lord Jesus stopped to pay tribute to the Old Testament Scripture and to proclaim that what he was about to do had been fully written of in advance in the scroll.

Hours could be spent here inspecting the familiar Old Testament prophecies and types that point so fully to the incarnate Messiah. But the great emphasis here, one we must not miss, is Christ's exuberant determination and eagerness to *obey* the Father—"Then I said, 'Behold, I have come to do your will, O God.'" Our Lord did not obey the Father grudgingly or under duress but with joy! Later, in 12:2, the writer tells us that Jesus endured the cross "for the joy that was set before him." The angels sang at the Incarnation (Luke 2:13ff.) because they were reflecting and expressing Christ's joy. He had come to die, and that could logically have produced an angelic dirge. But the angels gave out an anthem instead, because of the anthem of Christ's heart—"Then I said, 'Behold, I have come to do your will, O God.'" There is "in Deity Itself the joy of obedience: obedience which is a particular means of joy and the only means of that particular joy."[6] Jesus willed to be subordinate to God!

What is the application for us? Jesus' joyous resolve to obediently do God's will is the essence of the true sacrifice and worship that God desires. Jesus does what God desired from every worshiper in the old covenant. God did not want animal sacrifices. What he wanted and still wants is obedience! That is the *only* sacrifice that is acceptable to God.

Everything is ashes if we are not living in conscious obedience to God. Is there something you know God wants you to do, but you have been unwilling? Perhaps it is a kindness to perform—a confession to make—a gift to give—a commitment to fulfill—a task to perform. If you know what it is, say reverently to him, "Behold, I have come to do your will, O God."

The Results of Perfection (vv. 10–18)

The author introduces the results of Christ's willingness to do God's will by saying, "And by that will we have been sanctified through the offering of the body of Jesus Christ once for all" (v. 10). Jesus' sacrifice "once for all" is emphatic, and the writer wants us to see that its results are equally final, for the phrase "we have been sanctified" refers to an enduring, continuous state (perfect tense). Our salvation is a completed thing—a "done deal."[7]

From the writer's perspective, the comparative postures of Jesus (our Melchizedekian priest) and the Aaronic priests make the point. He explains:

> And every priest stands daily at his service, offering repeatedly the same sacrifices, which can never take away sins. But when Christ had offered for all time a single sacrifice for sins, he sat down at the right hand of God, waiting from that time until his enemies should be made a footstool for his feet. For by a single offering he has perfected for all time those who are being sanctified. (vv. 11–14)

Significantly, there were no chairs in the tabernacle—no provision whatsoever to sit down. Priests stood or kept moving, because their imperfect work was never over. But Jesus, in exact fulfillment of the Melchizedekian prophecies in Psalm 110:1—"The LORD says to my Lord: 'Sit at my right hand, until I make your enemies your footstool'"—sat down forever at the right hand of honor and power (cf. 1:3, 13; 8:1). Jesus rests. Our salvation, as we have said, is a "done deal." Our perfection is accomplished. And in the timelessness of eternity our holiness will go on and on.[8]

The preacher to the Hebrews finishes this great section with a brief recap of two perfections of the new covenant from Jeremiah 31 that were mentioned earlier in 8:10–12—namely, empowerment and forgiveness.

Empowerment

As to empowerment, we read, "And the Holy Spirit also bears witness to us; for after saying, 'This is the covenant that I will make with them after those days, declares the Lord: I will put my laws on their hearts, and write them on their minds . . .'" (vv. 15, 16; cf. Jeremiah 31:33). Instead of putting his laws on stone tablets, they are placed in the very center of the believer's being, so that there is an inner impulse that both delights in knowing his law and doing his will.

Shortly after the armistice of World War I, Dr. Donald Grey Barnhouse visited the battlefields of Belgium. In the first year of the war the area around the city of Mons was the scene of the great British retreat. In the last year of the war it was the scene of the greater enemy retreat. For miles west of the city the roads were lined with artillery, tanks, trucks, and other materiels of war that the enemy had abandoned in their hasty flight.

It was a lovely spring day. The sun was shining, and not a breath of wind was blowing. As he walked along, examining the war remains, he noticed leaves were falling from the great trees that arched along the road. He brushed at a leaf that had fallen against his chest. As he grasped at it, he pressed it in his fingers, and it disintegrated. He looked up curiously and saw several other leaves falling from the trees. Remember, it was spring, not autumn, nor was there enough wind to blow off the leaves. These leaves had outlived the winds of autumn and the frosts of winter. Yet they were falling that day, seemingly without cause.

Then Dr. Barnhouse realized why. The most potent force of all was causing them to fall. It was spring—the sap was beginning to run, and the buds were beginning to push from within. From down beneath the dark earth, roots were sending life along trunk, branch, and twig until it expelled every bit of deadness that remained from the previous year. It was, as a great Scottish preacher termed it, "the expulsive power of a new affection."[9]

This is what happens when God writes his will on our hearts. The new life within purges the deadness from our lives. Our renewed hearts pump fresh blood through us. The life of Christ in us—the same life that said "Behold, I have come to do your will, O God"—animates us!

You may be saying to yourself, "I don't think I can ever live the Christian life"—and you are right! But a new heart, the expulsive inner power of new affection, will make it possible. The sense that you cannot do it is precisely why you should come to Christ. In fact, it is the qualification!

Forgiveness

The other perfection of the new covenant mentioned here is forgiveness: "Then he adds, 'I will remember their sins and their lawless deeds no more.' Where there is forgiveness of these, there is no longer any offering for sin" (vv. 17, 18). Note the air of finality here—a completed sacrifice and complete forgiveness.

Amazingly, it is possible for people to think they believe what really in their heart they do not believe. It is possible to imagine they believe in the forgiveness of sins when they do not. Their belief is logical and theoretical but not actual. Then something happens, the truth appears clearer than ever before, they see it—and they believe with all their heart. Forgiveness follows belief.

It was said that Clara Barton, organizer of the American Red Cross, was never known to harbor resentment to anyone. On one occasion a friend recalled for her an incident that had taken place some years before, but Clara seemed not to remember. "Don't you remember the wrong that was done you?" asked her friend. Clara Barton answered calmly, "No, I distinctly remember forgetting that." Clara Barton willed to forgive and forget.

But God does even better. He really *does* forgive and forget—"I will remember their sins and their lawless deeds no more." Do you believe you believe it? Or do you truly believe it? Believe it!

What folly to leave one's living spouse for her lifeless portrait. On the one hand, you "possess" a living person of so many inches, of a definite weight, with her own aroma, brimming with thought and action. But you leave her for her lifeless photograph with its fixed and sealed expression. What an absurd thought!

But there is an exercise of even greater absurdity, and that is to leave her for nothing. This is the folly of our age. Christ's joyous shout upon leaving Heaven was for you and me: "Behold, I have come to do your will, O God.'" He died and rose to make you and me perfect, forgiving us completely and renewing our hearts. Heaven has been laid at our sinful feet. There can be no greater folly imaginable than to turn away from this to nothing. "Lord, to whom shall we go? You have the words of eternal life" (John 6:68).

Therefore, brothers, since we have confidence to enter the holy places by the blood of Jesus, by the new and living way that he opened for us through the curtain, that is, through his flesh, and since we have a great priest over the house of God, let us draw near with a true heart in full assurance of faith, with our hearts sprinkled clean from an evil conscience and our bodies washed with pure water. Let us hold fast the confession of our hope without wavering, for he who promised is faithful. And let us consider how to stir up one another to love and good works, not neglecting to meet together, as is the habit of some, but encouraging one another, and all the more as you see the Day drawing near.

10:19–25

26

Full Access/Full Living

HEBREWS 10:19–25

THOUGH WE DO NOT KNOW who the author of Hebrews was, we do know he was a preacher with flaming pastoral instincts. He did not do theology for *theoretical* ends, but rather for down-to-earth, *practical* purposes. So we come here to the great turning-point in Hebrews where the writer turns from the *explanation* of the superiority of the person and work of Christ to the application of it in the lives of the storm-tossed church. The shift can be stated in various ways: from *doctrine* to *duty,* from *creed* to *conduct,* from *precept* to *practice,* from *instruction* to *exhortation,* all of which mean one thing—the writer becomes very explicit regarding how Christians ought to live.

In making transition from instruction to exhortation, the preacher assumes that the foregoing ten chapters, truly believed, ought to have produced a profound dual confidence: confidence in one's *access* to God, and confidence in one's *advocate* before God.

Access (vv. 19, 20)

As he begins, he assumes matter-of-factly in the opening phrase that his hearers have a proper confidence in their divine *access*: "Therefore, brothers, since we have confidence to enter the holy places by the blood of Jesus, by the new and living way that he opened for us through the curtain, that is, through his flesh . . ." (vv. 19, 20). Their confident access comes from the torn curtain of Christ's crucified body. The rending of Jesus' flesh on the cross, which brought his death, perpetrated a simultaneous tearing from top to bottom of the curtain that had barred the way into the Holy of Holies (Matthew 27:51).

They walked confidently through the torn curtain of Christ, so to speak, into the presence of the Father.

Whereas before they could only have surrogate access through the high priest, who slipped behind the curtain once a year for a heart-pounding few minutes, they now had permanent access through the blood and torn body of Christ. Their confidence was certainly not a swaggering thing, but it was a real confidence in permanent access. This nicely complemented the preacher's earlier encouragement: "Let us then with confidence draw near to the throne of grace, that we may receive mercy and find grace to help in time of need" (4:16). They had deep confidence in their access to God.

Advocacy (v. 21)

This confidence in access is especially strong because it is coupled with a confidence in Christ's priestly advocacy: "since we have a great priest over the house of God" (v. 21). As we know, the appointments of the tabernacle and the daily vestments of the Aaronic high priests were specifically spelled out to Moses by God, because they were shadows of Christ's ultimate heavenly advocacy. God's instructions demanded that the Old Testament high priest wear twelve stones on his breastplate—over his heart—to represent his people (Exodus 28:21) and representative stones on his shoulder as well, for "Aaron shall bear their names before the LORD on his two shoulders for remembrance" (Exodus 28:12). Now Jesus, our ultimate advocate, bears our names not just over his body and heart, but in the very center of his being, for we are *in* him, our advocate! Even more, he is our constant high priest. His intercession never ceases!

See this access and advocacy, the dual sources of our confidence, together. See what strength they bring. Jesus is both the curtain (our access) and the priest (our advocate). His torn body and shed blood provides our access to the presence of the Father. And in our access he is our perpetual priestly advocate.

This was meant to make the ancient Church (and us) confidently point our ship into the high seas with strength and power. We are not only to exist in a hostile culture but to buck its waves. While arrogance can never be the Christian's way, confidence must mark his life. Listen to Paul's bold confidence:

> If God is for us, who can be against us? He who did not spare his own Son but gave him up for us all, how will he not also with him graciously give us all things? Who shall bring any charge against God's elect? It is God who justifies. Who is to condemn? Christ Jesus is the one who died—more than that, who was raised—who is at the right hand of God, who indeed is interceding for us. (Romans 8:31–34)

The logic here, seriously applied, pushes us to heights of confidence. It means more than God being graciously disposed toward us. It means we are victors. We may be defeated for a moment, but evil will never prevail. *Access* and *advocacy*—what confidence they bring!

When Chrysostom was brought before the Roman emperor, the emperor threatened him with banishment if he remained a Christian. Chrysostom replied:

> "You can not banish me for this world is my father's house." "But I will slay you," said the Emperor. "No, you can not," said the noble champion of the faith, "for my life is hid with Christ in God." "I will take away your treasures." "No, but you can not for my treasure is in heaven and my heart is there." "But I will drive you away from man and you shall have no friend left." "No, you can not, for I have a friend in heaven from whom you can not separate me. I defy you, for there is nothing you can do to hurt me."[1]

Draw Near to God (v. 22)

From the vantage-point of the remarkable confidence that ought to be every believer's, the preacher gives three sweeping exhortations, the first of which is to draw near to God. We can catch the force of the argument if we again consider verses 19–21, which lead up to it: "Therefore, brothers, since we have confidence to enter the holy places by the blood of Jesus, by the new and living way that he opened for us through the curtain, that is, through his flesh, and since we have a great priest over the house of God . . ." That is, because of the *confidence* we have from our grand *access* and *advocacy*, "let us draw near with a true heart in full assurance of faith, with our hearts sprinkled clean from an evil conscience and our bodies washed with pure water" (v. 22).

Under the old covenant, when priests were consecrated they were sprinkled with blood (Exodus 29:21). Also, when the old covenant began, the people had been sprinkled with blood (Exodus 24:8). But with the new covenant, when the people of this Hebrew church came to faith, their hearts were inwardly "sprinkled" with Christ's blood to cleanse them "from an evil conscience" (cf. 9:14). For the first time in their lives the guilt was completely gone, and their conscience rested easy. Then they were baptized and their "bodies washed with pure water"—an outward, visible sign of the inner sprinkling or cleansing they had experienced (cf. 1 Peter 3:21; Ephesians 5:25, 26).

To such lives the teacher's exhortation comes with great appeal and power: "Let us draw near with a true heart in full assurance of faith." The "heart" represents the whole inner life. There must be inner sincerity from one's whole being. One must be true, completely genuine, "wholehearted"

(Moffatt). Commentators have noted that although the language is different, the sixth Beatitude carries the same idea, where we are called to be "pure in heart" (Matthew 5:8).[2] There are to be no mixed motives or divided loyalties. There must be pure and unmixed devotion, sincere love for God.

Negatively, we can picture this idea from everyday life as we reflect on those people who, after being introduced to us, keep talking and smiling but at the same time looking behind and around us at other people and things. They really are not interested in us. They only see us as objects or a means for something they want. In our relationship with the God-man, such behavior is anathema. Positively stated, a "true" heart is represented in the words *focus* or *wholeheartedness*.

Jesus makes essentially the same point in John 4:23 when he says God desires those who worship "in spirit"—that is, those whose entire human spirit is engaged in worship.

This is how we are to draw near to God in prayer—real, genuine, absorbed. The preacher sees this as being of key importance to those who are being distracted by the menacing waves. He knows that essential to their survival is the ability to perpetually come to God in prayer that is sincere and wholehearted, true and engaged. If they do this, they will emerge victorious. They must prayerfully "draw near with a true heart in full assurance of faith." The wisdom of this exhortation is as relevant and necessary today as it was in the first century.

Hold to the Hope (v. 23)

The next exhortation flows naturally from the preceding because if we draw near to God, we will be disposed to heed the command to persevere in hope: "Let us hold fast the confession of our hope without wavering, for he who promised is faithful" (v. 23).

Hopelessness is the lot of the honest secularist. Bertrand Russell gave it famous expression in his book *A Free Man's Worship*:

> . . . the labours of the ages, all the devotion, all the inspiration, all the noonday brightness of human genius, are destined to extinction in the vast death of the solar system, and that the whole temple of Man's achievement must inevitably be buried beneath the debris of a universe in ruins . . . only within the scaffolding of the truths, only on the firm foundation of unyielding despair, can the soul's habitation henceforth be safely built.[3]

The "firm foundation of unyielding despair"? It doesn't sound very firm to the ear, or to the logical mind.

Most people, however, are not as cerebral as philosopher Russell. They base their lives, rather, on a vague, shapeless, subjective hope. Professor William M. Marston of New York University asked three thousand people, "What have you to live for?" He was shocked to discover that 94 percent were simply enduring the present while they waited for the future . . . waited for "something to happen" . . . waited for "next year" . . . waited for a "better time" . . . waited for "someone to die" . . . waited "for tomorrow."[4]

Hope springs eternal in the human breast:
Man never is, but always to be, blest.
                              Alexander Pope, "An Essay on Man"

So many people live on so little, surviving in this world, just putting one foot in front of the other as they depend on unsubstantiated, ungrounded "hope."

But the Christian's hope has substance! The hope that our text commends here in verse 23 is a conscious reference back to the writer's statement in 6:19, 20—"We have this as a sure and steadfast anchor of the soul, a hope that enters into the inner place behind the curtain, where Jesus has gone as a forerunner on our behalf." It is grounded in the life, death, resurrection, ascension, enthronement, and intercession of our Lord Jesus Christ. It is anchored at the right hand of God. It is so substantial and real that it is called an "anchor."

No ancient or modern sailor who knows what can happen during an ocean voyage would go to sea in a ship that carried no anchor, even today and even if the ship were the greatest and most modern vessel afloat. Every sailor knows that situations might arise when the hope of the ship and all her company will depend not on the captain, the crew, the engines, the compass, or the rudder, but on the anchor. When all else fails, there is hope in the anchor. It was so easy for Christians to appropriate this as their symbol because its very shape uses the form of the cross.

Literally, the author here commands, "And let us hold on *unbendingly* to the hope we confess, for he who promised is faithful." The anchor is not in the sea, but in Heaven, the celestial Holy of Holies. It is anchored in God's presence. As the winds pick up, as the ship bobs like a cork, as we sail through all life's troubles, we must hang on to the confession of our hope without wavering, for our hope is anchored in our access to and advocacy before God the Father. We must hang on with all we have. Such tenacity will endure any storm.

Consider One Another (vv. 24, 25)

The final exhortation in this section is to mutually consider one another, and it extends through verse 25, which is actually a participial phrase carrying on the thought of verse 24: "And let us consider how to stir up one another to love and good works, not neglecting to meet together, as is the habit of some, but encouraging one another, and all the more as you see the Day drawing near" (vv. 24, 25).

A father was showing his young son through a church building when they came to a plaque on the wall. Curious, the little boy asked, "Daddy, what's that for?" His father replied, "Oh, that's a memorial to those who died in the service." The little boy said, "Which service, Daddy, the morning or the evening?"[5]

People have a thousand reasons to stay away from church. This is not a new problem. The early Jewish church had had a fall-off in attendance due to persecution, ostracism, apostasy, and arrogance. Today persecution and ostracism may not be our experience, but people find many other reasons to absent themselves from worship, not the least of which is laziness. But de-churched Christians have always been an aberration, as St. Cyprian, St. Augustine, Luther, Calvin, and the various classic confessions repeatedly affirm.[6] There are solid Biblical reasons why no one should forego church.

Ontology

The first is "ecclesial ontology," the special existence—the being or presence—of Christ in the gathered church. This is dramatically portrayed in the first chapter of Revelation as Christ, holding seven stars in his right hand, walks among the seven golden lampstands that are emblematic of the church (Revelation 1:9–20). We meet Christ in a special way in corporate worship. It is true that a person does not have to go to church to be a Christian. He does not have to go home to be married either. But in both cases if he does not, he will have a very poor relationship.

Doxology

Next, if you absent yourself from church, you will encumber your ability to glorify God in worship. Congregational worship makes possible an intensity of adoration that does not as readily occur in solitude. On the tragic level, a mob tends to descend to a much deeper level of cruelty than individuals. It is also understood that the appreciation and enjoyment of an informed group of music lovers at a symphony is more intense than that of a single listener at home. This holds true for worship as well. Corporate worship provides a context where passion is joyously elevated and God's Word ministers with unique power.

Martin Luther spoke of this when he confided, "At home in my own house there is no warmth or vigor in me, but in the church when the multitude is gathered together, a fire is kindled in my heart and it breaks its way through."[7]

Theology

It is also true that giving up meeting with other believers hampers one's theology and doctrinal understanding. Paul, in Ephesians 3:18, 19, prays that the church in Ephesus "may have strength to comprehend with all the saints . . . and to know the love of Christ that surpasses knowledge." Great theological truths are best learned corporately—"with all the saints." Theology is to be done by the assembled church.

Psychology

Lastly, there is the matter of psychology—not in the sense of the study of the psyche, the soul—but rather its development. For example, the virtue of love enjoined by the second half of the Decalogue requires others for its development. One theoretically may be able to develop *faith* and *hope* while alone (though even this is questionable), but not *love*! Developing love is a communal activity of the church.

So for all these reasons—ontological, doxological, theological, psychological—it is impossible to be a good Christian while voluntarily absenting oneself from the assembled church. The author of Hebrews is pleading with his people not to make such a mistake, because he knows they would not survive. And neither would we. Laxity can destroy us, so we must beware.

What to do? The answer is in the exhortation that dominates this section: "And let us consider how to stir up one another to love and good works" (v. 24). This idea of stirring one another up is an exciting concept because the word translated "stir" is extremely strong. The RV translates it "provoke," the NEB "arouse." It is the word *paroxysmos*, from which we get *paroxysm*—a sudden convulsion or a violent emotion. Normally, as in the rest of the New Testament, this is not a pleasant word (for example, "a sharp disagreement"— *paroxysmos*—came between Paul and Barnabas, Acts 15:39; cf. 1 Corinthians 13:5). But here it has a pleasant sense of prodding our brothers and sisters toward love and good deeds.

Provoke One Another

The author wants us to take knowledge of one another as to how we might provoke each other to blessed paroxysms of grace. Here we suggest several ways we can be positive irritants.

Prayer

If we specifically pray for each other by name and pray for the development of volitional, selfless love—*agape*—and for specific good deeds, it will happen! It is as simple as that. Do you think your pastor or spouse or boss or whoever is grouchy? Pray that he or she will have an attack of niceness!

Example

A second powerful way to spur one another on to "love and good works" is by example. Oswald Chambers said, "It is a most disturbing thing to be smitten in the ribs by some provoker from God, by someone who is full of spiritual activity."[8] I believe Jim Elliot was this way when he was writing things like the following and living them out: "Oh, the fullness, pleasure, sheer excitement of knowing God on earth. I care not if I never raise my voice again for Him, if only I may love Him, please Him."[9]

It is a fact that loving God and man and doing good deeds are more readily caught than taught. To provoke others upward by example is the high road indeed.

God's Word

Of course, the Word of God is our basic primer for love and good deeds. When we internalize it, allowing God's Word to flow through us, we become conduits of its virtues and are gentle examples and provokers of grace.

Encouragement

Lastly, there is the responsibility to verbally spur others on through words of encouragement. Journalist Robert Maynard related the following story from his childhood in *The New York Daily News*: As a young boy Maynard was walking to school one day when he came upon an irresistible temptation. In front of him was a fresh piece of gray cement—a piece that had replaced a broken piece of sidewalk. He immediately stopped and began to scratch his name in it. Suddenly he became aware that standing over him with a garbage can lid was the biggest stone mason he had ever seen!

Maynard tried to run, but the big man grabbed him and shouted, "Why are you trying to spoil my work?" Maynard remembers babbling something about just wanting to put his name on the ground. A remarkable thing happened just then. The mason released the boy's arms, his voice softened, and his eyes lost their fire. Instead there was now a touch of warmth about the man. "What's your name, son?"

"Robert Maynard."

"Well, Robert Maynard, the sidewalk is no place for your name. If you want your name on something, you go into that school. You work hard and you become a lawyer and you hang your shingle out for all the world to see."

Tears came to Maynard's eyes, but the mason was not finished yet. "What do you want to be when you grow up?"

"A writer, I think."

Now the mason's voice burst forth in tones that could be heard all over the schoolyard. "A writer! A writer! Be a writer. Be a real writer! Have your name on books, not on this sidewalk."

Robert Maynard continued to cross the street, paused, and looked back. The mason was on his knees repairing the damage that Maynard's scratching had done. He looked up and saw the young boy watching and repeated, "Be a writer."[10]

There is amazing power in an encouraging word. You and I can change a life with a kind word. Encouragement is a Christian duty. Lives of provocation through prayer, example, Scripture, and encouragement are gifts the church needs desperately.

Hebrews 10:19–25 is no insignificant text. Its role in moving from *instruction* to *application* gives it huge significance. It tells us that if we have the proper confidence that comes from our *access* and *advocacy* before God, there are three things we must do for the sake of the church and her survival.

- We must draw near in prayer to God with a wholehearted sincerity. Our entire human spirit must be engaged in prayer and worship.
- We must hold on to the anchor of hope we possess. Our hope is in Jesus and is anchored in Heaven, where he intercedes for us. This is no cock-eyed optimism but tremendous reality.
- We must devote ourselves to the corporate church and do everything we can to provoke each other to love and good deeds.

If we do this, the church will ride high on every storm that comes! And we must do this more and more as we "see the Day drawing near."

For if we go on sinning deliberately after receiving the knowledge of the truth, there no longer remains a sacrifice for sins, but a fearful expectation of judgment, and a fury of fire that will consume the adversaries. Anyone who has set aside the law of Moses dies without mercy on the evidence of two or three witnesses. How much worse punishment, do you think, will be deserved by the one who has trampled underfoot the Son of God, and has profaned the blood of the covenant by which he was sanctified, and has outraged the Spirit of grace? For we know him who said, "Vengeance is mine; I will repay." And again, "The Lord will judge his people." It is a fearful thing to fall into the hands of the living God.

10:26-31

27

The Perils of Apostasy

HEBREWS 10:26–31

IT IS COMMONLY THOUGHT by those who have only a passing recognition of Jonathan Edwards that his famous sermon "Sinners in the Hands of an Angry God" was preached with sadistic glee to his bewildered congregation. The supposition is that Edwards enjoyed afflicting his people and that the sermon was preached with pulpit-pounding vehemence.

Such thinking is wide of the mark. Shouting was not Edwards's style. It is a matter of historical fact that Edwards quietly read his sermons from tiny pieces of paper he held up in front of him. Neither did Edwards enjoy such preaching. Rather, it was necessitated by the famous "halfway" covenant, an earlier Puritan attempt to keep as many people as possible under the influence of the church, though they were not professed believers. The church in Enfield contained baptized unbelievers who were barred from the Lord's Table. Ultimately Edwards was dismissed as pastor over the question of the admission of the unconverted to the Lord's Supper. Edwards was preaching for their souls, and also against the follies of the "halfway" covenant.

Therefore, we must understand that Jonathan Edwards's passionate love for God and his flock was the reason he employed every tool in his considerable stores of logic and metaphor to plead for his people's souls in "Sinners in the Hands of an Angry God." He was less concerned with God's wrath than with his grace, which was freely extended to sinners who repented.[1] Jonathan Edwards gave his people a whiff of the sulphurs of Hell that they might deeply inhale the fragrances of grace.

Edwards's intense concern joins him in heart with the preacher who wrote to the Hebrews some seventeen hundred years earlier. The stakes were identical—heaven or hell. And the symptoms, though not identical, were

267

similar as well—a declining regard for the church's authority, a willfulness to define one's relationship to the church in one's own terms, and, in some cases, quitting the church altogether. To such are addressed the thunderous warnings in verses 26–31, in which the brilliant writer summons his own prodigious logic and literary talents. To glimpse his passion, we can imagine ourselves as parents raising our children along a boulevard on which huge trucks regularly pass at great speed. Our warnings are couched in the most dramatic terms and lurid illustrations—"Do you know what happens to little children if . . ."—in the hope that somehow what we say will penetrate the imagination and thinking process of our children, so they will stay out of the deadly street!

The Terrors of Apostasy (vv. 26, 27)

The writer begins his plea by graphically outlining the terrors of apostasy. The opening terror is that it obviates Christ's atoning sacrifice: "For if we go on sinning deliberately after receiving the knowledge of the truth, there no longer remains a sacrifice for sins" (v. 26). This is the terror of no sacrifice! Now, the preacher is *not* saying that if believers persist in sinning deliberately, there will come a point where the effect of Christ's sacrifice runs out, and Christ would say, "I have paid for your sins up to this point, but I'm not prepared to pay for them any further."[2] Rather, what the writer is describing is a graceless, reprobate state characterized by two things—*deliberateness* and *continuance*.

We only have to look at our own hearts, or the actions of our offspring, to know what deliberate sin is like. Case in point: our two-year-old grandson, Joshua Simpson, recently climbed up on the kitchen counter to get at a forbidden stick of gum. But, alas, his father appeared several inches from Joshua's face, saying, "Joshua, you may not have the gum. If you eat that gum, I will spank you!" Joshua looked at the gum, then at his father, and back at the gum. Then he took the gum, *slowly* unwrapped it as he watched his dad, and put it in his mouth. Joshua got his spanking! But there was more, because a few minutes later he returned and took another stick, climbed down, ducked behind a corner to unwrap it—and got another spanking. The boy is a sinner, and so are we all.

Our text is talking about deliberate, intentional sin. In fact, the word "deliberately" stands first in the Greek for emphasis. Moreover, this deliberate sin is continual. The person persists in open rebellion against God and his Word.

Here is the point: this individual has received "the knowledge of the truth"—the content of Christianity as truth. He knows what God has done in Christ, and he understands it.[3] But he intentionally—knowingly—rejects it and willfully continues on in an unremitting state of sin—as an apostate. Calvin explains:

> The apostle describes as sinners not those who fall in any kind of sin, but those who forsake the Church and separate themselves from Christ. . . . There is a great difference between individual lapses and universal desertion of the kind which makes for a total falling away from the grace of Christ.[4]

What is in view is what Jesus calls the sin against the Holy Spirit (Matthew 12:32; Mark 3:29). It is the same thing as was described in 6:4–6:

> For it is impossible, in the case of those who have once been enlightened, who have tasted the heavenly gift, and have shared in the Holy Spirit, and have tasted the goodness of the word of God and the powers of the age to come, and then have fallen away, to restore them again to repentance, since they are crucifying once again the Son of God to their own harm and holding him up to contempt.

The ignorant cannot commit this sin. It cannot be committed inadvertently. It is a sin only "church people" can commit. For such, "there no longer remains a sacrifice for sins" because they have rejected the one and only valid sacrifice—Christ.

This terror is joined by a second great terror, because since there is no sacrifice, judgment follows: "But a fearful expectation of judgment, and a fury of fire that will consume the adversaries" (v. 27). This is an echo of Isaiah 26:11—"Let the fire for your adversaries consume them"—and is a gripping expression for judgment.

The point here is that those who have rejected Christ inherit a fearful expectation of judgment, whether or not they are aware of it. Some, of course, mask it, like Edward F. Prichard, a sometime politician and crook who used to say that when the last trumpet sounded, the Lord is not going to send people to Heaven or Hell. Rather, "He's going to take away their inhibitions, and everybody's going to go where he belongs."

Interesting thoughts, even amusing, when one is in good health. But it has proven far different with hardened apostates at the time of death when there comes "a fearful expectation of judgment." Take Voltaire, for example. Of Christ, Voltaire said, "Curse the wretch!" He once boasted, "In twenty years Christianity will be no more. My single hand shall destroy the edifice it took twelve apostles to rear." Ironically, shortly after his death the very house in which he printed his literature became the depot of the Geneva Bible Society.

The nurse who attended Voltaire said, "For all the wealth in Europe I would not see another infidel die." The physician Trochim, waiting with Voltaire at his death, said he cried out most desperately, "I am abandoned by God and man! I will give you half of what I am worth if you will give me six months' life. Then I shall go to hell and you will go with me."[5]

Or consider Thomas Paine, the renowned American author and enemy of Christianity who exerted considerable influence against belief in God and the Scriptures. He came to his last hour in 1809, a disillusioned and unhappy man. During his final moments on earth he said:

> I would give worlds, if I had them, that *Age of Reason* had not been published. O Lord, help me! Christ, help me! O God what have I done to suffer so much? But there is no God! But if there should be, what will become of me hereafter? Stay with me, for God's sake! Send even a child to stay with me, for it is hell to be alone. If ever the devil had an agent, I have been that one.[6]

Make no mistake about it—"if we go on sinning deliberately after receiving the knowledge of the truth, there no longer remains a sacrifice for sins, but a fearful expectation of judgment, and a fury of fire that will consume the adversaries." What an awesome duo these terrors make—no sacrifice for sin, and inexorable judgment! Many church attenders would do well to quake in fear like those in Enfield and Northampton lest they become hardened in unbelief so that they consciously reject Christ's work and become terminally apostate.

The Logic behind the Terrors (vv. 28, 29)

Next the preacher/writer turns to an *a fortiori* argument as he lays out the relentless logic behind the terrors he has identified, arguing from the lesser case of rejecting the Law to the greater case of rejecting the grace of Christ.

Lesser

Of the lesser offense he says, "Anyone who has set aside the law of Moses dies without mercy on the evidence of two or three witnesses" (v. 28). For example, Deuteronomy 17:2–7 stipulates regarding anyone accused of idolatry:

> If there is found among you, within any of your towns that the LORD your God is giving you, a man or woman who does what is evil in the sight of the LORD your God, in transgressing his covenant, and has gone and served other gods and worshiped them, or the sun or the moon or any of the host of heaven, which I have forbidden, and it is told you and you hear of it,

then you shall inquire diligently, and if it is true and certain that such an abomination has been done in Israel, then you shall bring out to your gates that man or woman who has done this evil thing, and you shall stone that man or woman to death with stones. On the evidence of two witnesses or of three witnesses the one who is to die shall be put to death; a person shall not be put to death on the evidence of one witness. The hand of the witnesses shall be first against him to put him to death, and afterward the hand of all the people. So you shall purge the evil from your midst.

The accusation had to be proved beyond doubt. One witness was not enough. But when there were two or three witnesses who agreed, it was over. No mercy whatsoever. No appeal. Certain death!

Greater

If such pitiless judgment came from rejecting the lesser old covenant, imagine the case with rejecting the greater new covenant: "How much worse punishment, do you think, will be deserved by the one who has trampled underfoot the Son of God, and has profaned the blood of the covenant by which he was sanctified, and has outraged the Spirit of grace?" (v. 29). This greater judgment comes from three immense travesties that characterizes all apostasy. First, they "trampled underfoot the Son of God." The January 1991 issue of *Harper's Magazine* carried a reproduction of an anti-Christian tract entitled *Dear Believer*, a "non-tract" published by the Freedom from Religion Foundation of Madison, Wisconsin. The tract variously attacked creation and miracles and then God himself, finally coming to Jesus and saying:

> And Jesus is a chip off the old block. He said, "I and my father are one," and he upheld "every jot and tittle" of the Old Testament law. He preached the same old judgment: vengeance and death, wrath and distress, hell and torture for all nonconformists. He never denounced the subjugation of slaves or women. He irrationally cursed and withered a fig tree for being barren out of season. He mandated burning unbelievers. (The Church has complied with relish.) He stole a horse. You want me to accept Jesus, but I think I'll pick my own friends, thank you.
>
> I also find Christianity to be morally repugnant. The concepts of original sin, depravity, substitutionary forgiveness, intolerance, eternal punishment, and humble worship are all beneath the dignity of intelligent human beings.

This tract captures the emotion of the word "trampled," which is a singularly powerful expression for disdain—as, for example, when the swine find your pearls and "trample them underfoot and turn to attack you" (Matthew

7:6; cf. Matthew 5:13; Luke 8:5). Figuratively, the metaphor portrays taking "the Son of God"—the highest accord given to Christ in Hebrews—and grinding him into the dirt.[7] Thus, turning away from Christ is an attack on his *person*.

Second, apostasy is an attack on Christ's *work*, for the one who has done this "has profaned the blood of the covenant by which he was sanctified" (v. 29). Hebrews 9 is especially a lyrical song about the superiority of Christ's blood. Because Christ's blood was nothing less than his divine life willingly offered, it could do what no animal's blood could do—namely, take away sin and bestow a clear conscience.

> Oh, precious is the flow
> That makes me white as snow;
> No other fount I know,
> Nothing but the blood of Jesus.

The sort of apostate pictured here had at one time *professed* faith in Christ, *listened* to the Word preached, and *celebrated* the Lord's Supper. Those initial acts "sanctified" him. As elsewhere in Hebrews, the idea of being sanctified refers to the initial act of being set apart for God.[8] But his faith, such as it was, was not internal and was not genuine, and now he consciously rejects Christ's work. "Jesus' blood," he says, "is common, just like any other man's. There is nothing special about it."

Third, having rejected the *person* and *work* of Christ, he also rejects the *person and work* of the Holy Spirit, as verse 29 concludes: "and has outraged the Spirit of grace." This is the only place in the New Testament where the Holy Spirit is called "the Spirit of grace" (but cf. Zechariah 12:10), and what a beautiful and fitting title it is. He *enlightens* our minds, he *seals* our hearts in adoption, he *regenerates* us with spiritual life, and he *grafts* us into the Body of Christ—all effects of grace. We ought to make note of this lovely ascription and use it devotionally. The Spirit of grace—the Holy Spirit of grace—gives and gives and gives!

To "outrage the Spirit of grace" is an immense act of hubris and arrogance (the Greek verb for "outraged" comes from the noun *hybris*). What had happened is that the Holy Spirit had come to the apostate, witnessed to him about spiritual reality, and courted his soul, but the apostate rejected the Spirit's witness with outrageous arrogance. Such persons deliberately close their eyes to the light, just as the Pharisees had done when they attributed the Spirit's works of mercy and power to Beelzebub—and thus their condemnation is the same:

Therefore I tell you, every sin and blasphemy will be forgiven people, but the blasphemy against the Spirit will not be forgiven. And whoever speaks a word against the Son of Man will be forgiven, but whoever speaks against the Holy Spirit will not be forgiven, either in this age or in the age to come. (Matthew 12:31, 32)

To reject the gracious work of "the Spirit of grace" renders one irremediably lost.

What frightening terrors lie behind apostasy: rejection of Christ's person, rejection of Christ's work, and rejection of the person and work of the Holy Spirit. Understanding this, the question of verse 29 explodes: "How much worse punishment, do you think, will be deserved by the one . . . ?" One thing is sure—there will be no mercy shown for the hardened apostate, just as there was no mercy shown to those who willfully transgressed the Law. But the greater severity is that breaking the old covenant brought *physical* death, while rejecting Christ brings *spiritual* death.

Some today reject this idea by employing a one-sided view of Christ. They say that Jesus' emblem was a lamb, that Jesus took little children in his arms and blessed them, that he sighed over the deaf and dumb and wept over Jerusalem. But they forget that the Lamb of God will come with wrath—in judgment (Revelation 6:16), that he told all who cause any of his little ones to sin that it would be better for them to be thrown into the sea with a large millstone tied around their neck, and that the same Jesus who wept over Jerusalem judged it.

Listen to Jesus' words on a number of different occasions:

So it will be at the end of the age. The angels will come out and separate the evil from the righteous and throw them into the fiery furnace. In that place there will be weeping and gnashing of teeth. (Matthew 13:49, 50)

And if your hand or your foot causes you to sin, cut it off and throw it away. It is better for you to enter life crippled or lame than with two hands or two feet to be thrown into the eternal fire. And if your eye causes you to sin, tear it out and throw it away. It is better for you to enter life with one eye than with two eyes to be thrown into the hell of fire. (Matthew 18:8, 9)

Then the king said to the attendants, "Bind him hand and foot and cast him into the outer darkness. In that place there will be weeping and gnashing of teeth." (Matthew 22:13)

Then he will say to those on his left, "Depart from me, you cursed, into the eternal fire prepared for the devil and his angels." (Matthew 25:41)

And these will go away into eternal punishment, but the righteous into eternal life. (Matthew 25:46)

And if your hand causes you to sin, cut it off. It is better for you to enter life crippled than with two hands to go to hell, to the unquenchable fire. (Mark 9:43)

And if your eye causes you to sin, tear it out. It is better for you to enter the kingdom of God with one eye than with two eyes to be thrown into hell, "where their worm does not die and the fire is not quenched" (Mark 9:47, 48)

But he [Jesus] looked directly at them and said, "What then is this that is written: 'The stone that the builders rejected has become the cornerstone'? Everyone who falls on that stone will be broken to pieces, and when it falls on anyone, it will crush him." (Luke 20:17, 18)

You cannot have the Jesus of the Scriptures without the doctrines of judgment and hell. "Think lightly of hell, and you will think lightly of the cross" (Spurgeon).

The Terror of Judgment (vv. 30, 31)

In verse 30, in order to drive home the terror of judgment, the author quotes loosely from the Song of Moses in Deuteronomy 32:35, 36—"For we know him who said, 'Vengeance is mine; I will repay.' And again, 'The Lord will judge his people'" (cf. Romans 12:19). The phrases appear to be proverbial and were undoubtedly understood by everyone in the church.[9] Clearly, judgment is *inevitable*, and it is *impartial*. There will be equal justice for all.

In the gallery of Antoine Wiertz in Brussels, there is a collection of the most astounding and overpowering paintings—most of them exposing the brutality and horrors of war and the cruelty of conquerors, but some of them heralding the Empire of Peace and the triumph of Christ.

Walking down the hall where these awesome paintings hang, one is suddenly brought to a halt by a great painting entitled *A Scene in Hell*. With folded arms and familiar cocked hat on his head, there stands the figure of a man. There is no name given, but there is no need, for he is recognized as the Little Corporal from Corsica. On his shadowed face there is a look of astonishment, with just a trace of dread and fear, as he beholds what is all around him. By the light of the flames of Hell burning all about him, you can see behind him the ranks of the slain in battle. Little children stretch out clenched fists at the emperor. Mothers, with agony on their countenances, surround him, holding up the bleeding, amputated arms and legs of the slaughtered. On the faces of the children, the wives, and the mothers are depicted rage, horror, hate, and infinite pain and sorrow. The scene is macabre, terrible, horrible! Yes, and that is just what Wiertz meant it to be, for it is Napoleon in Hell! The artist's moral imagination has tried to picture Napoleon with his just deserts, an equitable punishment for a man who caused so much pain.[10]

God's judgment will be based on what each has been given. Those with greater knowledge, such as the apostates in the Hebrew church and in the New England church in Jonathan Edwards's day, will be judged with greater stringency. Judgment will have an equity impossible with men, however, because God knows the very thoughts and intents of the heart.

Finally, we come to the grand statement of terror, "It is a fearful thing to fall into the hands of the living God" (v. 31). May we understand how dreadful and divine this is!

Divine Judgment

King David, after he had sinned against God by counting the number of fighting men in Israel and Judah, evidently viewed falling into God's hands as divine judgment, because when God commanded him to choose between three alternatives, his wise reply was, "Let us fall into the hand of the LORD, for his mercy is great" (2 Samuel 24:14). Very possibly this exact passage was on our author's mind and governed the form of the words he chose. However that may be, for the true believer there is nothing better than to fall repentantly into the hands of God. His hands are our hope!

> The hands of Christ are very frail
> For they were broken with a nail.
> But only those reach Heaven at last
> Whom those frail, broken hands hold fast.

Dreadful Judgment

But to fall into God's hands will be dreadful for those who have rejected him because, as we have mentioned, divine judgment will be *perfectly equitable*. The lurid picture of Napoleon does make the point. The horrible truth is that one will receive what is coming to him.

This will be dreadful because it involves *separation from God*. Union with God's nature is bliss, but separation from him is horror.[11]

It will be dreadful because it is *eternal*. If one could travel at the speed of light for one hundred years until he escaped this galaxy, and then travel for three thousand years at the speed of light to reach the next galaxy, repeating the process one hundred thousand million times until he reached every galaxy—eternity would have just begun!

The dread of eternal separation and punishment is inconceivably painful. This is an excruciating doctrine. Jonathan Edwards's metaphors were not too strong, for the Bible is true! Our lives do hang by a mere thread. Eternity gapes before us.

Wonderful Salvation

But the dreadful is met by the wonderful arms of Jesus, which he extends to us. Those arms were stretched wide on the cross so that he might embrace us. He was not only our atoning sacrifice, but he propitiates our sins, turning aside the Father's righteous wrath. Jesus today still has those same human, atoning, propitiating arms—and all we have to do is fall into them.

Be blessed now through faith in Christ—and fall into the arms and hands of the living God!

But recall the former days when, after you were enlightened, you endured a hard struggle with sufferings, sometimes being publicly exposed to reproach and affliction, and sometimes being partners with those so treated. For you had compassion on those in prison, and you joyfully accepted the plundering of your property, since you knew that you yourselves had a better possession and an abiding one. Therefore do not throw away your confidence, which has a great reward. For you have need of endurance, so that when you have done the will of God you may receive what is promised. For, "Yet a little while, and the coming one will come and will not delay; but my righteous one shall live by faith, and if he shrinks back, my soul has no pleasure in him." But we are not of those who shrink back and are destroyed, but of those who have faith and preserve their souls.

10:32–39

28

Keep On!

HEBREWS 10:32–39

NO GOOD PARENT ever enjoys disciplining his children. It is no fun to sit a child down and give him a good talking-to and then perhaps a swat or two or three. No parent likes to see a little lip quiver or tears well in blinking eyes and roll down a sad face. It is really true—there are times you would rather take the talking-to and even the spanking yourself.

But there is also very often a special sweetness in discipline (though certainly not all the time!). It comes when you take a hot-teared little person in your arms, hold him close, then brush away the tears and gently encourage him and tell him that you love him and that he can, and will, do better. This is a unique, healing, domestic sweetness.

Fortunately, this is not limited to the home but is also the experience of the family of God. Hebrews 10 shows this. In verses 26–31 the pastor had delivered one of the most chastening warnings in all of Scripture, concluding with the terrifying words, "It is a fearful thing to fall into the hands of the living God." There is no more aggressive, hard-hitting passage in God's Word. But now in verses 32–39 the writer figuratively takes his smarting, chastened listeners in his arms and bestows tender words of encouragement to keep on in the faith. St. Chrysostom saw the same thing here when he commented that the writer acts very much like a surgeon who comforts and encourages his patient after making a painful incision.[1]

The encouragement to continue on comes in two parts—first, to *remember* the past (vv. 32–34), and second, to *respond* in the present (vv. 35-39).

Remembering the Past (vv. 32–34)

The writer begins with a call to remembrance, saying, "But recall the former days when, after you were enlightened, you endured a hard struggle with sufferings" (v. 32). This was a challenge to recall how they had marvelously stood unmoved some fifteen years earlier during the persecution under the Roman Emperor Claudius in AD 49. A famous quotation from the historian Suetonius indicates the character of the Claudian persecution: "There were riots in the Jewish quarter at the instigation of Chrestus. As a result, Claudius expelled the Jews from Rome" (*Life of the Deified Claudius*, 25.4). Historians believe "Chrestus" is a reference to Christ and that the riots and expulsion occurred when Jewish Christians were banished from the synagogue by the Jewish establishment. No one had been killed (cf. 12:4), but it was nevertheless a wrenching time of humiliation and abuse.

The word translated "struggle" in our text is the Greek word *athlesis*, from which we derive our English word *athletic*. The persecution was like a hard-fought athletic contest viewed by a partisan crowd. There was nothing passive in their display. In fact, they showed superb spiritual athleticism as they stood their ground!

Such athleticism is a beautiful thing in the eyes of God and the church—as it was, for example, in the life of Hugh Latimer, the great English Reformer. On one notable occasion Latimer preached before Henry VIII and offended Henry with his boldness. So Latimer was commanded to preach the following weekend and make an apology. On that following Sunday, after reading the text, he addressed himself as he began to preach:

> Hugh Latimer, dost thou know before whom thou art this day to speak? To the high and mighty monarch, the king's most excellent majesty, who can take away thy life if thou offendest; therefore, take heed that thou speakest not a word that may displease; but then consider well, Hugh, dost thou not know from whence thou comest; upon whose message thou art sent? Even by the great and mighty God! who is all-present, and who beholdeth all thy ways, and who is able to cast thy soul into hell! Therefore, take care that thou deliverest thy message faithfully.

He then gave Henry the *same* sermon he had preached the week before—only with more energy![2] Latimer was superb! And his memory is a great treasure of the Church.

Here our writer is calling for a similar remembrance of those storied days when the little church had been magnificent—"But recall the former days when, after you were enlightened, you endured a hard struggle with sufferings."

Since the preacher knew that such remembering would help them remain steadfast in the faith, he attempted to help them recall the sequence and character of their stand amidst persecution.

"Sometimes [you were] publicly exposed to reproach and affliction" (v. 33a). The idea here is that they were made public theatre, because the word for "publicly exposed" (*theatrizo*) comes from *theatron*, "theater." They were ridiculed and taunted as a theatre of the absurd. Along with that, the "affliction" they endured was of the nature of being squeezed and pressured. Persecution was one thing, but sardonic, smiling, rung-dropping insults made it even more devastating.

"Sometimes [you were] partners with those so treated" (v. 33b). Here their spiritual athleticism leaps forth, because they transcended the normal tendency to be passive and actively joined in suffering together. What gallantry and honor! "I stand with my brothers and sisters here. If you insult them, you insult me!" Side-by-side, with arms locked, they chose to face persecution together.

"For you had compassion on those in prison" (v. 34a). That is, they literally had a "fellow-feeling" for or with those in prison. The same word is used in 4:15 of Christ's sympathy for us as our high priest! They lived out the later exhortation in Hebrews to "remember those who are in prison, as though in prison with them" (13:3). Even more, this was not *imagined* sympathy—it was *real*, because they visited their comrades in prison. In the first century prisoners had no means of survival apart from the visits of friends who brought food and water and clothing.[3] But such visiting placed one in grave danger. Yet they did it willingly—and in doing so some visited Christ who said, "For I was hungry and you gave me food, I was thirsty and you gave me drink . . . I was naked and you clothed me, I was sick and you visited me, I was in prison and you came to me" (Matthew 25:35, 36).

The writer continues, ". . . and you joyfully accepted the plundering of your property, since you knew that you yourselves had a better possession and an abiding one" (v. 34b). The human tendency is to hold on as hard as we can to what we have.

I once came across an ad that appealed to the desire of many to keep their household pets, which unfortunately do not have a lengthy life expectancy. The advertisement was for freeze-drying! According to the ad, most people who have their pets freeze-dried do so because they want to "keep their pets around a little longer." The process takes several months, and the pet will remain natural-looking for up to twenty years after being freeze-dried. The price for this service ranges from $400 for a small pet up to $1,400 for a pet the size of a golden retriever.[4] So, if your wish is to hang on to everything— even your dead dog—here's your chance!

But there is another way, the way of those in the early church who let go of their property—an amazing thing in itself, but even more amazing because they "joyfully accepted the plundering of [their] property." They found themselves exhilarated by the loss! Why? Because they knew they "had a better possession and an abiding one." They believed Jesus' words, "Do not lay up for yourselves treasures on earth, where moth and rust destroy and where thieves break in and steal, but lay up for yourselves treasures in heaven . . ." (Matthew 6:19, 20). They were "seek[ing] the city that is to come" (13:14)— "the heavenly Jerusalem" (12:22).

What an astounding remembrance the church was called to. They had experienced amazing spiritual athleticism in the oppression that took place during the springtime of their spiritual lives during the Claudian persecution. Now they are called upon to remember it, to call to mind the sequence of events and ponder their significance.

The reason for this is twofold. First, they will be challenged by their own past character. Second, they will be faced afresh with the power of God to sustain and deliver them.

This works! We may have *begun* well and now want to *end* well. If so, part of the secret is to *remember* well. We'll say more about this later, but first we must focus on what the text says about our present response.

Responding in the Present (vv. 35–39)

Respond in Confidence

The author's advice for responding to the present is to remain confident: "Therefore do not throw away your confidence, which has a great reward" (v. 35).

We have all heard of the famous high-wire aerialists the Flying Wallendas, and about the tragic death of their leader, the great Karl Wallenda, in 1978. Shortly after the great Wallenda fell to his death (traversing a seventy-five-foot high-wire in downtown San Juan, Puerto Rico), his wife, also an aerialist, discussed that fateful San Juan walk. She recalled: "All Karl thought about for three straight months prior to it was falling. It was the first time he'd ever thought about that, and it seemed to me that he put all his energies into not falling rather than walking the tightrope." Mrs. Wallenda added that her husband even went so far as to personally supervise the installation of the tightrope, making certain the guy wires were secure, "something he had never even thought of doing before."[5] Wallenda's loss of confidence portended and even contributed to his death, though his past performances gave him every reason to be confident.

Spiritually, no true Christian has to surrender to the "Wallenda factor" because our confidence rests not on ourselves but on God. The writer's charge to "not throw away your confidence" means not to cast away confident confession of Christ in the midst of opposition.[6] The positive corollary is to proclaim confidence in the midst of opposition—like Peter and John before the Sanhedrin (Acts 4:13) and Latimer before King Henry.

Respond in Perseverance

Next, one's confident response is to be followed by perseverance: "For you have need of endurance, so that when you have done the will of God you may receive what is promised" (v. 36).

I recall watching a high-school mile race in which one of the young runners took off like a shot out of a cannon and ran the first quarter in about fifty-four seconds, which positioned him about a hundred yards ahead of everyone else. He looked awesome. But predictably, he did not finish the race. What he needed was an *aggressive endurance*, a doggedness or steadfastness, as is recommended in our text. Such perseverance assures "what is promised"—that is, full salvation in Christ.[7] Perseverance does not earn salvation, but rather is prime facie evidence of saving grace.

Respond in Persevering Faith

The key to successful perseverance is faith. It is significant that in verses 37–39, as the preacher emphasizes the need of faith in order to persevere, he quotes from Habakkuk 2:3, 4—"For, 'Yet a little while, and the coming one will come and will not delay; but my righteous one shall live by faith, and if he shrinks back, my soul has no pleasure in him.' But we are not of those who shrink back and are destroyed, but of those who have faith and preserve their souls."

Originally God gave this exhortation to the prophet Habakkuk as the prophet repeatedly complained about the advances of injustice and the suffering of the righteous, God's bottom-line advice being that "the righteous shall live by his faith" (Habakkuk 2:4). "Live by faith, Habakkuk!" Later on in Habakkuk's writing, when the prophet had allowed this truth to sink in, he rose above his depression and complaint and sang this great song of faith: "Though the fig tree should not blossom, nor fruit be on the vines, the produce of the olive fail and the fields yield no food, the flock be cut off from the fold and there be no herd in the stalls, yet I will rejoice in the LORD; I will take joy in the God of my salvation" (Habakkuk 3:17, 18).

Here in Hebrews, though the quotation from Habakkuk is taken from the Septuagint's rearranged messianic rendering of the Hebrew text, the application is still the same—*the righteous will live by faith.* The meaning here in Hebrews is this: (1) Jesus is returning soon—"The coming one will come and will not delay" (v. 37); (2) the saved will persevere by faith—"But my righteous one shall live by faith" (v. 38a); (3) the lost will shrink back—"And if he shrinks back, my soul has no pleasure in him" (v. 38b).

Therefore, on the basis of this argument, we understand that the grand key for perseverance is *faith.* Knowing this, we are set up for the greatest exposition of the subject of faith found anywhere in Scripture—in chapter 11. But here we must also understand that Habakkuk's great song of faith is precisely what the young Hebrew church had experienced during the Claudian persecution when they "joyfully accepted the plundering of [their] property" (v. 34)—an experience very parallel to Habakkuk when he said that if there were no fruit or crops or flocks, "yet I will rejoice in the LORD; I will take joy in the God of my salvation. GOD, the Lord, is my strength; he makes my feet like the deer's; he makes me tread on my high places" (Habakkuk 3:18, 19).

Faith is everything. Paul quotes Habakkuk 2:4 in Romans 1:17 to explain that salvation is totally by faith: "For in it the righteousness of God is revealed from faith for faith, as it is written, 'The righteous shall live by faith.'" Here in Hebrews the writer quotes Habakkuk 2:4 to stress that the whole Christian life is to be lived by faith. It is *sola fide*, both for salvation and Christian living.

Think about that tiny storm-tossed church that had earlier triumphed in the Claudian persecution in AD 49 and is presently on the eve of the terrible Neronian persecution of AD 64. The writer has chastened them with a fiery warning (vv. 25–31) and now has sweetly encouraged them to do two things: (1) remember the past; (2) respond in the present with confidence and persevering faith.

The principles for enduring in triumph are universal and eternal. *Remembering* is the place to begin, as was shown to Israel after they crossed the Jordan. As all Israel stood gazing, the twelve select men solemnly descended the river's banks and approached the ark of the covenant in the middle of the empty riverbed. Then, kneeling at the priests' feet, each pried a large stone from the river bottom and began a reverent procession up the west bank and across the plain to Gilgal. To the symbol-oriented Israelites, the significance of the twelve stones was easily understood. They represented the twelve tribes of Israel and their deliverance from the river.

Arriving in Gilgal, the twelve men stacked the rocks into a small mound—a very unimpressive one, especially in comparison to the momentous event they commemorated. Having completed this, the twelve then each selected a stone from dry land and walked back to the ark, where they formed a duplicate mound on the riverbed. Then, for the first time in hours, the ark began to move as the weary priests who bore it slowly moved up the bank. When the last priest's foot crossed the edge, back roared the fabled Jordan, and a tumultuous cheer rolled across the great host of Israel.

The celebration in Gilgal must have been something to behold. The people rejoiced that the reproach of forty years of wandering was over. We can be sure that most of them danced and sang around their fires far into the night. Perhaps Joshua himself joined the dancing around the campfires, or perhaps he was too tired, but we can be sure of this—he returned to observe in the flickering light that mound of crude, unworked stones from the bottom of the Jordan.

God had done it! Again and again Joshua re-ran the mental tapes of that day through his mind. God was with him! God's power could do anything! Joshua's leadership was verified! He was God's man!

Joshua had much to think about as he viewed those stones, and he thought a lot about them over the years. Gilgal became the command headquarters for conquering the promised land. It was the place to which he frequently returned after victories, in the midst of battles, and after defeats such as that at Ai. Here he gathered wisdom and strength to go on, for here lay the stones of remembrance. It was much the same for the early church, and now for us.

We need to remember how God has helped us in the past. The writer to the Hebrews held up the church's stones of remembrance one by one. Each stone told them of two things—God's faithfulness, and the strength that had been theirs when they trusted him. All of us have such memories. We need to replay the tapes. It is a divine duty.

Finally, we need to respond in the present. Be confident! Do not succumb to the "Wallenda factor." Persevere in faith. Look back in faith. Look up in faith. "My righteous one," says God, "shall live by faith."

Now faith is the assurance of things hoped for, the con-viction of things not seen. For by it the people of old received their commendation. By faith we understand that the universe was created by the word of God, so that what is seen was not made out of things that are visible.

11:1–3

29

Faith Is . . .

HEBREWS 11:1–3

AS THE STORY GOES, a man despairing of life had climbed the railing of the Brooklyn Bridge and was about to leap into the river when a policeman caught him by the collar and pulled him back. The would-be suicide protested, "You don't understand how miserable I am and how hopeless my life is. Please let me jump."

The kindhearted officer reasoned with him and said, "I'll make this proposition to you. Take five minutes and give your reasons why life is hopeless and not worth living, and then I'll take five minutes and give my reasons why I think life is worth living, both for you and for me. If at the end of ten minutes you still feel like jumping from the bridge, I won't stop you."

The man took his five minutes, and the officer took his five minutes. Then they stood up, joined hands, and jumped off the bridge!

Gallows humor to be sure, but it is painfully parabolic of today's culture, which has abandoned its Christian roots for vacuous secularism. Indeed, if one factors God out of life's equation and adopts the view that we are little more than cosmic accidents, life, with its inevitable hardships and suffering, becomes hard to defend. In fact, suicide has been considered intellectually consistent, even stylish, by some existential intellectuals in recent years.

But for the Christian there is substantial reason for hope in this life and the life to come because of the promises of God's Word. In fact, 1 Peter 1:3 tells that we have been "born again to a living hope." The degree of our experience of hope is proportionate to the degree of our faith. The more profound our faith, the more profound our hope. A deeply intense faith spawns a deeply intense hope.

This was important to the writer of Hebrews because of the rising storm of persecution that was about to fall on the church. He knew that the key to survival was a solid faith and an attendant hope. That is why in 10:38 he quoted Habakkuk 2:4, "But my righteous one shall live by faith." There is a spiritual axiom implicit here: *faith* produces *hope*, and hope produces *perseverance*. Without faith one will inevitably shrink back.

This understood, the preacher launches into an eloquent song of faith that occupies the whole of chapter 11, beginning with a brief description of faith in verses 1–3 that is followed by a lyrical catalog of grand examples in verses 4–40. As we take up verses 1–3 and the theme of what "faith is," we must keep in mind that this is not an exhaustive definition, but rather a description of a faith that perseveres. We will consider faith under three headings: *Faith's Character*, v. 1; *Faith's Activism*, v. 2; and *Faith's Understanding*, v. 3.

Faith's Character (v. 1)

The character of faith is spelled out with great care in the famous lines of verse 1: "Now faith is the assurance of things hoped for, the conviction of things not seen." Faith's character is, in a word, *certitude*—a dynamic certainty about what God has promised. It is *not* a feeling, like the line from *Oklahoma*:

> O what a beautiful morning,
> O what a beautiful day.
> I've got a wonderful feeling,
> Everything's going my way!

It is not optimism or bootstrap positive thinking either. It is not a hunch. It is not sentimentality. An old song says, "You gotta have faith"—the sentiment being that if you somehow have faith in faith, you will be okay. And faith is not brainless. The cynical Ambrose Bierce wrongly described faith in his *Devil's Dictionary* as "belief without evidence in what is told by one who speaks without knowledge of things without parallel."

True faith is neither brainless nor a sentimental feeling. It is a solid conviction resting on God's words that makes the future present and the invisible seen. Faith has at its core a massive sense of certainty. The great Bishop Westcott says of verse 1, "The general scope of the statement is to indicate that the future and the unseen can be made real by faith."[1] What is the huge certainty of faith like?

Future Certitude

The first half of the verse expresses the future certitude that faith brings: "Now faith is the assurance of things hoped for." The word "assurance" is a translation of a single Greek noun—*hypostaseōs*, which literally means "That which stands under" or "foundation" and hence "substance." This word has appeared twice earlier in Hebrews where it was translated objectively ("nature") in 1:3 and subjectively ("confidence") in 3:14.[2]

The KJV here uses the objective translation: "Now faith is the substance of things hoped for." Likewise, the NEB says, "Faith gives substance to our hopes"—the idea being that faith grabs hold of what is hoped for, as something real and substantial. Along with the ESV, most other translations render the word subjectively—"the assurance" (RSV, ASV, NASB, NAB) or "the guarantee" (JB) or "being sure" (NIV). Actually the objective and subjective tenses of the word are not at odds because genuine faith does bring an assurance of what we hope for that is solid and substantive. The subjective certainty in our hearts has an objective solidity to it—*real certitude!* "Now faith is a solid sureness, a substantial certitude of what we hope for" (author's interpretive paraphrase).

The solid certainty is about the future—what we hope for. What are the things we hope for?

We hope for *Christ's return*—"waiting for our blessed hope, the appearing of the glory of our great God and Savior Jesus Christ" (Titus 2:13).

We hope for the *resurrection* because "according to his great mercy, he has caused us to be born again to a living hope through the resurrection of Jesus Christ from the dead" (1 Peter 1:3).

We hope for *glorification*—"but we know that when he appears we shall be like him, because we shall see him as he is. And everyone who thus hopes in him purifies himself as he is pure" (1 John 3:2, 3).

We hope to *reign* with him, for "if we endure, we will also reign with him" (2 Timothy 2:12). "And night will be no more. They will need no light of lamp or sun, for the Lord God will be their light, and they will reign forever and ever" (Revelation 22:5).

The believer's faith gives him such an inner certitude that the return of Christ, the resurrection, the glorification, a place in Heaven, and a coming reign all become present to him! As William Lane explains:

> Faith celebrates now the reality of the future blessings which make up the objective content of Christian hope. Faith gives to the objects of hope the force of present realities, and it enables the person of faith to enjoy the full certainty that in the future these realities will be experienced.[3]

Think of the staying power that comes to a life where, through faith, all the above are present realities! Church history illustrates this as it records that in the early days of persecution, a humble Christian was brought before the judges. He told them that nothing they could do could shake him because he believed that if he were true to God, God would be true to him. "Do you really think," asked the judge, "that the like of you will go to God and His glory?" "I do not think," said the man. "I *know*."[4]

Visual Certitude

The second half of verse 1 joins faith's future certitude to the parallel visual certitude that comes through faith, because faith means having "the conviction of things not seen." The KJV translates this, "the evidence of things not seen." These translations augment each other because the evidence by which a thing is proved brings conviction and certainty to the mind.

Our faith is the organ by which we are enabled to see the invisible order— and to see it with certainty, just as our eyes behold the physical world around us. What do we see? As we have mentioned, we see the future because it is made present to us through faith. But we also see more—namely, the invisible spiritual kingdom around us.

Genesis 28 records how Jacob, on that miserable night he fled from Esau into the wilderness, forlorn and alone, laid his weary head on a rock to sleep, and "he dreamed, and behold, there was a ladder set up on the earth, and the top of it reached to heaven. And behold, the angels of God were ascending and descending on it!" (Genesis 28:12). In a flash he saw what had been around him all the time—angelic commerce between Heaven and earth on his behalf! The account records, "Then Jacob awoke from his sleep and said, 'Surely the LORD is in this place, and I did not know it.' And he was afraid and said, 'How awesome is this place! This is none other than the house of God, and this is the gate of heaven'" (Genesis 28:16, 17). Jacob saw the unseen spiritual order, and that is what we see by faith.

> So to faith's enlightened sight
> All the mountain flamed with light.

There truly is an active spiritual order around us. If we could see it, it would change our lives! But we can see it, and we do see it! Faith brings visual certitude so that we have "the conviction of things not seen." I have never seen a flaming seraph or cherub or one of the lesser angels with my physical eyes. But I do see them every day through my eyes of faith. They are everywhere around me ministering to me and my family and my church—in fact, to all those who are God's elect children.

Faith brings a dynamic dual certitude to everyday life. First, there is *future certitude* as that which is to come becomes present to us. Second, there is a *visual certitude* as we see the invisible.

So here is the possibility we must consider if we are serious about following Christ: it is possible by faith to live in *future certitude*—to be present at Christ's return, to be present at our resurrection and glorification, to be present in Heaven, and to reign with him. It is also possible by faith to live in *visual certitude*—in the supernatural—to see all the mountain flaming with light—to see the traffic between Heaven and earth in our behalf. This is what our passage is calling us to, just as Abraham by faith put his stock in the future heavenly country, and just as Moses saw him who is invisible.

Faith's Activism (v. 2)

Having given us *faith's character* in verse 1, the writer now calls to mind *faith's activism* in verse 2: "For by it the people of old received their commendation." All the ancients in Israel who received divine commendation received it because of the character of their faith—their faith's *future certitude* as they were sure of what they hoped for—and their faith's *visual certitude* as they were certain of the invisible. This certitude produced a dynamic activism. Think of Shadrach, Meshach, and Abednego (alluded to in 11:34). They had nothing but God's word to rest on. They had no visible evidence that they would be delivered in this life. But they knew they would ultimately be delivered—they knew it so well that it was a present reality.

> Shadrach, Meshach, and Abednego answered and said to the king, "O Nebuchadnezzar, we have no need to answer you in this matter. If this be so, our God whom we serve is able to deliver us from the burning fiery furnace, and he will deliver us out of your hand, O king. But if not, be it known to you, O king, that we will not serve your gods or worship the golden image that you have set up." (Daniel 3:16–18)

There is no evidence that any of them had ever seen the invisible world at work around them, but they did see it by faith and were certain of it. Graciously, God did let them see it with their physical eyes when he delivered them. Remember Nebuchadnezzar's astonished words as he watched the trio in the flaming furnace:

> Then King Nebuchadnezzar was astonished and rose up in haste. He declared to his counselors, "Did we not cast three men bound into the fire?" They answered and said to the king, "True, O king." He answered and said, "But I see four men unbound, walking in the midst of the fire, and they are

not hurt; and the appearance of the fourth is like a son of the gods." (Daniel 3:24, 25)

The faith of the trio consisted simply in taking God at his word and living their lives accordingly. Things yet future, as far as their experience went, were *present* to their faith. Things unseen were *visible* to their individual eyes of faith.

And so it goes for every example in the great Hall of Faith of Hebrews 11—from Abel to Samuel to the unnamed heroes of the faith. And so it goes for us. By certain faith we will endure in blessed activism. And by certain faith we will receive God's commendation.

Faith's Understanding (v. 3)

Faith not only makes the future promises present and unveils the unseen—it also enlightens our understanding of the cosmos. "By faith," says the writer, "we understand that the universe was created by the word of God" (v. 3). As we have noted earlier in our studies of Hebrews, the universe is staggering in its size and glories. The nearest star in our very average galaxy, Alpha Centauri, is 25,000,000 miles away. Our glorious sun that fills our sky and lights our days is but a mere speck in our galaxy. The huge star Betelgeuse is 27,000,000 times larger than our sun. It would take fourteen 25,000,000-mile trips (the distance to Alpha Centauri) to travel the diameter of Betelgeuse. All that, and yet our galaxy is only one of a hundred thousand million other galaxies. The universe ought to cause us to praise God, as did the great astronomer Kepler, who constantly did so—especially when he discovered the third law of planetary motion and said, "I yield freely to the sacred frenzy; I dare frankly to confess that I have stolen the golden vessels of the Egyptians to build a tabernacle for my God far from the bounds of Egypt. If you pardon me, I shall rejoice; if you reproach me, I shall endure."[5]

But not all praise God. Many, in fact, employing the same scientific method, manage to deny the Creator. They are like the piano mice who lived all their lives in a large piano. The music of the instrument came to them in their "piano world," filling all the dark spaces with sound and harmony. At first the mice were impressed by it. They drew comfort and wonder from the thought that there was someone who made the music—though invisible to them—someone above, yet close to them. They loved to think of the Great Player whom they could not see.

Then one day a daring mouse climbed up part of the piano and returned very thoughtful. He had found out how the music was made. Wires were the secret—tightly stretched wires of graduated lengths that trembled and vibrated. They must revise all their old beliefs. None but the most conservative could any longer believe in the Unseen Player. Later another explorer carried the explanation further. Hammers were now the secret—great numbers of hammers dancing and leaping on the wires. This was a more complicated theory, but it all went to show that they lived in a purely mechanical and mathematical world. The Unseen Player came to be thought of as a myth, though the pianist continued to play.[6]

For the believer, those who know the Pianist, it is all so clear: "By faith we understand that the universe was created by the word of God, so that what is seen was not made out of things that are visible." We do not hold our breath to see if Stephen Hawking re-embraces the Big Bang theory. That theory is somewhat congenial to the Biblical account, but we do not need it. We know that God simply spoke the universe into existence: "By the word of the LORD the heavens were made, and by the breath of his mouth all their host. . . . For he spoke, and it came to be; he commanded, and it stood firm" (Psalm 33:6, 9). Moreover, he did it ex nihilo—out of nothing.[7] He did not have a rabbit, and he did not have a hat! By faith in God's Word we know for a certainty that every star was created by God—all 10,000,000,000,000,000,000,000, 000,000 (i.e., ten octillion)!

We smile, bemused at the story of the befuddled policeman joining hands with his depressed friend and jumping off the bridge. "Sure thing," we think, assuming such things do not happen. But that is exactly what so many ostensible believers do today as they uncritically imbibe the world's despair.

What is needed is a rebirth, or perhaps birth, of Hebrews 11 faith—the kind that is characterized by a dynamic twofold certainty: a *future certainty* that is so sure of what we hope for that it considers God's promises to be present—and a *visual certainty* that gives us "the conviction of things not seen." This is *certitude*—full belief in what we believe—bounding hope! Such a faith produces a dynamic activism such as that for which "the people of old received their commendation"—and a place in God's Hall of Faith. Finally, the certainty and activism of faith is crowned with a dynamic understanding of God's creatorship.

What is the benefit of all this? Certainly, the will to persevere. But also something else very important—the ability by God's grace to take the hand of the despairing and lead them away from the bridge to a life of certitude and love and life and understanding and action.

By faith Abel offered to God a more acceptable sacrifice than Cain, through which he was commended as righteous, God commending him by accepting his gifts. And through his faith, though he died, he still speaks.

11:4

30

Abel's Faith

HEBREWS 11:4

FIRST READ, without prior explanation, the story of Cain and Abel is mysterious and enigmatic. Adam and Eve had two sons: Cain, who went into agriculture—and Abel, who took up shepherding or animal husbandry. Both were religious men, and when it came time to worship each brought an offering appropriate to his profession—Abel from his flock, and Cain from his fields. But curiously, God favored Abel's sacrifice and rejected Cain's.

Cain, in turn, became angry. God warned him, "If you do well, will you not be accepted? And if you do not do well, sin is crouching at the door. Its desire is for you, but you must rule over it" (Genesis 4:7). But Cain nursed his rage and murdered Abel, whose blood cried out to God from the ground. The story ends in tragic closure: "Then Cain went away from the presence of the LORD and settled in the land of Nod, east of Eden" (Genesis 4:16). What a strange story, one thinks. What is the reasoning behind this primitive drama?

St. Augustine understood it and penetrated to its very core in his famous *City of God* when he explained: "Cain was the first-born, and he belonged to the city of men; after him was born Abel, who belonged to the city of God."[1] Augustine correctly saw that each was representative of radically different approaches to religion and to God. There was the way of Cain—a way of *unbelief* and of self-righteous, man-made religion. Jude 11 warns, "Woe to them! For they walked in the way of Cain." In contrast was the way of Abel—a way of *faith* described in the present text: "By faith Abel offered to God a more acceptable sacrifice than Cain, through which he was commended as righteous, God commending him by accepting his gifts. And through his faith, though he died, he still speaks" (11:4).

So the theme of this first example of faith in Hebrews 11 is a contrast of two cities, two streams—the two ways of faith and unbelief. As such, it provides unique insight into the anatomy of an authentic faith—a faith that endures. Abel's faith produced and was characterized by three things that are consecutively mentioned in verse 4: (1) authentic worship, (2) authentic righteousness, and (3) authentic witness.

By Faith: Authentic Worship

The authentic nature of Abel's worship is explicitly attributed to his faith in the opening sentence of our verse: "By faith Abel offered to God a more acceptable sacrifice [i.e., better worship] than Cain."

Approved through Obedience

To do a thing "by faith," you must do it in response to and according to a word from God. You hear God's word indicating his will, and "by faith" you respond in obedience. "Faith comes from hearing, and hearing through the word of Christ" (Romans 10:17).

From this we must understand that God evidently had given explicit instructions to Cain and Abel indicating that only animal sacrifices were acceptable. Very likely they learned this through their parents, Adam and Eve, because Genesis 3:21 indicates that after that couple's sin and fall, God provided garments of animals slain to clothe their nakedness—an implicit inference that animal blood was spilled in direct response to their sin. While it is true that the categories of ritual animal sacrifices were not established until Moses' time, the earliest believers nevertheless met at the altar on the basis of blood sacrifice (Genesis 8:20–22; 15:1–11).

Not only had God communicated his will regarding the necessity of animal sacrifices, but if, as we think, he communicated this first to Adam and Eve, then Cain and Abel had been conforming to the practice for some one hundred years, because Cain was 129 years old at this time![2] Moreover, Genesis 4:3 says, "In the course of time Cain brought . . . an offering," and "course of time" is literally "at the end of days" (Young's translation), indicating the end of a specific period of time—very possibly a time God had designated for regular sacrifice. Therefore, we surmise that both Cain and Abel had known God's word regarding the necessity of animal sacrifice ever since they were children and had obeyed it for years.

To this may be added the thought that Cain and Abel both understood the substitutionary atoning nature of the blood sacrifice because when God provided the skins to clothe their parents, he established the principle of covering sin through the shedding of blood. Abel's faith was an expression of his conscious need for atonement.[3]

But not so with Cain! He came his own way—"the way of Cain." By refusing to bring the prescribed offering, and instead presenting his garden produce, he was saying that one's own good works and character is enough. Cain may have reasoned, "What I am presenting is far more beautiful than a bloody animal. I myself would prefer the lovely fruits of a harvest any day. And I worked far harder than Abel to raise my offering. It took real toil and sweat. And it is even of greater market value! Enough of this animal sacrifice business, God. My way is far better!"

Cain's offering was a monument to pride and self-righteousness—"the way of Cain." Abel, on the other hand, believed and obeyed God: "By faith Abel offered to God a more acceptable sacrifice than Cain." He brought God what God wanted. This was acceptable worship.

Approved through Attitude

The other reason Abel's offering was accepted was his heart attitude. Cain's attitude puts it all in stark perspective. The Scriptures indicate that when God rejected Cain's offering, Cain became "very angry, and his face fell" (Genesis 4:5), thus revealing just how shallow his devotion was. And when God pleaded with Cain to desist and do what was right, warning him with powerful metaphorical language that sin was crouching like a monster at his door and desiring to have him (Genesis 4:6, 7), God's plea was met by ominous silence. Whereas Cain's mother had been talked into sin, Cain would not be talked out of it.

It seems that Cain was determined to stay angry. He liked being mad. And so it has been with Cain's children—like the famous author Henrik Ibsen, who was a specialist in anger, a man to whom anger was a kind of art form in itself. For example, when he wrote the ferocious play *Brand*, he recorded: "I had on my table a scorpion in an empty beer glass. From time to time the brute would ail. Then I would throw a piece of ripe fruit into it, on which it would cast itself in a rage and inject its poison into it. Then it was well again."[4] Cain too drew strength from his rage. The release of venom was his elixir. He would rather kill than turn to God's gentle pleadings and repent. So he directed his hatred for God at his brother Abel and killed him.

But Abel had come to God with a completely different spirit—a submissive, devoted heart. Abel brought some from "the firstborn of his flock and of their fat portions" (Genesis 4:4)—his best. This was in accord with the later directives of God's Word—for example, "Honor the Lord from your wealth, and from the first of all your produce" (Proverbs 3:9 NASB). God saw Abel's heart and was pleased with his motives, for "God loves a cheerful giver" (2 Corinthians 9:7).

How God desires devoted hearts in his worshipers! Jesus said that the time "is now here, when the true worshipers will worship the Father in spirit and truth, for the Father is seeking such people to worship him. God is spirit, and those who worship him must worship in spirit and truth" (John 4:23, 24). God longs for those who worship him with the complete devotion of their human spirits. In fact, nowhere in the entire corpus of Holy Scripture do we read of God's seeking anything else from a child of God. God desires sincere heart worship above all else! The psalmist recognized this and sang, "My heart is steadfast, O God! I will sing and make melody with all my being!" (Psalm 108:1)—saying in effect, "Everything in my human spirit shall be engaged in worshiping and praising you, O God." When the disciples harshly rebuked Mary for anointing Jesus' head and feet, he in turn rebuked them: "Leave her alone. . . . She has done a beautiful thing to me" (Mark 14:6).

It is very significant that this great chapter on faith begins with a worshiper—because worship is fundamental to everything else we do in life. As we shall see when we come to Abraham, everywhere he went, he built an altar. He knew that faith and service grow out of authentic worship.

So there we have it. The opening sentence of our text tells us that faith is essential to acceptable worship: "By faith Abel offered to God a more acceptable sacrifice than Cain." Why? First, because Abel's faith produced faithful *obedience* to God's expressed will and word. Cain did it his way, but Abel did it God's way. Abel brought God exactly what he asked for. Today if we would come to God we must come not with our own works, but rather with and through the sacrifice of Christ—the way of Christ, not "the way of Cain."

Second, we must come with the heart *attitude* with which Abel brought his "more acceptable sacrifice"—joyously giving his very best from his very first. This is what the Lord is looking for—followers who bring what he asks for with a joyous heart. This is approved, authentic worship, and it can only happen through faith!

By Faith: Authentic Righteousness

Having taught us that authentic *worship* comes through faith, the preacher in the next sentence shows that authentic *righteousness* also results from faith: "Through [his faith] he was commended as righteous, God commending him by accepting his gifts."

Just how God spoke well of (or attested) Abel's offerings is not indicated.

Jewish tradition and then Christian tradition have it that fire came down from Heaven and consumed Abel's offering but not Cain's. And Scriptures do record fire descending on acceptable offerings in at least five other instances (cf. Leviticus 9:23, 24; Judges 6:21; 13:19, 20; 1 Kings 18:30–39; 2 Chronicles 7:1). Such greats as St. Chrysostom, Thomas Aquinas, Martin Luther, John Owen, and Franz Delitzsch believe that fire did, indeed, descend on Abel's offering.[5]

And it is very likely—especially at this primal event. Perhaps it was memorably spectacular, like the experience of Manoah and his wife when fire fell from Heaven incinerating the sacrifice, and the angel of the Lord ascended in the flame! However it was, we do know that God spoke well of Abel's offerings and that on account of his faithful offerings he was "commended as righteous"—a right-living man. In fact, Jesus called him "righteous Abel" (Matthew 23:35). And St. John emphasized a life of love by contrasting Cain's evil actions with Abel's righteous actions (1 John 3:12). So Abel rightly has a huge reputation for righteous living.

Here's the connection: when there is authentic faith, which in turn authentically worships (obediently bringing to God what he asks for in joyful attitude), that faith will produce practical, living, authentic righteousness. James says essentially the same thing when he argues that faith and works are inseparable (cf. James 2:17, 18). True, living faith produces fruit—living action.

Faith and righteous works are like the wings of a bird. There can be no real life, no flight, with a single wing, whether works or faith. But when the two are pumping in concert, their owner soars through the heavens. Authentic faith produces an authentic life that flies high, like Abel of old.

By Faith: Authentic Witness

Now comes the final logic of Abel's faith: authentic faith produces an authentic witness—"And through his faith, though he died, he still speaks" (v. 4).

Among William Blake's most famous paintings is one depicting the murder of Abel. In the background lies Abel's muscular body, pale grey in death. In the foreground flees Cain. His body is moving away as he sprints by, but his torso is twisted back so that he faces the observer. His eyes are wide in terror, his mouth gaping in wrenching agony. And his hands are stopping up his ears in an attempt to shut out the wail of his brother's blood screaming from the ground. In Genesis we see Abel's blood crying for retribution! But here in the present text, it is Abel's illustrious example of faith that sweetly calls to us in profound witness—"And through his faith, though he died, he still speaks."

There is great power in example. St. Francis once called to one of his young monks, "Let's go down to the town to preach." The novice, delighted at being singled out to be the companion of Francis, quickly obeyed. They passed through the principal streets, turned down many of the byways and alleys, made their way out to some of the suburbs, and at length returned by a winding route to the monastery gate. As they approached it, the younger man reminded Francis of his original intention. "You have forgotten, Father," he said, "that we went down to the town to preach!" "My son," Francis replied, "we *have* preached. We were preaching while we were walking. We have been seen by many; our behaviour has been closely watched; it was thus that we preached our morning sermon. It is of no use, my son, to walk anywhere to preach unless we preach everywhere as we walk!"[6]

This could be genuinely said of Abel. Though none of his words have been preserved, he has been eloquently preaching for thousands and thousands of years about authentic faith.

And what does he say to us? First, that true faith spawns *authentic worship*—"By faith Abel offered to God a more acceptable sacrifice than Cain." It was "more acceptable" because it was *obedient* to God, giving him what he asked for. This tells us that we dare not bring anything to God until we bring the blood of Christ.

> Nothing in my hand I bring.
> Simply to the cross I cling.

It was "more acceptable" because it was presented with a *joyful attitude* of the heart—"And Abel also brought of the firstborn of his flock and of their fat portions" (Genesis 4:4). Faith produces authentic worship, which gives God what he wants with all one's heart. This is what God is looking for today.

Second, Abel's life witnesses to us that authentic faith produces a life of *authentic righteousness*—"Through [his faith] he was commended as righteous, God commending him by accepting his gifts." Abel walked his talk. His authentic faith produced authentic worship, which in turn produced authentic righteousness.

Third, Abel's life testifies that true faith's *worship* and *righteousness* produce an eternal *authentic witness*—"And through his faith, though he died, he still speaks."

This is what the world has always needed!

By faith Enoch was taken up so that he should not see death, and he was not found, because God had taken him. Now before he was taken he was commended as having pleased God. And without faith it is impossible to please him, for whoever would draw near to God must believe that he exists and that he rewards those who seek him.

11:5, 6

31

Enoch's Faith

HEBREWS 11:5, 6

ENOCH IS ONE of the truly mysterious figures in Scriptural history.

About Enoch

Enoch's Longevity

He was one of those long-lived antediluvians. That is, he lived before the deluge (Noah's great flood) and was early in the line of primal fathers who lived to incredible ages. Genesis 5:21–24 devotes only fifty-one words (in English) to describing Enoch:

> When Enoch had lived 65 years, he fathered Methuselah. Enoch walked with God after he fathered Methuselah 300 years and had other sons and daughters. Thus all the days of Enoch were 365 years. Enoch walked with God, and he was not, for God took him.

So we know that Enoch lived over three and a half centuries on this earth. This means that if Enoch's 365-year life span had ended in 1992, he would have been born in 1627—the year before Salem was founded by our Pilgrim fathers on Massachusetts Bay. That same year Francis Bacon published *New Atlantis* in London. On Enoch's hundredth birthday in 1727, young Jonathan Edwards would have been installed as assistant pastor to his grandfather, Solomon Stoddard, in Northampton, and the Danish explorer Vitus Bering would have discovered the strait between Asia and North America.

When Enoch celebrated his second century in 1827, Jedediah Smith blazed the first trail from Southern California to Fort Vancouver. And at the other end of the country, New Orleans would celebrate its first Mardi Gras when students from Paris introduced the Shrove Tuesday event.

In 1927, on his 300th birthday (the cake would have melted from the heat of the candles!), Charles Lindbergh would pilot the *Spirit of St. Louis* across the Atlantic to Paris, Babe Ruth would hit sixty home runs, and the first "talkie" (*The Jazz Singer* with Al Jolson) would be produced.[1]

And finally, in 1992, the whole world would know of his departure in one instant through satellite cable communication. Not only that, but Enoch's son, Methuselah, born when Enoch was sixty-five in 1692, would not die until the twenty-seventh century, AD 2661—at the ripe old age of 969 years (cf. Genesis 5:27).

The point of all this is that though Enoch's tenure was brief in comparison with that of his father and son, it is nonetheless an amazing stint of time—and those three-hundred-plus years were given to righteous living in the midst of a terribly evil antediluvian world that was destroyed precisely because of its depravity (cf. Genesis 6:11–13).

Not only that, but Enoch served as a prophet for over three centuries, preaching the unwelcome message of coming judgment. Jude 14, 15 records this, saying:

> Enoch, the seventh from Adam, prophesied, saying, "Behold, the Lord comes with ten thousands of his holy ones, to execute judgment on all and to convict all the ungodly of all their deeds of ungodliness that they have committed in such an ungodly way, and of all the harsh things that ungodly sinners have spoken against him."

Enoch was no wilting flower! His prophetic bloom remained fresh and full for three hundred years!

Enoch's Translation

Enoch was a man of immense age and character, but he is most famous for the incredible thing that happened to him, as described in the Genesis account: "Enoch walked with God, and he was not, for God took him" (Genesis 5:24). God translated him to be with himself without going through death. We know this because of the way Genesis 5 reads, with every one of the antediluvians' lives ending with the words, "and he died"—except for Enoch where it says, "and he was not, for God took him." This understanding is confirmed by Hebrews 11:5, which says, "By faith Enoch was taken up so that he should not see death, and he was not found, because God had taken him."

The Scriptures do not say exactly how this happened. Possibly God took Enoch up in a whirlwind as he did Elijah, the only other person in history who did not see death (cf. 2 Kings 2:1ff.). What a way to go!—like moving right up the whirling spiral of a Kansas tornado. Some ride! "Yeowww! Here I come, Lord!" Maybe he was just walking along, and *poof!*—he was no more. It is fun to speculate, but it is not speculation to say that "in a moment, in the twinkling of an eye" his perishable body put on an imperishable body (1 Corinthians 15:52, 53), because it is written that "flesh and blood cannot inherit the kingdom of God, nor does the perishable inherit the imperishable" (1 Corinthians 15:50).

We have already made some mention as to why Enoch was taken away— namely, the character of his life. Helpfully, Hebrews 11:5 is very explicit in exploring this, giving us two specific reasons he was taken. First, because of *his faith*—"By faith Enoch was taken up" (v. 5a). And second, because *he pleased God*—"Now before he was taken he was commended as having pleased God" (v. 5b).

Faith and pleasing God are opposite sides of the same coin, and it is profitable to examine each side.

Enoch's Walk

The fact that Enoch was taken because he "pleased God" refers to Enoch's walk with God, because 11:5 is based on the Septuagint for Genesis 5:24 (also in ESV: "Enoch walked with God"). "Walked with God" and "pleased God" mean the same thing.[2]

But the metaphor of walking more exactly reveals how Enoch pleased God. Walking with another person suggests a mutual agreement of soul, as the prophet Amos understood when he asked, "Do two walk together, unless they have agreed to meet?" (Amos 3:3). It is impossible to walk together unless there are several mutual agreements. To begin with, you must agree on the destination. Husbands and wives know that the paths to Bloomingdale's and Eddie Bauer are not the same! You cannot walk together and go to separate destinations. Enoch was heading in God's direction.

Of course, it is quite possible to be headed to the same destination but by separate paths. But again, two cannot walk together unless they have the same destination and follow the same path. This Enoch did with God!

There is one other requirement in walking together. Two must not only be traveling to the same *place* on the same *path*, but they must also go at the same *pace*. Enoch was in step with God. We too must "keep in step with the Spirit" (Galatians 5:25).

Enoch's great walk produced two wonderful things—fellowship and righteousness. When two walk toward the same *place* on the same *path* at the same *pace* for three hundred years, they are in fellowship! And this is the primary meaning of *walk*: fellowship, sacred communion.

Matching God stride for stride along the path of life while headed for the city of God also produced in Enoch a righteous walk. Malachi 2:6 describes such a walk: "True instruction was in his [Levi's] mouth, and unrighteousness was not found on his lips; he walked with Me in peace and uprightness, and he turned many back from iniquity" (NASB). Enoch walked in profound fellowship with God and had a profound righteousness. Thus, Enoch pleased God.

Warren Wiersbe writes,

> Enoch had been walking with God for so many years that his transfer to heaven was not even an interruption. Enoch had been practicing Colossians [chapter] three centuries before Paul wrote the words: ". . . keep seeking the things above. . . . Set your mind on the things above, not on the things that are on earth" (vv. 1, 2).[3]

It was little wonder that God took him!

Enoch's Faith

The other side of this coin, the primary side that so pleased God that he decided to take Enoch to Heaven, was *Enoch's faith*—"By faith Enoch was taken up so that he should not see death, and he was not found, because God had taken him" (11:5a). Though the Old Testament does not say Enoch had faith, the inspired author of Hebrews says that was his primary characteristic. Faith and a righteous walk with God are inseparably joined in the author's mind—just as he had observed about Abel in the previous verse: "By faith Abel offered to God a more acceptable sacrifice than Cain, through which he was commended as righteous" (11:4). The preacher is saying that *faith* precedes and produces the *walk* with God that so pleases him.

This understood, the way is now prepared for the great statement that the preacher has been leading up to: "And without faith it is impossible to please him [God]" (v. 6a). Notice that he does not say that "without faith it is *difficult* to please God," or "without faith you will have to work *extra-hard* to please God." He says categorically that it is *impossible*! This resonates with Paul's insistence that God cannot and will not be pleased apart from the righteousness that comes from God through faith (cf. Romans 3:21, 22; Philippians 3:9). Indeed, without this faith all are under the wrath of God (cf. Romans 1:17, 18; 2:5–8). Christians understand that "by grace you have been saved through faith. And this is not your own doing; it is the gift of God, not a result of works, so that no one may boast" (Ephesians 2:8, 9).

But the great emphasis here in 11:6 is on day-to-day practical faith, which is necessary for anyone, especially believers, in order to please God. In other words, if we are not living a life of faith, we cannot be pleasing to God. We *cannot* have God's smile on our lives without faith.

So the question we must pose, and which the text answers, is: what is the faith that pleases God like? The answer is twofold. It is a faith that believes, first, that *God "exists,"* and second, that he *"rewards"* those who diligently "seek him."

That He Exists (v. 6a)

"And without faith it is impossible to please him, for whoever would draw near to God must believe that he exists" (v. 6a). God's smile is only upon those who believe he exists! This involves three levels of belief.

The first level is simply that "he is"—as the Greek literally says. This is by no means a given in the modern day. The human race has descended from being pagan theists like the ancients to being modern pagan atheists. As Annie Dillard says, "We have drained the light from the boughs in the sacred grove and snuffed it in the high places and along the banks of sacred streams. We as a people have moved from pantheism to pan-atheism."[4]

In this, our modern culture does not even do as well as the demons, for there is not a demon in the universe who is an atheist (cf. James 2:19)! There are, no doubt, evil spirits of atheism, demons who have influenced and danced on the graves of atheists. But all demons are thoroughgoing monotheists, and Trinitarians to boot! So, believing "God is" is only the beginning.

But there is a second level of belief required to believe that "God is" (which comes from the fact that chapter 11 is a panoramic survey of the Old Testament)—and that is a belief in the great God of the Old Testament as the God who exists. We must believe in the Creator God of Genesis 1, who spoke creation into existence in symphonic sequence one note at a time until all creation stood in marvelous harmony—"when the morning stars sang together and all the sons of God shouted for joy" (Job 38:7).

We must believe in the personal Creator of Psalm 139 who knit us together in our mother's wombs (Psalm 139:13). As Job so beautifully celebrated, "Did you not pour me out like milk and curdle me like cheese? You clothed me with skin and flesh, and knit me together with bones and sinews. You have granted me life and steadfast love, and your care has preserved my spirit" (Job 10:10–12). We must believe that this personal God is!

Likewise, we must believe in the miracle-working God of the Old Testament. We must believe in the God who saved his people by rolling back the Red Sea as with a squeegee over a wet floor—who sent coveys of quail into Israel's camp so thick one could grab them from the air, and in the morning spread sweet manna like cake frosting on the ground—who parted the Jordan so that its bed ran dry down to the Dead Sea and who then brought down the walls of Jericho—and who surrounded his besieged servants with incendiary chariots chock-full of flaming angels. This kind of belief begins to activate the pleasure lines on the face of God.

But for us who live in the glow of the cross, there is a third level of belief incumbent upon us, and that is a belief in the massive God of the New Testament as revealed in Christ the Son. It is not a revelation of a greater God, but a greater revelation of God. "Long ago, at many times and in many ways, God spoke to our fathers by the prophets, but in these last days he has spoken to us by his Son" (1:1, 2). Jesus is God's final Word—his ultimate revelation.

Nowhere is this revelation made more clear than in Colossians 1:15–20, a great hymn to Christ.

Creator

The hymn celebrates Christ's being the Creator of everything: "For by him all things were created, in heaven and on earth, visible and invisible, whether thrones or dominions or rulers or authorities—all things were created through him and for him" (Colossians 1:16). In thinking about our solar system, we can glimpse the scale of things if we think of our sun as the size of an orange, which would make the earth the size of a grain of sand circling around the orange at thirty feet out. But within our galaxy would be one hundred thousand million oranges, each separated from its neighbor by a distance of a thousand miles. And there would be one hundred thousand million more galaxies like our own galaxy, each having one hundred thousand million oranges—and some of the oranges would be more than twenty-seven million times bigger than our orange.

Jesus made everything—"by him all things were created" (Colossians 1:16). Every crevice on every celestial "orange," every texture, every aroma, every shape, every size, every trajectory, every mite that crawls on or in each one—all were made by him.

Sustainer

Even more, he is not only Creator but Sustainer: "And he is before all things, and in him all things hold together" (Colossians 1:17). If one could travel at the speed of light for seventy-eight years to the Big Dipper's handle and the star Mizar, and then another 120 light-years along its handle to Alcaid, the handle's end, and then out past the Milky Way beyond the rim of our galaxy, our island universe, and then make a left turn and head off for a million light-years toward some black hole, and then come across a floating grain of stellar dust—it would all be held together by Christ, for "in him all things hold together." Similarly, if he spoke the word, everything would come apart in ultimate nihilism!

The Goal

And there is more, because Christ is also the goal of the universe: "All things were created through him and for him" (Colossians 1:16b). This is an astonishing statement. There is nothing like it anywhere else in Biblical literature. What is particularly dramatic is that "for him" has the sense of "toward him"—"all things have been created through him and *toward* him."[5] All creation is moving toward its goal in him. He is the Alpha and Omega, the beginning and the end, the first and the last. Everything in creation, history, and spiritual reality is moving toward him and for him.

The Lover of Our Souls

Lastly, he is the *lover of our souls*—"For in him all the fullness of God was pleased to dwell, and through him to reconcile to himself all things, whether on earth or in heaven, making peace by the blood of his cross" (Colossians 1:19, 20).

Our great God, Jesus Christ, reconciled us by his own blood on the cross! How could the Creator, sustainer, and goal of the universe do this? Why did he do this? Our minds become exhausted in contemplation of this, and we are driven to this explanation, for there can be no other: "For God so loved the world, that he gave his only Son, that whoever believes in him should not perish but have eternal life" (John 3:16). Christ loves us—and the cross is the measure of his love.

Now, if you truly believe that God is the Creator, sustainer, goal, and lover of your soul, then you believe in the God who is—who "exists"—and you are under his smile. He is grinning widely over you as you please him. Enoch believed that God is. To be sure, he didn't have the elegant charts of modern physics and astronomy at his disposal. But he believed in the awesome Creator and personal God of the Bible—he rested in that—and it changed his life.

We do not need any greater revelations or more grand and subtly nuanced doctrines. We simply need to believe what we believe. If we will *subjectively* begin to believe what we know to be *objectively* true—that he is the *Creator* of all creation—the *sustainer* of all—the *goal* of all, so that everything will be summed up in him—and that he is the *lover of our souls*—if we subjectively (on the inside) believe it, it will change our life. Do we truly believe?

That He Rewards (v. 6b)

Enoch's great faith, which led him to walk with God and please him, lies behind the final component of a faith that pleases God. Once we believe God exists, we must also believe "that he is a rewarder of them that diligently seek him" (KJV). Enoch was sure of this. It was implicit in his message of judgment:

> Behold, the Lord comes with ten thousands of his holy ones, to execute judgment on all and to convict all the ungodly of all their deeds of ungodliness that they have committed in such an ungodly way, and of all the harsh things that ungodly sinners have spoken against him. (Jude 14, 15)

This same God would also reward the godly. Enoch knew that God would be equitable to him.

Here is the great and grand point: Enoch lived in dark, hostile days that were uncongenial to his faith. Life was so inhospitable that finally, in the time of Noah:

> Now the earth was corrupt in God's sight, and the earth was filled with violence. And God saw the earth, and behold, it was corrupt, for all flesh had corrupted their way on the earth. And God said to Noah, "I have determined to make an end of all flesh, for the earth is filled with violence through them. Behold, I will destroy them with the earth." (Genesis 6:11–13)

However, Enoch resisted the sinful gravity of his culture and walked with God for over three hundred years! He set his goal on the city of God—God's *place*; so he walked the same *path*—striding in step with God's *pace*. Three hundred years of faithfulness!

Why was he able to do it? First, because he believed that God is, that "he exists" in all his creative and personal power. Second, because he believed that God "rewards" those who earnestly "seek him." Enoch was sure God would be equitable to him. As a result, there was great pleasure in Heaven—and God took him. Perhaps the stars echoed with God's joyous laughter.

The lesson was there for the early church, riding on the restless seas and moving toward persecution, and it is here for us: We can walk with God if we believe (1) that he exists, and (2) that he rewards those who earnestly seek him.

The question is, do we truly believe?

By faith Noah, being warned by God concerning events as yet unseen, in reverent fear constructed an ark for the saving of his household. By this he condemned the world and became an heir of the righteousness that comes by faith.

11:7

32

Noah's Faith

HEBREWS 11:7

RECENTLY *Time* magazine editor Lance Morrow penned some grim humor in expressing his despair at the world's ever deeper plunge into evil. Playing off the well-known persona of Willard Scott, the bright, cheerful weatherman of NBC's *Today Show,* he says:

I think there should be a Dark Willard.

In the network's studio in New York City, Dark Willard would recite the morning's evil report. The map of the world behind him would be a multicolored Mercator projection. Some parts of the earth, where the overnight good prevailed, would glow with a bright transparency. But much of the map would be speckled and blotched. Over Third World and First World, over cities and plains and miserable islands would be smudges of evil, ragged blights, storm systems of massacre or famine, murders, black snows. Here and there, a genocide, a true abyss.

"*Homo homini lupus,*" Dark Willard would remark. "That's Latin, guys. Man is a wolf to man."

Dark Willard would . . . add up the moral evils—the horrors accomplished overnight by man and woman. Anything new among the suffering Kurds? Among the Central American death squads? New hackings in South Africa? Updating on the father who set fire to his eight-year-old son? Or on those boys accused of shotgunning their parents in Beverly Hills to speed their inheritance of a $14 million estate? An anniversary: two years already since Tiananmen Square.

The only depravity uncharted might be cannibalism, a last frontier that fastidious man has mostly declined to explore. Evil is a different sort of gourmet.[1]

Here's the weather in your part of the country: acid rain is falling on Chicago today . . . tornado funnels expected over the western suburbs.

Dark Willard is right. The world is in bad shape. Most of it is dark, with a few mottled areas and some bright spots. Of course, this is because of what humans are—sinners who are tainted in every part of their persons with sin. Most are not as bad as they can be. But apart from God's grace, many have descended deep into darkness, though through God's grace there are yet bright spots in this world.

What a depressing job poor Willard has, we think. But it could be worse. Think how it would have been for a pre-diluvian Dark Willard! Except for one tiny point of light, the entire forecast would have been darkness. Remember God's assessment of Noah's days in Genesis 6—"The LORD saw that the wickedness of man was great in the earth, and that every intention of the thoughts of his heart was only evil continually" (Genesis 6:5). As bad as our world is today, this cannot yet be said of it. True, all humans are depraved and are naturally given to evil thoughts. But it is not true that "every intention" of the thoughts of every man and woman's heart are "only evil continually."

But this, indeed, was the pre-diluvian assessment and forecast. Every forming, every purposing of their thoughts (as the Hebrew suggests) was evil.[2] Moreover, the debasement was universal, as the account further describes: "Now the earth was corrupt in God's sight, and the earth was filled with violence. And God saw the earth, and behold, it was corrupt, for all flesh had corrupted their way on the earth" (Genesis 6:11, 12).

Dark Willard's pre-diluvian forecast would have been monotonously routine:

Darkness,
Darkness everywhere
And not
A light to spare.

Except for one minuscule pinpoint emanating from the wilds of Palestine.

Thus we read, "So the LORD said, 'I will blot out man whom I have created from the face of the land, man and animals and creeping things and birds of the heavens, for I am sorry that I have made them.' But Noah found favor in the eyes of the LORD" (Genesis 6:7, 8). Noah was the sole ray of light in a world gone dark! It is this singular man, and his great faith amidst the darkness of an unbelieving world, that we will now consider.

Faith's Certainty

Faith must have something to believe—and in this case it was a warning from God because our text tells us Noah was "warned by God concerning events as yet unseen." The primary unseen thing he was warned about was, of course, that the earth's population was going to be destroyed by a monstrous cataclysmic flood—judgment by water (cf. Genesis 6:17). Implicit in this was a second thing not seen and certainly never dreamed of—that God was going to deliver Noah and his family through a great ark that Noah himself was going to build. In fact, the Genesis account records God's explicit instructions: "This is how you are to make it: the length of the ark 300 cubits, its breadth 50 cubits, and its height 30 cubits" (Genesis 6:15). In terms we can visualize, it would be one and a half football fields long, about as wide as a football field, and about four stories high.

Now imagine how this all came down on this pre-diluvian farmer. The only floods he had ever seen, if indeed he had seen any,[3] were the wadi washers that came from an occasional thunderstorm. And he had certainly never set his eyes on anything as big as the ark, much less a ship! But he heard God's word, and he considered it (some respected scholars, such as the famous Bishop Westcott, think God's words were also heard by others)[4]—and after thinking for a moment *he alone believed* God!

As to what took place inside him, we are given clear instruction because here the phrase "warned by God concerning events as yet unseen" is meant to direct us back to the opening verse of the chapter: "Now faith is the assurance of things hoped for, the conviction of things not seen." Inwardly Noah came to possess *visual certitude*. He saw a terrible mountain of water come and cover the entire earth, destroying "all flesh in which is the breath of life" (Genesis 6:17). And he saw an immense ark of cypress wood, the work of his hands, riding high on the tempest.

This visual certitude was combined with a *future certitude*, for he had "the assurance of things hoped for"—namely, the promise of salvation for him and his family. Thus, a dynamic certainty swept over his soul. *He believed God.* He saw the unseen flood. For him the future promise of salvation was so real, it was present. And this great belief was combined with trust in God, so that he became a man of towering faith. Faith is always more than certainty of belief. Faith is belief plus trust. In an instant Noah entrusted everything to God.

Long ago, before the flood, the standard for faith was set in the midst of a midnight of unbelief. Faith hears God's word and believes with a profound certainty that makes the promise present so that the believer actually sees it and rests everything on God. Faith still requires that we believe God's word and rest our lives on it.

Faith's Obedience

The next great thing we see about Noah's faith is that it brought obedience—the obedience of faith—as evidenced when Noah began to build the ark: "By faith Noah, being warned by God concerning events as yet unseen, in reverent fear constructed an ark for the saving of his household." There on a broad expanse of dry land, presumably far from the ocean, somewhere in the Fertile Crescent, Noah began to lay the ship's great keel. Here the words of our text provide two beautiful insights into the nature of Noah's obedience.

Reverent Obedience

First, he obeys "in reverent fear," which I believe is better translated as "holy reverence," because fear does not fit Noah or the context in Genesis.[5] Noah obeys, not because he dreads the consequences of disobedience, but because of the sweet reverence he has for God. If there is any "fear" here, it is that of holy regard and devotional awe. Noah's obedience is built on a warm heart for God—not a servile fear, but a loving fear like that of a child who does not want to displease his father.

Noah's reverent obedience tells us that at the very heart of a life of obedience, there must be, and there always is, a holy reverence for God. We need to beware of obedience that is unemotional, that leaves our hearts beating at the same rate as before we believed. A reverent heart is a holy point of light in a dark world, for it is an obedient heart.

Practical Obedience

Understanding that faith's obedience is fueled by a reverent heart, we must next understand that obedience must always be practical. Noah got right down to doing what God had told him and "constructed an ark for the saving of his household." The Genesis account adds, "Noah did this; he did all that God commanded him" (Genesis 6:22; cf. 7:5). He followed the blueprints implicitly.

As Noah finished the incredible 450-foot keel and began to install some of the ark's ribs, we can imagine the abuse he took! How many "Noah jokes" and clever jibes do you think people could come up with in 120 years? Imagine the insults and taunts and amusement that came at the expense of Noah and his own. "How many of Noah's children does it take to . . . ?" But Noah maintained his practical obedience, doing exactly what God said, for 25 . . . 50 . . . 75 . . . 100 . . . 120 years—until the ark lay like a huge coffin on the land.

Faith always obeys! It obeys with a *reverential* heart in ways eminently *practical*. And true faith always acts! Bringing this down to where we live, we understand that there was no way Noah could truly believe that the flood was coming without doing what God told him to do to save his family. And, therefore, we must ask ourselves if *we* truly believe God's word—that he is coming in judgment—if we do nothing to bring salvation to those around us.

Faith's Witness

There is a beautiful sequence that emanates from true faith: faith involves certitude of *belief*, which produces *obedience*, which in turn produces *witness*. And this is precisely what Noah's faith did because his witness condemned the world—"By this he condemned the world," or as the NEB has it, "through his faith he put the whole world in the wrong." This he did by the witness of his *word* and *life*.

Word Witness

The Apostle Peter tells us that Noah was "a herald of righteousness" (2 Peter 2:5). This means that for 120 years while he labored on the ark, he preached to all who would listen. Perhaps sometimes he preached from the construction scaffolding to the curious "tire kickers" who came out to gawk. Other times, no doubt, he went on preaching missions throughout the countryside. His message was a call to faith in God, repentance, and righteous living. The ancient *Sibylline Oracles* imagined this passionate address from his lips:

> Faithless men, maddened by passion, do not forget the great things God has done; for the immortal all-provident Saviour knows all things, and he has commanded me to be a messenger to you, lest you be destroyed by your madness. Sober yourselves, cease from your evil practices and from murderous violence against each other, soaking the earth with human blood. Reverence, my fellow mortals, the supreme and unassailable Creator in heaven, the imperishable God who dwells on high. Call upon him, all of you (for he is good) to be merciful to you all. For this whole vast world of men will be destroyed with water and you will then utter cries of terror. Suddenly the elements will turn against you and the wrath of Almighty God will come upon you from heaven.[6]

Life Witness

So Noah faithfully preached righteousness for twelve decades—one long pastorate! But along with this was the witness of his life. His continual preparation of the ark was a constant visual witness that judgment was coming. But there was also the powerful witness of the way he lived his life, because Noah was a profoundly righteous man.

Francois Mauriac, in his novel *Viper's Tangle*, has his lead character, an alienated non-Christian named Louis, write to his religious self-righteous wife about how the witness of a righteous, pure boy awakened a sense of evil in his own heart:

> Your paraded principles, your assumptions, your airs of disgust, your pursed mouth would never have given me any consciousness of evil, such as was conveyed to me by that boy, all unknown to myself. It was not until long afterwards that I realised this.[7]

Such was the effect of Noah's life.

What a powerful witness Noah was in the *word* and the *life* he preached. Both eloquently condemned the world and put it in the wrong.

Some people were probably reproved by Noah's word and walk. Some may have even begun to long for righteousness. But, sadly, not one person responded in a century-plus of such consistent witness. In fact, the world became progressively darker.

The abiding lesson? True faith witnesses both by *word* and by *life*. But the results must be left to God.

Faith's Inheritance

Next, a faith like Noah's makes one heir to a grand inheritance, as our text indicates in its closing line: "By this he condemned the world and became an heir of the righteousness that comes by faith."

Objective Righteousness

This is the author of Hebrews' one and only use of "righteousness" in the objective, Pauline sense of righteousness that comes from God through faith. I like to call it an *alien* righteousness because "alien" stresses the fact that it does not come from man, but is an objective gift from God. The great Pauline texts often repeat the phrase "righteousness of God." For example:

> For I am not ashamed of the gospel, for it is the power of God for salvation to everyone who believes, to the Jew first and also to the Greek. For in it the *righteousness of God* is revealed from faith for faith, as it is written, "The righteous shall live by faith." (Romans 1:16, 17)

But now the *righteousness of God* has been manifested apart from the law, although the Law and the Prophets bear witness to it—the *righteous-*

ness of God through faith in Jesus Christ for all who believe. (Romans 3:21, 22)

Similarly, in Philippians 3:9 Paul expresses a desire that he might "be found in him, not having a righteousness of my own that comes from the law, but that which comes through faith in Christ, *the righteousness from God* that depends on faith."

The sublime result of receiving this "alien" righteousness is that we become *the righteousness of God*, as it says in 2 Corinthians 5:21—"For our sake he made him to be sin who knew no sin, so that in him we might become the righteousness of God."

The point we must see here is that this righteousness from God is necessary for salvation. Self-generated righteousness is never enough. Moreover, we can never earn salvation, for it comes by faith, as the verses cited above emphasize. Romans 1:17—"the righteousness of God is revealed from faith for faith." Romans 3:22—"The righteousness of God [comes] through faith in Jesus Christ." Philippians 3:9—"the righteousness from God that depends on faith."

The only way we can obtain this righteousness is by faith in Christ (*belief* that he died for our sins, plus *trust* in him alone for our salvation).

Subjective Righteousness

When we have true faith and receive the *objective* gift of righteousness and salvation from God, it enacts in us a growing *subjective* righteousness (a righteousness that grows from within). And this is precisely what happened to Noah, as Genesis 6:9 beautifully testifies: "Noah was a righteous man, blameless in his generation. Noah walked with God." He was "righteous" within. He was "blameless." He "walked with God" toward the same *place* on the same *path* at the same *pace*. He lived a beautiful life that pleased God.

Faith's Salvation

Noah was saved by faith—his faith led to his salvation. There came the day when the rain began—it continued for forty days without stopping—and the pre-diluvians began to think perhaps Noah was not so crazy. Noah got into the ark, and the jokes stopped for good as the water rose to the pre-diluvians' knees and over their still lips.

Just as God came to the pre-diluvians through Noah, he comes today to us post-diluvians through the words of his Son who says:

> For as were the days of Noah, so will be the coming of the Son of Man. For as in those days before the flood they were eating and drinking, marrying

and giving in marriage, until the day when Noah entered the ark, and they were unaware until the flood came and swept them all away, so will be the coming of the Son of Man. (Matthew 24:37–39)

Dark Willard's forecasts are not promising. The world is still very much as it was in the early 1960s when the Kingston Trio used to sing:

> They're rioting in Africa
> They're starving in Spain.
> There are hurricanes in Florida
> And Texas needs rain.
> The whole world is seething
> With unhappy souls.
> The French hate the Germans.
> The Germans hate the Poles.
> The Poles hate the Yugoslavs,
> South Africans hate the Dutch,
> And I don't like anybody very much.[8]

But in this dark world there is light wherever there is faith. The light comes from those who believe God's Word with such faith that they are sure of what they hope for (*future certitude*) and certain of what they do not see (*visual certitude*)—which together produce a *dynamic certitude* of faith.

Those who are granted this sure faith are also graced with the *objective* righteousness that comes from God and thus are granted a perfect standing before him. Objective righteousness, in turn, makes it possible to live in *subjective* righteousness—manifested in Noah-like obedience and witness.

This faith, of course, is a saving faith that will deliver the faithful from the judgment to come.

The truth has always been, and ever shall be, "my righteous one shall live by faith" (10:38; cf. Habakkuk 2:4).

How about you? How about me? Are we walking by faith?

By faith Abraham obeyed when he was called to go out to a place that he was to receive as an inheritance. And he went out, not knowing where he was going. By faith he went to live in the land of promise, as in a foreign land, living in tents with Isaac and Jacob, heirs with him of the same promise. For he was looking forward to the city that has foundations, whose designer and builder is God. By faith Sarah herself received power to conceive, even when she was past the age, since she considered him faithful who had promised. Therefore from one man, and him as good as dead, were born descendants as many as the stars of heaven and as many as the innumerable grains of sand by the seashore. These all died in faith, not having received the things promised, but having seen them and greeted them from afar, and having acknowledged that they were strangers and exiles on the earth. For people who speak thus make it clear that they are seeking a homeland. If they had been thinking of that land from which they had gone out, they would have had opportunity to return. But as it is, they desire a better country, that is, a heavenly one. Therefore God is not ashamed to be called their God, for he has prepared for them a city.

11:8–16

33

Abraham's Faith

HEBREWS 11:8–16

WITHOUT ANY DOUBT Abraham is the greatest example of faith in the Bible. Of course, others such as Enoch and Noah lived extraordinary lives of faith, but none are so closely chronicled as that of Abraham. And we do not find such detail about the inception, progress, and ultimate display of faith as is given regarding Abraham in his epic life as recorded in Genesis 12—25. His faith was so celebrated in Old Testament times that the Levitical prayer of confession extolled God and lauded Abraham's faith: "You are the LORD, the God who chose Abram and brought him out of Ur of the Chaldeans and gave him the name Abraham. You found his heart faithful before you. . . ." (Nehemiah 9:7, 8).

The New Testament likewise holds him up as the great example of faith and the father of all who truly believe: ". . . just as Abraham 'believed God, and it was counted to him as righteousness' . . . Know then that it is those of faith who are the sons of Abraham" (Galatians 3:6, 7; cf. Hebrews 2:16). James adds that because of Abraham's faith, Abraham was called "a friend of God" (James 2:23). Abraham is thus the undisputed paragon of faith. And so, because of the greatness of Abraham's faith, we have much to gain from his example, which is given extended coverage in Hebrews' great Hall of Faith.

Our knowledge of Abraham extends back to the nineteenth century BC. Scripture indicates he was a citizen of the city of Ur, located on the Euphrates River in what is today southern Iraq. Ur was already an ancient city in Abraham's time and boasted an elaborate system of writing, sophisticated mathematical calculations, educational facilities, and extensive business and religious records. The city was dominated by a massive three-staged Ziggurat built by Ur-Nammu during the beginning of the second millennium BC. Each stage was colored distinctively, with the top level bearing the silver one-roomed shrine of Nammu, the moon-god. The royal cemetery reveals that ritual burials were sealed with the horrors of human sacrifice.[1] So Ur, advanced as it was, was nevertheless in the bonds of darkest paganism. And Abraham, as an idolater (Joshua 24:2), was a part of its conventional social and religious structure.

We also know from Stephen's speech before the Sanhedrin that there in Ur of the Chaldeans, "The God of glory appeared" to Abraham, and that the Lord delivered this singular message: "Go out from your land and from your kindred and go into the land that I will show you" (Acts 7:2, 3). We know, too, what happened inside Abraham, because the universal pattern of faith, which introduces the discussion of faith in the opening verse of chapter 11, was activated in his heart. He believed God's word with a certainty so powerful that he regarded the future promise as virtually present. "Now faith is the assurance of things hoped for." He became so certain that God had called him and would lead him to a land where he would establish a great people that the future promise was transposed to the present. Philo of Alexandria said Abraham considered "things not present as beyond question already present by reason of the sure steadfastness of him that promised them."[2]

This *future certitude* was coupled with Abraham's *visual certitude* as he had "the conviction of things not seen"—that is, he saw God's promise fulfilled in his mind's eye. Thus Abraham experienced the characteristic *dynamic certitude* of real faith: "Now faith is the assurance of things hoped for, the conviction of things not seen." Certainty welled in Abraham's heart right there in the pagan city of Ur. Abraham believed God!

Faith and the Promised Land (vv. 8–10)

Having seen what happened *inside* Abraham when he heard God's promise about the land, we now note what happened on the *outside*—namely, he obeyed God. "By faith," reads verse 8, "Abraham obeyed when he was called to go out to a place that he was to receive as an inheritance. And he went out, not knowing where he was going."

Faith Obeys

It is important to note that Abraham's believing life began with an immediate act of obedience. Faith and obedience being inseparable in man's relation to God, Abraham would never have obeyed God's call if he had not truly taken God at his word. Abraham's obedience was thus an *outward* evidence of his *inward* faith. His obedience was so prompt that the Greek text presents

Abraham as setting out on his journey while the word of God was still ringing in his ears.[3] What is more, the text adds that "he went out, not knowing where he was going." It was not until later that his destination was revealed to be the land of Canaan.[4] There was a glorious element of abandon in Abraham's faith! And it cost. Martin Luther remarked:

> It was hard to leave his native land, which it is natural for us to love. Indeed, love for the fatherland is numbered among the greatest virtues of the heathen. Furthermore, it is hard to leave friends and their companionship, but most of all to leave relatives. . . . And then it is clear that with his obedience of faith Abraham gave a supreme example of an evangelical life, because he left everything and followed the Lord. Preferring the Word of God to everything and loving it above everything.[5]

Faith spawns reflexive steps of obedience. It steps out. We must not imagine that we have faith if we do not obey. Are we truly obeying God's word to us? Has he been calling us to a specific task or action, but we have passively ignored it? Where is our faith?

Faith Sojourns

Having shown that it was by faith that Abraham obeyed, setting out for the promised land, the writer adds that it was also by faith that he was able to be a sojourner in the promised land: "By faith he went to live in the land of promise, as in a foreign land, living in tents with Isaac and Jacob, heirs with him of the same promise" (v. 9). God had promised the land of Canaan to Abraham, but during his life (and the lives of his sons, Isaac and Jacob) God "gave him no inheritance . . . not even a foot's length" (Acts 7:5). The only land Abraham ever owned was Sarah's tomb, a cave in a field in Machpelah near Hebron, which he bought from Ephron the Hittite (Genesis 23).

To get a feel for what this was like, imagine God promising you and your descendants the land of Guatemala, and then in obedience traveling there and living the rest of your life in your camper, along with your sons' families in their campers, moving from place to place. You remain an alien for the remainder of your sojourn, without full citizenship rights, a perpetual outsider.

The word for Abraham's existence was *dissonance*—he never fit in. His religion was different and far above that of the land. He was a monotheist, and his neighbors were polytheistic pagans. His standards of morality were rooted in the character of God, while theirs came from the gods they themselves had created. His worldview invited repeated collisions with that of the inhabitants. He was always living in conscious dissonance.

What a lesson for us! The life of faith demands that we live in dissonance with the unbelieving world. A life of faith is not anti-cultural, but counter-cultural. Thus, a vibrant faith is always matched with a sense of dis-ease, a pervasive in-betweenness, a sense of being a camper. This does not mean, of course, that Abraham was separate from culture. To the contrary, the Genesis record reveals he was deeply involved in the politics of the land. But there was always that dissonance. He was never at home!

The parallels between Abraham's experience and that of the Christian are easy to see, because the Christian has the promise of an ultimate land. In fact, every believer is called to step out in faithful obedience and to follow Christ as he leads on to that land. All of us are, by faith, to obey and go as God directs, though we do not know where the path will take us. All of us are, by faith, to become willing sojourners, living in constant dissonance with the world as we await our final inheritance. It is a dangerous thing when a Christian begins to feel permanently settled in this world.

Have we stepped out in obedience to our individual call? Are we living in such a way in this world that there is the discomfort of dissonance?

Abraham *went out*, and Abraham *camped out*. But in his obedience and sojourn he was overall (with some famous exceptions) a patient "happy camper." Why? Because of his ultimate faith-perspective—"For he was looking forward to the city that has foundations, whose designer and builder is God" (v. 10). Literally the Greek reads, "For he was looking for the city which had the foundations"—the idea being that he was looking for the *only* city with enduring foundations.[6] There was simply no other!

This city was, and is, totally designed by God. "Builder," *demiourgos*, signifies the one who does the actual work. The city was designed in God's mind and built with his hands. The city "owes nothing to any inferior being" (Morris).[7] Significantly, it was a "*city*," a place that is intrinsically social. As Bishop Westcott observed, "The object of his desire was social and not personal only."[8] There he would not only see God, but he would dwell with believers in harmony rather than dissonance (cf. 12:22–24). No more camping! No more dis-ease. No more alienation. No more pilgrim life.

How much more our faith would be strengthened to step out and sojourn if we, like Abraham, would continue "looking forward to the city that has foundations, whose designer and builder is God." Soon the writer to the Hebrews will greatly expand this thought—much to our souls' benefit.

Faith and the Promised Son (vv. 11, 12)

Having explained how Abraham's faith worked in relation to the promise of the land, the writer now begins to explain Abraham's faith and the obtaining of a promised son:

> By faith Sarah herself received power to conceive, even when she was past the age, since she considered him faithful who had promised. Therefore from one man, and him as good as dead, were born descendants as many as the stars of heaven and as many as the innumerable grains of sand by the seashore. (vv. 11, 12)

Some other translations along with the ESV make Sarah and her faith the subject of verse 11—for example, the RSV: "By faith Sarah herself received power to conceive. . . ." But this is implausible because the phrase "received power to conceive" literally is "power for the deposition of seed/sperm" (*dynamin eis katabolen spermatos*), a patently male function. Thus Abraham has to be the subject of the sentence.

This is the view of nearly all contemporary New Testament scholars including F. F. Bruce, Leon Morris, and Simon Kistemaker. Most believe the misunderstanding is due to a wrong accent mark in the Greek that incorrectly renders "Sarah herself" as a nominative and not as dative. The corrective dative translation gives the right sense: "By faith he [Abraham] also, together with Sarah, received power to beget a child when he was past age, since he counted him faithful who had promised."[9]

The point is, it was biologically impossible for Abraham, as well as Sarah, to have children at the time the promise of a son was reaffirmed to them with the giving of the covenant of circumcision (Genesis 17). Abraham was ninety-nine years old, and his bride was ninety (cf. Genesis 17:1, 24)! Sarah's personal assessment was, "I am worn out, and my lord is old" (Genesis 18:12). The assertion that he was "as good as dead" (perfect passive participle) in verse 12 is exactly the same in the Greek as in Romans 4:19, where Paul said that Abraham "considered his own body, which was as good as dead (since he was about a hundred years old), or when he considered the barrenness of Sarah's womb."

Faith's Conception

Abraham knew the situation and that it was humanly impossible, but he came to faith. Some people are under the impression that when a person has faith, he inwardly agrees to ignore the facts. They see faith and facts as mutually exclusive. But faith without reason is *fideism*, and reason without faith is *rational-*

ism. In practice, there must be no reduction of faith to reason. And likewise, there must be no reduction of reason to faith. Biblical faith is a composite of the two. Abraham did not take an unreasonable leap of faith.

How did Abraham come to such a massive exercise of faith? He weighed the human impossibility of becoming a father against the divine impossibility of God being able to break his word and decided that since God is God, nothing is impossible. In other words, he believed that "[God] is, and that he is a rewarder of them that diligently seek him" (11:6 KJV). Thus he became certain that God would do what he said—dynamic certitude! He had *visual certitude* as he saw that promised baby boy in his mind's eye and *future certitude* as he saw it as present.

Faith's Optimism

George Sweeting, a past president of Moody Bible Institute, once gave this memorable definition of optimism: "Optimism is when an 85 year-old man marries a 35 year-old woman and moves into a 12-room house next to an elementary school!" But I have a better definition for him: Optimism is when a ninety-nine-year-old man and his ninety-year-old bride hear God say they are going to be parents and believe their offspring will fill, not a schoolhouse, but the whole earth—that they will be "as many as the stars of heaven and as many as the innumerable grains of sand by the seashore" (v. 12)!

We are not to indulge in *fideism*—faith without reason—or *rationalism*—reason without faith. We are to rationally assess all of life. We are to live reasonably. When we are aware that God's Word says thus-and-so, we are to rationally assess it. Does God's Word actually say that, or is it man's fallible interpretation? And if God's Word does indeed say it, we must then be supremely rational, weighing the human impossibility against the divine impossibility of God being able to break his word. And we must believe.

Faith to the End (vv. 13-16)

Finishing by Faith

The next section is introduced by the author's statement that Abraham, Sarah, and Isaac finished well. "These all," he says, "died in faith, not having received the things promised, but having seen them and greeted them from afar" (v. 13a). Death is the final test of faith, and they all passed with flying colors, living by faith right up to the last breath. The beauty of their dying was that they died in faith though never receiving the fullness of the universal blessing that had been promised. The reason they could do this was, they saw the unseen—they were certain of what they did not see. The patriarchs could see through the eye of faith the ultimate fulfillment of the promises, like sailors who become content they can see their final destination on the horizon. Land ahoy!

Along with this they recognized and accepted the dissonance of being a camper in this world—they "acknowledged that they were strangers and exiles on the earth" (v. 13b). They embraced the life of a pilgrim as the only proper way for them to live.

> This world is not my home
> I'm just a passing through
> My treasures are laid up
> Somewhere beyond the blue
> The angels beckon me
> From heaven's open door
> And I can't feel at home
> In this world anymore.

They died well because by faith they embraced the dissonance and saw the far-off fulfillment of the promise. This is how we, too, can die well.

Living by Faith

The subject of finishing by faith is rounded off by advice for living by faith— specifically by setting one's eyes on a heavenly country. "For people who speak thus," writes the author, "make it clear that they are seeking a homeland. If they had been thinking of that land from which they had gone out, they would have had opportunity to return. But as it is, they desire a better country, that is, a heavenly one" (vv. 14–16a).

When Abraham and his family admitted they were aliens, they were making it clear they were not in their home country. And so it might be supposed that they longed to go back. And if in fact their hearts were still in the old country, they could have returned. But they did not! The reason is, they had a "desire [for] a better country, that is, a heavenly one." And it is this spiritual longing that enabled them to persevere in faith.

May this example not be wasted on us! Paul tells us in Philippians that "our citizenship [*politeuma*] is in heaven" (Philippians 3:20). In Ephesians he says, "So then you are no longer strangers and aliens, but you are fellow citizens [*sumpolitai*] with the saints and members of the household of God" (Ephesians 2:19). We are supernaturalized citizens, and our citizenship is not only with one another, but is rooted in Heaven! Paul again alludes to this reality when he says:

If then you have been raised with Christ, seek the things that are above, where Christ is, seated at the right hand of God. Set your minds on things that are above, not on things that are on earth. For you have died, and your life is hidden with Christ in God. When Christ who is your life appears, then you also will appear with him in glory. (Colossians 3:1–4)

Being willing to do this greatly enables a life of faith!

And what will be the result? Our text beautifully answers, "Therefore God is not ashamed to be called their God, for he has prepared for them a city" (v. 16b). Because the patriarchs believed God's word with dynamic certitude—because when God called Abraham to leave Ur, he believed and obeyed—because aged Abraham believed God when he said he would be a father, "God is not ashamed to be called their God." In fact, God later proclaimed to Moses, "I am [present tense] . . . the God of Abraham, the God of Isaac, and the God of Jacob" (Exodus 3:6).

No higher tribute could be paid to any mortal. But God proudly claims whoever trusts and obeys him, and they can humbly insert their name in the divine proclamation, "I am the God of _____!"

Just after the turn of the century, pioneer missionary Henry C. Morrison was returning to New York after forty years in Africa. That same boat also bore home the wildly popular President Theodore Roosevelt. As they entered New York harbor, the President was greeted with a huge fanfare. Morrison felt rather dejected. After all, he had spent four decades in the Lord's service. But then a small voice came to Morrison, saying, "Henry . . . you're not home yet."

And was the voice ever right, for God had prepared a city far greater than the Big Apple for Henry Morrison. God says, "I am the God of Henry C. Morrison. And here, Henry, are the keys to the city!"

With faith, it *is* possible to please God!

By faith Abraham, when he was tested, offered up Isaac, and he who had received the promises was in the act of offering up his only son, of whom it was said, "Through Isaac shall your offspring be named." He considered that God was able even to raise him from the dead, from which, figuratively speaking, he did receive him back. By faith Isaac invoked future blessings on Jacob and Esau. By faith Jacob, when dying, blessed each of the sons of Joseph, bowing in worship over the head of his staff. By faith Joseph, at the end of his life, made mention of the exodus of the Israelites and gave directions concerning his bones.

11:17–22

34

Abraham's and the Patriarchs' Faith

HEBREWS 11:17–22

WHEN AGED ABRAHAM, just one year short of a century, was told by God that he must change Sarai's name to Sarah ("princess") because she was going to have a son and thus would become the mother of many nations, "Abraham fell on his face and laughed and said to himself, 'Shall a child be born to a man who is a hundred years old? Shall Sarah, who is ninety years old, bear a child?'" (Genesis 17:17). Abraham, of course, had earlier come to believe he would have an heir and innumerable offspring (cf. Genesis 15:4–6). But the assertion that two old nonagenarians (ninety-year-olds) would have a baby struck his funny bone, and, though properly prostrate before God, he could not help laughing. However, his incredulous laughter was only momentary, for when God explained that the birth would take place the following year, Abraham believed with all his heart, as 11:11 has made so clear: "By faith he [Abraham] also, together with Sarah, received power to beget a child when he was past age, since he counted him faithful who had promised" (literal translation).

A short time later when Sarah, listening at the door of their tent, overheard three mysterious guest-angels tell Abraham that about the same time next year they would be parents, the old princess inwardly chuckled.

So Sarah laughed to herself, saying, "After I am worn out, and my lord is old, shall I have pleasure?" The LORD said to Abraham, "Why did Sarah laugh and say, 'Shall I indeed bear a child, now that I am old?' Is anything too hard for the LORD? At the appointed time I will return to you, about this time next year, and Sarah shall have a son." But Sarah denied it, saying, "I did not laugh," for she was afraid. He said, "No, but you did laugh." (Genesis 18:12–15)

So the great prince and princess, the father and mother of all who believe, fell to incredulous laughter as a prelude to profound faith.

There is divine poetry here, because God had the last laugh (and a very gentle and joyous laugh it was), for God specified that the baby boy be called "Isaac," which means "he laughs" (cf. Genesis 17:19). And when Isaac was born, "Sarah said, 'God has made laughter for me; everyone who hears will laugh over me'" (Genesis 21:6). Sarah was ninety-one years old, and she had given birth to her *first* child! She laughed, Abraham laughed, laughter filled all the tents—and Heaven smiled!

Isaac's name was a sure prophecy of what he brought to life. The old couple would take baby Isaac in their age-spotted hands and hold him close before their wrinkled visages, and their eyes would light as the smile lines drew taut—they would chuckle—and baby Isaac would laugh. If there ever were doting parents, Abraham and Sarah were surely prime examples. The boy was everything to them—the amalgam of their bodies and souls, the miraculous fulfillment of prophecy, the hope of the world. Isaac's every move was lovingly chronicled—his first word, the first step, his likes and dislikes, his tendencies. And as he grew to boyhood and on toward manhood, Abraham and Sarah would see aspects of their younger selves in their son—perhaps Abraham's height and carriage and Sarah's stride and grace.

There can be no doubt that either parent would have died in an instant for Isaac. They were so utterly proud of their son—"laughter."

Abraham's Obedience (Genesis 22:1–18)

A Call to Obedience

Over the years Abraham had learned to respond to God's voice. So, Abraham's quick and courteous reflex to God's address in Genesis 22:1 is most natural: "After these things God tested Abraham and said to him, 'Abraham!' And he said, 'Here I am'"—the sense being, "at your service" or "ready."[1]

But the brightness in the old patriarch's response faded when he heard God's charge: "Take your son, your only son Isaac, whom you love, and go to the land of Moriah, and offer him there as a burnt offering on one of the mountains of which I shall tell you" (Genesis 22:2). Immediate horror fell on Abraham's soul, and revulsion repeatedly welled up in dark waves of emotional nausea. God was calling him to put Isaac to death with his own hand, and to then incinerate the remains as a burnt offering to God. This divine command was contrary to everything in Abraham—his common sense, his natural affections, his lifelong dream. He had no natural interest and no natural sympathy for this word from God. The only thing natural was his utter revulsion!

A Journey of Obedience

But Abraham knew God had spoken. So at the first gleam of dawn, without a word to poor old Sarah, Abraham saddled his donkey, quietly summoned two trusted servants, split wood for the sacrificial pyre, roused Isaac, and began the three-day journey to Moriah. Finally seeing the mountain in the distance, he bid his servants to stay with the donkey (he knew they would surely oppose him if they saw the plan unfold) and informed them that he and Isaac would "worship" and return (cf. Genesis 22:3–5).

Then Abraham and Isaac began their ascent of Mt. Moriah. Abraham placed the wood on his strapping young son and slipped the dagger into his belt. Thus lovable, talkative Isaac, happy to be alone with his father, and Abraham, preoccupied and wearier than he had ever felt, began the climb. "So they went both of them together. And Isaac said to his father Abraham, 'My father!'" (Genesis 22:6, 7a). Isaac used the patronymic "*Abi (Abba)*," which could well be translated, "Daddy" or "Dearest Father." "*Abi?*" "[Abraham] said, 'Here I am, my son.' He said, 'Behold, the fire and the wood, but where is the lamb for a burnt offering?' Abraham said, 'God will provide for himself the lamb for a burnt offering, my son.' So they went both of them together" (Genesis 22:7b, 8). Abraham felt older than any man who had ever lived. How he managed the ascent, only God knows!

A Sacrifice of Obedience

With leaden hands Abraham gathered stones and piled them into a rough altar and arranged the wood atop it. Then Abraham's whole existence began to play to the cadence of a heartbeat—the slow pumping music of his son's brief life. No one really knows how old Isaac was (tradition generally has regarded him as a grown man, though there is no proof). He could have been a teenager or an adult. I personally think he was young, which accounts for his apparent naiveté during the journey. However that may be, one thing is sure—Isaac must have cooperated with his ancient father because he could have certainly outrun Abraham or overpowered him if necessary.

When Abraham made his terrible intention known, Isaac began to shudder. Both wept aloud as Isaac submitted himself to be bound for slaughter upon the altar. Abraham's heart pounded, and he gasped for air. His wet eyes closed in darkness as he raised the blade to its apex and his fingers tightened for the plunge. But then Heaven spoke:

> But the angel of the LORD called to him from heaven and said, "Abraham, Abraham!" And he said, "Here I am." He said, "Do not lay your hand on the boy or do anything to him, for now I know that you fear God, seeing you have not withheld your son, your only son, from me." And Abraham lifted up his eyes and looked, and behold, behind him was a ram, caught in a thicket by his horns. And Abraham went and took the ram and offered it up as a burnt offering instead of his son. So Abraham called the name of that place, "The LORD will provide"; as it is said to this day, "On the mount of the LORD it shall be provided." (Genesis 22:11–14)

And then there was light and fire . . . And laughter rolled from the top of Moriah across the Promised Land!

Abraham's Faith (Hebrews 11:17–19)

Faith's "Sacrifice"

The story of Abraham's offering of Isaac is, of course, a story of towering faith. And the writer of Hebrews takes great pains to display the anatomy of such faithful obedience. "By faith," he says, "Abraham, when he was tested, offered up Isaac, and he who had received the promises was in the act of offering up his only son, of whom it was said, 'Through Isaac shall your offspring be named'" (vv. 17, 18).

The author states implicitly that Abraham's faith produced *immediate obedience* because the phrase "when he was tested, [he] offered" indicates that his obedience came at the same instant he heard the call to offer Isaac.[2] The Genesis account corroborates this when it says, "Abraham rose early in the morning, [and] saddled his donkey" (Genesis 22:3). He did not stall, and he did not procrastinate. There was no arguing with God, no bargaining, no equivocating. Abraham had learned well from the lessons of life—for example, his own wasted sojourn in Haran, or the unforgettable tragedy of Lot's wife. Therefore, his obedience was immediate and explicit. Though every fiber of his natural being rebelled against what God was calling him to do, though his feet felt like lead, he did not turn aside. What amazing faith!

Not only that, but he really did "sacrifice" Isaac. The Greek perfect tense is used when the text says that he "offered up Isaac "—and the perfect tense refers to a completed action in past time. This means that the *sacrifice actually took place* as far as Abraham's resolve and obedience were concerned. From the divine perspective, as well as from Abraham's perspective, Abraham did it! But immediately the *same* verb is used in the imperfect tense in the following statement—he "was in the act of offering up his only son"—indicating that it did not physically happen.[3] The point is, in terms of obedience to God, Abraham did it. He completely offered his beloved Isaac, the laughter and joy of his life.

Faith's Reasoning

How was Abraham able to do this? Our text gives the memorable answer, "He considered that God was able even to raise him from the dead, from which, figuratively speaking, he did receive him back" (v. 19). The word for "considered" is *logisamenos*, from which we get the word *logarithm*. It means "to calculate or compute." The idea is that Abraham used his stores of logic to reason the situation out. He didn't indulge in *fideism*—faith without reason, blind faith. He was eminently logical—almost mathematical—in his reasoning.[4]

And his logic was audacious. God had said that Abraham would have children as numerous as the stars and the sand—and Abraham believed God (Genesis 15:5, 6). God had said that through Isaac the great covenant and blessing would come—and Abraham believed God even though his body was "as good as dead" (11:12; cf. 11:1; Genesis 17:15–22; Romans 4:18–21). Abraham knew Isaac had come through a miraculous prophetic fulfillment of God's word. He also knew Isaac had no children and, in fact, was not even married. Yet God had clearly told him to sacrifice Isaac. There was no mistake or misunderstanding. Therefore, Isaac was as good as dead! And from Abraham's perspective it was now God's problem, for God's word through Isaac had to be fulfilled. Abraham's breathtaking logic was: God could and would raise the dead. There had never been a resurrection, but he knew God *had* to bring Isaac back to life. There was no other way. God would keep his word! "Stay here with the donkey," he told his servants, "*I and the boy* will go over there and worship and come again to you" (Genesis 22:5).

Think of this in the context of the categories Hebrews 11 supplies. Abraham's faith rested upon *the greatness of God*. He believed that God "exists and that he rewards those who seek him" (11:6). Abraham's faith also was grounded on *the creative power of God*. By faith he understood that "the universe was created by the word of God, so that what is seen was not made out of things that are visible" (11:3). He knew that God could bring forth the living out of nothing. In fact, his body had been "as good as dead" when he fathered Isaac (11:12). Abraham's faith was characterized with the *dynamic certitude* of verse 1: "Now faith is the assurance of things hoped for, the conviction of things not seen." So certain was he of God's promise through Isaac that he saw it as present!

What astounding faith! No wonder he is the father of all who believe. No wonder he is called the friend of God.

Some of us may be thinking, "But this is so far beyond me. How could I ever rise to such great heights of faith? Abraham is one-of-a-kind—*sui generis*. Men like him only come along every one or two millennia!" But we must understand that Abraham's great faith did not begin with the offering of Isaac. Certainly he did begin in faith (as all spiritual life must) when he stepped out from Ur and began his sojourn. And it was a great act of faith to believe God's promise that he and Sarah would be parents when they were both "as good as dead."

But we must also remember the down times in Abraham's life, his lapses of faith—for example, the occasions on which he lied to save his own skin, saying Sarah was his sister (Genesis 12:13; 20:11–13) or when, impatient for an heir, he and Sarah took matters into their own hands and engaged Hagar to become the mother of Ishmael (Genesis 16:1–15).

We must understand that it was through ups and downs that Abraham grew in faith—until he became capable of the ultimate display. The Spanish philosopher Miguel de Unamuno wrote these perceptive words: "Those who believe that they believe in God, but without passion in their hearts, without anguish in mind, without uncertainty, without doubt, without an element of despair even in their consolation, believe only in the God idea, not God Himself."[5] We must understand, then, that "faith" that never doubts is a dead faith because it is never exercised. As believers, we are sinners who have trusted in God, notwithstanding our sin and weakness, and we are called to ascend to a dynamic certitude that profoundly believes and obeys God's word, as did Abraham. But the road to strong faith is never smooth. Faith will be tested. Inevitably there will be times of uncertainty and doubt and even despair. But the soul that clings to God will experience growth and notable triumphs of faith.

Abraham's Legacy (vv. 20–22)

When Abraham died, he was succeeded by patriarchs who were nevertheless similarly imperfect men—Isaac, Jacob, and Joseph. But what impresses the writer of Hebrews is that when they came to what they considered to be their final hour, they had a faith that looked beyond death—they were sure of what they hoped for and certain of what they did not see (cf. 11:1). They all were convinced that death would not frustrate God's purposes—that his word would be fulfilled.

Isaac's Faith

"By faith," says the preacher, "Isaac invoked future blessings on Jacob and Esau" (v. 20). Actually, when he pronounced the blessing, Isaac meant to give the blessing of the firstborn to Esau, but he was deceived (Genesis 27). Nevertheless, after the blessing was given to Jacob, Isaac knew that it was binding and would not fail. In fact, he later blessed Jacob with full knowledge of what he was doing (cf. Genesis 27:33; 28:1–4). The main thing is that by faith Isaac knew his blessing would be perfectly fulfilled in the future.

Jacob's Faith

Next the author says, "By faith Jacob, when dying, blessed each of the sons of Joseph, bowing in worship over the head of his staff" (v. 21). Aged Jacob, leaning on his staff, had Joseph bring his sons to be blessed. The older Manasseh was placed by his right hand in order to receive the greater blessing, and the younger Ephraim on his left. But Jacob, responding to the direction of God, crossed his hands, reversing the blessings (Genesis 48:17–20). Thus, by faith in God's word he was sure about the future even though it was contrary to human convention. Nothing, he was convinced, would thwart God's purposes. And, indeed, in the course of time the tribe of Ephraim became a leader in Israel.

Joseph's Faith

The last patriarch mentioned here, Joseph, was sure nothing would annul God's promise that Israel would one day possess the land. "By faith Joseph, at the end of his life, made mention of the exodus of the Israelites and gave directions concerning his bones" (v. 22). This is remarkable because he had left Canaan when he was seventeen (Genesis 37:2) and lived in Egypt until his death at the age of 110 (Genesis 50:26). But in fulfillment of his faith's directive, Joseph's mummy was carried out of Egypt by Moses (Exodus 13:19) and later was buried in Shechem by Joshua when he conquered the land (Joshua 24:32). The overall point is that all these patriarchs ended well, for they had learned to trust God's bare word. They were sure regarding what would happen after their deaths.

But Abraham is the transcending example. When he raised his trembling hand above the shuddering body of his son, it was because he had learned the logic of faith: first, that God's word never fails, and second, that it must be obeyed at all costs. So the questions for us are:

Does God's Word Say It?

Not does the pastor say it, or does the committee say it. Rather, is it the clear teaching of God's Word—the Scriptures? And, as a point of fact, most of God's Word is very clear as to what it means. As Mark Twain said, it is not what we do not understand about God's Word that troubles us; it is what we do understand! While there are some inscrutable passages in the Bible, most of it is perfectly clear. The perspicacity of Scripture was one of the great principles of the Reformation. So we can, and must, ascertain what God's Word says.

Do We Believe It?

Do we believe what God's Word says about Jesus? "In the beginning was the Word, and the Word was with God, and the Word was God. He was in the beginning with God. All things were made through him, and without him was not any thing made that was made" (John 1:1–3).

Do we believe what it says about salvation? "Jesus said to him, 'I am the way, and the truth, and the life. No one comes to the Father except through me'" (John 14:6).

Do we believe what it says about judgment? "Then I saw a great white throne and him who was seated on it. From his presence earth and sky fled away, and no place was found for them. And I saw the dead, great and small, standing before the throne, and books were opened. Then another book was opened, which is the book of life. And the dead were judged by what was written in the books, according to what they had done. And the sea gave up the dead who were in it, Death and Hades gave up the dead who were in them, and they were judged, each one of them, according to what they had done. Then Death and Hades were thrown into the lake of fire. This is the second death, the lake of fire. And if anyone's name was not found written in the book of life, he was thrown into the lake of fire" (Revelation 20:11–15).

Do we believe what it says about riches? Jesus said, "Do not lay up for yourselves treasures on earth, where moth and rust destroy and where thieves break in and steal, but lay up for yourselves treasures in heaven, where neither moth nor rust destroys and where thieves do not break in and steal. For where your treasure is, there your heart will be also" (Matthew 6:19–21).

Do we believe what it says about purity? "For this is the will of God, your sanctification: that you abstain from sexual immorality; that each one of you know how to control his own body in holiness and honor, not in the passion of lust like the Gentiles who do not know God; that no one transgress and wrong his brother in this matter, because the Lord is an avenger in all these things, as we told you beforehand and solemnly warned you" (1 Thessalonians 4:3–6).

And finally, do we obey God's Word?

By faith Moses, when he was born, was hidden for three months by his parents, because they saw that the child was beautiful, and they were not afraid of the king's edict. By faith Moses, when he was grown up, refused to be called the son of Pharaoh's daughter, choosing rather to be mistreated with the people of God than to enjoy the fleeting pleasures of sin. He considered the reproach of Christ greater wealth than the treasures of Egypt, for he was looking to the reward. By faith he left Egypt, not being afraid of the anger of the king, for he endured as seeing him who is invisible. By faith he kept the Passover and sprinkled the blood, so that the Destroyer of the firstborn might not touch them. By faith the people crossed the Red Sea as on dry land, but the Egyptians, when they attempted to do the same, were drowned.

11:23–29

35

Moses' Faith

HEBREWS 11:23-29

THE BOOK OF DEUTERONOMY ends with Moses' unparalleled epitaph:

> And there has not arisen a prophet since in Israel like Moses, whom the
> LORD knew face to face, none like him for all the signs and the wonders
> that the LORD sent him to do in the land of Egypt, to Pharaoh and to all
> his servants and to all his land, and for all the mighty power and all the
> great deeds of terror that Moses did in the sight of all Israel. (Deuteronomy
> 34:10–12)

To all Jews, Moses was the greatest of all men. According to one early tradition, Moses had higher rank and privilege than the ministering angels.[1]

He was Israel's greatest *prophet*. God communicated directly to him and
testified regarding their relationship:

> If there is a prophet among you, I the LORD make myself known to him in a
> vision; I speak with him in a dream. Not so with my servant Moses. He is
> faithful in all my house. With him I speak mouth to mouth, clearly, and not
> in riddles, and he beholds the form of the LORD. (Numbers 12:6–8)

This is why his face was luminous when he descended Mt. Sinai with the Ten
Commandments.

He was Israel's greatest *lawgiver*. Virtually everything in their religion
recalled his name.

He was Israel's great *historian*. Moses authored everything from Genesis
to Deuteronomy.

He was considered Israel's greatest *saint*, for Scripture says he was "very
meek, more than all people who were on the face of the earth" (Numbers

12:3). This is perhaps most amazing of all because often those who have accomplished great things are anything but humble. But Moses was the humblest of the entire human race!

He was Israel's greatest *deliverer.* His feats are wonderfully chronicled throughout the book of Exodus.

Significantly, in regard to Moses' deliverance of Israel from Egypt, his liberating work was a huge act of faith from beginning to end. And this is what the author of Hebrews focuses on in verses 23–29 in the great Hall of Faith. Here we have the anatomy of a faith that delivers others and sets them free. This insightful teaching had special relevance to the ancient church suffering in its own inhospitable "exile" in the Roman Empire. Certainly this section has direct relevance for every believing soul who senses any dissonance with the unbelieving world.

Moses' faith is conveniently explained under five brief sections, each successively introduced with "By faith."

By Faith: Moses' Preservation (v. 23)

The initial faith we are shown is not Moses' faith, but the heroic faith of his parents: "By faith Moses, when he was born, was hidden for three months by his parents, because they saw that the child was beautiful, and they were not afraid of the king's edict" (v. 23). Both parents were from the tribe of Levi (cf. Exodus 2:1), and Exodus 6:20 tells us that their names were Amram and Jochebed and that they also had another son—Aaron, who would be high priest. They also had a daughter—Miriam, the prophetess.

The couple's marriage came at a dark time for Israel—when the oppression of the Egyptians had become utterly diabolical. First, Pharaoh had commanded the Hebrew midwives to murder all males immediately upon birth. When that plan failed, his command became more crude and effective—all newborn baby boys were to be tossed into the Nile as food for the crocodiles (cf. Exodus 1:15–22).

Nevertheless, Jochebed conceived. Interestingly, Josephus says the pregnancy was accomplished by Amram's obedience to a vision in which God told him he would have a son who would deliver his people. Says Josephus:

> These things revealed to him in vision, Amram on awaking disclosed to Jochabel(e), his wife; and their fears were only the more intensified by the prediction in the dream. For it was not merely for a child that they were anxious, but for that high felicity for which he was destined.[2]

Josephus' account is not inspired revelation, though some respected commentators believe something like this may have led to their faith.[3]

However that may be, when baby Moses came, his parents' faith was in full force: "By faith Moses, when he was born, was hidden for three months by his parents, because they saw that the child was beautiful." This seems an odd reason, especially in the light of universal parental experience. All my children were "beautiful" and extraordinary—and so were all yours! Right? Amram and Jochebed had nothing on us!

Obviously, there was something about him that was more than beautiful. Possibly there was something unique about his presence that confirmed God's word. John Calvin wisely remarked:

> It seems contrary to the nature of faith that he says that they were induced to do this by the beauty of his form. We know that Jesse was rebuked when he brought his sons to Samuel in the order of their physical excellence, and certainly God does not hold us to external appearances. I reply that the parents of Moses were not induced by his beauty to be touched with pity and save him as men are commonly affected, but there was some sort of mark of excellence to come, engraved on the boy which gave promise of something out of the ordinary for him.[4]

The point is, the parents were so encouraged in their faith by the extraordinary nature of their child that they hid him for three months. And then, when it became impossible to conceal his presence, they came up with a creative plan that floated him right into Pharaoh's palace! Jochebed took a papyrus basket, coated it with pitch, put her beautiful baby in it, placed it in the reeds where Pharaoh's daughter bathed, and set big sister Miriam there to watch.

Baby Moses, of course, melted the heart of Pharaoh's daughter. And as she cooed over him, up popped big sister with the brilliant suggestion of a surrogate nurse. Result: Jochebed got paid to nurse her own baby and to raise him during his early years!

So Moses was preserved by his parents' heroic faith. But there is more, for he was also nurtured by their faith. There in the slave hut of his parents Moses was surrounded by the pure atmosphere of faith. There he became aware of his own origins. There he was taught to fear God. And there he was made conscious of his call to deliver his people. Stephen informs us in his great sermon (Acts 7:25) that when Moses made his first attempt to defend his people, "[Moses] supposed that his brothers would understand that God was giving them salvation by his hand."

What encouragement there is here for any who are attempting to try to raise a godly family in today's secular desert. Moses was preserved by his parents' faith. Their faith, their prayers, their bravery, and their creativity saved him. And more, he became a great man of faith through their faith. His experience was exactly that of the preacher who gave his mother the tribute, "My mother practices what I preach!" Moses preached and practiced the faith he saw at home as a child. Those of us who are parents and grandparents and aunts and uncles and teachers not only have great power, but also immense responsibility to the children in our lives. Israel's deliverance began with an obscure couple believing God in the midst of darkness. Think what a faith like that could accomplish today!

By Faith: Moses' Identification (vv. 24–26)

There is a time lapse of some forty years between verse 23 and the second "by faith," which covers verses 24–26. Here we see how Moses identified with his people by faith.

His identification began with a *negative choice*: "By faith Moses, when he was grown up, refused to be called the son of Pharaoh's daughter" (v. 24). Moses was known by the royal designation "son of Pharaoh's daughter"—a title of self-conscious dignity that is emphasized here in the Greek by the absence of definite articles.[5] A modern equivalent might be Duke of York.

To be such during Egypt's Nineteenth Dynasty would have meant immense prestige and wealth. Any pleasure that the oriental or occidental mind could conceive of was his for the asking. Such privilege could be personally deluding, as Boris Pasternak observed of the Russian aristocracy in *Dr. Zhivago* when the doctor remarked that wealth "could itself create an illusion of genuine character and originality."[6] But Moses suffered no such delusions. He was a mature man—an adult. And as such, he publicly refused the title—thus committing a grievous and dangerous insult to Pharaoh. Faith is courageous!

True faith will announce its discord whenever God and conscience call for it. Believers can love their culture, and there is much to love in most cultures, but they will refuse to be identified with the godless zeitgeist or spirit of the age.

Moses' negation was, of course, also motivated by a *positive act of his will*: "[He chose] rather to be mistreated with the people of God than to enjoy the fleeting pleasures of sin" (v. 25). Moses' sin, had he remained part of the Egyptian system, would have been apostasy—for he would have had to abandon the truth. There is no doubt that the pleasures of sin in Egypt were substantial. But like all physical pleasures, they were only pleasurable for a moment. The pleasures of sin are like a Chinese dinner. No matter how much you eat, you are hungry again in a couple of hours!

So rather than embracing Egypt's evanescent pleasures, Moses consciously chose "to be mistreated with the people of God." Moses believed that Israel stood in unique relationship with the living God and had a unique role to play in world history. Moses chose the most exciting path he could possibly take. To him, life in the brilliance of the Egyptian court was a dull, ignoble thing when compared with the society of mistreated Israel.

Christians, likewise, must absorb Moses' wisdom because the Church is the only thing that will outlive this world. The elements will melt with a fervent heat, and everything will become ashes—but the Church will go on and on. When the 10,000,000,000,000,000,000,000,000,000 stars of the universe are only burned-down, flickering candles, it will still be springtime for the Church!

How could Moses turn his back on Egyptian delights and embrace the affections of his stigmatized people? The answer reveals his faith: "He considered the reproach of Christ greater wealth than the treasures of Egypt, for he was looking to the reward" (v. 26). When Moses identified with Israel, he was aligning himself with the people with whom Jesus Christ had been identified from their inception. He had always been one with his people. "In all their affliction he was afflicted" (Isaiah 63:9). Thus, Moses' identification with the disgrace of the messianic people was an identification with Christ[7]—he endured disgrace for the sake of Christ.

The great truth for us is that Moses could do this because "he was looking to the reward." Here the author again takes us back to the foundational truth of verse 1: "Now faith is the assurance of things hoped for." Moses was, quite simply, sure of his reward. He was so certain that it was what we have called *future certitude*.

This is what will enable us to refuse to be called the sons and daughters of Pharaoh and to forego the fleeting pleasures of sin and to identify with God's people and their struggles. If we truly believe in the reward, as did Moses and the saints, we will do just fine. Paul said, "I consider that the sufferings of this present time are not worth comparing with the glory that is to be revealed to us" (Romans 8:18). A couple of paragraphs later he said:

> And we know that for those who love God all things work together for good, for those who are called according to his purpose. For those whom he foreknew he also predestined to be conformed to the image of his Son, in order that he might be the firstborn among many brothers. And those

whom he predestined he also called, and those whom he called he also justified, and those whom he justified he also glorified. (Romans 8:28–30)

Similarly, he encouraged the Corinthians:

So we do not lose heart. Though our outer self is wasting away, our inner self is being renewed day by day. For this light momentary affliction is preparing for us an eternal weight of glory beyond all comparison, as we look not to the things that are seen but to the things that are unseen. For the things that are seen are transient, but the things that are unseen are eternal. (2 Corinthians 4:16–18)

These are the things we must believe!

I know what would produce such faith in each one of us. Sixty seconds in Heaven. Fifteen seconds to view the face of Christ (though it would be impossible to move our gaze after such a short time). Fifteen seconds to survey the angelic host. Fifteen seconds to glimpse Heaven's architecture. And fifteen seconds to behold the face of a loved one now glorified. That is all it would take. But God is not going to do that for any of us. I could pray until I was blue in the face, and I wouldn't get a second in Heaven until eternity.

I know what else would do it, and that is simply what Moses did: *believing God's word*. And we can all do that now. If we are having trouble believing, we ought to read these passages carefully, then ask God for the capability to believe, and then *believe*!

By Faith: Moses' Separation (v. 27)

Next, the author explains that Moses' forty-year separation from Egypt in the land of Midian[8] was also a result of faith: "By faith he left Egypt, not being afraid of the anger of the king, for he endured as seeing him who is invisible" (v. 27). Here again the author references the second half of his essential definition of faith in verse 1: "Now faith is . . . the conviction of things not seen"—*visual certitude*.

The paradoxical phrase "seeing him who is invisible" does not mean he saw God with the naked eye. Faith's eye saw what the physical eye is incapable of seeing. But there did also come a time when God was so pleased with Moses' spiritual vision that he graced him with physical vision of a part of God's glory (cf. Exodus 33:18–23) and spoke to him face-to-face (cf. Exodus 33:9–11; Numbers 12:7, 8).

I personally believe that "seeing him who is invisible" is *not* extraordinary. Rather, it is ordinary, normal Christianity. In fact, if you do not see the unseen, you are abnormal and below the divinely ordained norm.

Christianity is supernatural, and it is to be lived supernaturally. Elisha's prayer is just as relevant today for the church as it was when he prayed it over his anxious servant: "Then Elisha prayed and said, 'O LORD, please open his eyes that he may see.' So the LORD opened the eyes of the young man, and he saw, and behold, the mountain was full of horses and chariots of fire all around Elisha" (2 Kings 6:17).

By Faith: Moses' Salvation (v. 28)

The last of the ten plagues that secured Israel's exodus from Egypt was the destruction of all the male firstborn of both man and beast (cf. Exodus 12:12). But God provided a way of salvation for his people. They were directed through Moses to slaughter a lamb, take some hyssop and dip it in the lamb's blood, and daub the blood on the top and sides of the doorways of their homes. Homes so anointed would be under God's protection, and the destroyer would not be permitted to enter (cf. Exodus 12:21–23). So our text reads, "By faith he kept the Passover and sprinkled the blood, so that the Destroyer of the firstborn might not touch them" (11:28).

The point is that Moses and Israel so believed God that they obeyed God to the letter. As Raymond Brown notes:

> The instructions were strange, the demands costly (a lamb without blemish) and the ritual unprecedented, but they did precisely as they were told. In simple faith they *kept the Passover.* They relied on the God who had spoken to them through his servant: "Then the people of Israel went and did so; as the Lord had commanded Moses and Aaron, so they did" (Exodus 12:1–3, 28).[9]

But what is even more remarkable is that the phrase "by faith he kept the Passover" actually means that he *instituted* the Passover (perfect tense). Moses actually instituted the Passover "as a statute forever" to be done year after year (Exodus 12:14)—which means that Moses never doubted in the least that the people would be delivered from Egypt! He had nothing to go on but God's word, but he believed it implicitly. Moses' massive faith saved Israel!

By Faith: Moses' (and Israel's) Deliverance (v. 29)

The final "by faith" in our section is charitable to a fault if it is read without reference to Moses: "By faith the people crossed the Red Sea as on dry land, but the Egyptians, when they attempted to do the same, were drowned" (v. 29). The reason this is overly charitable is that Israel did not show faith but held back in craven fear, decrying Moses:

> They said to Moses, "Is it because there are no graves in Egypt that you have taken us away to die in the wilderness? What have you done to us in bringing us out of Egypt? Is not this what we said to you in Egypt: 'Leave us alone that we may serve the Egyptians'? For it would have been better for us to serve the Egyptians than to die in the wilderness." (Exodus 14:11, 12)

Their faithlessness is corroborated by the fact that all of them later died in the desert because of their lack of faith, with the exception of Joshua and Caleb.

Actually it was Moses' faith that rallied them and secured their deliverance: "Moses said to the people, 'Fear not, stand firm, and see the salvation of the LORD, which he will work for you today. For the Egyptians whom you see today, you shall never see again. The LORD will fight for you, and you have only to be silent'" (Exodus 14:13, 14). This eventuated in Moses' preeminent display of faith when he stretched his hand out over the Red Sea, and the Lord drove back the waters with a strong east wind, and Israel passed through as on dry land (cf. Exodus 14:21, 22).

What a sublime fact we have here! One man's faith can be so authentic and effectual that it can elevate a whole people and secure their deliverance! In lesser ways we have seen this in the lives of such people as Martin Luther and John Wesley and Jonathan Edwards. This truth holds great promise for us. Vibrant, authentic faith can elevate our families, churches, and communities. It is not too much to say that it can even be the vehicle for corporate deliverance! Never underestimate the power of real faith!

Moses' peerless life shouts faith from beginning to end.

- By faith—the faith of Amram and Jochebed—Moses was *preserved* and nurtured.
- By faith Moses *identified* with his oppressed people as he turned his back on Egypt and took on the stigma of Israel.
- By faith Moses *separated* from Egypt for forty years so God could prepare him to be a deliverer.
- By faith Moses obtained the *salvation* of his people by instituting the Passover.
- By faith Moses effected the *deliverance* of Israel through the Red Sea.

What does this all mean to us? We understand what it meant to the early Jewish church, which saw itself in a kind of "exile" set amidst the mounting hostility of Roman culture. What was going to get them through their "Egypt" was faith—believing God's word about the promise of future reward and seeing the unseen. This is what is necessary to survive.

Our culture is becoming increasingly philistine—so much so that I am convinced that simple Biblical faith will soon become so abhorrent to popular culture that faithful Christians will be persecuted.

I am further convinced that some, by God's grace, will draw upon Moses' example and will thereby gain strength to live for God. Moses prevailed because:

- He believed in God's promise of reward.
- He lived a normal Christian life—he saw the unseen.

He who has ears to hear, let him hear!

By faith the walls of Jericho fell down after they had been encircled for seven days.

11:30

36

Joshua's and His People's Faith

HEBREWS 11:30

ISRAEL HAD CROSSED THE JORDAN. Virtually nothing remained before the campaign for possession of the land of Canaan would begin. War loomed only hours away. Behind the masses of God's people, the flooding Jordan blocked all retreat. Before them rose the ominous ramparts of Jericho, her gates sealed tight, her men of war on the walls. Most of the Israelites had never seen a fortified city, and with what we know of the recurrent pessimism of this people, we can be sure that fear ran high in the camp—despite the great things God had done for them.

Humanly speaking, Joshua bore all the lonely responsibility of the leadership of his fickle, frightened people. How he would have liked to have Moses there to talk to. But there was no Moses. Joshua had sole authority. He needed to get away to pray, to meditate, to plan the conquest.

A Divine Encounter

So Joshua stole out of the camp in the darkness to view Jericho for himself and to seek God's guidance. The Hebrew word that tells us Joshua was "by Jericho" (Joshua 5:13) expresses the idea of immediate proximity.[1] He was very close, perhaps close enough to feel the oppression of the city described as "fortified up to heaven" (cf. Deuteronomy 1:28).

There he remained in the night—brooding, meditating, patrolling, his eyes wide to the darkness—when he detected some movement on which he fixed his eyes. What he saw set his heart racing and adrenaline pumping, for there stood a warrior in full battle-dress, his sword bare and gleaming blue in the moon's light.

A less courageous man would have bolted—but not Joshua. His hand was very likely upon his own sword as he strode forward, calling out to the menacing figure, "Are you for us, or for our adversaries?" (Joshua 5:13). In other words, "Which side are you on—ours or the enemy's? Because if you are from Jericho, it will be steel against steel!" Joshua was no armchair general!

There was no way Joshua could have anticipated the sublimity that lay ahead. He certainly did not know that the next few minutes would become a spiritual milestone in his life.

Joshua's ringing challenge, "Are you for us, or for our adversaries?" was met by an answer that put him flat on his face: "No; but I am the commander of the army of the LORD. Now I have come" (Joshua 5:14). I believe (along with Calvin and Keil and Delitzsch) that this "commander of the army of the LORD" was a theophany, an appearance of Jehovah in the form of an angelic messenger.

I am convinced of this for several reasons. First, Joshua was told to take off his sandals. This very same command had been given to Moses *by God* from the burning bush:

> "Take your sandals off your feet, for the place on which you are standing is holy ground." And he said, "I am the God of your father, the God of Abraham, the God of Isaac, and the God of Jacob." And Moses hid his face, for he was afraid to look at God. (Exodus 3:5, 6)

Joshua realized, through the command to take off his sandals, that this "commander" was the same God who had spoken to Moses. Second, the "commander" who spoke to Joshua is identified as "the LORD" in Joshua 6:2–5: "And the LORD said to Joshua . . ." Third, as Origen said in his Sixth Homily on Joshua, "Joshua knew not only that he was of God, but that he was God. For he would not have worshiped him, had he not recognized him to be God."[2] These three reasons convince me that "the commander of the army of the LORD" was God in angelic form—the angel of the Lord.

This encounter with God served to steel Joshua and arm him for the conquering of Jericho, for very specific reasons. He saw not only that God was with him, but God's mystic appearance—with his sword pulled from his scabbard and held ready for battle—was indelibly printed on Joshua's consciousness. God would fight for him! He knew that whatever the enemy mobilized, it would be matched and exceeded by heavenly mobilization. It was this same awareness that galvanized Philipp Melanchthon, the primary theologian of the Reformation, for the immense battles he fought, for his favorite verse was Romans 8:31: "If God is for us, who can be against us?" Melanchthon is said to have referenced this verse many times in his writings—and on his death bed. It was his repeated (victorious!) refrain.

Also, Joshua's encounter with God left him steeled by fully informing him regarding what God wanted him to do in taking Jericho:

> And the LORD said to Joshua, "See, I have given Jericho into your hand, with its king and mighty men of valor. You shall march around the city, all the men of war going around the city once. Thus shall you do for six days. Seven priests shall bear seven trumpets of rams' horns before the ark. On the seventh day you shall march around the city seven times, and the priests shall blow the trumpets. And when they make a long blast with the ram's horn, when you hear the sound of the trumpet, then all the people shall shout with a great shout, and the wall of the city will fall down flat, and the people shall go up, everyone straight before him." (Joshua 6:2–5)

What was the effect of all this upon Joshua? In a word, it produced the bedrock faith that introduces Hebrews 11—"Now faith is the assurance of things hoped for, the conviction of things not seen"—faith's *dynamic dual certitude*. He had incredible *visual certitude*, for he had seen the unseen. His conviction regarding the invisible would gird him in every battle. He had awesome *future certitude* regarding what he hoped for—namely, the fall of Jericho and the taking of the Promised Land. He was sure those walls would fall! And this dual certitude made him the great General Joshua, the son of Nun—or to give it a more martial ring, Field Marshal Joshua Von Nun!

Joshua's dynamic sureness enabled him to lead Israel to victory. And here we must emphasize again that, as with Moses' believing parents and Moses himself, one person's faith can make all the difference for God's people. As we shall see, Joshua's faith was communicated to and elevated the whole nation's faith—and so can yours and mine. No matter where we are planted—whether it is behind a machine or a desk or in a house—if we live a life of dynamic certainty regarding God's Word, we will elevate and energize others to live as they ought. One person's faith can raise the level of a whole church.

That morning, as the bright rays of the early sun illuminated the thousands of orderly arranged tents of his people, Joshua knew what he had to do—and in the storied days that followed, he did it. The writer of Hebrews tells us, in a simple sentence, "By faith the walls of Jericho fell down after they had been encircled for seven days" (v. 30). This is the key to the spiritual understanding of the fall of Jericho: *the walls of Jericho fell because of the faith of Joshua and his people*. It was the greatest corporate act of faith in

Israel's history, one never to be exceeded. And as such, it forms an extended object lesson for us. Let us consider faith's factors.

The Obedience of Faith

The Lord himself had given *explicit* instructions to Joshua that demanded *implicit* obedience (cf. Joshua 6:2–5; 6–10). They detailed the order and conduct of the famous procession around Jericho. The precise order was: soldiers, then seven priests carrying seven rams' horns called shofars, then (significantly in the middle) the ark of the covenant on the shoulders of more priests, then the people, and finally the rearguard of soldiers.

The conduct of this unusual procession was likewise carefully specified. During the first six days they were to march once around the walls each day, maintaining absolute silence while the priests blared intermittently on their shofars. On the seventh day they were to maintain silence as they circled the walls *seven* times—until Joshua gave the command to "shout" (Joshua 6:10).

Absurdity

By any outside estimation these instructions were ridiculous! The uniform witness of military history is that the foe is conquered by force. City walls are cleared by bombardment. Then they are scaled by ladders and ropes. Gates are smashed by battering rams, troops taken by sword. Cities do not fall by mystics making bad music on rams' horns! When the Canaanites got a good look at the procession, they undoubtedly exploded in incredulous laughter and then hoots and catcalls. They could not believe their eyes. What fools these Israelites were—clowns! And secretly some of the Hebrews agreed.

Belief

But though the instructions looked foolishly contrary to human logic, Israel, as a corporate body, believed. Why their uncharacteristic faith? Obviously because of their recent experience in watching the Jordan dry up when the ark penetrated its boundary. The freshness of that recent miracle made them receptive to faith. The other reason, already touched upon, was the faith and character of Joshua. The iron certitude of Field Marshall Joshua Von Nun energized them all!

Thus, Israel really did believe God was going to give them Jericho. When the writer of Hebrews, under the inspiration of the Holy Spirit, says, "By faith the walls of Jericho fell down," he means that the Israelites actually did have faith. They were not pretending to believe. Theirs was not a bogus faith. As they marched silently around the wall, they did believe the walls would come tumbling down! Their faith pleased God because they were believing "that he exists and that he rewards those who seek him" (11:6).

Obedience

The evidence that they believed God's word is that they *obeyed* it. It was a little after dawn. The sun had lifted just above the horizon. Joshua had assembled his elders and had given them the instructions of the divine "commander." Now they were moving quickly throughout the camp, calling the people together. Soon a long procession began to wind from the camp. Though it was vast in number, it did not include all the people, but involved a representative delegation from each tribe.

The ordered procession made its way toward the walled city in silence, broken only by the discordant, elephantine blasts of the shofars. The trip from Gilgal to Jericho took about two hours, although Jericho was encircled in about twenty-five to thirty minutes.

Joshua kept the Israelites well beyond the range of Jericho's archers, but of course not beyond the taunts of the increasing number of her inhabitants who lined her walls. Yet Israel never broke silence. The strange parade continued its absurd procession for six consecutive days. The Amorites shouted on, but the grim silence of the circling fools began to wear on them.

The enduring object lesson here is that a life of faith is evidenced by a life of obedience to God's word, even when it seems absurd. Paul's comments in his second letter to the Corinthians (10:3, 4) are appropriate here: "For though we walk in the flesh, we are not waging war according to the flesh. For the weapons of our warfare are not of the flesh." To the unbelieving mind, the Christian's weapons appear not only impotent but ridiculous. Who ever stormed a walled city wearing truth for his war belt, righteousness for a breastplate, the good news for shoes, faith for a shield, salvation for a helmet, the Bible for a sword? Come on! This is the armament of clowns—fools' armor.

But God gives us directions in his Word on how to meet our Jerichos, instructions that are folly to human logic.

- A man is filling out his income tax form and realizes that if he lists his extra hidden income, it will put him in a higher tax bracket and he will not have money to pay his taxes. He is up against a dark wall indeed. He has a choice to make—do what is logical (just like everyone else does) or be absurdly truthful, trusting God to take care of him.
- A student is doing poorly in class. He needs a B to get into grad school, and as he works on his final exam he realizes it is not going to happen. But he

notices that his neighboring A student is working in such a way that he can read all his answers without being seen. What to do? Rationalize and say "God provides!" or be a fool, fixing his eyes on his own miserable dunce paper, trusting God to work things out as he sees fit?

- You have been wronged by an enemy. Now you have the chance to do him ill, and he will never know who did it. Everyone would applaud you for it if they knew you did it. And you know that you can get away with it. But you remember the words of Jesus, "You have heard that it was said, 'You shall love your neighbor and hate your enemy.' But I say to you, Love your enemies and pray for those who persecute you" (Matthew 5:43, 44). Will you join the fools' parade and actually pray for blessing on the one who has wronged you?

The Scriptures reveal a spiritual law: disobedience reveals our unbelief, but obedience to God evidences our faith. When difficult circumstances assail us, unbelief draws from the arsenals of the world, whereas faith causes us to take up the armor of God and join the absurd march around Jericho. Any Jerichos facing you? Are you wavering between God's way and the world's way of meeting it? Do you believe God's Word? The authenticity of your belief will be determined by the weapon you choose.

The Focus of Faith

The first great dimension of Israel's victorious faith is *obedience*. The second factor is the *focus* of Israel's faith.

The centerpiece of the narrative here is the golden ark of the covenant—*God's presence*. The account mentions the ark no less than eleven times! The ark was borne, as we have noted, in the exact middle of the procession, with the priests' horns blasting constantly as heralds of God's presence. This is what shofars were used for—just as they had earlier been sounded at Mt. Sinai to announce the presence of God (cf. Exodus 19:16). It was God's presence that circled Jericho those seven days, and it was his presence that would bring its fall.

Central to Israel's great exercise of faith was the awareness that God was with them, leading them. We must emphasize that they were *not* imagining this. God was truly present. But he manifested himself specially through the ark. And the realization that he was physically in their midst had a massive impact on the Israelites' exercise of faith.

In John Bunyan's church in Bedford, England, there is a poem framed on the wall of the anteroom from which the preacher exits to walk to the pulpit. It reads:

Enter this door
As if the floor
Within were gold,
And every wall
Of jewels, all
Of wealth untold,
As if a choir,
In robes of fire
Were singing here;
Nor shout, nor rush,
But hush,
For God is near.

And so he is! This is what we need. This is what will enable us to conquer the evil opposition that confronts us—a sense that God is specially with us. If on a given Sunday morning we suddenly had the ability to see the unseen, we would see angels among us—maybe sitting next to us in human form. Perhaps if the preaching were good, we might see angels with their Bibles out listening intently, for Peter tells us that "angels long to look" into these things (1 Peter 1:12). The Greek gives the idea of them bending over or stooping to search the mysteries of God's Word. And the writer of Hebrews says, "Are they not all ministering spirits sent out to serve for the sake of those who are to inherit salvation?" (1:14).

As the Israelites encircled Jericho, the Canaanites saw nothing more than a ragtag people carrying a golden box, but the Israelites saw the unseen. Their focus was on God, and they knew God's special presence went with them. This is faith's focus. This is the focus that brings down enemy walls!

A Declaration of Faith

It must have been very difficult for the Israelites to keep silent during those first six days. Their enemies practiced no restraint—we can be sure of that. Moreover, not one stone in the walls had loosened, there were no cracks in the city wall up to Heaven, and the citizenry was far from saying uncle.

It must, then, have been a great relief on the seventh day when Joshua ordered them to rise early and circle Jericho seven times, finishing with a great shout at his cue. Joshua 6:15–17, 20 describe the climactic event:

> On the seventh day they rose early, at the dawn of day, and marched around the city in the same manner seven times. It was only on that day that they marched around the city seven times. And at the seventh time, when the priests had blown the trumpets, Joshua said to the people, "Shout, for the LORD has given you the city. And the city and all that is within it shall be

devoted to the Lord for destruction. Only Rahab the prostitute and all who are with her in her house shall live, because she hid the messengers whom we sent."

When the trumpets sounded, the people shouted. And at the sound of the trumpet, when the people gave a loud shout, the wall collapsed, every man charged in, and they took the city.

That was the voice of faith. It was the outward expression of the Israelites' inward confidence in the power of God. Conquering faith declares itself. Faith that does not do so is not faith at all. "For with the heart one believes and is justified, and with the mouth one confesses and is saved" (Romans 10:10). Ancient Job announced, "I know that my Redeemer lives, and at the last he will stand upon the earth. And after my skin has been thus destroyed, yet in my flesh I shall see God, whom I shall see for myself" (Job 19:25–27). The lips declare what is within. What do our lips say about our faith?

Surely that was some shout there at Jericho! All their repressed human emotions came forth in a cry heard all the way to Gilgal, and the walls came tumbling down. Literally, "the wall fell in its place."

- True faith *obeys* God and his Word, even when it seems absurd. It rejects the world's armament and dons the ridiculous armor of God. It marches confidently in a fools' army—to victory.
- True faith *focuses* upon God and sees the unseen. It cultivates a special sense of his presence—that he is with his people—and refuses to divert its focus.
- True faith *declares* itself to a fallen world.

How is our faith? These things happened as an example for us who still fight the battles of faith. By learning from them, we too can achieve victory in the Lord, and he will cause impossible walls to tumble before us.

By faith Rahab the prostitute did not perish with those who were disobedient, because she had given a friendly welcome to the spies.

11:31

37

Rahab's Faith

HEBREWS 11:31

WE HAVE CONSIDERED the amazing faith of Joshua and the people of Israel as they followed God's seemingly absurd instructions—and saw the great city of Jericho fall flat on its face! But not all the faith was outside the city.

Faith inside Jericho

The collapse was complete, except for one small section from which a scarlet cord hung in the wake of the concussion. It was the cord of faith. Hebrews 11:30, 31 tells us, "By faith the walls of Jericho fell down after they had been encircled for seven days. By faith Rahab the prostitute did not perish with those who were disobedient, because she had given a friendly welcome to the spies."

During those last seven days, all faith's factors—which we examined in the previous chapter—had developed and swelled through Rahab's growing soul.

Obedience

She gave implicit *obedience* to the explicit directions given her by God through the spies. She kept all her family in her home, just as she had been told. Though some of them very likely questioned her wisdom, she did not capitulate, but rather insisted that they remain. Her obedience bears testimony to an amazing faith. Rahab's obedience matched that of the encircling Israelites.

Focus

Day after day Rahab rose to the trumpeting of the shofars as they announced the approach of God and the ark, then peered out over her scarlet cord. The

Israelites silently and knowingly stared back, and she rested her faith in the fact that God really was with them. Hers was a focused faith. Perhaps she recited to her family something of the testimony she had given to the spies:

> I know that the LORD has given you the land. . . . For we have heard how the LORD dried up the water of the Red Sea before you when you came out of Egypt, and what you did to the two kings of the Amorites who were beyond the Jordan, to Sihon and Og, whom you devoted to destruction. And as soon as we heard it, our hearts melted, and there was no spirit left in any man because of you, for the LORD your God, he is God in the heavens above and on the earth beneath. (Joshua 2:9–11)

By faith, like Noah and Moses before her, Rahab saw the unseen, and that changed her whole life.

Declaration

Finally, there was the *declaration*, the shout of faith. Earlier she had declared her faith to Israel's spies. And because of this she probably shouted out in concert with her new people, for faith declares itself.

The story of Rahab will bring us immeasurable encouragement and fuel for faith.

The Faith of Rahab

First we will consider some background to the story of Rahab. The older faithless generation of Israelites had perished in the wilderness. God had buried Moses in a secret place in one of the valleys of Moab and made Joshua the leader of his people. Now Israel had to spy out the land and consecrate itself to the great work before her. Joshua 2:1–3 describes the spies' mission:

> And Joshua the son of Nun sent two men secretly from Shittim as spies, saying, "Go, view the land, especially Jericho." And they went and came into the house of a prostitute whose name was Rahab and lodged there. And it was told to the king of Jericho, "Behold, men of Israel have come here tonight to search out the land." Then the king of Jericho sent to Rahab, saying, "Bring out the men who have come to you, who entered your house, for they have come to search out all the land."

This reconnaissance was extra-perilous because Jericho was a walled city situated in an open valley, and its inhabitants, the Amorites, were on special alert. The ominous massed presence of Israel at the Jordan had made them suspicious of everyone and everything.

Accordingly, the spies took every precaution, carefully disguising themselves, discarding anything characteristically Hebrew, and doing their best to appear Canaanite-Amorite in clothing and speech. They approached the city with great caution. The Jordan was flooding, so they probably traveled to the north where the fords were easier, then turned southwest to enter Jericho from the west side—the side away from the Israeli presence. This was advantageous because they would have the cover of the caves in the mountains west of Jericho, and the king would be less likely to detect infiltration from that side.[1]

Apparently unnoticed, they slipped through Jericho's gates, and, in a premeditated, studied attempt to "get lost" in the city, sought hiding in the house of a prostitute named Rahab. Lodging in such a place was characteristic of traveling merchants, and the spies felt their chances of escaping notice were best served there.

But the strategy failed in two respects. First, someone saw them enter Jericho and followed them to Rahab's house. Second, the prostitute immediately discerned their identity.

From all appearances everything had fallen apart, and they were doomed. The king was searching for them. They could not retreat back into the city. And if they jumped through the window, horsemen would easily run them down on the plain. It looked like their time had come, except for one totally unexpected thing—*the faith and good works of a prostitute*. God's agents were saved by a madame, the proprietress of a bordello, a woman who sold her body for money, who submitted to any man who crossed her doorway if he had the cash. Some try to tone down the facts, but the New Testament is clear—she was a *pornee*, a prostitute (see James 2:25; Hebrews 11:31). So unanticipated, and so extraordinary, was this prostitute's courageous faith that she is included in the Hall of Faith in Hebrews 11, along with the likes of Enoch, Noah, Abraham, and Moses: "By faith Rahab the prostitute did not perish with those who were disobedient, because she had given a friendly welcome to the spies" (v. 31).

It is most significant that the final person to receive individual commentary in the list of champions of faith is a woman and a Gentile and a prostitute.[2] Rahab's faith, a *prostitute's faith*, is given as an example for all who desire to have true faith—especially those who know they are sinners and who deep down want to be pleasing to God.

We are going to look at this from three revealing angles: (1) *Faith's work*—its demonstration, (2) *Faith's formation*—its nature and development, and (3) *Faith's reward*—its astounding benefits.

Faith's Work

Faith's Lie

Verses 4, 5 of Joshua 2 present a very awkward truth—Rahab's first work of faith was a lie!

> But the woman had taken the two men and hidden them. And she said, "True, the men came to me, but I did not know where they were from. And when the gate was about to be closed at dark, the men went out. I do not know where the men went. Pursue them quickly, for you will overtake them."

Actually Rahab told three lies in one. First, she said she did not know where they came from. Secondly, she said they had gone. And finally, she said she did not know where they were. So here we have it—a lie was the first work of Rahab's faith!

Does this mean it is okay to lie in certain situations? I personally do not think so, though some highly respected theologians do.[3] I agree with Calvin, who comments on Rahab's deception:

> As to the falsehood, we must admit that though it was done for a good purpose, it was not free from fault. For those who hold what is called a "dutiful lie" to be altogether excusable, do not sufficiently consider how precious truth is in the sight of God. Therefore, although our purpose be to assist our brethren, to consult for their safety and relieve them, it never can be lawful to lie, because that cannot be right which is contrary to the nature of God. And God is truth. . . . On the whole, it was the will of God that the spies should be delivered, but He did not approve of saving their lives by falsehood.[4]

The Scripture does, of course, record the lies of saints such as Abraham (Genesis 12:10–20), but it never approves such deception. Rather, God's Word uniformly condemns falsehood and calls us to be men and women of truth. Moreover, the life of Christ, our model *par excellence*, provides us with the supreme example of truthfulness. Our Lord never lied or deceived anyone. And as members of his Body, we are obligated to do our best to live according to his example.

Nevertheless, Rahab's calculated lie was a stupendous act of true faith, for her subsequent actions—when she assisted the spies in their escape through the window and cleverly advised them to hide three days in the hill country—put her life in deadly peril (cf. Joshua 2:15, 16). In fact, if the king had gotten wind of her doings, her death would have been immediate and terrible. Rahab's faith was great and deserves the status it has been given.

We must consider Rahab's lie against the backdrop of her pagan culture and lowly profession. She had no knowledge of the revelation given to Israel at Sinai. We can be sure that godly morality and its radical truth ethic had not penetrated her pagan mind. True, she possessed a moral conscience, but it was not informed by God's word. Hence it very likely did not occur to her that she was doing wrong. I am not saying that her lie was okay or that people are better off not knowing what is right and what is not. But I am saying that God recognized the motive behind the act—and that motive was faith!

The lessons Rahab leaves us are many, and one we should particularly keep in mind is that we must be sympathetic and patient with the character of recent converts. It is a matter of historical fact that John Newton, the author of "Amazing Grace," composer of the famous Olney hymns, and one of the early fathers of the evangelical movement in the Church of England, continued to participate in the slave trade for over a year after his dramatic conversion.[5] Faith and sin mingled without conscious contradiction in his new life.

This is often characteristic today of those coming out of our Biblically ignorant post-Christian culture. One of my long-time missionary friends tells how he came to Christ in the midst of a hard-drinking business environment—and how he fortified himself with six martinis to get the courage to share Christ the first time! An inebriated evangelist? Rahab would have understood this completely.

Often real faith is salted with sin, and God finds faith where we do not (and often cannot) see it. We should be slow to judge sin and quick to perceive faith.

Faith's Trust

The classic symbol that revealed Rahab's great faith was the scarlet cord she hung from her window over the wall of Jericho. Joshua 2:17–20 record how the two spies promised her safety if she would display that cord in her window. They vowed that everyone in the house would survive if the red cord were in place. Rahab's faith invited their saving work. Joshua 2:21 says she replied, "'According to your words, so be it.' Then she sent them away, and they departed. And she tied the scarlet cord in the window."

Recent scholarship has suggested that the scarlet rope may have been the mark of a prostitute and that Rahab lived, so to speak, in the "red rope" district. It is also noted that since the Hebrew word for "rope" is the same word for "hope"—and most often means "hope"—there may be an intentional pun here: the "rope" is the prostitute's "hope" for customers! But now that

Rahab has confessed Jehovah as God, her scarlet "rope" signified a new kind of "hope"—that of deliverance by God.[6]

Be that as it may, the scarlet cord tells us that Rahab's faith, though incipient and uninformed, was *completely trusting*. If the Israelites failed to return and conquer the city, she would soon be found out. The gathering of her family into her home would be interpreted for what it was, someone would talk, and she and her kind would go down to their graves in terrible agony. But Rahab completely believed that judgment was coming and that salvation awaited her. So she let down the scarlet cord in profound trust.

Here a word about the scarlet cord is in order. Too much has been made of it typologically, as the history of interpretation reveals. Some of the church fathers, such as Clement of Rome, thought the red cord was a symbol of the blood of Christ and that Rahab was a symbol of the Church because through it she obtained safety for her family.[7]

This type of allegorization is still quite popular. A member of my family recalls listening to a flannelgraph story in which the spies were depicted as escaping down the red cord! Following this, the teacher stretched out a red cord as a symbol, not only of the blood, but of the bloodline of Christ.

Having said this, I would like to suggest there is a direct connection with the Passover, which had occurred forty years earlier. Then, you will remember, the Israelites were commanded to gather all their family into the house (just as Rahab did) and paint lamb's blood around the door, so that when the death angel came and saw the blood, all inside would be spared (Exodus 12:21–23). What happened with Rahab parallels this closely, and it seems likely that the spies (though not Rahab) were quite aware of the symbolism. In both cases the red upon the door or the window evidenced the faith of those inside. Francis Schaeffer explains further: "When the children of Israel were about to leave Egypt, they were given the blood of the Passover Lamb under which to be safe. When the people were about to enter the land, they were met by a different, but parallel sign—a red cord hanging from the window of a believer."[8]

What great trust flowed from Rahab's faith. Rahab's sequestering of her family and patiently awaiting the outcome showed her trust. She stood alone against the whole of her culture, something few of us in our contemporary culture have had to do. She, like Moses before, saw the unseen when no one else did (cf. 11:27). Oh, did she believe!

Faith's Work

The Apostle James, in the second chapter of his letter, tells us that true faith produces works, and he gives two examples—first Abraham and then Rahab.

He presents them as parallels. Of Abraham he says, "Was not Abraham our father justified by works when he offered up his son Isaac on the altar?" (James 2:21). Of Rahab he then says, "And in the same way was not also Rahab the prostitute justified by works when she received the messengers and sent them out by another way?" (James 2:25).

James's point in these two examples is the same. Abraham demonstrated his faith at great cost. He willingly offered up his own son. Rahab's faith was likewise costly. She risked everything. Faith is not a barren intellectual process. True faith issues in action—even when it costs! Is our faith real? Can it be seen in our actions? Are we willing to let it cost us something? We can, and will, if it is real. Rahab's faith was salted with sin. She did not understand everything. But she trusted God—and her faith worked as she sent out the spies and lowered the scarlet cord. True faith works!

Faith's Formation

We wonder at such great faith, and we wonder where Rahab got it. Abraham Kuyper, the great Biblical scholar who delivered one of the most brilliant of the Stone Lectures at Princeton, and who also served as Prime Minister of the Netherlands from 1901–1905, explains:

> The people who in Rahab's time most frequently used such houses of prostitution were the traveling merchants. From them she had repeatedly heard of the marvelous nation which was approaching from Egypt, and of the God of Israel who had perfected such striking miracles.[9]

Rahab heard that there was only one God, Jehovah. She heard bits and snatches about Israel's destiny. She heard, perhaps derisively, of the nation's high ethical and moral code. Perhaps she had become disillusioned with the culture around her. She was treated as chattel. She had seen life at its worst. All of this together made her open to truth and faith. No doubt, fear contributed to the formation of her faith. Fear is an inevitable and natural consequence of sensing that God's justice leaves us in the wrong. Rahab knew she was a sinner. She was ready for faith. The testimony of the spies opened her to faith. Rahab would immediately have sensed the difference between the Israelite visitors and the clients who normally frequented her house. The spies were not sensualists but holy men of impeccable morals. She had never seen this before. They were sure of their God. Their ethos confirmed the reality of what she had been hearing from the merchants. She was spiritually enticed.

These inner workings coalesced with her disillusionment and fear to produce faith. Rahab's speech in Joshua 2:9–11 is a grand song of belief in the one God:

> I know that the LORD has given you the land, and that the fear of you has fallen upon us, and that all the inhabitants of the land melt away before you. For we have heard how the LORD dried up the water of the Red Sea before you when you came out of Egypt, and what you did to the two kings of the Amorites who were beyond the Jordan, to Sihon and Og, whom you devoted to destruction. And as soon as we heard it, our hearts melted, and there was no spirit left in any man because of you, for the LORD your God, he is God in the heavens above and on the earth beneath.

Jericho had stood for hundreds of years. Today it is still the earliest fortified town known to scholarship.[10] Its inhabitants thought it invincible. But Rahab heard God's word, and though she was encased by her ancient pagan culture, which appeared to be eternal, she believed! That is why her faith has been immortalized. "By faith Rahab the prostitute did not perish with those who were disobedient, because she had given a friendly welcome to the spies."

Truly, we can never tell where faith will be found. And Rahab's example tells us there is hope for people where we would never dream of it. When Jesus came, he said to the Pharisees, "Truly, I say to you, the tax collectors and the prostitutes go into the kingdom of God before you. For John came to you in the way of righteousness, and you did not believe him, but the tax collectors and the prostitutes believed him" (Matthew 21:31, 32).

There is no one who is too bad or too ignorant to be saved! Some are not only doing drugs but dealing them—dealing death to others. Some have prostituted their sexuality—doing anything with anyone. But anyone can come to faith, like Rahab in her house, and be saved. Rahab's story means there is hope for all us sinners with our incipient, imperfect, stumbling, selfish faith. This ought to cause us to shout for joy!

Faith's Reward

Rahab's faith garnered three rewards.

ENCOURAGEMENT

First, Israel was encouraged—"Then the two men returned. They came down from the hills and passed over and came to Joshua the son of Nun, and they told him all that had happened to them. And they said to Joshua, 'Truly the LORD has given all the land into our hands. And also, all the inhabitants of the land melt away because of us'" (Joshua 2:23, 24). The children of Israel were encouraged through Rahab's great confession of faith (Joshua 2:9–11). They were uplifted by the positive report that the spies brought back, and they were strengthened by the miraculous deliverance given to the two spies through the prostitute.

SALVATION

The second reward of Rahab's faith was her own salvation. This came initially as physical salvation, as Joshua 6:22–25 records:

> But to the two men who had spied out the land, Joshua said, "Go into the prostitute's house and bring out from there the woman and all who belong to her, as you swore to her." So the young men who had been spies went in and brought out Rahab and her father and mother and brothers and all who belonged to her. And they brought all her relatives and put them outside the camp of Israel. And they burned the city with fire, and everything in it. Only the silver and gold, and the vessels of bronze and of iron, they put into the treasury of the house of the LORD. But Rahab the prostitute and her father's household and all who belonged to her, Joshua saved alive. And she has lived in Israel to this day, because she hid the messengers whom Joshua sent to spy out Jericho.

Rahab did not initially have saving faith in the spiritual sense, but as she joined with Israel she completely believed and became a full member of God's covenant people. Ultimately Rahab's faith saved her in every way.

GLORIFICATION

The third reward of Rahab's faith may be spoken of as her glorification. Here her story becomes lyrical—an "impossible dream." Not only did Rahab live in Israel the rest of her life, but she married an Israelite and became an ancestor of Jesus Christ. Matthew's genealogy of Jesus bears out the incredible truth: ". . . and to Ram was born Amminadab; and to Amminadab, Nahshon; and to Nahshon, Salmon; and to Salmon was born Boaz by Rahab; and to Boaz was born Obed by Ruth; and to Obed, Jesse; and to Jesse was born David the king" (Matthew 1:4–6 NASB). And Christ came from David's lineage!

Nahshon, Rahab's father-in-law, was one of the twelve princes who made a special offering at the raising of the tabernacle. Numbers 7:12 says, "He who offered his offering the first day was Nahshon . . . of the tribe of Judah." Nahshon was a great prince of Judah, and so was his son Salmon, who married Rahab.

How unutterably beautiful! The Amorite prostitute became a believer and then the wife of a prince of Judah. Rahab was a princess and ancestor of Christ!

Predictably, but nevertheless amazing, some have been uncomfortable with Rahab's being in the genealogy of Christ. Josephus tried to make her out to be an "innkeeper" (*Ant.* V. 1:2, 7), and some have referred to her as a "landlady" or "formerly a fallen woman." As we have seen, she was a *pornee* and nothing else. I think it is wonderful that she belongs to Christ's blood-line. In fact, it fits perfectly, for the whole human race is guilty of spiritual prostitution! Furthermore, all of us have had our lapses. Jesus did not come from a sinless human line. Every person in it was a sinner in need of salvation, including Rahab and the Virgin Mary!

Anyone who looks down on Rahab had better beware, for it is obvious that such a person has a defective doctrine of sin and does not understand the depth of human iniquity or the heights of the grace of God. All of us stand in Rahab's place in front of a holy God. And many of us are worse, because she had such little knowledge. We must at least be as wise as Rahab, who though she understood little did understand that she was under God's judgment and sought redemption.

Hebrews 11:31 cites Rahab as an example of one who was saved by faith. James 2:25 says she was saved by works. There is no contradiction, for Rahab was saved by a faith that produced works. There is eternal wisdom for us here in Rahab's faith—especially from the enlightening angles from which we have considered it.

Conclusions

Faith comes to us in response to God's Word—"faith comes from hearing" (Romans 10:17). On this point, we have incredible advantage over Rahab. We have the whole Bible, not just a fragmentary story from the lips of traveling merchants. And the message we hear is not just of judgment but of love and salvation—"For God so loved the world, that he gave his only Son, that who-ever believes in him should not perish but have eternal life. For God did not send his Son into the world to condemn the world, but in order that the world might be saved through him" (John 3:16, 17).

Also unlike Rahab, we are surrounded by people of faith who have trusted Christ and can lead us in the way everlasting. There are people who will pray for us, counsel us, even give of their resources to help us grow in faith. The quality of their lives alone draws us upward. Our advantages in forming faith are huge.

Further, God does not expect perfection from us. He knows how weak we are. He forbears with us. But he does expect us to act on our faith—even if it is one step at a time—even if it is a stumbling faith. He expects us to hang the scarlet cord in our windows, announcing our faith in this dark world, and to trust him alone for our salvation. He expects a faith that works.

Regarding reward, I would mention only this: we become not only beneficiaries of Christ's atoning blood, but part of his bloodline as members of his mystical body—we are "in Christ" (a term used no less than 168 times in the New Testament). He calls us brothers and sisters and himself our elder brother (cf. 2:11). We have been made royalty and will reign with him forever and forever!

And what more shall I say? For time would fail me to tell of Gideon, Barak, Samson, Jephthah, of David and Samuel and the prophets—who through faith conquered kingdoms, enforced justice, obtained promises, stopped the mouths of lions, quenched the power of fire, escaped the edge of the sword, were made strong out of weakness, became mighty in war, put foreign armies to flight. Women received back their dead by resurrection. Some were tortured, refusing to accept release, so that they might rise again to a better life. Others suffered mocking and flogging, and even chains and imprisonment. They were stoned, they were sawn in two, they were killed with the sword. They went about in skins of sheep and goats, destitute, afflicted, mistreated—of whom the world was not worthy—wandering about in deserts and mountains, and in dens and caves of the earth. And all these, though commended through their faith, did not receive what was promised, since God had provided something better for us, that apart from us they should not be made perfect.

11:32–40

38

Triumphant Faith

HEBREWS 11:32-40

AS WE NOW COME TO THE END of the Hall of Faith, we see that it has been a consistent exposition of what faith is, as was defined in the opening verse of chapter 11: "Now faith is the assurance of things hoped for, the conviction of things not seen." Therefore, faith is a *dynamic certainty* made up of two certitudes: a *future certitude* that makes one sure of the future as if it were present, and a *visual certitude* that brings the invisible within view. One hears God's Word and so believes it that its future fulfillment becomes subjectively present and visible to the spiritual eye.

This grand certainty characterized each of the sixteen heroes thus far presented and was the ground of their triumphs. By faith the heroes of old were enabled to live so as to deserve the testimony that they were "righteous" (v. 4), that they "pleased God" (v. 5), and that they were people of whom God was "not ashamed" (v. 16). And all of them experienced triumphs over great difficulties.

This chapter was composed by the preacher/writer with the hope of steeling the tiny, expatriate Hebrew church against the persecution that was mounting against them and was soon to fall in the genocidal waves of horror orchestrated by the mad emperor Nero. And, indeed, those who did persevere did so because of their profound faith in the promises of God's Word. So we must understand that Hebrews 11 was not just an entertaining and inspiring aside, but was essential life-and-death teaching for the Hebrew church. It may well be the same for us and our children.

Recent history has again reminded us that no dictatorship or democracy is eternal. Freedom, and especially religious freedom, is fragile. Moreover, dark forces are at work in our culture to the extent that it has become politically correct to "call evil good and good evil" (Isaiah 5:20). A case in point is homosexual "marriages" and "families," ideas that received extensive uncritical positive coverage in the *Chicago Tribune* in a recent article entitled "The Gay Baby Boom."[1] It is also a matter of record that New York City schools include in the teachers' resource books for first-graders (the "see Jane go to school, see Jane read" level) that approvingly portray homosexual "marriages" and "families" ("Meet Johnny's parents, Dave and Lance").

To the purveyors of this approved cultural agenda, Judeo-Christian morality is reactionary. And if any of us think that being reactionary is a safe thing, consider what the social engineers have done to reactionaries in the recent times. There is only one unforgivable sin in the eyes of the popular moral pundits, and that is intolerance. "The one thing we will not tolerate is intolerance. It is un-American. In fact, it is un-Christian," goes the specious logic. But Jesus was intolerant—and his followers must humbly follow his loving example. It is more than possible—it is highly probable—that the church, once pampered, may become the church persecuted.

Is everything, then, hopeless? No, not at all. A church that lives in the *dynamic certitude* that comes from believing God's Word can have a profound effect on culture—as salt and as light. So the church that is sure of God and sure of his Word will foster great hope. But even if culture proceeds down its neo-pagan path, even if it becomes Neronian in its treatment of the church, there remains substantial hope for those who possess Hebrews 11 faith—for they will be empowered to persevere and will sometimes experience astounding victories.

The preacher concludes chapter 11 with a dazzling rush of encouragement as he quickly describes the empowerment that comes through faith to believers who are either winners or even apparent losers in this life.

Empowered for Triumph (vv. 32–35a)

The Empowered

The writer begins by listing half a dozen obvious winners who were empowered for victory: "And what more shall I say? For time would fail me to tell of Gideon, Barak, Samson, Jephthah, of David and Samuel and the prophets" (v. 32).

At God's direction *Gideon* underwent a remarkable divestment of power in preparation for his phenomenal victory over the Midianites. Obediently he reduced his troops from 32,000 to 10,000 to 300. Then the 300, armed with trumpets and pitchers that concealed torches, routed the Midianites whose "camels were without number, as the sand that is on the seashore in abundance" (Judges 7:12). Gideon's feat was a stupendous act of faith.

Likewise, *Barak*, obeying God's word as given through Deborah, sallied forth to meet the great army of Sisera with its 900 chariots of iron and myriads of troops, Barak himself having only 10,000 men drawn from just two of Israel's tribes, Naphtali and Zebulun (Judges 4:6). But his token army was victorious. Once again faith carried the day.

Normally we do not think of *Samson* as a man of faith, but rather a great dunce whose moral brain waves had gone flat! But there was a subterranean substance of faith in Samson. He knew God had given him power to deliver his people from the Philistines—though he frittered it away. But once blinded, he regained his spiritual perspective, and in a great act of faith he prayed and received strength to avenge himself (Judges 16:25–30).

Neither would we imagine *Jephthah* as a man of faith because of his infamous and foolish vow to sacrifice his own daughter (Judges 11:30–39). Nevertheless, this illegitimate son, this outcast Hebrew Robin Hood, was called back to save Israel—which he did through his faith in God. He conquered because of his faith—notwithstanding that his raw uninformed faith tragically was perverted so that it became the source of his rash and wrongful vow to sacrifice "whatever comes out from the doors of my house to meet me" (Judges 11:31).

King *David*, on the other hand, is well-known for his acts of faith, not the least of which was his challenge and defeat of Goliath, to whom he cried, ". . . the LORD saves not with sword and spear. For the battle is the LORD's, and he will give you into our hand" (1 Samuel 17:47). Towering faith!

The prophet *Samuel* had lived a life of faith since he was a little "boy clothed with a linen ephod" (1 Samuel 2:18), serving Eli in the house of the Lord. Through faith he fearlessly delivered God's word to anyone anywhere at anytime—even the sinning King Saul (1 Samuel 15:22, 23). This faithful proclamation was the hallmark of all true prophets.

Viewed together, this dynamic half-dozen bore remarkable similarities to one another. Each lived in a time when faith was scarce—definitely the minority position. During the days of the judges, "everyone did what was right in his own eyes" (Judges 21:25), and this ethic was very much alive during the transfer to the monarchy. From Gideon to David, each battled overwhelming odds—Gideon with his three hundred against an innumerable host—young David against the giant. Each stood alone *contra mundum*. And most significantly, perhaps, each of these heroes had a flawed faith. John Calvin remarked:

There was none of them whose faith did not falter. Gideon was slower than he need have been to take up arms, and it was only with difficulty that he ventured to commit himself to God. Barak hesitated at the beginning so that he had almost to be compelled by the reproaches of Deborah. Samson was the victim of the enticements of his mistress and thoughtlessly betrayed the safety of himself and of all his people. Jephthah rushed headlong into making a foolish vow and was over-obstinate in performing it, and thereby marred a fine victory by the cruel death of his daughter.

And to this we could add that David was sensuous (2 Samuel 11:1ff.), and Samuel lapsed into carelessness in domestic matters (1 Samuel 8:1ff.). Calvin concludes:

In every saint there is always to be found something reprehensible. Nevertheless although faith may be imperfect and incomplete it does not cease to be approved by God. There is no reason, therefore, why the fault from which we labour should break us or discourage us provided we go on by faith in the race of our calling.[2]

How encouraging! There is hope for every man, woman, and child of us. Faith's empowerment is not beyond any of us. As believers we have untapped faith capacities that will surprise not only others but, most of all, ourselves. We each possess interior spiritual nitroglycerin that faith can detonate.

The Empowerments

To further strengthen his argument regarding the power that faith brings to life, the preacher lifts his focus from the empowered to the empowerments that they and others experienced. He lists nine empowerments grouped in three successive groups of three.[3]

The first three give the broad *empowerments* of authentic faith: "who through faith conquered kingdoms, enforced justice, obtained promises" (v. 33a). This was not only the corporate experience of the half-dozen, but the general experience of the preceding sixteen members of the Hall of Faith.

The second trio lists some of the forms of personal *deliverances* that they experienced: "who . . . stopped the mouths of lions, quenched the power of fire, escaped the edge of the sword" (vv. 33b, 34a). Samson, David, and Beniah all shut the mouths of lions through physical force. Samson, barehanded, took a charging lion by the jaws and ripped it apart. David grabbed a sheep-stealing lion by the beard and thrust it through. Beniah descended into a pit on a snowy day and dispatched another king of the beasts. But Daniel is the preeminent example, through his faith and prayer (Daniel 6:17–22).

Shadrach, Meshach, and Abednego trusted God and thus coolly conversed in a blazing furnace while the awe-struck king looked on (Daniel 3:24–27). King David, as well as the prophets Elijah and Elisha, escaped the sword, as did many others (1 Samuel 18:10, 11; 1 Kings 19:8–10; 2 Kings 6:31, 32; Psalm 144:10).

The third triad tells about the astounding *power* that came by faith: "[who] were made strong out of weakness, became mighty in war, put foreign armies to flight. Women received back their dead by resurrection" (vv. 34b, 35a). Elijah stretched himself out three times on the dead form of the son of the widow of Zarephath and cried to God for his life—and then carried the child alive down to his distraught mother (1 Kings 17:17–24). Elisha, his understudy, accomplished a similar feat for the Shunammite woman's son— "putting his mouth on his mouth, his eyes on his eyes, and his hands on his hands . . . the flesh of the child became warm" (2 Kings 4:34).

Three triads—nine empowerments—what power comes through faith! This was important to know and believe under the darkening skies of Nero's impending pogrom. The examples of the empowered six and the litany of the triads of empowerments that have come to the church ought to make one thing very clear: God delights to effect mighty triumphs through people of faith. Faith pleases God—and faith empowers.

God can deliver the faithful anytime he wants from anything! Noah's family was delivered from a flood that drowned all the rest of the human race. Moses and Israel walked through the Red Sea. Joshua and Israel crossed the flooded Jordan. Rahab survived the fallen walls. Gideon prevailed while outmanned a thousand to one. God can deliver us triumphantly from anything if he so pleases—sickness, professional injustice, domestic woe, the growing oppression of a neo-pagan culture—*whatever!* And he will do it again and again and again. But remember, it is always "by faith" in his Word.

But the parallel truth is, God has not promised wholesale deliverance *in this life* for his people at all times and in every situation. Not all of us will be "winners" in this life. From the world's point of view some people of faith are huge "losers."

Empowered for Perseverance (vv. 35b–39)

Now to balance the record, the writer changes the emphasis by showing that faith also provides a different empowerment—the power to persevere to the end.

Perseverance in Persecution

The switch comes abruptly in the middle of verse 35 and on through 36 where the writer describes the power to persevere in persecution: "Some were tortured, refusing to accept release, so that they might rise again to a better life. Others suffered mocking and flogging, and even chains and imprisonment." The apparent reference here is to the Maccabean persecution because the word for "tortured" has etymological reference to the *tympanum*, a large drum or wheel on which Maccabean victims were stretched and beaten or even dismembered. Second Maccabees details the gruesome torture of a ninety-year-old priest, Eleazar, who refused to eat swine's flesh (2 Maccabees 6:18–31), and then goes on to recount the even more revolting accounts of the systematic torture of seven brothers for the same reason (2 Maccabees 7:1–42).

Each of them could have been released if they had compromised, but each categorically refused—the reason being, as our text explains, "so that they might rise again to a better life" (v. 35b). Better? How can one resurrection be "better" than another? Is one slow and another like a rocket launching? What is meant here? It is a better resurrection because it is a resurrection not just back to life on this earth, as happened to women's sons mentioned in verse 35a, but a resurrection to everlasting life in the world to come.

Significantly, the Maccabean accounts of the torture of the seven brothers carry the words of heroic encouragement by their mother based on her hope of the resurrection:

> I do not know how you came into being in my womb. It was not I who gave you life and breath, nor I who set in order the elements within each of you. Therefore the Creator of the world, who shaped the beginning of man and devised the origin of all things, will in his mercy give life and breath back to you again, since you now forget yourselves for the sake of his laws. (2 Maccabees 7:22, 23)

The point of these macabre examples is that through faith God's children can experience triumphant perseverance—even preferring torture to compromise and release.

Perseverance to Death

The preacher moves on to explicitly remind his little church that some of the faithful persevered even to death: "They were stoned, they were sawn in two, they were killed with the sword" (v. 37a). Since stones are plentiful in Palestine, they were often the murderous weapons of choice against the prophets. Jesus mourned this fact, crying out: "O Jerusalem, Jerusalem, the city that kills the prophets and stones those who are sent to it! How often would I have gathered your children together" (Matthew 23:37).

As to being sawed asunder, there is no record of this happening to a martyr in the Bible. However, the writer here draws on a non-Biblical *haggadah* in *Ascension of Isaiah*, which asserts that the prophet Isaiah was sawn in two by the false prophets of Manasseh, who stood by "laughing and rejoicing," and that "he neither cried aloud nor wept, but his lips spake with the Holy Spirit until he was sawn in twain" (5:1, 2, 14).[4]

And, of course, untold numbers of the faithful were devoured in a more conventional manner by the sword. So we see that although some "escaped the edge of the sword" through faith (v. 34), others, equally faithful, suffered its pain. But through faith they persevered to death, whether stoned or sawed or stabbed. What power!

Perseverance in Deprivation

Lastly, there were those of the faithful who knew deprivation: "They went about in skins of sheep and goats, destitute, afflicted, mistreated—of whom the world was not worthy—wandering about in deserts and mountains, and in dens and caves of the earth" (vv. 37b, 38). The calculated irony here is that the world has rejected such people, and yet the world does not deserve to have them even if it were to accept them.

So much for the prosperity gospel! Here are saints who are so holy and so full of faith that the world is not worthy to contain them, and yet they are called to persevere in persecution, deprivation, and death. Not only that, but the reason they are able to persevere *is* their great faith! Christians under the oppressive old paganism of Roman culture were to take note, and so must we in the darkening neo-paganism of our day.

Now, what was the result for those who were faithful in persecution, deprivation, and death? Beautifully, it was and is the same as for those who experienced great public triumphs in their lives (the Noahs and Moseses and Gideons).

First, they were "commended through their faith" (v. 39a). This is the way the chapter began—"Now faith is the assurance of things hoped for, the conviction of things not seen. For by it the people of old received their commendation" (vv. 1, 2)—and this is how it ends. All the faithful (the known and unknown, the famously triumphant and those who anonymously persevered in suffering) were "commended through their faith." God forgets no one who loves and serves him! It is his great pleasure to commend faith!

The second result is that none—that is, none of the great triumphant members of the Hall of Faith or those who persevered without earthly triumphs—"receive[d] what was promised" (v. 39b). Although many promises had been given and fulfilled in their lifetimes, they did not receive the great promise—namely, the coming of the Messiah and salvation in him. Every one of the faithful in Old Testament times died before Jesus appeared. They entered Heaven with the promise unfulfilled.[5]

Why is this? The answer is given in our final verse: "God had provided something better for us, that apart from us they should not be made perfect" (v. 40). No one was "made perfect" under the old covenant, because Christ had not yet died. They were saved, but not until Jesus' work on the cross was complete could salvation be perfect. Their salvation looked ahead to what Christ would do. Ours looks back to what he has done—and ours is perfect.

The surpassing excellence of this is that the faithful of all the ages would not be made perfect apart from Christians. As Leon Morris says:

> Salvation is social. It concerns the whole people of God. We can experience it only as part of the whole people of God. As long as the believers in Old Testament times were without those who are in Christ, it was impossible for them to experience the fullness of salvation. Furthermore, it is what Christ has done that opens the way into the very presence of God for them as for us. Only the work of Christ brings those of Old Testament times and those of the new and living way alike into the presence of God.[6]

All the faithful of all the ages are made perfect in Christ. We are all in it together—from Abel to Rahab—from Paul to Billy Graham.

And the message to the embattled little church, and to us, is: *how great our advantage!* Right here, while we walk on earth, we have the perfection of Christ. And it is so much better under the new covenant. We now have a high priest who has offered a perfect sacrifice for our sins once and for all. Our Savior/priest sits at the right hand of the Father and prays for us. We have, then, a better hope!

How much easier it is for us to walk in faith—even if the walk is down the shadowy roads of neo-pagan culture. We are called to a *dynamic certainty* on the basis of God's Word. It is a *future certainty* that makes the future as if it were present. It is a *visual certainty* that brings the invisible into view.

This is survival truth! We must not succumb to the delusion that gentle rain and sunshine will continue to fall on the church in America as the culture sinks further into neo-paganism. What foolishness! How ahistorical. What ego! What hubris to imagine that the church will sail untouched through the bloody seas.

Those who have ears, let them hear God's steeling Word through the saints of old!

Therefore, since we are surrounded by so great a cloud of witnesses, let us also lay aside every weight, and sin which clings so closely, and let us run with endurance the race that is set before us, looking to Jesus, the founder and perfecter of our faith, who for the joy that was set before him endured the cross, despising the shame, and is seated at the right hand of the throne of God. Consider him who endured from sinners such hostility against himself, so that you may not grow weary or fainthearted.

12:1–3

39

Consider Him

HEBREWS 12:1-3

ON A SUNDAY MORNING during my first year as pastor of College Church (in Wheaton, Illinois), as I stood in the pastors' room before the first service going over the notes of a sermon I was not very confident about, the chief elder burst into the room, flushed with enthusiasm. "Pastor, I have the most wonderful thing to tell you—Alan Redpath is in the congregation this morning, sitting there with Stephen Olford!" Both men are famous British preachers who had pastored here in America—Dr. Redpath at Moody Church in Chicago and Dr. Olford at Calvary Baptist in New York City. Both these men had been held up as paragons of pulpit excellence in my seminary homiletics classes. I responded disingenuously with something like, "Oh, that's . . . wonderful"—and then began to pore even more nervously over my notes.

Now, I always prepare as thoroughly as possible and have always tried to do my best regardless of the situation, but I do remember consciously crossing and dotting my homiletical "t's" and "i's" that morning—though it is to be feared that my sermon was eminently forgettable! But my point is, the presence of notable witnesses is motivating, whatever one's activity may happen to be.

On an earlier occasion during my seminary years, when I was working a swing-shift in a factory in Los Angeles, I made the acquaintance of a law student who played tennis, and Larry King and I talked a lot of tennis during breaks. Soon we began to exchange a little tennis "trash" about who was the best, which after some weeks eventuated into a casual "we'll find out" tennis match. And the game was fairly casual until Larry's wife, Billy Jean King, showed up and began to do a little of her own talking. She was not impressed. Predictably, our shots became crisper, and we began to sweat more—all, of course, with a conscious male "who cares!" casualness! Wimbledon champion Billy Jean's presence definitely elevated the game.

Golfers, think what would happen to your concentration if Arnold Palmer joined your foursome! Or imagine the adrenaline if while shooting some hoops, Michael Jordan appeared saying, "Mind if I join you?" Every ounce of "wanna be" in our mortal bodies would suddenly be on the court! The presence of the pros, the Hall of Famers, is innately elevating.

On a far more exalted level the truth also obtains, for the author of Hebrews paints an awesome picture of one's spiritual observers in an attempt to motivate and instruct his faltering little church to persevere.

The scene is a great coliseum. The occasion is a footrace, a distance event. The contestants include the author and the members of his flock and, by mutual faith, *us*. The cloud of witnesses that fills the stadium are the great spiritual athletes of the past, Hall of Faith members—every one a gold medal winner. They are *not* live witnesses of the event, but witnesses by the fact that their past lives bear witness to monumental, persevering faith that is like Abel's faith: "though he died, he still speaks" (11:4).[1]

Everywhere one looks in the vast arena, there is a kind face nodding encouragement, saying, "I did it, and so can you. You can do it. You have my life for it!" Moses strokes his long beard and smiles. Rahab winks and gives a royal wave.

Your heart is really pumping. You are afraid. And with all your being you want to do well. What to do? Our text eloquently answers with a challenge that can be summarized in four succeeding imperatives.

Divest! (v. 1a)

The call to divestment is clearly spelled out in the opening line: "Therefore, since we are surrounded by so great a cloud of witnesses, let us also lay aside every weight, and sin which clings so closely" (v. 1a). The divestment here, the throwing off of everything, has reference to the radical stripping off of one's clothing before a race, as in the Greek custom of the day. And the writer orders a double divestment—first, of all hindrances, and second, of sin.

Divest Sin

The sin that we are especially commanded to cast off is described as "sin which clings so closely," which is an apt description of what sin repeatedly does. A phenomenon of nature, repeated billions of times, provides an ongoing allegory of sin's billion-fold pathology. Perhaps you have seen it yourself while lying on the grass by a sundew plant when a fly lights on one of its leaves to taste one of the glands that grow there.[2] Instantly three crimson-tipped, finger-like hairs bend over and touch the fly's wings, holding it firm in a sticky grasp. The fly struggles mightily to get free, but the more it struggles, the more hopelessly it is coated with adhesive. Soon the fly relaxes, but to its fly-mind "things could be worse," because it extends its tongue and feasts on the sundew's sweetness while it is held even more firmly by still more sticky tentacles. When the captive is entirely at the plant's mercy, the edges of the leaf fold inward, forming a closed fist. Two hours later the fly is an empty sucked skin, and the hungry fist unfolds its delectable mouth for another easy entanglement. Nature has given us a terrifying allegory.

But the most sobering thing we see here is that the "*sin* which clings so closely" to us refers to the specific sin(s) each of us, individually, is most likely to commit—a "besetting sin" as it is termed in the older translations. We each have characteristic sins that more easily entangle us than others. Some sins that tempt and degrade others hold little appeal for us—and vice versa. Sensuality may be the Achilles' heel for many men, but not all. Another who has gained victory over such sin may regularly down jealousy's deadly nectar, not realizing it is rotting his soul. Dishonesty may never tempt some souls, for guile simply has no appeal to them, but just cross them and you will feel Satan's temper!

What sin is it that so "easily" (NIV) entangles you or me? Covetousness? Envy? Criticism? Laziness? Hatred? Lust? Unthankfulness? Pride? Whatever sin it is, it must be stripped off and left behind.

Divest Hindrances

Our divestment must go even further as we "lay aside every weight"—literally, "the weight that hinders." Not all hindrances or weights are sin, however. In fact, what is a hindrance to you may not be a hindrance in any way to someone else. A hindrance is something, otherwise good, that weighs you down spiritually. It could be a friendship, an association, an event, a place, a habit, a pleasure, an entertainment, an honor. But if this otherwise good thing drags you down, you must strip it away. For example, there may be an ostensibly harmless place (a forest, a store, an apartment, a city) that, because of your past sins, still lures you downward. Such a place must be tossed aside and forgotten.

This image is extreme. If we are to finish well in faith, we must strip our souls naked of "every weight, and sin which clings so closely" to us. The benevolent knowing faces of the witnesses beckon us to do so. We will never run well without doing this. What is called for here, I believe, is a conscious, systematic divestment of all sins and hindrances—a divestment that is regularly performed. Remember, all it takes is *one* sin or *one* hindrance to sabotage the runner's soul!

Run! (v. 1b)

Properly divested, there remains one great thing to do—and that is run: "and let us run with endurance the race that is set before us" (v. 1b).

Run the Course

We each have a specific course mapped out for us, and the course for each runner is unique. Some are relatively straight, some are all turns, some seem all uphill, some are a flat hiking path. All are long, but some are longer. But the glory is, each of us (no exceptions!) can finish the race "that is set before us." I may not be able to run your course, and you may find mine impossible, but I can finish my race and you yours. Both of us can finish well if we choose and if we rely on him who is our strength and our guide!

We can experience the same satisfaction the Apostle Paul did as he neared the finish line:

> I have fought the good fight, I have finished the race, I have kept the faith. Henceforth there is laid up for me the crown of righteousness, which the Lord, the righteous judge, will award to me on that Day, and not only to me but also to all who have loved his appearing. (2 Timothy 4:7, 8)

Is that not a comforting and inviting thought? There is no doubt that we can finish "the race that is set before us"—and finish it with satisfaction.

Run with Perseverance

The secret is to "run with endurance." Here the example of Bill Broadhurst is instructive. In 1981 Bill entered the Pepsi Challenge 10,000-meter race in Omaha, Nebraska. Surgery ten years earlier for an aneurysm in the brain had left him paralyzed on his left side. Now, on that misty July morning, he stands with twelve hundred lithe men and women at the starting line.

The gun sounds! The crowd surges forward. Bill throws his stiff left leg forward, pivots on it as his foot hits the ground. His slow *plop-plop-plop* rhythm seems to mock him as the pack races into the distance. Sweat rolls down his face, pain pierces his ankle, but he keeps going. Some of the runners complete the race in about thirty minutes, but two hours and twenty-nine minutes later Bill reaches the finish line. A man approaches from a small group of remaining bystanders. Though exhausted, Bill recognizes him from pictures in the newspaper. He is Bill Rodgers, the famous marathon runner, who then drapes his newly won medal around Bill's neck. Bill Broadhurst's finish was as glorious as that of the world's greatest, though he finished last. Why? Because he ran with endurance. As William Barclay described this as:

> That determination, unhasting and unresting, unhurrying and yet undelaying, which goes steadily on, and which refuses to be deflected. Obstacles will not daunt it; delays will not depress it; discouragements will not take its hope away. It will halt neither for discouragement from within nor for opposition from without.[3]

It is quite within the reach of every one of us to manifest positive, conquering patience—putting one heavy foot in front of the other until we reach the glorious end. The race is not for sprinters who flame out after 100 or 200 or 400 meters. It is for faithful plodders like you and me. Fast or slow, strong or weak—all must persevere.

Focus! (v. 2)

Focus on Jesus

Now, stripped bare of any weights or sin and running with perseverance, we are given the focus that will ensure our finishing well—and that is, of course, Jesus: ". . . looking to Jesus, the founder and perfecter of our faith" (v. 2a).

By insisting that we focus on Jesus, instead of the name Christ, the writer is calling us to focus on Jesus' humanity as we saw it here on earth. Jonathan Edwards remarked beautifully concerning this that we are to "take notice of Christ's excellence which is a . . . feast."[4] And so it is! We are to focus on him first as "founder" (*archegos*—literally, "pioneer") of our faith. Jesus is the pioneer and founder of all faith in both the Old and New Testaments. He initiates all faith and bestows it (cf. Ephesians 2:8–10).

But, still more, he is the "perfecter of our faith." His entire earthly life was the very embodiment of trust in God (2:13). He perfected living by faith. He lived in total dependence upon the Father (10:7–10). It was his absolute faith in God that enabled him to go through the mocking, crucifixion, rejection, and desertion—and left him perfect in faith. As F. F. Bruce has said, "Had he come down by some gesture of supernatural power, He would never have been hailed as the 'perfecter of faith' nor would He have left any practical example for others to follow."[5] But the sublime fact is, he endured everything by faith, and thus he is uniquely qualified to be the "founder and perfecter" of the faith of his followers.

Do we sense the need of faith to run the race? Then we must "look to Jesus, the founder and perfecter of our faith." That is, as the Greek suggests, we must deliberately lift our eyes from other distracting things and focus with utter concentration on him—and continue doing so.[6] This is fundamental to a life of faith and finishing the race!

Focus on Jesus' Attitude

Along with this we ought to focus on Jesus' attitude—"who for the joy that was set before him endured the cross, despising the shame" (v. 2b). Some people wrongly imagine that because Jesus was a divine man, the physical and spiritual sufferings of the cross were somehow less for him. What wrong-headed thinking, as John Henry Newman so brilliantly explained:

> And as men are superior to animals, and are affected by pain more than they, by reason of the mind within them, which gives a substance to pain . . . so, in like manner, our Lord felt pain of the body, with a consciousness, and therefore with a keenness and intensity, and with a unity of perception, which none of us can possibly fathom or compass, because His soul was so absolutely in His power, so simply free from the influence of distractions, so fully directed *upon* the pain, so utterly surrendered, so simply subjected to the suffering. And thus He may truly be said to have suffered the whole of His passion in every moment of it.[7]

So we must let the full force of the text's statement here in Hebrews—he "endured the cross"—sink into our souls. The *physical* pain he endured was absolute. But the spiritual pain was even greater because his pure soul, which knew no sin, became sin for us, inducing a heretofore unknown pain. And we must also absorb the fact that he "endured the cross, despising the shame." That is, he thought nothing of its shame—he dismissed it as nothing.

How and why could he do this? Because of "the joy that was set before him"—which was rooted in his coming super-exaltation when he sat "at the right hand of the throne of God" (v. 2c). His exaltation, with all that it means for his people's shalom and for the triumph of God's purpose in the universe, was "the joy that was set before him." We can list some specific aspects of his joy. There was the joy of his reunion, as it were, with the Father. What an exalted thought—Heaven's homecoming! Imagine the joy! David's words suggest the idea: "In your presence there is fullness of joy; at your right hand are pleasures forevermore" (Psalm 16:11). Then there was the joy of being crowned with honor and glory and having all things put under his feet (2:6–8; cf. Psalm 8:4–6). There was also the joy before him of bringing many sons to glory—making us part of his joy (2:10).

Our blessed and glorious Lord lived his earthly life in faith's *dynamic certitude*. "Now faith is the assurance of things hoped for [*future certitude*], the conviction of things not seen [*visual certitude*]." Our blessed Lord fixed his eyes not on "the things that are seen but to the things that are unseen. For the things that are seen are transient, but the things that are unseen are eternal" (2 Corinthians 4:18)—and thus his joy was the "eternal weight of glory" (2 Corinthians 4:17).

Now on this matter of focus, understand this: even though the great gallery of past saints witnesses to us, our central focus must be Jesus—*sola Jesu!* Focus on him as the "founder" and originator of faith. Focus on him as the divine human "perfecter" of faith. Focus on the joy that enabled him to endure the awesome agony of the cross and dismiss as nothing the shame. Focus on his joyous exaltation—and the fact that you are part of the joy.

Consider! (v. 3)

In capping his famous challenge to finish well, the writer gives the idea of focusing on Jesus a dynamic twist by concluding: "Consider him who endured from sinners such hostility against himself, so that you may not grow weary or fainthearted" (v. 3). The phrase "grow weary or fainthearted" was sports lingo in the ancient world for a runner's exhausted collapse.[8] Thus, the way for the Christian runner to avoid such a spiritual collapse was to "consider him"—that is, to carefully calculate (we derive our word *logarithm* from the Greek word translated "consider") Jesus and his endurance of opposition from the likes of Caiaphas, Herod, and Pilate. We are to remember his confidence and meekness and steel-like strength in meeting his enemies.

No one can miss the superb wisdom of this passage: we must be totally absorbed with Jesus. This requires negation—turning away from those things that distract us—and then the positive act of consciously focusing and meditating on Jesus. This is why we must read and re-read the Gospels. This is why our worship must be Christocentric. This is why *he* must be the measure of all things.

If we are believers, we are in the race, and we are surrounded by a great cloud of lives whose examples call for our best—the *patriarchs* (Abraham, Isaac, Jacob), the *prophets* (Moses, Elijah, Samuel, Daniel, Jeremiah), the *apostles* (Peter, John, Paul), the *martyrs* (Stephen, Polycarp, Cranmer, Elliott, Saint), the *preachers* (Luther, Calvin, Wesley, Spurgeon), the *missionaries*

(Carey, Taylor, Carmichael), our *departed family members*, and on and on. Their faces invite us to finish well.

So the imperatives are before us:

- We must *divest* ourselves of all hindrances and sins. Figuratively speaking, if our foot hinders us, we must chop it off; if our eye causes us to sin, we must gouge it out (cf. Matthew 5:29, 30). We will not finish the race apart from radical divestment.
- We must *run* with patient perseverance the race that is marked out individually for each of us. We must put one foot in front of the other, refusing to quit—unhasting, unresting, constant.
- We must *focus* on Jesus as "the founder and perfecter of our faith." Jesus must cover the entire sky. He must be the center and horizons of our sight. Such vision will insure for us faith's beginning and end.
- We must *consider* him and how he lived amidst contradiction and follow his example.

In your struggle against sin you have not yet resisted to the point of shedding your blood. And have you forgotten the exhortation that addresses you as sons? "My son, do not regard lightly the discipline of the Lord, nor be weary when reproved by him. For the Lord disciplines the one he loves, and chastises every son whom he receives." It is for discipline that you have to endure. God is treating you as sons. For what son is there whom his father does not discipline? If you are left without discipline, in which all have participated, then you are illegitimate children and not sons. Besides this, we have had earthly fathers who disciplined us and we respected them. Shall we not much more be subject to the Father of spirits and live? For they disciplined us for a short time as it seemed best to them, but he disciplines us for our good, that we may share his holiness. For the moment all discipline seems painful rather than pleasant, but later it yields the peaceful fruit of righteousness to those who have been trained by it.

12:4–11

40

Divine Discipline

ON AUGUST 7, 1954, during the British Empire Games in Vancouver, Canada, one of the greatest mile-run match-ups ever took place. It was touted as the "miracle mile" because Roger Bannister and John Landy were the only two sub-four-minute milers in the world. Bannister had been the first man ever to run a four-minute mile. Both runners were in peak condition.

Dr. Bannister, who is today Sir Roger and master of an Oxford college, strategized that he would relax during the third lap and save everything for his finishing drive. But as they began the third lap, John Landy poured it on, stretching his already substantial lead. Immediately Bannister adjusted his strategy, increasing his pace and gaining on Landy. The lead was cut in half, and at the bell for the final lap they were even.

Landy began running even faster, and Bannister followed suit. He felt he was going to lose if Landy did not slow down. Then came the famous moment (replayed thousands of times in print and celluloid) as at the last stride before the home stretch the crowds roared. Landy could not hear Bannister's footfall and thus compulsively looked back—a fatal lapse of concentration. Bannister launched his attack, and Landy did not see him until he lost the lead. Roger Bannister won the "miracle mile" that day by five yards.

Landy's lapse serves as a modern visualization of what the writer of Hebrews implicitly warned against in his earlier charge to "run with endurance the race that is set before us, fixing our eyes on Jesus, the author and perfecter of faith" (Hebrews 12:1, 2 NASB). Those who look away from Christ—the end-goal of our race—will never finish well. And this was exactly what was happening to some treading the stormy waters mounting around the early church. They had begun to take their eyes off Christ and to fix them instead on the hardships challenging them.

When these Hebrew Christians first came to Christ, the Savior filled their lives from horizon to horizon. It was a delightful, joyous fixation. But that initial rush of joy began to be assaulted by hardships. Some of their lifelong friendships cooled to estrangement. They were no longer welcome in the synagogue. Some lost their jobs as they were squeezed out of the family business. Others were assaulted by domestic stress, as even husband and wife relationships became strained over the matter of Christ. And to boot, their newfound faith did not shield them from the common vicissitudes of life—they suffered reversals, accidents, illness, and death just like everyone else.

As a result, not a few were distracted. Those increasingly longer looks away from Christ left some off-stride. Others stumbled here and there, and tragically a few had quit altogether. They were, in fact, a microcosm of many in the modern church who have lost their focus through hardship—who say, "It all began so well. But I didn't expect this. I had problems before I became a Christian, but nothing like this. Thanks for the offer of the abundant life, but I have an abundance of problems already! You go ahead. I think I'll take a breather."

The preacher/writer now attempts to encourage people like these.

Gentle Reproach for Faltering Endurance (vv. 4–6)

He begins this section with a pair of gentle reproaches. First, he reminds them that life is not as bad as some may suppose. "In your struggle against sin," he says, "you have not yet resisted to the point of shedding your blood" (v. 4). Jesus, of course, had suffered death because of his decision to stay on track—all the way to the cross. And some of the heroes of the faith so memorably praised at the end of chapter 11 had paid the ultimate price as well. But though the Hebrew church had experienced severe persecution early on, under the Emperor Claudius, no one had yet been martyred. The parallels with the modern church in the West are plain to see. The tides of neo-paganism are rising, but none of us have resisted to the point of spilling blood.

Then, like now, was no time to be discouraged—especially considering the great examples of those who have remained steadfast amidst far greater hardships. "Cut the melodrama," the writer seems to be saying, "I don't see any bodies lying around."

The preacher's other reproach was this: they had failed to recall and reassure themselves with God's Word—"And have you forgotten the exhortation that addresses you as sons?" (v. 5a). Of course, this is an even more common sin of the modern church—which, the pollsters tell us, cannot name the books of the Bible or locate the Ten Commandments or the Beatitudes, much less tell us what they are. This also brings us to the indisputable axiom, *we cannot be profoundly influenced (or encouraged) by that which we do not know*. The comfort and strength of God's Word will avail us not at all if we do not *know* it. Many today do not know enough of God's Word to survive a skinned knee! Knowing God's Word is essential for spiritual survival, as the preacher earlier insisted in his letter: "Therefore we must pay much closer attention to what we have heard, lest we drift away from it" (2:1).

Having reproached his congregation for forgetting God's Word, the preacher calls for their attention in a special word of encouragement that addressed them specifically as God's children. This is taken from the Greek rendering of Proverbs 3:11, 12. Verse 5 represents verse 11 of Proverbs 3, which clearly warns those undergoing hard times of two opposite pitfalls of *disdain* and *dismay* regarding divine discipline. Regarding the perils of *disdain*, "My son, do not regard lightly the discipline of the Lord" (v. 5b). The fact is, many who experience the unpleasantness of discipline choose to remain indifferent as to its significance. They vaguely intuit that they are experiencing discipline, but refuse to meditate upon what it might mean. They make light of it—they blow it off! It is better not to think too much about one's hardships, they say to themselves, or they might have to do something about them. Better to just ignore them. By refusing to consider their deep waters, their lives remain perpetually shallow.

The other pitfall is *dismay*—"nor . . . be weary when reproved by him" (v. 5c). Far from being indifferent to discipline, there are some who are overwhelmed by it all. They are paralyzed—just as the runners described in verse 3 came to "grow weary or fainthearted" and collapsed on the track. Such giving up is inexcusable because none of God's children will ever be tested beyond their strength (cf. 1 Corinthians 10:13).

So we see that when disciplined we must not afford ourselves either the luxury of *disdain* or of *dismay*. Why? Because discipline is the telltale sign of being loved by God and in family relationship to him—"For the Lord disciplines the one he loves, and chastises every son whom he receives" (v. 6). In other words, if we cop out in respect to the Lord's discipline either by *disdain* (making light of it) or *dismay* (fainting away), we are turning our back on the personal evidence of his love and relationship to us. Discipline is the divinely ordained path to a deepening relationship with God and a growing love with him. It is the only path! Thus to refuse discipline is to turn our back on growth and love. Therefore we must heed God's words of encouragement to us—

especially as they are given in the following verses, which are an elaboration of Proverbs 3:11, 12.

Gentle Challenge to Sustained Endurance (v. 7a)

To begin with, the truth of the Proverbs passage elicits a command: "It is for discipline that you have to endure" (v. 7a). Jesus "endured" (v. 2), and it is imperative that we "endure."

The word "discipline" comes from a root word generally meaning "to teach or instruct as one would a child" (cf. Acts 22:3; 1 Timothy 1:20; Titus 2:12). Often it means "to correct or punish"—as it means here (cf. v. 10; Luke 23:16, 22). Broadly, it signifies much of what we would think of as discipline for the purpose of education. We experience God's education through hardship or affliction.

Significantly, God's discipline of his children never involves his wrath. Every reference in the New Testament on the subject indicates that God's wrath rests upon and is reserved for the unbelieving.[1] God has no such thoughts toward his own—no thoughts of calamity. Theodore Laetsch, the Old Testament scholar, makes a most perceptive comment regarding this:

> His plans concerning his people are always thoughts of good, of blessing. Even if he is obliged to use the rod, it is the rod not of wrath, but the Father's rod of chastisement for their temporal and eternal welfare. There is not a single item of evil in his plans for his people, neither in their motive, nor in their conception, nor in their revelation, nor in their consummation.[2]

So the preacher to the Hebrews, who exhorts his flock to "endure" their hardships as "discipline," is enjoining them to a most positive pursuit that has as its goal the very growth of their souls.

God's discipline takes three distinct forms—namely, corrective discipline, preventative discipline, and educational discipline[3]—though there are surely other distinctives of discipline that extend beyond these classifications.

Corrective Discipline

Sometimes God's children undergo corrective judgment that comes directly from God's love. King David is a prime exhibit here. His adultery and resulting homicide brought down stiff judgment. The son of his illicit union died, and violence attended his home (cf. 2 Samuel 12:10). His son Amnon raped his half-sister Tamar. Absalom murdered Amnon and then, in league with Bathsheba's father Ahithophel, staged a rebellion. This was a stiff corrective, but David did learn from it and grew in grace. Consider Psalm 51, and also the chastened wisdom of Psalm 119:

> Before I was afflicted I went astray,
>   but now I keep your word. . . .
> It is good for me that I was afflicted,
>   that I might learn your statutes. (Psalm 119:67, 71)

Likewise, in New Testament times the Corinthian church underwent God's corrective discipline when some of its believers suffered illness and even death because they were profaning the Lord's Supper through their greedy, self-centered indulgence and, in some cases, outright drunkenness. Paul explained, "When we are judged by the Lord, we are disciplined so that we may not be condemned along with the world" (1 Corinthians 11:32). Harsh correctives, but they come from a heart of fatherly love.

Preventative Discipline

It is a fact of forestry that very often when small trees are cleared away, some of the big trees will subsequently come down. Why? The smaller trees shielded the larger trees from nature's assaults, and thus the large trees never developed the strength to stand alone. Just so, God regularly allows his children to undergo hardships to prevent their falling.

For example, the Apostle Paul was a humble man. Nevertheless, God gave him a thorn in the flesh to keep him from becoming conceited because of the great revelations God had given him (2 Corinthians 12:7, 8). Paul prayed for it to be removed but later thanked God as he realized how his thorn had protected him.

This same realization enabled D. D. Matheson to pray: "Thou Divine Love, whose human path has been perfected by sufferings, teach me the value of any thorn . . . and then shall I know that my tears have been made a rainbow, and I shall be able to say, 'It was good for me that I have been afflicted.'" Preventative discipline, properly understood, is seen as a substantial grace.

Educational Discipline

A careful reading of the story of Job reveals that his afflictions came not as corrective discipline or preventative discipline but for his education. This is majestically confirmed by Job's own words at the end of his ordeal: "'Hear, now, and I will speak; I will ask You, and You instruct me.' I have heard of You by the hearing of the ear; but now my eye sees You; therefore I retract, and I repent in dust and ashes" (Job 42:4–6 NASB). Job's afflictions, coupled with his dialogue with God, gave him a stupendous revelation of God far beyond that of his contemporaries. From Job's example we understand that discipline may not come because one is doing poorly, but because he is doing well (cf. Job 1:1)! Job was, in fact, a spiritual athlete. And because of his excellence, God (like a wise coach) brought greater stress and challenge to Job so that he might ascend to undreamed of levels of spirituality.

So we see that all the hardships that come the believer's way are loving discipline and are, in effect, either *corrective* or *preventative* or *educational*. We must remember this! As James Moffatt said, "To endure rightly, one must endure intelligently."[4] If we have an informed, intelligent, Biblical understanding of the afflictions that come our way, and we believe God's Word, we will endure. The *correction* of David, the *prevention* of Paul, the *education* of Job—this is sanctifying grist for the reflective heart.

Gentle Reasons for Sustained Endurance (vv. 7b–11)

From here the writer goes on to provide more reasons for the intelligent embrace of and endurance in affliction.

A Paternal Reason

The primary one is that discipline is a sign of God's paternity—it is evidence that we are his children. "God is treating you as sons," he says, "For what son is there whom his father does not discipline? If you are left without discipline, in which all have participated, then you are illegitimate children and not sons" (vv. 7b, 8).

John Perkins, the remarkable preacher and social activist, gives a poignant and deeply instructive account in his book *Let Justice Roll Down* of his father's deserting him when he was a boy.

> I knew then that Daddy was going away without me. But I still didn't turn back. So once more he came back and whupped me a last time.
>
> Just then my Auntie came up. She must have missed me and followed after me. I stood there between the two of them, neither one saying anything. Then she took me by the hand and dragged me away, back down the tracks toward home.
>
> I looked back once, but Daddy was already gone. And with him went my newfound joy in belonging, in being loved, in being somebody for just a little while. Years would pass before I would know this joy again.
>
> I cried all the way back to the house, holding tightly to Auntie with one hand and carrying my heart with the other.

> What was Daddy really thinking, what was in his mind that day he left me? I never found out. I never ever really had a chance to talk with Jap in the few times I saw him again before he died.
>
> But I do know that, even when he punished me for following him that afternoon, he was admitting we had some sort of *relationship*.[5]

Even in this terribly disordered relationship, a failed father's egregious discipline was a telltale sign of his paternity. The Scriptures affirm this primal impulse: "Whoever spares the rod hates his son, but he who loves him is diligent to discipline him" (Proverbs 13:24). And, "The rod and reproof give wisdom, but a child left to himself brings shame to his mother" (Proverbs 29:15).

The ancient world found it incomprehensible that a father could possibly love his child and not punish him. In fact, a real son would draw more discipline than, say, an illegitimate child for the precise reason that greater honor and responsibility were to be his. The ultimate example of this is, of course, Jesus who as the supreme Son "learned obedience through what he suffered. And being made perfect, he became the source of eternal salvation to all who obey him" (5:8, 9). There is no doubt about it—the hardships and disciplines we endure are signs of our legitimacy and ought to be embraced as telltale signs of grace.

An A Fortiori *Reason*

Another reason we should opt for the intelligent acceptance of enduring hardship as discipline is the *a fortiori* argument from the lesser to the greater: "Besides this, we have had earthly fathers who disciplined us and we respected them. Shall we not much more be subject to the Father of spirits and live?" (v. 9). Respect and submission characterized ancients in regard to their *natural* fathers—and it developed a disciplined productive life in the child. But, *a fortiori*, how much more should we submit to our *supernatural* Father and live a life that is life indeed! Submission to the discipline of our *temporal* fathers brought good things, but how much more will come through submission to the discipline of our *eternal* Father. Conscious submission to our divine Father is essential to truly live in the here and now and to have an ever-deepening experience of the abundant life.

Those who live life to the fullest are those who do not buck God's discipline but rather knowingly embrace it. If your spiritual life is static and unfulfilling, it may be because you are consciously or unconsciously resisting God's discipline. If so, God's Word to you is, *submit* to him and begin to truly live!

A Sanctifying Reason

Next, the author argues for our continued endurance of affliction by giving us a sanctifying reason for it: "For they disciplined us for a short time as it seemed best to them, but he disciplines us for our good, that we may share his holiness" (v. 10). Every earthly father, if he is candid, will admit he has meted out imperfect discipline at best. All fathers have learned by doing. Sometimes we were too severe, other times too lax. Sometimes we showed favoritism. Sometimes we punished the wrong child. Sometimes a child "got it" because the boss had "given it" to us. But God has never made such a mistake. No discipline of his was ever capricious or ill-informed or ill-tempered. None of his discipline has ever been misplaced.

Moreover, all the disciplines of the heavenly Father have one grand aim, which is nothing less than to make his people like him—holy (cf. Leviticus 19:2; Matthew 5:48; 1 Peter 1:15, 16). In Christ we have been made "partakers of the divine nature" (2 Peter 1:4), and as partakers, God chastens us so that we will partake even more. The most holy of us are those who have properly endured the most discipline. What a gift, then, discipline is! Jonathan Edwards says of such people:

> They are holy by being made partakers of God's holiness, Heb. xii. 10. The saints are beautiful and blessed by a communication of God's holiness and joy, as the moon and planets are bright by the sun's light. The saint hath spiritual joy and pleasure by a kind of effusion of God on the soul.[6]

What more could we wish in this life?

A Hedonistic Reason

The writer concludes his train of thought by giving a hedonistic, pain/pleasure reason for enduring discipline. First, concerning *pain*: "For the moment all discipline seems painful rather than pleasant" (v. 11a). That is certainly true whatever the level of discipline—a spanking, a privilege suspended, a possession removed, an injury, an illness, a persecution. Moreover, we would be patently weird if we enjoyed the pain—pious masochists. But eventually there comes the *pleasure*: ". . . but later it yields the peaceful fruit of righteousness to those who have been trained by it" (v. 11b).

Blessed hedonism! "The peaceful fruit of righteousness" comes to believers who endure under discipline—not just the objective, imputed righteousness of God (2 Corinthians 5:21), but a subjective, day-to-day righteous life. To the eyes of onlookers the believer's righteous life becomes apparent—as he more and more shows the character of God. But that is just half of the crop, the other half being a harvest of peace—*shalom.* As Isaiah wrote, "The effect of righteousness will be peace, and the result of righteousness, quietness and trust forever" (Isaiah 32:17). Peace—*shalom*—means not only quietness of soul but wholeness. As Richard John Neuhaus says: "It means the bringing together of what was separated, the picking up of the pieces, the healing of wounds, the fulfillment of the incomplete, the overcoming of the forces of fragmentation. . . ."[7] It is Heaven's peace experienced now in an unpeaceful world. Some harvest!

This only comes through enduring hardship as discipline. It does not come through fighting the hard things in life, but from accepting them as discipline from God.

Hardships will do one of two things to us. They will *distract* our focus from Christ, forcing us into a spiritual "Landy's lapse"—so that we are slowed down, or even drop out of the race. Or they will *intensify* our focus on Christ, so that we "run with endurance the race that is set before us, fixing our eyes on Jesus the author and perfecter of faith" (Hebrews 12:1, 2 NASB). If we do this, we will neither *despise* the Lord's discipline nor *dismay* and lose heart (cf. v. 3). We will understand that the disciplines we endure are evidences of the love and relationship God has for us (cf. v. 6).

And thus we will do our best to endure, embracing the reasons we ought to endure hardship as discipline.

- We embrace the *paternal reason* because discipline proves that God is our Father and we are his children!
- We embrace the *a fortiori reason* because discipline makes us live life that is life indeed!
- We embrace the *sanctifying reason* because discipline makes us like God—holy!
- We embrace the *hedonistic reason* because though there is pain now, later it produces a double harvest of righteousness and peace!

This is why we keep our eyes on Jesus and keep running!

Therefore lift your drooping hands and strengthen your weak knees, and make straight paths for your feet, so that what is lame may not be put out of joint but rather be healed. Strive for peace with everyone, and for the holiness without which no one will see the Lord. See to it that no one fails to obtain the grace of God; that no "root of bitterness" springs up and causes trouble, and by it many become defiled; that no one is sexually immoral or unholy like Esau, who sold his birthright for a single meal. For you know that afterward, when he desired to inherit the blessing, he was rejected, for he found no chance to repent, though he sought it with tears.

12:12–17

41

Failing Grace

HEBREWS 12:12–17

WRITER AND SOMETIMES MARATHONER ART CAREY described in a memorable piece for the *Philadelphia Inquirer* his experience of "hitting the wall" and then going on to finish the Boston Marathon. We pick up his story midstride:

> By now, the rigors of having run nearly twenty miles are beginning to tell. My stride has shortened. My legs are tight. My breathing is shallow and fast. My joints are becoming raw and worn. My neck aches from all the jolts that have ricocheted up my spine. Half-dollar-size blisters sting the soles of my feet. I'm beginning to feel queasy and light-headed. I want to stop running. I have "hit the wall."
>
> Now the real battle begins. Up the first of many long inclines I start to climb—one-two, one-two, one-two, right-left, right-left, right-left. I keep watching my feet move, one after the other, hypnotized by the rhythm, the passage of the asphalt below . . . shoulder cramps, leaden legs, seething blisters, dry throat, empty stomach, stop—keep moving—must finish. . . . A radio-listening spectator reports that the race is over. Six miles away, Bill Rodgers has won again. His ordeal is done; the most intense of my own is about to begin.
>
> "Heartbreak Hill"—the last, the longest and the steepest, a half-mile struggle against gravity designed to finish off the faint and faltering. Hundreds of people stand along the hill, watching . . . [urging] the walkers to jog, the joggers to run, the runners to speed on to Boston. . . . Slowly, ever so slowly, the grade begins to level out. . . .
>
> The last four miles are seemingly endless. Some runners, their eyes riveted catatonically to the ground, trudge alone in their bare feet, holding in their hands the shoes that have blistered and bloodied their feet. Others team up to help each other, limping along, arm-in-arm, like maimed and battle-weary soldiers returning from the front.

Finally, the distinctive profile of the Prudential Building looms on the horizon. I begin to step up my pace. Faster, faster . . . smoother, smoother. Suppress the pain. Finish up strong. Careful—not too fast. Don't cramp. . . .

I can see the yellow stripe 50 yards ahead. I run faster, pumping my arms, pushing off my toes, defying clutching leg cramps to mount a glorious, last-gasp kick . . . 40 yards, 30 yards, 20 yards . . . cheers and clapping . . . 10 yards . . . finish line . . . an explosion of euphoria . . . I am clocked in at two hours, 50 minutes and 49 seconds. My place: 1,176. I find the figures difficult to believe, but if they are accurate, then I have run the best marathon of my life.

While times and places are important, and breaking a personal record is thrilling (especially as you grow older), the real joy of the Boston Marathon is just finishing . . . doing what you have set out to do.[1]

According to Holy Scripture, as we have it in Hebrews 12, the marathoner's grit and finishing joy are metaphorical of what we Christians, ancient and modern, are called to in this life. The spiritual life is a long-distance run (vv. 1–3). Though we will "hit the wall" many times, we are called to "tough it out," realizing that the hardships we endure are disciplines that enable us to share in God's holiness (cf. vv. 4–11).

The author's transcending desire is that his flock, and indeed the Church universal, will finish well. So he expounds the metaphor further in verses 12–17 with specific advice on what to do (vv. 12–14) and what to guard against (vv. 15–17) in order to finish well.

Finishing Well—What to Do (vv. 12–14)

Run Tough

The telltale signs of flagging energy are drooping arms, flopping hands, and wobbling knees that reduce the runner's stride to a mincing gait. These signs were proverbial in Biblical culture for mental and spiritual slowdown. Isaiah encouraged his despairing, stumbling people by saying, "Strengthen the weak hands, and make firm the feeble knees. Say to those who have an anxious heart, 'Be strong; fear not! Behold, your God will come'" (Isaiah 35:3, 4). Job was heartened by Eliphaz, the Temanite who reminded him, "Behold . . . you have strengthened the weak hands. Your words have upheld him who was stumbling, and you have made firm the feeble knees" (Job 4:3, 4).

So here the preacher, like an attentive coach, employs the proverbial exhortation, "Therefore lift your drooping hands and strengthen your weak knees" (v. 12). The command to "strengthen" comes from the word from which we derive our English word *orthopedic*. The sense is, "make upright or straight"—or in modern coaching terms, "Straighten up! Get those hands and feet up! Suck it in!"

Of course, he is not promoting a do-it-yourself, bootstrap Christian life. But Christians must will to tough it out by God's grace. Life for the believer is full of repeated hardships that come as divine discipline. In fact, these disciplines are substantive signs that we are authentic sons and daughters (cf. vv. 7, 8). But they still require grit every bit analogous to the determined marathoners. Muscular Christianity is a must! Run tough!

Run Tough Together

Toughing it out is essential, but there is still more to the idea because this toughness is not meant to be a solo venture. In the next verse the writer alludes to Proverbs 4:25–27 as he calls his people to corporate toughness in helping one another to run well: "Make straight paths for your feet, so that what is lame may not be put out of joint but rather be healed" (v. 13). Here the ESV translates *orthos* as "straight," other translations say "level,"[2] but the idea remains clear—to put the paths in better order so as to make the race easier for the lame—"so that what is lame may not be put out of joint."[3]

The point is, every consideration should be made to help everyone finish the race. The bloodied, blistered Boston marathoners teaming up to help each other, limping along arm-in-arm, are a vivid metaphor of this idea. But the church should include not only the weak assisting the weak, but also the strong teaming up with the weak in what Bishop Westcott called "the duty of mutual help."[4]

Hebrews is full of this idea of helping each other make it: "But exhort one another every day, as long as it is called 'today,' that none of you may be hardened by the deceitfulness of sin" (3:13). "Therefore, while the promise of entering his rest still stands, let us fear lest any of you should seem to have failed to reach it" (4:1). "Let us therefore strive to enter that rest, so that no one may fall by the same sort of disobedience" (4:11). "And we desire each one of you to show the same earnestness to have the full assurance of hope until the end" (6:11) ". . . not neglecting to meet together, as is the habit of some, but encouraging one another" (10:25).

I believe Art Carey is right in saying, "The real joy of the Boston Marathon is just finishing"—and I am even more sure that the real joy of the race set before us will be in the finishing.

When by His grace
I shall look on his face

That will be glory,
Be glory for me.

But I also believe there is a double joy—and that is finishing together! As we run the race, we must exorcise the wretched curse of American individualism that so hinders the church. Sure, we have to be tough. We have to "gut it out" by God's grace. But we also have to hang tough *together*. The strong among us must hold up the dangling hands and wobbling knees of the weak with our prayers and acts of mercy. Those who are strong must make straight paths for the weak by the exemplary direction of their lives. The lives of the strong must keep the weak on the right road. Their lives must never cause the weak to stumble. We have to run tough, and we have to run together!

Run After Peace and Holiness

As we run we are encouraged to a dual pursuit—namely, peace and holiness: "Strive for peace with everyone, and for the holiness without which no one will see the Lord" (v. 14). Our experience tells us that though we may have peace with God, we do not always have peace with all men and women. Commitment to Christ incurs the enmity of the world. "If the world hates you," said Jesus, "know that it has hated me before it hated you" (John 15:18). If we follow Christ, we must expect conflict. But how unexpected and disheartening it is when conflict is encountered in the church! There is a passage in Tolkien's *The Fellowship of the Ring* in which God-fearing elves join with God-fearing dwarves to oppose the Dark Lord. But immediately they begin to quarrel, calling down plagues on each other's necks. Then one of the wiser of the company, Haldir, remarks, "Indeed in nothing is the power of the Dark Lord more clearly shown than in the estrangement that divides all those who still oppose him."[5]

Conflict in the church brings glory to Satan and disgraces our God. Few things will grieve God more and impede the great race more than conflict in the Body of Christ. In fact, conflict in the church—and the failure to pursue peace—is the most public reason so many never finish. Satan too often infiltrates committees and elders' homes and parsonages, paralyzing those who ought to be setting the pace for others.

So as we run the race we must pursue peace with "everyone"—both Christians and non-believers alike. The word "strive" or "pursue" is an uniquely aggressive word. It is often used in the sense of "to chase after one's enemies—to persecute."[6] We must chase after peace! Other Scriptures further enjoin the aggressive pursuit of peace, urging us to "[be] eager to maintain the unity of the Spirit in the bond of peace" (Ephesians 4:3), and to "pursue what makes for peace" (Romans 14:19). Similarly, Romans 12:18 says, "If possible, so far as it depends on you, live peaceably with all." And, of course, there is the grand dominical beatitude, "Blessed are the peacemakers, for they shall be called sons of God" (Matthew 5:9). Those who pursue peace *will* to forgive and *will* to forget and *will* to be kind and *will* to be thoughtful and *will* to help others and *will* to pray for their enemies!

The preacher has linked the pursuit of peace with the pursuit of practical holiness (purity of soul) because he sees a logical association between them. Significantly, Jesus made the same association between peace and purity by joining them in successive beatitudes. "Blessed are the pure in heart" is followed by "Blessed are the peacemakers" (Matthew 5:8, 9). Character and peace are woven together as a single garment of the soul. Ultimately it is holy people who finish the race, for it is they who "shall see God" (Matthew 5:8) at his glorious return or in the glory that comes with death.

The application is clear: the way to finish well in life's marathon is to pursue peace and holiness—to give it our best—to "strive for peace with everyone, and for the holiness without which no one will see the Lord." We must learn the "runner's lean," stretching ourselves forward to peace, extending our entire beings toward holiness!

Finishing Well—What to Guard Against (vv. 15–17)

As the writer continues his advice about finishing well, he turns from the positive charges (regarding running tough, running tough together, and running after peace and holiness) to negative admonitions about what to guard oneself against. The warnings come in three successive clauses.[7]

Gracelessness

The first clause is in verse 15a and warns against what we shall call gracelessness: "See to it that no one fails to obtain the grace of God." Grace is the divine attitude of benevolence God has toward his children. The image that helps me to picture this is that of a brimming pitcher in God's hand tilted to pour blessing on us. The Apostle James says essentially this when he declares, "But he gives more grace" (James 4:6)—literally, "great grace." Thus we confidently know there is always more grace for the believer. Earlier in 4:16 the preacher/writer urged us, "Let us then with confidence draw near to the throne of grace, that we may receive mercy and find grace to help in time of need."

The unchanging truth is, we can have no need that outstrips his grace, and we never will! Even if we fall into deep sin, greater grace is available, as Paul said: "But where sin increased, grace abounded all the more" (Romans 5:20b). "For daily need there is daily grace; for sudden need, there is sudden grace; for overwhelming need, there is overwhelming grace," wrote John Blanchard.[8]

Because of this, what a tragedy gracelessness is—and hence the warning, "See to it that no one fails to obtain the grace of God" (literally, "falls short of the grace of God")—the idea being that of "falling behind, not keeping pace with the movement of divine grace which meets and stirs the progress of the Christian."[9]

And how does this gracelessness come to afflict a child of grace? First and primarily, through unconfessed sin. Lack of confession, in effect, places a hand against the tilted pitcher with a tragic power that omnipotence refuses to overcome.

Secondly, one often misses the grace of God by a self-imposed famine of God's Word. For millennia God has watered the lives of his people with his Word. Those who do not read and meditate on it are self-condemned to a state of spiritual anorexia.

A third way to gracelessness is the absenting of oneself from the fellowship of the church, Christ's Body. The movement of divine grace through Christ's Body is meant to be a corporate experience. A section of Paul's prayer for the church in Ephesians 3:17–19 explains the important truth that it is together "with all the saints" that we "comprehend . . . what is the breadth and length and height and depth . . . [of] the love of Christ" and, indeed, go on to "be filled with all the fullness of God." Our capacity to understand God's Word and to experience his grace is vitally linked to our participation in church "with all the saints." It is in rich community that we experience grace upon grace.

Beautifully here in our text "See to it" is a plural command, making it everyone's responsibility to make sure no one misses the grace of God. Moreover, "See to it" is an unusual word that bears the sense of oversight (in fact, we derive the word *bishop* from this verb).[10] The idea is: "All of you, act like bishops in seeing that no one succumbs to gracelessness." We are called to some sanctified "meddling" in each other's lives. We must consciously involve ourselves in the Body of Christ, assuming responsibility for seeing others go on in grace, and also humbly receiving their loving care for us. We all need grace to finish the race!

'Tis grace hath brought me safe thus far,
And grace will lead me home.

Apostasy

The next clause calls the church to steel itself against idolatry and apostasy if it is to finish well, warning the believers to beware "that no 'root of bitterness' springs up and causes trouble, and by it many become defiled" (v. 15b). The image of idolatry as a bitter root comes from Deuteronomy 29:18, where the Lord formally warned his people against apostasy: "Beware lest there be among you a man or woman or clan or tribe whose heart is turning away today from the LORD our God to go and serve the gods of those nations. Beware lest there be among you a root bearing poisonous and bitter fruit." The phrase in our text that depicts the root's apostatizing growth is freighted with even further insight because it describes a hidden seed that takes root and grows slowly, so that only time reveals what it is.[11] Virtually every church has such bitter roots, and it is the height of arrogance to imagine otherwise.

The call here is for vigilance. Certainly this does not enjoin a witch hunt. The Lord specifically warned against such a response because such actions would tear out real wheat with the weeds (Matthew 13:24–30). Nevertheless, we must be alert. Every fellowship of any size has a few "bitter roots" who follow false gods and subtly poison those around them. If we are to run well, the price is vigilance—especially in the good times.

Appetites

The next verse indicates there are two appetites that can torpedo the race—the *sexual* appetite and the *physical* appetite: "See to it . . . that no one is sexually immoral or unholy like Esau, who sold his birthright for a single meal" (vv. 15, 16). Here the writer asserts in clearest terms that Esau was sexually immoral, calling him a *pornos*, from which we get the word *pornography*. Interestingly, the Old Testament does not say he was a fornicator unless it is implied in his marrying the two Canaanite daughters of Heth, who subsequently made life miserable for his parents (cf. Genesis 26:34, 35). Rabbinical tradition, however, both Palestinian and Hellenistic, paints Esau as a man completely subject to his libido.

Philo of Alexandria in his *Questions and Answers on Genesis* made this observation regarding Esau: "The hairy one is the unrestrained, lecherous, impure and unholy man."[12] The Palestinian Targum on Genesis 25:29 describes him as coming home exhausted on the same day he sold Jacob his birthright and saying that on "that day he had committed five transgressions," one of which was adultery with a betrothed maiden.[13]

The indictment from extra-Biblical literature parallels the revelation of

Holy Scripture—that Esau was a *pornos* subject to the whims of his tomcat nature—the archetype of the modern-day testosterone man. His essential sensuality made God quite unreal to him—as lust always does.[14]

This goes hand in glove with the text's second assertion that he was "unholy," *bebelos*, a man who had no regard for God, whose focus was only on physical pleasures. Calvin says of such that they are:

> . . . those in whom the love of the world so holds sway and prevails, that they forget heaven as men who are carried away by ambition, addicted to money and riches, given over to gluttony, and entangled with other kinds of pleasures, and give the spiritual kingdom of Christ either no place or the last place in their concerns.[15]

Remember Esau's story in Genesis 25? He grew up to be a big, hairy, red-headed lout whose focus was *fun* (hunting), *food*, and *females*, as Hebrews here asserts. Big "Red" (for that is what his nickname "Edom" meant) came in from the field hungry after hunting and found Jacob cooking some lentil stew. So he motioned, "Let me eat some of that red stew, for I am exhausted!" (Genesis 25:30), to which Jacob made the incredible proposition, "Sell me your birthright now" (Genesis 25:31), only to be followed by Esau's even more incredible flip response, "I am about to die; of what use is a birthright to me?" (Genesis 25:32). Unbelievable! Old sweaty Red chose a cheap meal over the divine promise.

Esau was completely earthbound. All his thoughts were on what he could touch, taste, and suck. Instant gratification was his rule of thumb. He was void of spiritual values. Godless!

Esau was like a living beer commercial—bearded, steroid-macho, with two things on his mind: sexual pleasure and physical pleasure—food, drink, sports, and sleep. "Hey, you only go around once. You have to get it while you can." He was the prototype of modern godlessness—like the forty-five-year old man who had spent all his post-college years devoted to money and when asked, "How is it with your soul?" answered candidly, "My soul? I don't even know whether I have one." Tragic!

In Esau's pathetic case he went on to lose his birthright and blessing (cf. Genesis 27). And there was no remediation, because the text concludes, "For you know that afterward, when he desired to inherit the blessing, he was rejected, for he found no chance to repent, though he sought it with tears" (v. 17). If Esau sought forgiveness (and perhaps he did), God would have given it to him. But there was no way Esau's pleading could undo what was done. He had to live with the consequences. He could never possibly finish as well as he had begun.

God's message to all who are in the race is so clear: Sexual and physical appetites, given free rein, will ruin our race. Sure, we can repent of any sin, but Esau-like sins will leave deficiencies that can never be regained. How tragic, then, that so many today are selling a glorious finish for a cheap meal!

Art Carey's lyrical note on completing the Boston Marathon went like this: "The real joy of the Boston Marathon is just finishing . . . doing what you have set out to do. It is like climbing Mount Everest, hitting a home run during the World Series, or scoring a touchdown during the Super Bowl."

And it may well be. But if that is so, can you imagine what it is going to be like, after life's numerous "heartbreak hills" and bloody feet, when we cross the tape having finished well with our eyes fixed on "Jesus, the founder and perfecter of our faith" (12:2)?

Do we want to finish well? Then here is what we must do:

- *Run tough*—"Therefore lift your drooping hands and strengthen your weak knees" (v. 12).
- *Run tough together*—"Make straight paths for your feet, so that what is lame may not be put out of joint but rather be healed" (v. 13).
- *Run after peace and holiness*—"Strive for peace with everyone, and for the holiness without which no one will see the Lord" (v. 14).

And here is what we must guard against:

- *Gracelessness*—"See to it that no one fails to obtain the grace of God . . ." (v. 15a).
- *Apostasy*—". . . that no 'root of bitterness' springs up and causes trouble, and by it many become defiled" (v. 15b).
- *Appetites*—". . . that no one is sexually immoral or unholy like Esau, who sold his birthright for a single meal" (v. 16).

The joy of the Christian's marathon will be finishing. May we finish well!

For you have not come to what may be touched, a blazing fire and darkness and gloom and a tempest and the sound of a trumpet and a voice whose words made the hearers beg that no further messages be spoken to them. For they could not endure the order that was given, "If even a beast touches the mountain, it shall be stoned." Indeed, so terrifying was the sight that Moses said, "I tremble with fear." But you have come to Mount Zion and to the city of the living God, the heavenly Jerusalem, and to innumerable angels in festal gathering, and to the assembly of the firstborn who are enrolled in heaven, and to God, the judge of all, and to the spirits of the righteous made perfect, and to Jesus, the mediator of a new covenant, and to the sprinkled blood that speaks a better word than the blood of Abel.

12:18–24

42

Marching to Zion

HEBREWS 12:18–24

AS WE HAVE SEEN in the three preceding studies of this chapter, Hebrews 12 presents wisdom for living the Christian life by employing the metaphor of a long-distance race. Following Christ of necessity involves enlisting in a lifelong spiritual marathon. Success in this great race is dependent on the careful cultivation of spiritual athleticism. Verses 1–3 presented the basics—that we must run with perseverance *divested* of sin and hindrances and *focused* on "Jesus, the founder and perfecter of our faith." Verses 4–11 further advised us regarding how to endure the race's hardships as spiritual discipline and make the most of it. Verses 12–17 instructed us positively on what to do and negatively on what to guard against if we wish to finish well.

One of the facts that comes through loud and clear is that marathoning is tough. Spiritual runners experience the spiritual equivalents of what the Boston marathoner regularly undergoes—bone grinding against raw bone, searing half-dollar-sized blisters, "hitting the wall" so that each step is like running through warm caramel. Sometimes, like modern marathoners, they are encouraged by those along the way, just as the spectators who line Boston's "Heartbreak Hill" encourage the walkers to jog and the joggers to run, cheering, "Pick up those feet. You can do it!" Because of such encouragement, runners finish well.

But there is an experience the spiritual runner undergoes that is virtually unknown to those involved in a mere physical race—and that is the jeering of carping distracters. This was the experience of the early Hebrew church and of virtually all who have subsequently followed in its footsteps. Specifically, in that day Jewish Christians were being taunted by their newly estranged relatives and friends and synagogue officials for leaving the historic Jewish faith. As they followed Christ and attempted to put one foot in front of the other, as they ascended their own spiritual "heartbreak hills," they were hearing discordant voices: "You are on the wrong path. You are headed away from Sinai and Jerusalem. You have left your heritage in Abraham and Moses. You have forsaken your nation that has had the great blessings of God. You will never make it!"

The writer addresses such thinking in verses 18–24 by contrasting where his people have come from with where they have come to and are indeed going. The contrast is between Mounts Sinai and Zion—the old and new covenants—terror and joy—distance and closeness.

From Sinai's Law (vv. 18–21)

Essential to understanding the contrast, we must see that the giving of the Law at Mount Sinai was an awesome *physical* display, as depicted in Exodus 19:16–19, 20:18, 19, and Deuteronomy 4:11, 12. The prelude to the divine fireworks at Sinai involved the people's consecration as directed by God (cf. Exodus 19:10–15). They washed their clothing (Exodus 19:10, 11, 14) and abstained from sexual relations, so as to be ceremonially clean (Exodus 19:15). They also observed God's orders that no man or beast touch the mountain on pain of death by stoning or arrows (Exodus 19:12, 13).

The stage remained set for three days. Then on the morning of the third day, the people saw a thick cloud cover the top of Sinai illumined by gold veins of lightning with accompanying thunder rolling down the slopes, plus a deafening trumpet blast that reduced everyone to trembling (Exodus 19:16). Whether the trumpet sound was natural or unnatural cannot be determined. Personally I believe it was supernatural because it was heard by all the million plus in the camp and because the giving of the Law was attended by "ten thousands of holy ones" (Deuteronomy 33:2). Hundreds of thousands of angels hovered invisibly around and over Sinai, and some, I think, were blowing celestial horns.

Whatever the case, Moses led his people from their tents to the foot of the mountain, and this is what they saw: "Now Mount Sinai was wrapped in smoke because the LORD had descended on it in fire. The smoke of it went up like the smoke of a kiln, and the whole mountain trembled greatly. And as the sound of the trumpet grew louder and louder, Moses spoke, and God answered him in thunder" (Exodus 19:18, 19). Imagine what it must have been like to be there: the ground is unsteady under your feet due to perpetual seismic tremors—the sky is black in deep darkness except for the radiating forks of lightning in the gloom and the fire blazing from the top of Sinai "to the heart of heaven" (Deuteronomy 4:11)—celestial shofars blare more and more loudly in primal moans—Moses speaks, and God answers him with a voice like thunder. The only thing that matches the incredible display you are witnessing is the seismic trauma in your heart!

The people were visibly, physically assaulted with the holiness and majesty of God. This palpable divine display on Sinai communicated far more than any speech or written word ever could—and all Israel, young and old, could understand.

In addition to providing a glimpse of God's holiness, the blazing fire atop Sinai emphasized that his holiness rendered him a judge—"a consuming fire" (cf. Deuteronomy 4:24; Hebrews 12:29). The effect of these physical signs was to display in no uncertain terms the absolute unapproachableness of God. The mountain was so charged with the holiness of God that for a man to touch it meant certain death. Even if an innocent animal wandered to the mountain, it would contract so much holiness that it became deadly to the touch and had to be killed from a distance by stone or arrow.[1]

The salutary effect upon those at the foot of Sinai was substantial—it instilled a proper fear of God. As Moses explained, "God has come to test you, that the fear of him may be before you, that you may not sin" (Exodus 20:20). It was patently remedial. To understand that God is holy and that one is a sinner is to stand at the threshold of grace. Moreover, the giving of the Ten Commandments in this awesome context—and Israel's failure to keep them—served to emphasize the people's impotence and doom, which is a further grace, however negative the experience may be.

But this said, the great problem with the trip to Sinai was that while men and women could come to see God's holiness and their sinfulness, the Law provided no power to overcome sin.

> To run and work the law commands,
> Yet gives me neither feet nor hands.

Understanding this, the writer's explanation that they have come to a better mountain than Sinai makes sense: "For you have not come to what may be touched." Zion, to which they had come, is a spiritual mountain, whereas Sinai was a physical mountain that could be touched only at pain of death.

> For you have not come to what may be touched, a blazing fire and darkness and gloom and a tempest and the sound of a trumpet and a voice whose words made the hearers beg that no further messages be spoken to them. For they could not endure the order that was given, "If even a beast touches

the mountain, it shall be stoned." Indeed, so terrifying was the sight that Moses said, "I tremble with fear." But you have come to Mount Zion. . . ." (vv. 18–22a)

In effect, the writer is admonishing his people as they attempt to run with perseverance the race that is marked out for them to not listen to the voices of their old friends who are still immersed in the futile pursuit of attempting to live up to Sinai, but rather to do everything in their power to maintain a straight path to Zion's grace.

There is an early passage in *Pilgrim's Progress* in which Christian, amidst the difficulties of trying to walk the narrow path to Zion, is lured away by Mr. Worldly Wiseman's counsel and directed toward the futility of Sinai. Bunyan writes:

> So Christian turned out of his way to go to Mr. Legality's house for help; but, behold, when he was got now hard by the hill, it seemed so high, and also that side of it that was next the wayside did hang so much over, that Christian was afraid to venture farther, lest the hill should fall on his head; wherefore there he stood still, and wotted not what to do. Also his burden now seemed heavier to him than while he was in his way. There came also flashes of fire out of the hill that made Christian afraid that he should be burnt: here, therefore, he sweat and did quake for fear. And now he began to be sorry that he had taken Mr. Worldly Wiseman's counsel; and with that, he saw Evangelist coming to meet him, at the sight also of whom he began to blush for shame.[2]

And, of course, Mr. Evangelist got him back on track, and the race continued on to Zion, the heavenly Jerusalem.

Today few Christians, especially Gentiles, are in danger of turning back to Sinai per se and embracing the Levitical corpus of the Old Testament. Sinai, with its fiery mountain and its code, is simply too daunting. Instead we fabricate our own mini-Sinais with a series of mini-laws that reflect nothing of the fiery presence and that are, we think, well within the reach of our unaided powers. If one is an evangelical, one's little legalisms reflect something of Biblical ethics, however faintly. If one is liberal, the little legalisms will simply reflect cultural consensus about popular causes.

But whether evangelical or liberal, our legalisms—our mini-Sinais—are always *reductionist*, shrinking spirituality to a series of wooden laws that say, "If you will do those six or sixty or six hundred things, you will be godly." And, of course, legalism is always *judgmental*. How easily our hearts imagine that our lists elevate us, while at the same time providing us with a convenient rack on which to stretch others in merciless judgment.

To Zion's Grace (vv. 22–24)

From Mount Sinai we now switch to Mount Zion and the sublimest description anywhere of what we come to under grace. It is lyrical and has the feel of an early confession regarding the church. Perhaps the little Hebrew church sang or chanted its words in the months that followed as it attempted to run the race amidst the ensuing Neronian persecution. There follows now seven sublimities.

First, we come to the *city of God*—"But you have come to Mount Zion and to the city of the living God, the heavenly Jerusalem" (v. 22a). Mount Zion was the location of the Jebusite stronghold that David captured and made the religious center of his kingdom by bringing to it the golden ark of God—God's presence with his people. When Solomon built the temple and installed the ark, Zion/Jerusalem became synonymous with the earthly dwelling-place of God. In Christ we have come to its *heavenly counterpart*, the spiritual Jerusalem from above. In one sense, this is still to come (cf. 13:14, "but we seek the city that is to come"), but we have also already arrived there in spirit.

Christians are *now* citizens of the heavenly city and enjoy its privileges. Paul wrote, "But our citizenship is in heaven, and from it we await a Savior, the Lord Jesus Christ" (Philippians 3:20). We are in Zion by virtue of our incorporation in Christ, for "[God] raised us up with him and seated us with him in the heavenly places in Christ Jesus" (Ephesians 2:6).

Sure, the fiery presence is there, but we have the requisite holiness and access of Christ. And what is more, we are in Zion for good. "But you have come to Mount Zion" is in the perfect tense, emphasizing our permanent, continuing state. This is why the seemingly endless miles of life's marathon and the inevitable "heartbreak hills" do not stop us. We are in Zion and marching—marathoning—to Zion!

Second, as the church we meet *angels*—"But you have come . . . to innumerable angels in festal gathering" (v. 22). Moses tells us that "ten thousands of holy ones" attended the giving of the Law (Deuteronomy 33:2), and from Daniel we hear that "A thousand thousands served him [the Ancient of Days—God], and ten thousand times ten thousand stood before him" (Daniel 7:10). David said, "The chariots of God are twice ten thousand, thousands upon thousands" (Psalm 68:17). In the church we come to these dizzying thousands of angels.

They are everywhere—mighty flaming spirits, "ministering spirits sent out to serve for the sake of those who are to inherit salvation" (1:14), passing in and out of our lives, moving around us and over us just as they did with Jacob of old. Sometimes they protect God's elect—for example, the "tall men in shining garments" who surrounded Mr. and Mrs. John G. Paton years ago in the New Hebrides—or the "tall soldiers with shining faces" who protected missionary Marie Monsen in North China—or, on another occasion, the "huge men, dressed in white with flaming swords" who surrounded the Rift Valley Academy—and on another the "hundreds of men dressed in white, with swords and shields" who stood guard over a hut shielding Clyde Taylor, who would one day found the National Association of Evangelicals. Similarly, a missionary from the church I pastor, Carol Carlson, serving in China in 1922, learned why the bandits never attacked her compound—there were "men in white walking up and down the wall."[3]

At other times, angels preside over the apparent earthly tragedy of God's people. Olive Fleming Liefeld in her book *Unfolding Destinies* tells how two young Auca Indians, Dawa and Kimo, heard singing after witnessing the martyrdom of the five missionaries in the jungles of Ecuador. "As they looked up over the tops of the trees they saw a large group of people. They were all singing, and it looked as if there were a hundred flashlights."[4]

But the grand emphasis of our passage is not so much the angels' care of us, but rather our joining them in festal assembly. The word translated "festal gathering" was used in ancient culture to describe the great national assemblies and sacred games of the Greeks. Whereas at Mount Sinai the angels blew celestial trumpets that terrified God's people, we are to see ourselves on Mount Zion as dressed in festal attire and worshiping in awe side by side with these shining beings!

Third, we come to *fellow-believers*—"to the assembly of the firstborn who are enrolled in heaven" (v. 23a). Jesus is the firstborn par excellence, and by virtue of our union with him *we* are firstborn.[5] All the rights of inheritance go to the firstborn—to us who are "fellow heirs with Christ" (Romans 8:17). Bishop Westcott says we are "a society of 'eldest sons' of God."[6] There are no second or third or fourth sons and daughters in the church. We all get the big inheritance!

And there is more. As firstborn, our names are written in Heaven along with the firstborn who are already there. In other words, there is an amazing solidarity between the Church Triumphant in Heaven and the Church Militant here on earth. We are all the Body of Christ! The family is never broken. It simply keeps growing and going on and on—a bulging assembly of rich first sons and daughters.

Fading is the world's best pleasure
All its boasted pomp and show;
Solid joys and lasting treasure
None but Zion's children know.

John Newton
"Glorious Things of Thee Are Spoken," 1779

Fourth, we come to *God*—"and to God, the judge of all" (v. 23b). Although the scene in Zion to which we come is a joyous festival, it is not a casual thing. We come to Zion to meet the God of Sinai, who is Judge of all. We understand regarding him that "no creature is hidden from his sight, but all are naked and exposed to the eyes of him to whom we must give account" (4:13). We also know that he said, "'Vengeance is mine; I will repay.' And again, 'The Lord will judge his people.' It is a fearful thing to fall into the hands of the living God" (10:30, 31).

Knowing this, we come before him in awe because he is the Judge. But we do not come in craven dread, because his Son has borne the judgment for us. This is our *highest delight*—to gather before God! It is a miracle of grace.

Fifth, we come to the *Church Triumphant*—"to the spirits of the righteous made perfect" (v. 23c). As we have noted, though they are in Heaven, we share a solidarity with those who have gone before. The same spiritual life courses through us as through them. We share the same secrets as Abraham and Moses and David and Paul. Here is an amazing thing—they died millennia before us, but God planned, according to 11:40, "that apart from us they should not be made perfect." They waited for centuries for the perfection we received when we trusted Christ, because that came only with Christ's death—"by a single offering he has perfected for all time those who are being sanctified" (10:14). Because of Christ's work we are not one whit inferior to the patriarchs, for through Christ we are all equal in righteousness!

Sixth, we come—"to *Jesus*, the mediator of a new covenant" (v. 24a). Significantly, Christ's human name, redolent in the Incarnation, is used here because we have come to the man "*like* us, and the man *for us*."[7] Moses was the mediator of the old covenant, but as great as he was, he trembled fearfully at Mount Sinai (cf. v. 21). But through Jesus, the mediator of the new covenant, we draw near with confidence. The promises of the new covenant are sure, for they are in Jesus. He is the source and dispenser of all for which we hope. He is *in* us, and we are *in* him.

Savior, if of Zion's city,
I through grace a member am,

Let the world deride or pity,
I will glory in Thy name.

John Newton
"Glorious Things of Thee Are Spoken," 1779

Seventh, we come to forgiveness because of *sprinkled blood*—"and to the sprinkled blood that speaks a better word than the blood of Abel" (v. 24b). Abel's warm blood cried from the ground for vengeance and judgment, but Christ's blood shouts that we are forgiven and have peace with God. *Hallelujah!* Oh, the eloquence of Jesus' blood! It says that what was impossible for us has happened. It says that you and I are forgiven!

As fellow-pilgrims in the great marathon, we must not veer off course toward Sinai, because Jesus has met Sinai's great demands for holiness and perfection at Calvary atop Mount Zion.

To run and work the law commands,
Yet gives me neither feet nor hands;
But better news the gospel brings;
It bids me fly, and gives me wings.

The Scriptures tell us that in the Church "you have come" (*right now!*) to these seven sublime realities:

- To the City of God
- To myriads of angels
- To fellow-believers
- To God
- To the Church Triumphant
- To Jesus
- To forgiveness

If this does not create a wellspring of thanksgiving in our hearts and make us want to march to Zion, what will?

See that you do not refuse him who is speaking. For if they did not escape when they refused him who warned them on earth, much less will we escape if we reject him who warns from heaven. At that time his voice shook the earth, but now he has promised, "Yet once more I will shake not only the earth but also the heavens." This phrase, "Yet once more," indicates the removal of things that are shaken—that is, things that have been made—in order that the things that cannot be shaken may remain. Therefore let us be grateful for receiving a kingdom that cannot be shaken, and thus let us offer to God acceptable worship, with reverence and awe, for our God is a consuming fire.

12:25–29

43

A Consuming Fire

HEBREWS 12:25–29

DURING CHRISTIANITY'S SECOND CENTURY, a notable heretic by the name of Marcion came to power in Asia Minor. Though he was excommunicated early on, his destructive teaching lingered for nearly two centuries. Marcion taught the total incompatibility of the Old and New Testaments. He believed there was a radical discontinuity between the God of the Old Testament and the God of the New Testament—between the Creator and the Father of Jesus. So Marcion created a new Bible for his followers that had no Old Testament and a severely hacked-up New Testament that consisted of only one Gospel (an edited version of Luke) and ten select and edited Pauline epistles (excluding the Pastorals). His views were spelled out in his book *Antitheses*, which set forth the alleged contradictions between the Testaments. Tertullian in his famous *Against Marcion* wrote a five-volume refutation.

But Marcionism never completely died out, and in the nineteenth century, especially, with the rise of liberalism, it underwent a revival among those who wished to separate what they considered to be the crude and primitive parts of the Old Testament from the New. Friedrich Schleiermacher, the eighteenth- and nineteenth-century father of liberalism, said the Old Testament has a place in the Christian heritage only by virtue of its connections with Christianity. He felt it should be no more than an appendix of historical interest. Adolph Harnack argued that the Reformers should have dropped it from the canon of authoritative writings. Likewise, there are thousands today who have rejected the Old Testament either formally or in practice.

The error of this kind of approach was pointed out by another liberal, Albert Schweitzer, who demonstrated that such thinking amounts to choosing aspects of God that fit one's man-made theology. Men project their own thoughts about God back up to him and create a god of their own thinking. Anyone who is in touch with modern culture knows that this kind of reasoning—Marcionism—is alive and well.

What does this have to do with us who hold both Testaments to be the inerrant, infallible Word of God? Very much! You see, Marcionism is subtly alive in the evangelical enterprise's understanding of God. Of course, it is true that the New Testament gives us a fuller revelation of God and that we do not live under the Old Testament. Nevertheless, the God we worship is still the *same God*. But, sadly, many Christians today are so ignorant of their Bibles, especially the Old Testament, that they have a tragically sentimentalized idea of God—one that amounts to little more than a Deity who died to meet their needs; the sin question is minimized or ignored. The result is the incredible paradox of evangelicals who "know Jesus" but who do not know who God is—unwitting Marcionites!

The remedy for this travesty is the Bible, specifically Sinai in the old covenant and Zion in the new covenant—each of which present a vision or an *aesthetic* for understanding God.[1]

From Mount Sinai we learn, in Moses' words, that God is a consuming fire—"Take care, lest you forget the covenant of the LORD your God. . . . For the LORD your God is a consuming fire, a jealous God" (Deuteronomy 4:23, 24). The vision is stupendous—a mountaintop blazing with "fire to the heart of heaven" (Deuteronomy 4:11)—cloaked with a deep darkness—lightning illuminating golden arteries in the clouds—celestial rams' horns overlaying the thunder with mournful blasts—the ground shaking as God's voice intones the Ten Commandments. God is transcendentally "other," perfectly good and holy. He radiates wrath and judgment against sin. God cannot be approached.

This is the vision for the heart of every believer—"the LORD your God is a consuming fire." It is the corrective so needed in today's church that has shamefully trivialized worship, turning it into a self-assured farce. Here God's divine intention in creating Sinai is obvious because "a picture is worth a thousand words." Flaming Mount Sinai shows us God!

Of course, the other mountain, Mount Zion of the New Testament, completes the picture. There we see God's love as God the Son takes all of his people's transgressions on himself so that he became sin (2 Corinthians 5:21; cf. Galatians 3:10,11, 13)—writhing under its load like an impaled serpent (cf. Numbers 21:4–8). There on the cross we see God the Son dying for our sins and extending forgiveness to all who will believe in him, trusting his work alone for salvation. What a vision we are bequeathed from Calvary: God with his arms nailed wide as if to embrace all those who come to him—his blood covering the earth, speaking a better word than the blood of Abel (12:24)—the consuming love of God. Mount Zion, crowned by Golgotha, shows us God!

Both mountains—Sinai and Zion—reveal the true God. Neither can be separated from the other. God is not the God of one hill but of both. Both visions must be held in blessed tension within our souls—consuming fire and consuming love. This will save us from the damning delusion of Marcion!

It is this great twin-peaked God to whom we come as we marathon onward "to Mount Zion and to the city of the living God, the heavenly Jerusalem" (12:22). The massive dual revelation of the mountains is meant to shape our pilgrimage. The question we must ask is, how then are we to march? What are we to do? The answer? *Obey* and *worship*.

Obedience (vv. 25–27)

Effectual Word

We ought to obey because God's word is unstoppably *effectual*: "See that you do not refuse him who is speaking. For if they did not escape when they refused him who warned them on earth, much less will we escape if we reject him who warns from heaven" (v. 25). This is what is called in logic an *a fortiori* argument, an argument that argues that what is true in the lesser case will be even more true in the greater. In the lesser case, God's earthly warning at Sinai first suffered subtle refusal by the Israelites when they "beg[ged] that no further messages be spoken to them" (12:19; cf. Exodus 20:19)—though their refusal there at Sinai was more from fear than from outright rejection of God. However, in the years that followed, they explicitly refused God's word by repeated disobedience during the four decades of wandering in the wilderness. So grievous was their disobedience that Numbers 14:29 records that God pronounced judgment in that everyone who was twenty and older would die in the desert. And, indeed, none did escape except faithful Caleb and Joshua. A million plus corpses littered the desert.

Considering the inexorable penalty for disobeying God's earthly message, how much greater will the penalty be in the greater instance of disobeying his heavenly message of grace through his Son (cf. 1:2)? Surely no one will escape! This, of course, has been the writer's message all along. In 2:3a he warned, "How shall we escape if we neglect such a great salvation?" Later in 10:28, 29 he said much the same thing, emphasizing greater punishment:

> Anyone who has set aside the law of Moses dies without mercy on the evidence of two or three witnesses. How much worse punishment, do you think, will be deserved by the one who has trampled underfoot the Son of

God, and has profaned the blood of the covenant by which he was sanctified, and has outraged the Spirit of grace?

The message is so clear: we had better obey God's Word because his
threat that no one who disobeys will escape is ineluctably effectual. It is a
"done deal." No person will escape who refuses the gospel! God is a relentless "consuming fire."

Final Word

If this is not sufficient reason to obey the God of the two mountains, there is
another, and that is that his word is *final*, as the writer goes on to explain: "At
that time his voice shook the earth, but now he has promised, 'Yet once more
I will shake not only the earth but also the heavens.' This phrase, 'Yet once
more,' indicates the removal of things that are shaken—that is, things that
have been made—in order that the things that cannot be shaken may remain"
(vv. 26, 27).

The initial historical event where God's voice shook the earth was at
Mount Sinai when he verbally spelled out the Ten Commandments with a
thunderous voice. Imagine how terrifying it was to have the ground under
one's feet tremble in response to God's audible word. There were no sleepers
in the congregation at Sinai!

But there is an infinitely greater shaking coming, an eschatological cosmic shaking of the whole universe, and it too will be triggered by God's word.
Here the writer has quoted God's promise from Haggai 2:6—"Yet once more
I will shake not only the earth but also the heavens" (v. 26b)—indicating that
every created thing will be shaken to utter disintegration. This is in accord
with what the Scriptures teach us about the power of God's word. Genesis
says he created everything by his word as he spoke the universe into existence.
Therefore, one "little word" from him can and will fell creation!

The psalmist tells us that creation is transitory: "Of old you laid the foundation of the earth, and the heavens are the work of your hands. They will perish, but you will remain; they will all wear out like a garment" (Psalm 102:25,
26; cf. Hebrews 1:10–12). Isaiah says of the future, "Therefore I will make
the heavens tremble, and the earth will be shaken out of its place, at the wrath
of the LORD of hosts in the day of his fierce anger" (Isaiah 13:13). And Peter
identifies it with the day of the Lord: "But the day of the Lord will come like
a thief, and then the heavens will pass away with a roar, and the heavenly bodies will be burned up and dissolved, and the earth and the works that are done
on it will be exposed" (2 Peter 3:10). Think of it! All one hundred thousand

million galaxies—each containing at least that many stars—each galaxy one hundred light-years across—will hear the word and shake out of existence! Just a little word from God, and it is done.

The reason for this is clearly spelled out: "in order that the things that cannot be shaken may remain" (v. 27b). The people of God, as a part of the order of those things that are unshakable, will survive. But everything else in the universe will be shaken and therefore purged. Everything that is wrong will be eradicated. No sin, no imperfection will remain. Then there will be a blessed reconstruction—"Then I saw a new heaven and a new earth, for the first heaven and the first earth had passed away" (Revelation 21:1).

To those who are obedient this is good news. And the writer means it to be a powerful encouragement to the beleaguered little church to which he writes, in which some feel as though their lives are being shaken to pieces by Rome. "Stand firm amidst the Roman tremors," he seems to be saying, "because the ultimate shaking is coming when Rome and indeed the entire present evil order will fall into oblivion. And you, as part of the new order, will survive. Take heart!" On the other hand, to those who are ignoring God's word and drifting further away, this was a disquieting revelation and a challenge to obedience.

But to all, including us, there is here a mighty call to obey God's word, because it is *effectual* and *final*. No Israelite who disobeyed God's earthly word survived the desert, and how much more will that be the case with those who disobey the heavenly word through Christ. God's word is effectual—it never fails. And God's word is final. It started the universe, and it will stop it! So the command to all us pilgrims in verse 25 comes with great force: "See that you do not refuse him who is speaking."

Are you refusing God? Has he been speaking to you, but you have been ignoring his word? What folly! His word is *effectual*, and it is *final*.

Worship (vv. 28, 29)

After obedience, the other great "to do" that comes from the two mountains is worship: "Therefore let us be grateful for receiving a kingdom that cannot be shaken, and thus let us offer to God acceptable worship, with reverence and awe, for our God is a consuming fire" (vv. 28, 29). Charles Colson, in his book *Kingdoms in Conflict*, relates:

> In 1896, the . . . planners of St. John the Divine in New York city envi-
> sioned a great Episcopal cathedral that would bring glory to God. Nearly
> a century later, though the immense structure is still under construction,

it is in use—in a way that its planners might well have regarded with dismay.

St. John's Thanksgiving service has featured Japanese Shinto priests; Muslim Sufis perform biannually; Lenten services have focused on the ecological "passion of the earth" . . . St. John the Divine has ceased to be a house of the one God of the Scriptures, and has become instead a house of many gods. Novelist Kurt Vonnegut Jr. wrote for the cathedral's centennial brochure that "the Cathedral is to this atheist . . . a suitable monument to persons of all ages and classes. I go there often to be refreshed by a sense of nonsectarian community which has the best interest of the whole planet at heart. . . ."

Dean James Morton has encountered opposition, but he defends it saying:

This cathedral is a place for people like me who feel constricted by the notion of excluding others. What happens here—the Sufi dances, the Buddhist prayers—are serious spiritual experiences. We make God a Minnie Mouse in stature when we say these experiences profane a Christian church.[2]

The Scriptures, however, would argue that it is Dean Morton who has made the great God of Sinai and Zion into a mousy deity whose only "virtue" is sub-Biblical toleration. It is difficult to conceive how much farther one could depart from the awesome God of the Scriptures—a God who tolerates no other gods before him, who forbids idolatry and demands the holiness of his people. Instead of giving his people a golden calf, the cathedral dean has given them a Mickey-Mouse reflection of popular culture—a profoundly vapid idolatry.

Note our text well! It says that "our God is [not was!] a consuming fire." The God of Zion is the same God as the God of Sinai. God has not changed. To some of us, the troubles faced by some of the great religious traditions may seem far removed. But the truth is, similar problems are common in the more independent, evangelical traditions. One Sunday morning a friend of mine visited a church where, to his amazement, the worship prelude was the theme song from the Paul Newman/Robert Redford movie *The Sting*, entitled (significantly, I think) "The Entertainer." The congregation was preparing for divine worship while cinematic images of Paul Newman and Robert Redford in 1920s garb hovered in their consciousness! Absurd!

And that was just the prelude, for what followed was an off-the-wall service that made no attempt at worship, the "high point" being the announcements when the pastor (inspired, no doubt, by the rousing prelude) stood unbeknownst behind the unfortunate person doing announcements making "horns" behind his head with his forked fingers and acting Bozo-like for the congregation. This buffoonery took place in a self-proclaimed "Bible-believing church" that ostensibly worships the holy Triune God of the Bible!

But what was in the pastor's and people's minds? What did they really think of God? How could anyone do such things and understand who God is? The answer is, they were modern evangelical Marcionites whose ignorance of Holy Scripture had so edited God that divine worship had become man-centered vaudeville—and poor slapstick at that!

Granted, Christians ought to laugh—they ought to have the best sense of humor on this planet. And Christians ought to enjoy life. But they must also know and understand that God remains "a consuming fire" and that acceptable worship takes place when there is authentic "reverence and awe." This is God's Word!

When we come to worship, we must keep both mountains in view—the approachable Zion with its consuming love, and the unapproachable Sinai with its consuming fire—and then come in reverent boldness.

Everything depends on how we see God. If we see him Scripturally we will experience awe and reverence—and there will be times when we are overwhelmed with the numinous as our souls are engaged by God. Our heart's desire for ourselves and those around us ought to be that: (1) they be regenerated, (2) they have a radical Biblical vision of God, a sense of his holiness and transcendence, and (3) this will inform all of life—their worship, their sense of mission and evangelism, their stewardship, their affirmation and delight in creation, their relationships, their sexual ethics—everything!

We members of the unshakable kingdom are meant to worship with thankful hearts. Our pulses should race with thanksgiving—"Thanks be to God for his inexpressible gift!" (2 Corinthians 9:15). Whatever we do or wherever we go, we must be "giving thanks always and for everything to God the Father in the name of our Lord Jesus Christ" (Ephesians 5:20).

It is so easy to succumb to focusing on one mountain at the expense of the other. But theological balance is the key. Our God is both unapproachable and approachable.

The twin peaks of our spiritual life demand two things as we march to Zion: *obedience* and *worship*. Let us obey his Word implicitly, for it is *effectual*—it never fails, and it is *final*—it will shake the whole universe. Let us worship him with reverence and awe and thanksgiving!

Let brotherly love continue. Do not neglect to show hospitality to strangers, for thereby some have entertained angels unawares. Remember those who are in prison, as though in prison with them, and those who are mistreated, since you also are in the body.

13:1–3

44

Ecclesial Ethics

HEBREWS 13:1–3

MUCH OF THE NEW TESTAMENT, especially the epistles, follows the common pattern of giving theological instruction followed by practical application—theology, then *practicality*. The change can be expressed in many ways—from *exposition* to *exhortation*, from *creed* to *conduct*, from *doctrine* to *duty*, from the *indicative* to the *imperative*. This characteristic movement took place in Hebrews in the shift between chapters 11 and 12 where the writer began to exhort his people regarding their duty to run the great race marked out for them.

Yet, while the continental divide in Hebrews is between chapters 11 and 12, there are numerous mini-divides that follow the theology-to-practicality pattern. One such divide follows closely in the switch from chapter 12 to chapter 13. Chapter 12 builds to an intensely theological crescendo with the statement that "God is a consuming fire," which is then met by the intensely *practical* command that opens chapter 13—namely, to "Let brotherly love continue." So now we move from *fire* to *function*—from *vertical* to *horizontal*—from *love for God* to *love for the church*.

The implication is clear: what we think about God has everything to do with our relationship to each other and with the world. For example, this logic is built into the very structure of the Ten Commandments. The first four are intensely vertical and theological, followed by six that are intensely horizontal and ethical. This is why worship is so important—because a proper grasp of God will guide our footsteps in the world.

So the question that our text answers is this: understanding that God is both the consuming fire of Mount Sinai and the consuming love of Mount

Zion, how ought we to live—especially in the church? What ought our ecclesial ethics to be?

Volitional Love (v. 1)

The answer begins with the command given in verse 1: "Let brotherly love continue."

There had been an evident flagging of brotherly affection among the members of the tiny Jewish congregation as it rode the increasingly hostile seas of Roman culture. History and experience show that persecution and the accompanying sense of dissonance with pagan and secular culture can bring two opposite effects. One is to draw God's people together, but the other is to promote disaffection. For example, in the 1830s two New York Christians, Reverend John McDowall and Mr. Arthur Tappan, were drawn together in their battle against the abuse of women fallen to prostitution, and the two men formed the Magdalen Society. But when their work began to probe too close to the heart of New York society, both found that they could "scarcely go into a hotel, or step for a moment on board a steamboat, without being annoyed by . . . angry hissing."[1] This, along with threats from Tammany Hall and derisive newspaper coverage that branded Mr. Tappan as "Arthur D. Fanaticus," brought immense stress upon the two men, which served to exacerbate their differences and finally ended their friendship.[2]

I have witnessed the same phenomenon when ministering in Europe at a conference attended by some expatriate Eastern Europeans who under lengthy persecution had become increasingly rigid, legalistic, and judgmental. I learned then that persecution can definitely have a spiritual downside.

The structure of the command here to "Let brotherly love continue" suggests that the brotherly and sisterly bonds in the little church were dangerously frayed among some of the members.[3] This was not the way they had begun because initially the fresh experience of salvation in Christ had brought with it the discovery of a shared paternity, the joyous sense of being brothers and sisters with the same Father, and the experience of *philadelphia*—the word used here, meaning "brotherly love."

At first, this love had come to those new believers as naturally as one's first steps, very much like Paul's allusion to the similar experience of the Thessalonians: "Now concerning brotherly love [*philadelphia*] you have no need for anyone to write to you, for you yourselves have been taught by God to love one another" (1 Thessalonians 4:9). For these new Christians, loving other believers was as easy as falling off a log. They could not wait to get to church where they could drink in the fellowship of the godly. The fellowship of their new brothers and sisters was delectably mysterious to them, and they rejoiced in plumbing the depth of each other's souls.

Indeed, their brotherly love was a telltale sign of their salvation. As the Apostle John would later write: "We know that we have passed out of death into life, because we love the brothers" (1 John 3:14). Their impulse to brotherly love provided a sweet, inner self-authentication. It also announced to the world that their faith was the real thing, for Jesus had said, "By this all people will know that you are my disciples, if you have love for one another" (John 13:35).

What a glorious phenomenon brotherly love is—a sense of the same paternity (a brotherly and sisterliness taught by God, a desire to climb into each other's souls), a sweet inner authentication, and the sign of the real thing to the world.

But it had been waning in the little house-church with the years of stress and uncertainty. Some of the brethren had grown weary of each other. And a few actually seemed to exchange mutual hatred.

What to do? The answer given here is utterly volitional—they were to *will* to practice brotherly love! Inwardly this requires that we will to consider the stupendous implications of our shared generation—that we truly are brothers and sisters (the terms are not merely sentimental but are objective fact)—that though we are millions, we share only one Father—that we will still be brothers and sisters when the sun turns to ice—that God is pleased when brothers and sisters dwell together in unity (cf. Psalm 133 and John 17).

Outwardly, we must will to say and do only those things that will enhance our *philadelphia*. To paraphrase Will Rogers, we must so order our lips that we would not be afraid to sell the family parrot to the pastor—or to any other Christian friend.

We must will to love one another. George Whitefield and John Wesley did this even though they disagreed in matters of theology. Whitefield's words say it all:

> My honored friend and brother . . . hearken to a child who is willing to wash your feet. I beseech you, by the mercies of God in Christ Jesus our Lord, if you would have my love confirmed toward you . . . Why should we dispute, when there is no possibility of convincing? Will it not, in the end, destroy brotherly love, and insensibly take from us that cordial union and sweetness of soul, which I pray God may always subsist between us? How glad would the enemies of our Lord be to see us divided. . . . Honored sir, let us offer salvation freely to all by the blood of Jesus, and whatever light God has communicated to us, let us freely communicate to others.

The will to let brotherly love remain—this is a divine duty.

Volitional Hospitality (v. 2)

In March 1990 Clark and Ann Peddicord, Campus Crusade for Christ representatives in Germany, gave this report in a personal letter:

> Last week the former communist dictator, Erich Honecher, was released from the hospital where he had been undergoing treatment for cancer. There is probably no single person in all of East Germany that is more despised and hated than he. He has been stripped of all his offices and even his own communist party has kicked him out. He was booted out of the villa he was living in; the new government refused to provide him and his wife with accommodation. They stood, in essence, homeless on the street. . . . It was Christians who stepped in. Pastor Uwe Holmer, who is in charge of a Christian help-center north of Berlin, was asked by Church leaders if he would be willing to take them in. Pastor Holmer and his family decided that it would be wrong to give away a room in the center that would be used for needy people, or an apartment that their staff needed; instead, they took the former dictator and his wife into their own home. It must have been a strange scene when the old couple arrived. The former absolute ruler of the country was being sheltered by one of the Christians whom he and his wife had despised and persecuted. In East Germany there is a great deal of hate toward the former regime and especially toward Honecher and his wife, Margot, who had ruled the educational system there for 26 years with an iron hand. She had made sure that very few Christian children were able to go on for higher education. There are ten children in the Holmer family and eight of them had applied for further education in the course of the past years: all had been refused a place at college because they were Christians, in spite of the fact that they had good or excellent grades in school. Pastor Holmer was asked why he and his family would open their door to such detestable people. . . . Pastor Holmer spoke very clearly, "Our Lord challenged us to follow him and to take in all who are weary and heavy laden—both in soul and in body. . . ."[4]

The story is a miracle, for no one, apart from the grace of God and the example of Christ and the instruction of the New Testament, would stoop to do such a thing. Pastor Holmer was certainly informed by God's Word, and perhaps even the teaching here of 13:2—"Do not neglect to show hospitality to strangers, for thereby some have entertained angels unawares."

We may wonder, why this teaching on hospitality, and what motivated it some two thousand years ago? For starters, inns were proverbially miserable places from earliest antiquity on. In Aristophanes' *The Frogs*, Dionysus asks Heracles if he can tell him which inn has the fewest fleas. Plato, in *The Laws*, instances an innkeeper keeping his guests hostage. And Theophrastus puts innkeeping on the level of running a brothel.[5]

Thus inns were not congenial or healthy places for Christians. This, coupled with the fact that many Christians had suffered ostracism by both society and family, necessitated Christian hospitality—which was happily provided by brothers and sisters who could do so. Predictably, such hospitality was sometimes abused. The first-century pagan satirical writer Lucian describes how his Elmer Gantry-like protagonist Proteus Peregrinus took advantage of naive Christians, reporting that "he left home, then, for a second time, to roam about, possessing an ample source of funds in the Christians, through whose ministrations he lived in unalloyed prosperity" (*The Passing of Peregrinus*, 16).[6]

Significantly, such abuses became so common that the *Didache*, an early Christian handbook, gave this advice:

> Let every Apostle who comes to you be received as the Lord, but let him not stay more than one day, or if need be a second as well; but if he stays three days, he is a false prophet. And when an Apostle goes forth let him accept nothing but bread till he reach his night's lodging; but if he ask for money, he is a false prophet." (11:4–6)[7]

The effect of all this was that some Christians had noticeably cooled in their hospitality. As the country song says: "Fool me once—shame on you! Fool me twice—shame on me!"

To counter this destructive trend among his congregation, the writer again frames his advice as a command: "Do not neglect to show hospitality to strangers" (v. 2a)—or more exactly, "Do not forget to show love to strangers." In the Greek there is even a beautiful assonance between the words for brotherly love (*philadelphia*) and love for strangers (*philozenia*). The writer has phrased his language for maximum impact.

To him, hospitality was so important that he tantalized his people with an enchanting possibility—"for thereby some have entertained angels unawares" (v. 2b). The primary reference here was no doubt to the cheerful hospitality Abraham extended to three strangers who unbeknown to him were angels— one of whom was no less than Jehovah himself (Genesis 18)! The Hebrew mind would recall a chain of similar encounters—perhaps Gideon's encounter with the angel under the oak in Ophrah (Judges 6:11ff.), or Manoah's unstinting hospitality to the angel unaware who then announced that he and his wife would give birth to Samson (Judges 13).

By presenting the delectable possibility of hosting a real angel, the preacher was not promoting hospitality on the chance that one might luck out and get an angel, but was simply saying that the possibility of its happening indicated how much God prizes hospitality in his people.

The fact is, some of us have entertained angels! Hebrews 12:22 says that in coming to Zion, "You have come . . . to innumerable angels in festal gathering." That hasty hamburger topped with raw onions and served to a hungry stranger may have rested in a celestial stomach—and with no heartburn! Bishop Westcott was right: "We only observe the outside surface of those whom we receive. More lies beneath than we can see."[8]

The Scriptures consistently place a high premium on hospitality. Paul says, "Contribute to the needs of the saints and seek to show hospitality" (Romans 12:13). Peter choruses, "Show hospitality to one another without grumbling" (1 Peter 4:9). No one must ever think for a moment of being a Christian leader but not practicing hospitality—"Therefore an overseer must be above reproach . . . self-controlled, respectable, hospitable . . ." (1 Timothy 3:2; cf. Titus 1:8).

Why this great premium on opening one's home and life to others? There is a reason beyond meeting each other's occasional material needs—it is in each other's homes that we really get to know one another. In fact, you can never really know another person without being in his or her abode. In one's home, over the table, relaxed amidst the decor and accoutrement of one's persona—that is where exchange is naturally enhanced and brotherly love elevated. Sharing a blessed meal at the family table can be quasi-sacramental. It binds us together in the reality that everything comes from Christ.

And finally, there is another reason for hospitality—sharing love with strangers who do not know Christ. East German dictator Erich Honecher was no angel, that is for sure! But I think some angels dropped in to Pastor Holmer's home. I also believe that if Erich and Margot Honecher ever became Christians, the primary earthly medium will have been humble Christian hospitality! The writer's unadorned point stands firm: we must *will* to be hospitable.

Volitional Empathy (v. 3)

Herman Melville in his novel *White Jacket* has one of the ship's sailors became desperately ill with severe abdominal pain. The ship's surgeon, Dr. Cuticle, waxes enthusiastic at the possibility of having a real case to treat, one that challenges his surgeon's ability. Appendicitis is the happy diagnosis. Dr. Cuticle recruits some other sailors to serve as his attendants.

The poor seaman is laid out on the table, and the doctor goes to work with skillful enthusiasm. His incisions are precise, and while removing the diseased appendix he proudly points out interesting anatomical details to his seaman-helpers who had never before seen the inside of another human. He is completely absorbed in his work and obviously a skilled professional. It is an impressive performance, but the sailors—without exception—are not impressed but are rather appalled. Why? Their poor friend, now receiving his last stitch, has long been dead on the table! Dr. Cuticle had not even noticed.[9] Cold Dr. Cuticle—a man with ice water in his veins—was insensitive and void of empathy.

But such is never to be the case with Christians, as the writer to the Hebrews further commands: "Remember those who are in prison, as though in prison with them, and those who are mistreated, since you also are in the body" (v. 3). In this respect, the little Jewish church had earlier excelled, as the preacher averred in 10:32–34:

> But recall the former days when, after you were enlightened, you endured a hard struggle with sufferings, sometimes being publicly exposed to reproach and affliction, and sometimes being partners with those so treated. For you had compassion on those in prison, and you joyfully accepted the plundering of your property, since you knew that you yourselves had a better possession and an abiding one.

And how important their sympathetic caring had been, because those suffering the abuse of prison were virtually dependent on the church for survival.

The early church had a remarkable reputation in the pagan community for caring for its own. Lucian, again, has his bogus Christian, Proteus Peregrinus, tossed into prison, and, satirical as Lucian was, the sympathetic care of Christians shines. Says Lucian, the Christians

> . . . left nothing undone in the effort to rescue him. Then, as this was impossible, every other form of attention was shown him, not in any casual way but with assiduity; and from the very break of day aged widows and orphan children could be seen waiting near the prison, while their officials even slept inside with him after bribing the guards. The elaborate meals were brought in, and sacred books of theirs were read aloud. (*The Passing of Peregrinus*, 12)[10]

Similarly, *The Apology of Aristides* describes Christians' care for the incarcerated, saying:

> If they hear that any of their number is imprisoned or oppressed for the name of their Messiah, all of them provide for his needs, and if it is pos-

sible that he may be delivered, they deliver him. If there is among them a man that is poor or needy, and they have not an abundance of necessaries, they fast two or three days that they may supply the needy with their necessary food.[11]

How beautiful the church had been and would continue to be!

But here we see the preacher giving his people a profound prod to a sublime empathy—an empathy so deep that they would will to project themselves into the inner life of those suffering mistreatment and imprisonment. The unadorned empathy commanded here was not based on the esoteric truth that Christians are members of each other in Christ, but rather on the truth of shared humanity. Project your humanity into the place where their humanity now is—in suffering or in prison.

This call is especially relevant to us modern Christians who have had our empathizing faculties increasingly dulled by the electronic media that assault us daily with images of suffering narrated with the professional, detached nonchalance of the network anchors.

We must *will* to identify with the imprisoned and mistreated. None of us can excuse ourselves by rationalizing that we are not empathetic by nature. We are to labor at an imaginative sympathy through the power of God!

In summary, we are to stand at the foot of the two mountains and gaze reverently at God's consuming fire and consuming love. We are to drink it in with all its mysterious paradox—for in it lies the vision of God.

But having gazed upward we turn from the *vertical* to the *horizontal*, from the *indicative* to the *imperative*—the ethics of a life aglow with God. And here we must will to obey the imperatives—God's commands.

- We must will to practice brotherly love, *philadelphia*: "Let brotherly love continue" (v. 1). We must will to contemplate the fact of our mutual generation, its profundity and eternity. Our words and actions must be committed to enhancing brotherly love.
- We must will to practice love of hospitality, *philozenia*—a love for strangers: "Do not neglect to show hospitality to strangers, for thereby some have entertained angels unawares" (v. 2). Open hearts and open houses are the Christian way. Hospitality builds the Body of Christ and opens the door to a lost world.
- We must will to be empathetic, to be imaginatively sympathetic: "Remember those who are in prison, as though in prison with them, and those who are mistreated, since you also are in the body" (v. 3). The will to have imaginative sympathy will make our hearts like that of the Master and will encourage an authentic Christian walk.

Let marriage be held in honor among all, and let the marriage bed be undefiled, for God will judge the sexually immoral and adulterous. Keep your life free from love of money, and be content with what you have, for he has said, "I will never leave you nor forsake you." So we can confidently say, "The Lord is my helper; I will not fear; what can man do to me?"

13:4–6

45

Personal Ethics

HEBREWS 13:4–6

FROM THE BEGINNING TO THE END OF HEBREWS, the abiding concern of the author has been to so instruct the tiny Hebrew church that it would stay afloat on the increasingly hostile seas of first-century Roman culture. Their ship was a microscopic dot on the massive billows of the official pagan/secular enterprise—and eminently vulnerable. It appeared to outside eyes that the external forces could sink it at will.

But the author knew that the internal threat to the church was far more deadly. In fact, he knew that it could ride out any storm if things were right on the inside. That is why, in our preceding study (13:1–3), the preacher so strongly emphasized ecclesial ethics, instructing his people on how to treat those on board the ship—the church. Specifically, he advised, first, brotherly love, then hospitality, and then the necessity of sympathetically identifying with those in the church who were undergoing suffering.

Now in the present text, verses 4–6, he becomes even more intimate in his advice, giving very personal ethical directives about *marriage*, *money*, and one's *mind-set*. He knows that nothing will sink a church faster than moral wavering in respect to sex, materialism, or mental outlook. Here is intimate advice regarding how to keep our ship afloat. It is so essential that any church that ignores it will founder and possibly even sink.

Advice about Marriage (v. 4)

The advice about marriage is direct and unequivocal: "Let marriage be held in honor among all, and let the marriage bed be undefiled, for God will judge the sexually immoral and adulterous" (v. 4).

443

Marriage and Honor

Here the command to honor marriage is directed at those who dishonored it in two opposite ways—*asceticism* and *libertinism*. Some first-century Christian ascetics considered "virginity as necessary to Christian perfection."[1] This later developed in the second century into the Montanist movement, which later spawned celibate monasticism. To such, those who choose marriage choose inferior spirituality. Marriage was thus implicitly dishonored. But the greatest assault on marriage's honor came from the libertines who saw marriage as irrelevant as they pursued unbridled sexual fulfillment.

These first-century extremes foreshadowed the modern contempt for marriage. For example, Count Leo Tolstoy embraced a perverse marital asceticism late in life, claiming that the responsibilities of marriage impeded his progress in moral perfection. Since he had a large family, this was a remarkable assertion. In an outburst to his daughter Tanya written in 1897 he said:

> I can understand why a depraved man may find salvation in marriage. But why a pure girl should want to get mixed up in such a business is beyond me. If I were a girl I would not marry for anything in the world. And so far as being in love is concerned, for either men and women—since I know what it means, that is, it is an ignoble and above all an unhealthy sentiment, not at all beautiful, lofty or poetical—I would not have opened my door to it. I would have taken as many precautions to avoid being contaminated by that disease as I would to protect myself against far less serious infections such as diphtheria, typhus or scarlet fever.[2]

Tolstoy's wide acceptance, and his radical chic style, gave his ideas unusual weight among the avant-garde culture-shapers of the early twentieth century and ultimately provided grist for subsequent secular attacks by both heterosexuals and homosexuals on marriage. Today radical secular wisdom claims that marriage impedes self-actualization—an unforgivable sin in modern eyes.

However, the main attacks today are mostly libertine. For many, "marriage" is at best a provisional arrangement between two people (sexual orientation is irrelevant) that can be dissolved whenever one wishes, for any reason. To be sure, conventional attitudes toward marriage are not as extreme, though there is a growing skepticism regarding love and marriage. As one person sarcastically put it, "Love: temporary insanity curable by marriage."

But for those of us who live under the authority of God's Word, marriage is an ordinance of God. Genesis proclaims, after God gave Eve to Adam, "Therefore a man shall leave his father and his mother and hold fast to his wife, and they shall become one flesh" (Genesis 2:24). Marriage is patently heterosexual and indissoluble. As Jesus said, "What therefore God has joined together, let not man separate" (Matthew 19:6). Jesus honored marriage by performing his first miracle at a wedding (John 2:1ff.). The Holy Spirit further honored it in Ephesians 5 by using it to portray the relationship of Christ and his church (Ephesians 5:23–32).

Therefore, in the words of our text, "Let marriage be held in honor among all"—or more literally, "Let marriage be precious to all of you." As Christians we celebrate marriage. We joyfully surround a couple as out of their depth they make those wild sacred promises to each other. And we celebrate the mystery with ancient invocations and feasting. Marriage is divinely given and deserves our greatest honor!

Marriage and Purity

Indispensable, of course, to the honor of marriage is purity, and thus the text adds, "and let the marriage bed be undefiled" (v. 4b). "Bed" is used here as a euphemism for sexual intercourse, and in demanding that it be kept "unde-filed" "our author is referring in sacrificial terms to married chastity."[3] The bed—the sexual relationship—is an altar, so to speak, where a pure offering of a couple's lives is made to each other and to God.

This was radical stuff in the pagan context—and Christians lived it out. When Pliny was sent by the Roman Emperor Trajan to govern the province of Bithynia and looked for charges against the Christians, he had to report back that on the Lord's Day, "They bound themselves by oath, not for any criminal end, but to avoid theft or adultery, never to break their word. . . ."[4] Christian sexual morality was unique in the pagan world and a source of wonder. And it has become increasingly so today in a world that considers adultery irrelevant, purity abnormal, and sex a "right" (however and with whomever one may get it) and that has invented the egregious term "recreational sex."

We Christians are called to be outrageously pure—to be a source of wonder and even derision to this glandular world.

Marriage and Judgment

That we are called to radical purity is nothing to trifle with because the call concludes, "for God will judge the sexually immoral and adulterous" (v. 4c). This means that everyone—ostensible Christians and non-Christians alike—will be judged for adultery (extramarital sexual relations) and sexual immo-rality (other illicit sexual relations, including perversions). Further, those who have taken up adulterous lifestyles and remain unrepentant will suffer ultimate judgment and damnation, for despite their insistence that they are "Christians," they are self-deceived. God's Word is terrifyingly clear:

> Or do you not know that the unrighteous will not inherit the kingdom of God? Do not be deceived: neither the sexually immoral, nor idolaters, nor adulterers, nor men who practice homosexuality . . . will inherit the kingdom of God. (1 Corinthians 6:9, 10)

> For you may be sure of this, that everyone who is sexually immoral or impure, or who is covetous (that is, an idolater), has no inheritance in the kingdom of Christ and God. Let no one deceive you with empty words, for because of these things the wrath of God comes upon the sons of disobedience. (Ephesians 5:5, 6)

> For this is the will of God, your sanctification: that you abstain from sexual immorality . . . the Lord is an avenger in all these things, as we told you beforehand and solemnly warned you. For God has not called us for impurity, but in holiness. (1 Thessalonians 4:3–7)

> But as for the cowardly, the faithless, the detestable, as for murderers, the sexually immoral, sorcerers, idolaters, and all liars, their portion will be in the lake that burns with fire and sulfur, which is the second death. (Revelation 21:8; cf. 22:15)

All who are living in serial adultery or fornication and are unrepentant are under God's wrath and ultimate judgment regardless of what they assert about a salvation experience.

The judgment God metes out has both a future and a present reality. In the future, unbelieving sensualists will stand before the Great White Throne and be judged accordingly (cf. Revelation 20:11ff.), and Christians will stand before the Judgment Seat of Christ where their works will be judged (cf. 2 Corinthians 5:10; 1 Corinthians 3:11–15).

Notwithstanding the inexorable coming of the future judgment, the fact remains that infidelity and its attendant sexual immoralities also regularly inflict judgment in the present. Significantly, Paul tells us, "Flee from sexual immorality. Every other sin a person commits is outside the body, but the sexually immoral person sins against his own body" (1 Corinthians 6:18). *Physical* misery grimly follows immorality in the present epidemics of herpes and AIDS. *Mental* firestorms afflict millions in the form of guilt, self-hatred, and ego disintegration. *Relational* wars are the proverbial result of sensuality—alienation, estrangement, hatred, and sometimes murder. *Societal* degradation follows—jungle ethics, brutalization, illegitimate children, abortion. Anyone who imagines that unrepentant adultery and sexual immorality will go unpunished is in La-la Land. It is happening right now from every angle, and in addition a terrible judgment awaits, for all unrepentant sinners will stand before God, who is "a consuming fire" (12:29; cf. 10:27).

But what does this have to do with the survival of the church? Everything! I can think of no more efficient way to sink that ship than through adultery and sexual immorality. The reasons are elementary. Immorality perverts theology. I have seen this time and time again with preachers—famous and unknown. They become involved in a secret affair (perhaps several) and yet keep on preaching. But over time an amazing phenomenon takes place—they unconsciously detach themselves from truth. Like the ancient Averroists, they divide truth, so that there is a truth for them and another truth for others. They may not articulate this, but they become practical relativists, and their relativism so eats away at their belief that many, after the trauma of discovery, leave the faith. Tragic shipwreck!

The damage to the church is immense. Preachers caught in such sins suffer a reduction in spiritual ethos. They increasingly sound like old-time railroad conductors who loudly invite people to embark to destinations they themselves have never visited and to which they are incapable of traveling. Powerlessness becomes the hallmark of their rhetoric.

And, of course, they discredit the Word. I can think of no better way to damn the soul of a junior-higher who is just beginning to experience spiritual stirrings than through the fall of a pastor, Sunday school teacher, or other spiritual leader. There can be no more efficient way to dampen the spiritual aspiration of a young family man than adulterous leaders. Because such sin is a particularly lethal sin against the church, I have at times prayed this with my ministerial colleagues: "Lord, if adultery would lie in the future for any of us should we continue to live—then take us home now." Better dead than damage the church!

So, if we want to keep the ship afloat, we must hear and heed God's Word: "Let marriage be held in honor among all, and let the marriage bed be undefiled, for God will judge the sexually immoral and adulterous" (v. 4).

Advice about Money (v. 5)

The second corresponding part of the writer's advice for keeping the church shipshape has to do with money: "Keep your life free from love of money, and be content with what you have, for he has said, 'I will never leave you nor forsake you'" (v. 5). The author knew that those who loved the world would not stand firm in a storm—that those with the greatest affection for wealth would be the first to turn aside when they understood that losses and crosses would come from sailing with Christ.

Not Covetousness . . .

Covetousness is plainly forbidden here and elsewhere in the Scriptures. "Keep your life free from love of money," begins the command. The Scriptures present a desire for wealth as a danger. After Jesus' encounter with the rich young man, Mark tells us:

> And Jesus looked around and said to his disciples, "How difficult it will be for those who have wealth to enter the kingdom of God!" And the disciples were amazed at his words. But Jesus said to them again, "Children, how difficult it is to enter the kingdom of God! It is easier for a camel to go through the eye of a needle than for a rich person to enter the kingdom of God." And they were exceedingly astonished, and said to him, "Then who can be saved?" Jesus looked at them and said, "With man it is impossible, but not with God. For all things are possible with God." (Mark 10:23–27)

Jesus' point was that it is impossible for a man who trusts in riches to get into Heaven, because a rich man trusts in himself! However, by the grace of God it is possible. God's grace can change hearts. At the end of the Sermon on the Mount Jesus recommended:

> Do not lay up for yourselves treasures on earth, where moth and rust destroy and where thieves break in and steal, but lay up for yourselves treasures in heaven, where neither moth nor rust destroys and where thieves do not break in and steal. For where your treasure is, there your heart will be also. (Matthew 6:19–21)

Miserly hoarding casts a metallic, lifeless heart. A few verses later Jesus concludes, "No one can serve two masters, for either he will hate the one and love the other, or he will be devoted to the one and despise the other. You cannot serve God and money" (Matthew 6:24).

Wealth has its disadvantages. It is difficult to have it and not trust in it. Material possessions tend to focus one's thoughts and interests on this world alone. It can enslave so that one becomes possessed by possessions, comforts, and recreations. Jesus said, "the deceitfulness of riches and the desires for other things enter in and choke the word" (Mark 4:19).

Though wealth has its intrinsic disadvantages, the preacher here is not forbidding wealth but the love of money. In one sense, such love is no respecter of persons. It can equally afflict a homeless man sleeping on a grate or the man occupying the penthouse sixty stories above him. But, this said, it is difficult not to love what you have spent your life collecting. Paul warned Timothy, "For the love of money is a root of all kinds of evils. It is through this craving that some have wandered away from the faith and pierced themselves with many pangs" (1 Timothy 6:10).

The warning stands for all of us to hear, for we are rich people. It is a special warning for the captains or helmsmen of the church—those who are to pilot others through the storms. "Therefore an overseer must . . . not [be] a lover of money" (1 Timothy 3:2, 3). Do not even entertain the tiniest thought of church leadership if you are a lover of money.

. . . But Contentment

The covetous, those who love money, will never be content. The author of Ecclesiastes informs us, "He who loves money will not be satisfied with money, nor he who loves wealth with his income" (Ecclesiastes 5:10). Our hearts resonate with the wisdom of these ancient words. C. H. Spurgeon amplifies this thought:

> It is not possible to satisfy the greedy. If God gave them one whole world to themselves they would cry for another; and if it were possible for them to possess heaven as they now are, they would feel themselves in hell, because others were in heaven too, for their greed is such that they must have everything or else they have nothing.[5]

A story received from ancient times tells of a king who was suffering from a certain malady and was advised by his wise men that he would be cured if the shirt of a contented man were brought to him to wear. The search began for a contented man, but none could be found. So emissaries were sent to the edge of the realm, and after a long search a man was found who was truly content. But he had no shirt! The consensus of enduring wisdom is that contentment comes from a source other than things or possessions.

The Christian knows that true contentment comes from resting in God's care, and this is evident when we follow the flow of verse 5: "And be content with what you have, for he has said, 'I will never leave you nor forsake you'" (v. 5c). In other words, "Christians, be content because you have God—and he will never forsake you!"

Where in the Old Testament did God say he would never leave us or forsake us? Only occasionally explicitly, but everywhere implicitly! God told Jacob as he fled from Esau to Bethel, "I am with you. . . . I will not leave you" (Genesis 28:15). Moses encouraged the Israelites, "Be strong and courageous. Do not fear or be in dread of them, for it is the LORD your God who goes with you. He will not leave you or forsake you" (Deuteronomy 31:6, cf. vv. 7, 8). When Joshua was called to take over Moses' leadership, God said, "I will be with you. I will not leave you or forsake you" (Joshua 1:5). David instructed Solomon, "Do not be afraid and do not be dismayed, for the LORD God, even my God, is with you" (1 Chronicles 28:20).

In no situation will God leave us, nor for any reason will he leave us. He will not leave us even for a little while. He may seem to hide his face, but he will not leave us.

> The soul that on Jesus hath lean'd for repose,
> I will not, I will not, desert to his foes;
> That soul, though all hell should endeavour to shake,
> I'll never, no never, no never forsake.
>
> Rippon's Hymns, *1787*

We will be content if we truly embrace the fact that we have God! The Apostle Paul was content. Destitute of worldly possessions, Paul sublimely speaks of himself as "having nothing, yet possessing everything" (2 Corinthians 6:10). "I know how to be brought low," he told the Philippians, "and I know how to abound. In any and every circumstance, I have learned the secret of facing plenty and hunger, abundance and need" (Philippians 4:12). And then to Timothy, he gave this jewel: "But godliness with contentment is great gain, for we brought nothing into the world, and we cannot take anything out of the world. But if we have food and clothing, with these we will be content" (1 Timothy 6:6–8).

A boatload of discontented materialists—lovers of money—will not do well in the coming storms. Those who always want more will turn away from God when their Christianity brings material subtraction rather than addition. On the other hand, those who are content—who have found their ultimate treasure in the unflagging presence and care of God—will sail on!

Today only those who adopt a head-in-the-sand/Pollyanna view will doubt that the tides of secular culture are becoming increasingly hostile and restless. Right now traditional Judeo-Christian sexual morality regarding marriage, fidelity, sexual orientation, and unborn life is considered reactionary by the dominant culture-shapers. The day is fast approaching when those who hold to Christian sexual ethics will be social pariahs.

Heavy seas are ahead, and there are two things that could keep the church from riding the storm—wrong thinking on *sex* and on *money*. It is of the greatest importance that we honor marriage as God's divinely given ordinance. It is imperative that we keep the marriage bed pure so we will not undergo judgment and lose our authenticity and power. Having refused sensual seduction, we must also resist the vacuous seduction of money. Our contentment must announce to our fellow-Christians and the world that Christ is with us and for us—and that he is enough!

Furthermore, our mind-set must be crowned with matchless confidence: "So we can confidently say, 'The Lord is my helper; I will not fear; what can man do to me?'" (v. 6). This is the mind-set that will ride the waves no matter what—just as Chrysostom did when he was brought before the Roman emperor and was threatened with banishment:

> "Thou canst not banish me for this world is my father's house." "But I will slay thee," said the Emperor. "Nay, thou canst not," said the noble champion of the faith, "for my life is hid with Christ in God." "I will take away thy treasures." "Nay, but thou canst not for my treasure is in heaven and my heart is there." "But I will drive thee away from man and thou shalt have no friend left." "Nay, thou canst not, for I have a friend in heaven from whom thou canst not separate me. I defy thee; for there is nothing that thou canst do to hurt me."[6]

Remember your leaders, those who spoke to you the word of God. Consider the outcome of their way of life, and imitate their faith. Jesus Christ is the same yesterday and today and forever. Do not be led away by diverse and strange teachings, for it is good for the heart to be strengthened by grace, not by foods, which have not benefited those devoted to them. We have an altar from which those who serve the tent have no right to eat. For the bodies of those animals whose blood is brought into the holy places by the high priest as a sacrifice for sin are burned outside the camp. So Jesus also suffered outside the gate in order to sanctify the people through his own blood. Therefore let us go to him outside the camp and bear the reproach he endured. For here we have no lasting city, but we seek the city that is to come. Through him then let us continually offer up a sacrifice of praise to God, that is, the fruit of lips that acknowledge his name. Do not neglect to do good and to share what you have, for such sacrifices are pleasing to God.

13:7–16

46

Sustaining Wisdom

HEBREWS 13:7-16

WHEN I FIRST MET JOE BAYLY it was late in his life and early in my ministry—a number of years ago when I was called to pastor College Church in Wheaton, Illinois, a church of which Joe had been a member for over twenty years. My first glimpse of Joe was as he sat Quaker-bearded with his wife, Mary Lou, on the front pew smiling benignly (like the face on the oatmeal box) and listening to my forgettable candidating sermon. How would I fare, I wondered, with this imposing personality, the author of the sometimes acerbic *Eternity Magazine* column "Out of My Mind"?

Happily, I learned the smile was real and that Joe Bayly cared little about where I came from, though he was concerned about who I was. Indeed, among the first things he said to me was in reference to the church's highly educated congregation: "Just remember, Pastor, we all slip our trousers on one leg at a time." Joe was put off by anyone and anything that smacked of condescension—especially smarmy, condescending preachers! He was, in fact, a spiritual populist because he truly believed that he could learn from everyone—and so he treated all his acquaintances with equal respect.

As it turned out, Barbara and I became close friends of Joe and Mary Lou, so that in addition to our occasional meals together, our family was regularly included in the Bayly family gatherings during the holidays and such memorable events as sipping apple cider while Joe sat in his rocking chair and read aloud Truman Capote's haunting *A Christmas Memory*.

But what stands out most about the Bayly get-togethers was the conversation between Joe and his grown children and anyone else at the table. Joe had brought his children up to reason Biblically and logically about everything, so conversation was always laced with spirited, cheerful family forthrightness. If you had the temerity to state your viewpoint, you had better be ready to defend it. "You believe that?" No quarter was extended, especially to Joe himself.

Joe was profoundly Biblical in his thinking. And, of course, this is one of the reasons Joe was something of a gadfly to the evangelical enterprise. No bromides, trendy or conventional, ever fell from Joe Bayly's pen because he was rigorously orthodox and Biblical and therefore gloriously radical!

Joe Bayly was a prophet—a voice of sanity in an upside-down world. His writings were always penetrating, whether humoring us to greater idealism and faith as he did in *I Saw Gooley Fly* or steeling us for the future with the Orwellian chill of *Winterflight*. Where principle was involved, Joe was a straight shooter and a fighter. And this left him with his share of enemies. But agree or disagree—like him or not—he was never equivocating or disingenuous. His trademark—clarity and economy of expression—left no doubt about where he stood.

He personally made us feel safe. Amidst the confusion there was always Joe Bayly, who rejected weak-minded reasoning and would think things through, kindly telling us what he thought—right or wrong. Joe's bracing effect was to make us stand up for what we believed.

As his pastor, I witnessed firsthand his belief in the church. For years he team-taught the Covenant Class, a transgenerational Sunday school class of grandparents, parents, their college-age children, and singles, including unmarried, divorced, and widowed. The Bayly home regularly hosted numerous singles. Though super-busy, Joe also served as prophet, writer, poet, preacher, business executive, and elder.

Joe Bayly always brought with him a sense of the numinous—that life is supernatural and that there is always more. To be sure, this had much to do with the early death of three of his children. But it was also due to his radical Biblical mind-set, for he volitionally set his mind on things above. I remember hearing him say in his final sermon at College Church, "Oh, God, burn eternity into my eyeballs. Help me to see all of this life through the perspective of eternity." God used Joe Bayly to do this for thousands of us.

Perhaps once a month I say to my wife, "I miss Joe Bayly," and we smile and agree that no one has come to replace him—at least for us.

Remember Spiritual Leaders (v. 7)

Why this consciously sainted biographical memory? The reason is to draw our attention to the indispensable wisdom enjoined in the opening verse of our text: "Remember your leaders, those who spoke to you the word of God. Consider the outcome of their way of life, and imitate their faith" (v. 7). From this we see that my memory of Joe Bayly is not only a Biblical exercise but is divinely commanded. Why? Because considering Joe Bayly's life and its outcome and humbly attempting to imitate it will encourage me to straighten up and sail right! His conscious commitment to point his ship into the winds of culture, if that is where Scripture points, puts steel in my walk. His sailing style, the trim of his sails, the tilt of his vessel are all salutary to my soul.

Significantly, this is beautifully consistent with the purpose of chapter 13, which is to strengthen the little Hebrew church so it will ride out the coming storms of persecution. A church that adequately recalls its godly leaders and considers the outcome of their way of life and attempts to imitate that way of life will sail well! Remembering, considering, and imitating the virtues of departed believers is of greatest spiritual importance both to one's family and to the broader family of the Body of Christ. Doing so will certainly help keep the boat afloat.

Remember Jesus Christ (v. 8)

Departed saints, of course, bless the memory of those who have known them, but they are no longer available for counsel. I cannot talk to Joe Bayly! But Jesus Christ is always available, for as the writer adds in what is perhaps the most famous verse in Hebrews, "Jesus Christ is the same yesterday and today and forever" (v. 8).

What a contrast with the changeableness of us humans and of life here on earth. The cycle from birth to death is a testament to our human mutability. The supple, sweet flesh of a newborn prospers like a flower and then fades and wrinkles and is finally cast off in death. Human personality never ceases changing. Some freshen with time, others sour, most do a little of both. Relationships wax and wane. To meet one twenty years from now may be to meet another person. Forests rise and stand for a millennium—and fade into deserts. Rivers cut canyons and disappear. Newtonian physics, with its straight lines and right angles, is replaced by Einstein's elegant curves of relativity.[1] The only thing that is sure is change! We humans appear for a little while to laugh and weep and work and play, and then we are gone. This is a melancholy thought at best. Our souls long for something solid.

But the great truth is, God does not change, and neither does the Holy Spirit or the Son, Jesus Christ. In fact, the very same Old Testament Scriptures and wording that describe God the Father's immutableness are applied directly to Christ (cf. Psalm 102:27 and Hebrews 1:12; Isaiah 48:12 and Revelation 1:17). This means that though the Savior has ascended into Heaven and dwells in that splendor, he is the same! He is the same in his wrath and his love and mercy and compassion and tenderness as he was here on earth. *Yesterday* Jesus "offered up prayers and supplications, with loud cries and tears, to him who was able to save him from death" (5:7). *Today* he is a high priest before the Father who is able to sympathize with our weakness because "in every respect [he] has been tempted as we are, yet without sin" (4:15). And *forever* this same Jesus "always lives to make intercession for them" (7:25).[2] Our priest is eternally the same and eternally contemporary. We need not fear opinion changes or mood swings in Jesus!

> I stay myself on Him who stays
> Ever the same through nights and days.[3]

No matter what lies ahead in this always-changing world with its drifting continents and fading suns—no matter what the seas may bring, we must sustain ourselves with this double-focus—remembering those who have gone before and focusing on Jesus Christ, our eternal, unchangeable contemporary. Those who truly do this will navigate the roughest seas.

A Sustaining Understanding (vv. 9–14)

The little Jewish church was not only harried by the imminent threat of persecution, but was also assailed within by the succumbing of some in the congregation to a strange teaching that combined esoteric eating practices with their Christian faith. No one knows exactly what the practices were, though we do know that some held that their sacred menu would make them better Christians.

Understanding Christ's Nourishment

To such the writer/preacher warns, "Do not be led away by diverse and strange teachings, for it is good for the heart to be strengthened by grace, not by foods, which have not benefited those devoted to them. We have an altar from which those who serve the tent have no right to eat" (vv. 9, 10). Those who imagined that spiritual growth came through a special menu had not only become ignorant of the necessity of grace for growth, but they actually blocked strengthening grace by their proud little rules.

Grace, like the earth's water system, operates on gravity—the spiritual "gravity of grace." Just as the waters of Niagara roll over the falls and plunge down to make a river below, and just as that river flows ever down to the even lower ranges of its course, then glides to still more low-lying areas where it brings life and growth, so it is with God's grace. Grace's gravity carries it to the lowly in heart, where it brings life and blessing. Grace goes to the humble.

This is the spiritual law behind Proverbs 3:34, which James 4:6 quotes: "'God opposes the proud, but gives grace to the humble.'" The unbowed soul standing proudly before God receives no benefit from God's falling grace. It may descend upon him, but it does not penetrate, and drips away like rain from a statue. But the soul lying before God is immersed—and even swims— in a sea of grace. So while there is always more grace, it is reserved for the lowly and the humble. Legalisms, even "little" ones such as dietary rules, impede grace. Humility invites the elevating weight of grace!

Actually, the grace we imbibe comes directly from the cross of Christ, for in verse 10 the preacher adds, "We have an altar from which those who serve the tent have no right to eat," referring to the cross because in a Christian context the sacrifice must be on the cross—the sacrificial altar of our faith.[4] Our spiritual food is nothing less than the life of Christ!

The force of these thoughts is phenomenal. Jesus Christ is eternally the same and eternally contemporary. Therefore, do not get mixed up with strange teaching such as that leading to spiritual diets. Our nourishment comes from grace, which comes directly from the altar—the cross of Christ. This meal goes to the humble!

Understanding Christ's Accessibility

The meal, the work of the cross, also goes only to those "outside the camp"— those who do not subscribe to the old Jewish system. Here the preacher uses a very Hebrew argument to make his point: "For the bodies of those animals whose blood is brought into the holy places by the high priest as a sacrifice for sin are burned outside the camp. So Jesus also suffered outside the gate in order to sanctify the people through his own blood" (vv. 11, 12).

The logic goes like this: the sacrifices offered on the Jewish great Day of Atonement were a prophetic type for the sacrifice of Christ, the Lamb of God who takes away the sin of the world (John 1:29). On the Day of Atonement a bull was slain to atone for the sins of the priest and his family, and a lamb likewise was sacrificed for the sins of the rest of the people. The blood of these sacrifices was taken into the Holy of Holies, but both the carcasses were taken outside the camp and burned up (Leviticus 16:27). Therefore, those under the old sacrificial system could not partake of this great offering as a meal.

But Jesus, the ultimate atoning lamb, was sacrificed outside the camp— outside Jerusalem's walls, on Golgotha—as an offering to God. This means two great things: (1) All those who remained committed to the old Jewish system were excluded from the benefit of partaking of Christ's atoning death. And, (2) Jesus' death outside the camp means that he is accessible to anyone in the world who will come to him. Jesus planted his cross in the world so all the world could have access. And there he remains permanently available!

There thus remains only one thing to do, and so the writer exhorts us: "Therefore let us go to him outside the camp and bear the reproach he endured. For here we have no lasting city, but we seek the city that is to come" (vv. 13, 14). The cities of the earth—all earthly institutions—will fall apart. Only the heavenly Zion will remain. We must go, flee to him outside the camp, and willfully embrace his "reproach," for such an act is worth doing a million times over! Thus Jesus Christ, who is "the same yesterday and today and forever," becomes our constant meal—our food, our drink, our life—and we will receive from him grace upon grace upon grace. And because he is outside the camp, he will always be accessible. In fact, he is with us, in us, and coming to us! This understanding that he *nourishes* us and is *accessible* to us will help us keep on course.

A Sustaining Lifestyle (vv. 15, 16)

There is one final thing that will sustain us, and that is how we live—our lifestyle—specifically, *worship* and *work*. Or as Coventry Patmore put it, to be "Mary in the house of God/A Martha in our own."

Worshiping Christ

We must make worship the first priority of living: "Through him then let us continually offer up a sacrifice of praise to God, that is, the fruit of lips that acknowledge his name" (v. 15). We all need to be like Mary—at Jesus' feet looking up so that he fills the whole horizon. She worshiped him "in spirit" (John 4:23, 24) because her whole being was passionately engaged in giving him worth. In fact, in a sublime moment she gave her very best for him as *snap!* went the alabaster flask, and she poured her fortune onto Jesus. Jesus said, "She has done a beautiful thing to me" (Mark 14:6).

Here our text is very specific about what he wants. It is a sacrifice—"a sacrifice of praise to God, that is, the fruit of lips that acknowledge his name." He wants us to say it. He wants to hear us verbally praise him.

> O God, I love Thee, I love Thee—
> Not out of hope of heaven for me
> Nor fearing not to love and be
> In the everlasting burning.
> Thou, Thou, my Jesus, after me
> Didst reach Thine arms out dying,
> For my sake sufferedst nails and lance,
> Mocked and marred countenance,

Sorrows passing number
Sweat and care and cumber,
Yea and death, and this for me,
And Thou couldest see me sinning:
Then I, why should not I love Thee;
Jesus so much in love with me?
Not for heaven's sake; not to be
Out of hell by loving Thee;
Not for any gains I see;
But just that Thou didst me
I do and I will love Thee:
What must I love Thee, Lord, for then?—
For being my King and God. Amen.

Gerard Manley Hopkins
"O Deus Ego Amo Te"

Working for Christ

Mary must be balanced by Martha in our souls: "Do not neglect to do good and to share what you have, for such sacrifices are pleasing to God" (v. 16). True worship always involves giving ourselves in the service of Christ and others (cf. Romans 12:1; James 1:27; 1 John 3:17, 18). We may participate in an elegant call to worship and prayer, heartily sing the *Gloria Patri*, solemnly repeat the Apostles' Creed, join together in a grand hymn, reverently pray the Lord's Prayer, and attentively listen to the Word, but if we do not do good to others and share what we have, none of it gives pleasure to God. But worship coupled with work—this brings God's pleasure and the winds of the Holy Spirit to our sails so we can ride the most daunting waves.

Sustaining power for the storms of life? How to keep the Good Ship Grace seaworthy?

- First, we must have a sustaining *memory* of two things: (1) a considered memory of the Joe Baylys in our lives and a resolve to humbly imitate their virtues by God's grace; and even more, (2) the measured memory that "Jesus Christ is the same yesterday and today and forever"—that his sustaining love for us will never ever vary. These dual memories will help us stay on course.
- Second, we need a sustaining *understanding* of the nourishment and access Christ provides us. He nourishes us from the cross, resulting in grace and more grace. And he remains outside the camp—in the world—perpetually accessible and inviting.
- Third, there must be a sustaining *lifestyle* that worships like Mary and works like Martha.

These are the keys to safe navigation in a dangerous world!

Obey your leaders and submit to them, for they are keeping watch over your souls, as those who will have to give an account. Let them do this with joy and not with groaning, for that would be of no advantage to you. Pray for us, for we are sure that we have a clear conscience, desiring to act honorably in all things. I urge you the more earnestly to do this in order that I may be restored to you the sooner.

13:17–19

47

Responsibility toward Leadership

HEBREWS 13:17–19

IN 1987 BARBARA AND I coauthored a book entitled *Liberating Ministry from the Success Syndrome*, targeted to encourage fellow-ministers and Christian workers in their labors for Christ, especially those ministering in less visible places. The book chronicled our early struggle in a small church and how we came to grips with "success," first Biblically and then practically. The result was a surprising flood of letters and phone calls asking for prayer and advice and also invitations to speak. So over the last five years we have spoken to numerous denominational conferences and gatherings of pastors, both old-line and independent, from Maine to California.

In our travels we discovered this: pastors as a group are one of the most hurting and abused segments of our society. This is not an isolated observation. Bill Waldrop, executive director of Advancing Churches and Missions Commitment (ACMC), and his wife, Doris, in their wide travels on behalf of church missions have witnessed the same thing. The four of us have shared our observations at some length. Perhaps the reason we see this so much is that as interlopers we are "safe" to talk to. We are not a part of our listeners' denominations, we do not run in their circles, we have few mutual acquaintances, and best of all, we will be gone shortly afterwards! So, very often after a few congenial remarks a pastor and wife will ask to "talk," and we hear it all—and much of it would tax the credulity of the uninitiated.

Why such pain for so many in ministerial leadership experience? Here are a few reasons:

Christian media. Millions of Christians spend hours daily listening to Christian radio where they hear a top handful of Christian preachers and teachers giving their best stuff, edited and packaged with artistically

461

interspersed background music. Though once isolated, farmers today plow their fields tuned in with headphones while their wives listen to the same programs one after another—sometimes for eight hours a day as they go about their household duties. When they come to church on Sunday they find the fare to be pedestrian and dull in comparison. So at the door the pastor hears things like: "That was interesting, pastor . . . Eh . . . I have a tape by Dr. Frank Lee Terrific that is along the same line. I think you should listen to it. In fact, here it is." The pastor smiles and says, "Thank you." He gets the message but also senses a reduction of his esteem and authority.

Big business mentality. Another source of abuse of those in ministry is a rung-dropping, business-world mentality that divides its world into big fish and small-fry. This mind-set regards the captains of, say, the food industry as fit subjects for veneration, whereas the proprietors of a mom-and-pop grocery store are scarcely worthy of notice. The result in such minds is that the proprietors of a mom-and-pop church are, well, shall we say, lightweights.

American individualism and subjectivism. American individualism is proverbial. And millions of Christians are afflicted with an underlying attitude that imagines we can each go it alone—without the church or anyone else. If we have the Lord, we need nothing else. In fact, this line of thinking can even conclude that bowing to any human spiritual authority will result in a reduction of one's own spirituality. This reaches its destructive apex when a person says, "Well, that's what you think, pastor. But my opinion is as good as yours." The truth is, one's opinion may be even better than the pastor's. But the appeal to the magisterium of one's subjective opinion is a specious appeal. One's opinion is only as good as or better than another's if it is supported by Scripture and rigorous logic. Pastoral authority evaporates where individualism and subjectivism reign.

So, we see that leadership is difficult in the modern church because the ever-present radio has inbred in some an implicit disregard for local pulpits. The disregard has been further fed by a worldly business mentality that regards bigger as worthy of more respect. Mix in the anti-authoritarian strain of American individualism and subjectivism, and it all adds up to a leadership crisis for the modern church and an entire generation of beat-up clergy. No wonder that in so many places the church is awash, drifting aimlessly, and at the mercy of the hostile seas of neo-pagan culture.

What is the answer? Helpfully the essential remedy is provided in 13:17–19, where the preacher/writer gives instruction about the church's responsibility toward leadership. Although the specific dynamics of the early church's anti-authoritarian mind-set differed from ours, the writer gives principles that are relevant to today's church. His advice helped keep the early church afloat, and it will do the same now for those wise enough to take heed.

Obedience (v. 17)

Obedience Commanded

The writer's wisdom was two-fold, the first being an admonition to obedience: "Obey your leaders and submit to them, for they are keeping watch over your souls, as those who will have to give an account. Let them do this with joy and not with groaning, for that would be of no advantage to you."

Clearly, all Christians are called to obedience and submission to authority—a call that demands careful definition. We must understand that this does not mean unqualified blanket obedience—the kind that made it possible for Jim Jones to murder more than nine hundred of his followers by ordering them to drink poisoned Kool-Aid. Neither does it provide the basis for authoritarian churches, like some of the contemporary house-churches whose members submit virtually every decision of their lives to the elders. I have seen this type of authoritarianism take the most draconian forms, as in one instance the leader ordered all members of the church to cease wearing any modern blend of fabrics, such as dacron and cotton or wool and rayon, because Leviticus 19:19 ordered the Israelites, "You shall not . . . . wear a garment of cloth made of two kinds of material." "About that shirt, Brother Hughes . . . let's see the tag."

Of course, this call to obedience was never meant to entice anyone to contradict Biblical morality or individual conscience. It was, instead, a call to an obedient heart, as we shall see.

Why Obedience?

But before we consider that, it is helpful to consider the reason for this emphasis on obedience. The answer, first, is that leaders are accountable to God—"for they are keeping watch over your souls, as those who will have to give an account" (v. 17b). The sense here is that "they and no other keep watch over your souls."[1] In addition, the words "keeping watch" literally mean "to keep oneself awake." So the idea may well mean that some of the leaders had lost sleep over certain people in the church.[2] Thomas Aquinas cited the shepherds in the Nativity story as an illustration of such care—"keeping watch over their flock by night" (Luke 2:8).[3] The pastors to which the writer calls his people to submit were good, energetic, conscientious, caring shepherds.

Moreover, their watching over their people was motivated by the awareness that they "will have to give an account" to God for the way they care for the flock. The sobering fact is, spiritual responsibility brings with it a higher level of responsibility and judgment. As James wrote, "Not many of you should become teachers, my brothers, for you know that we who teach will be judged with greater strictness" (James 3:1).

How and why do teachers incur greater judgment? The answer is, if we claim to have an informed knowledge of God's Word for God's people, and further claim that we are charged to deliver it, we are more responsible to deliver it clearly and to obey it. I, by virtue of my professed calling and study of God's Word, will undergo a stricter judgment than many Christians. Increased responsibility means increased accountability. Jesus followed up the Parable of the Foolish Manager by saying, "Everyone to whom much was given, of him much will be required, and from him to whom they entrusted much, they will demand the more" (Luke 12:48).

Every one of us—no exceptions—will stand before the *Bema*, the Judgment Seat of Jesus Christ. The Bible is clear that while believers will *not* stand in judgment for their sin (Romans 8:1), and salvation is a free gift (Ephesians 2:8, 9), the works of believers will nevertheless be judged. "For we must all appear before the judgment seat of Christ" (2 Corinthians 5:10). "So then each of us will give an account of himself to God" (Romans 14:12). The picture the Bible gives of this judgment is one of individual believers presenting their lives' works to Christ in the form of buildings. The eternal foundation of each building is Christ, but the structures vary. Some are made totally of wood, hay, and straw. Others are of gold, silver, and precious stones. Still others are composite structures of all the elements. Each life will be publicly subjected to the revealing torch of Christ's judgment, and with the flames will come the moment of truth:

> Now if anyone builds on the foundation with gold, silver, precious stones, wood, hay, straw—each one's work will become manifest, for the Day will disclose it, because it will be revealed by fire, and the fire will test what sort of work each one has done. If the work that anyone has built on the foundation survives, he will receive a reward. If anyone's work is burned up, he will suffer loss, though he himself will be saved, but only as through fire. (1 Corinthians 3:12–15)

While all Christians will be at the *Bema*, professed leaders and teachers of the church will undergo a stricter judgment. Leaders will answer for their care of souls.

So we see that the rationale for obedience was very clear for the Hebrew church. (1) Their leaders were so committed to watching over the souls under their care that they lost sleep. And (2) they were doing this with the powerfully motivating knowledge that they would answer to God for how well they did it. Such care invites obedience from God's people.

And if that is not sufficient reason, the author gives another, which is that obedience will make life better for all concerned: "Let them do this with joy and not with groaning, for that would be of no advantage to you" (v. 17c). The fact is, leadership can be a pain. The words "not with groaning" is an accurate literal translation.[4] I am sure Moses groaned over the disobedience of his people when after the exodus he brought them to Rephidim where, being out of water and supplies, they began to rebel (cf. Exodus 17:1–7). But forty years later when the *same thing* happened at Kadesh so that the people seemed to be lip-syncing their earlier rebellion—"Why have you brought the assembly of the LORD into this wilderness, that we should die here, both we and our cattle?" (Numbers 20:4)—his old bones must have really groaned!

All leaders know this pain. Phillips Brooks, one-time Episcopal Bishop of Boston, said:

> To be a true minister to men is always to accept new happiness and new distress. . . . The man who gives himself to other men can never be a wholly sad man; but no more can he be a man of unclouded gladness. To him shall come with every deeper consecration a before untasted joy, but in the same cup shall be mixed a sorrow that it was beyond his power to feel before.[5]

A heart that can know and accept such pain is a glory to God.

> O give us hearts to love like Thee,
> Like Thee, O Lord, to grieve
> Far more for others' sins than all
> The wrongs that we receive.[6]

But along with the pain comes joy from obedient charges. "Let them do this with joy and not with groaning." The Apostle John wrote, "I have no greater joy than to hear that my children are walking in the truth" (3 John 4). Paul expressed much the same when he encouraged the Philippians to live for Christ in this world "so that in the day of Christ I may be proud that I did not run in vain or labor in vain" (Philippians 2:16). Later in the same book he referred to them as "my joy and crown" (Philippians 4:1). Ministry can be a pain—but its pleasures are incredible.

Of course, obedience is good for the people as well, as is implicit in the writer's negative understatement regarding disobedience: "For that [i.e., being a groaning, disobedient burden] would be of no advantage to you." It would not be an advantage in this life because the strife that comes to the church through disobedience would not only impede the leaders but *everyone's* spiritual growth. And at the Judgment Seat of Christ the disadvantage would be monumental!

So the reasons to submit to spiritual authority are substantial: (1) God-appointed leaders are fulfilling the high charge of watching over their congregation's souls. (2) Such leaders must answer to God at the Judgment Seat for their work. And, (3) believers' obedience will bring joy instead of pain—and will work to preserve their soul's advantage. Slavish, blind obedience is not called for here, but a respectful, submissive spirit is. Christians are to be discerning in their hearing of God's Word. They must never accept something as true just because a preacher or leader says it. At the same time, they are to be eager to obey and to submit to authority. Such ought to be one's first impulse when the leader and the people are right with God. Such churches will sail well, because all hands will be coordinated to point the ship in a single direction.

Prayer (vv. 18, 19)

Prayer Commanded

From the necessity of obedience the author naturally switches to the command to pray: "Pray for us, for we are sure that we have a clear conscience, desiring to act honorably in all things" (v. 18). The writer's conscience is clear because he has performed well in his spiritual duties toward his friends. His conscience has made him confident toward both men and God. Similarly, Paul could write, "For our boast is this, the testimony of our conscience, that we behaved in the world with simplicity and godly sincerity, not by earthly wisdom but by the grace of God, and supremely so toward you" (2 Corinthians 1:12). And, "By the open statement of the truth we would commend ourselves to everyone's conscience in the sight of God" (2 Corinthians 4:2). What a boon a clear conscience is! When the conscience is clear, one can ask wholeheartedly for the prayers of all the saints.

The preacher's specific request—"I urge you the more earnestly to do this in order that I may be restored to you the sooner" (v. 19)—reflects his simple faith in prayer. If they fail to pray, his return to them may be slowed or possibly never take place. But if they pray, he expects that their prayers will speed his restoration, just as Daniel's prayers brought the return of the angel Gabriel to aid him (cf. Daniel 10:12–14). He believed in prayer!

We are to pray for our leaders. It is recorded that D. L. Moody, founder of Moody Bible Institute, repeatedly appropriated the wisdom of this command. For example, during his great turn-of-the-century evangelistic endeavors he often wired R. A. Torrey at the school asking for prayer, and in response the faculty and students would pray late into the evening and sometimes all night—bringing great power to Moody's faraway ministries.[7] After Moody's death, Torrey himself preached in many countries backed up by an immense chain of prayer. In Australia, 2,100 home prayer groups met for two weeks before he arrived. As a result, there was great power in his preaching, and many lives were changed.[8]

Charles Haddon Spurgeon, the peerless Victorian preacher of London, told his vast congregation as he concluded his sermon delivered May 27, 1855:

> My people! shall I ever lose your prayers? Will ye ever cease your sup-plications? . . . Will ye then ever cease to pray? I fear ye have not uttered so many prayers this morning as ye should have done; I fear there has not been so much earnest devotion as might have been poured forth. For my own part, I have not felt the wondrous power I sometimes experience.[9]

If we desire power in our lives and in our churches, we must pray. Likewise, if we desire our or others' preaching to be more than exegesis and rhetoric, we must pray.

How different the modern church would be if the majority of its people prayed for its pastors and lay leadership. There would be supernatural suspensions of business-as-usual worship. There would be times of inexplicable visitations from the Holy Spirit. More laypeople would come to grips with the deeper issues of life. The leadership vacuum would evaporate. There would be more conversions.

Will we commit ourselves to pray for our pastors and their colleagues and their layleaders—especially those who chair the boards and committees and teach children in Sunday school and lead other important ministries? I suggest three headings for your prayers: (1) devotional, (2) domestic, and (3) professional. This single commitment could ensure ongoing vitality for our churches. No doubt about it!

It is an indisputable fact—pastors as a group are one of the most abused and hurting segments of modern society. Admittedly, sometimes the misery is self-inflicted due to sloth and ineptness. But more often it comes from the factors previously considered.

And this personal *angst* of the clergy is superseded by an even greater tragedy—the mournful fact that tens of thousands of churches are not sailing well. Many are listing dangerously, some are dead in the water, and the skeletal remains of some rest on the bottom. What is the answer? The writer has not given us all of it, but he has given two huge pillars of support.

- *Obedience.* We are to obey our leaders—"Obey your leaders and submit to them, for they are keeping watch over your souls, as those who will have to give an account. Let them do this with joy and not with groaning, for that would be of no advantage to you" (v. 17). Slavish, unthinking obedience? No! Rather, the *will* to obey, to be respectful, to be supportive—to be a cheerful team player.
- *Prayer.* This obedience is to be oiled by prayer—"Pray for us, for we are sure that we have a clear conscience, desiring to act honorably in all things. I urge you the more earnestly to do this in order that I may be restored to you the sooner" (vv. 18, 19).

What power this will bring! As Paul said, "On him we have set our hope that he will deliver us again. You also must help us by prayer, so that many will give thanks on our behalf for the blessing granted us through the prayers of many" (2 Corinthians 1:10b, 11).

Now may the God of peace who brought again from the dead our Lord Jesus, the great shepherd of the sheep, by the blood of the eternal covenant, equip you with everything good that you may do his will, working in us that which is pleasing in his sight, through Jesus Christ, to whom be glory forever and ever. Amen. I appeal to you, brothers, bear with my word of exhortation, for I have written to you briefly. You should know that our brother Timothy has been released, with whom I shall see you if he comes soon. Greet all your leaders and all the saints. Those who come from Italy send you greetings. Grace be with all of you.

13:20–25

48

Soaring Benedictions

HEBREWS 13:20–25

THE BOOK OF HEBREWS closes with one of the most exquisite and soaring of all Scriptural benedictions. Multiple millions of worshipers have been dismissed with the pastor's upraised hand and the sonorous words that begin, "Now may the God of peace . . ."

In its original setting it was especially appropriate for the expatriate Hebrew church as it battened down its hatches, trimmed its sails, and pointed its prow into the ominous rising seas of Roman persecution that would explode full-fury under Nero's infamy. Its appropriateness comes from the fact that the benediction and doxology of verse 21 flows from a grand foundational statement in verse 20 regarding what comes from the God they serve—namely, his *peace*, his *eternal covenant*, and his *risen Shepherd*. So we will do a little digging into the foundation and then explore the benediction that rises from it.

Foundation of the Soaring Benediction (v. 20)

His Peace

Peace is intrinsic to the character and existence of God. God is called "the God of peace" at least five other times in the New Testament (Romans 15:33; 16:20; 2 Corinthians 13:11; Philippians 4:9; 1 Thessalonians 5:23). These citations, along with the opening invocation of our text, "Now may the God of peace," reference two marvelous aspects of that peace. First, we see his divine tranquility—the eternal repose in God's being. And secondly, it references his *shalom*. God's peace is more than the absence of conflict, it is more than tranquility. It is completeness, soundness, welfare, well-being, wholeness.

Invoking God as "the God of peace" is parallel to Jeremiah 29:11, which reads literally, "'For I know the plans I am planning for you,' declares the Lord, 'plans for *shalom* and not for calamity, to give you a future and a hope'" (based on NASB). Significantly, this promise of *shalom* was given to God's covenant people at the beginning of the Babylonian captivity when it appeared that the seas of the Gentile world had inundated God's people for good.

Therefore, the title "the God of peace" at the end of Hebrews comes as a consciously appropriate benediction to fearful, restless hearts—"Your God is a God of peace, and he will pick up the pieces no matter what happens—he will heal your wounds and fulfill what is lacking. No storm will sink you!" He gives us *his* peace. Jesus said, "Peace I leave with you; my peace I give to you. Not as the world gives do I give to you" (John 14:27a). He gives us his repose of soul. Are we flirting with fantasy to make such a dazzling assertion? Absolutely not! The promise of Jesus' peace came from his own lips. Notice also that after promising his peace he said, "Let not your hearts be troubled, neither let them be afraid" (John 14:27b).

What a salve to the harried church!

The truth for all of us who are his children is that our God is "the God of peace," and his plans for every one of us are for *shalom*, well-being. None of his children are an exception and never will be!

His Eternal Covenant

The second component is his eternal covenant/promise, referenced in the qualifying phrase that follows: "by the blood of the eternal covenant." Specifically, the foundation for our highest dreams is the everlasting, unbreakable new covenant promise earlier quoted in 8:10 where God says, "I will put my laws into their minds, and write them on their hearts, and I will be their God, and they shall be my people" (cf. Jeremiah 31:31–34). The promise is nothing less than a renewed heart and a personal relationship with God through the atoning work of God the Son and the indwelling of God the Holy Spirit. We have his word for it that all this is ours if we come to him!

And this covenant, this promise, is eternal. It will never be replaced by another as it once replaced the old covenant. It was established by the blood of the ultimate Lamb of God, whose atoning death was ratified and verified by his resurrection. The writer's friends were being encouraged to remember that whatever came, no matter how high the seas, his new covenant promise would never change or fail. The eternal covenant granted them eternal life.

The stars shine over the mountains,
The stars shine over the sea,

The stars look up to the mighty God.
The stars shall last for a million years
A million years and a day,
But God and I will live and love
When the stars have passed away.
When the stars are gone.

Robert Louis Stevenson

His Risen Shepherd

We have seen, as we move toward the great benediction, that we have God's peace and God's eternal promise. The remaining element is his risen Shepherd. The middle clause of verse 20 tells us that God "brought again from the dead our Lord Jesus, the great shepherd of the sheep." The shepherd metaphor is one of the most spiritually sumptuous in all of God's Word. It reveals volumes about us (the sheep) and about the Lord (our Shepherd). As to our "sheepness," Dr. Bob Smith, long-time philosophy professor at Bethel College in Minnesota, used to humor his point home regarding our human state by insisting that the existence of sheep is *prima facie* evidence against evolution. Sheep are so unintelligent and obtuse and defenseless, they could not have possibly evolved—the only way they could have survived is with shepherds!

Certainly we must admit that we are sheep. But even more, we must note that Jesus took up the term *shepherd* and applied it to himself (cf. Mark 14:27). Jesus' shepherd heart welled with compassion, for Mark tells us, "When he went ashore he saw a great crowd, and he had compassion on them, because they were like sheep without a shepherd" (Mark 6:34). Even more, his good shepherd's heart caused him to give everything: "I am the good shepherd. I know my own and my own know me, just as the Father knows me and I know the Father; and I lay down my life for the sheep" (John 10:14, 15).

But here our writer tells us that he is not only a "good shepherd"—he is also "the great shepherd of the sheep." Why? Because he is a risen Shepherd—"brought [back] again from the dead." As the great risen Shepherd, his compassion and protection are mediated from a position of an unparalleled display of power! He, our Shepherd, is exalted at the right hand of the Father. All other shepherds pale by comparison. There is none like our "great shepherd." Our risen Shepherd lives not only to give us life, but to tend us so that we will be sheep who bring him glory. This means that our grandest spiritual desires are never audacious and that any spiritual aspirations less than the loftiest are not grand enough. What security and what challenge the fact of our risen "great shepherd" brings to our souls.

Now reflect for a moment on the richness of our foundation from God: (1) We have his peace/*shalom*. (2) We have his unbreakable, immutable eternal promise. And, (3) we have his risen Shepherd's care. We have his peace, his promise, his care. This grand foundation can now bear the weight of the loftiest benedictions of his people and the ascription of glory to God.

Expression of the Soaring Benediction (v. 21)

His Equipping

The writer's petition is richly phrased and to the point: "[May God] equip you with everything good that you may do his will" (v. 21a). The richness of this request is in the word "equip," which can mean "to perfect," "to make good," or "to mend." According to Montefiore, "There is a flavour of all these meanings here."[1]

My three grandsons, who are between the ages of three and six, and I have experienced the idea lodged in this word on our occasional fishing trips. Excited little hands and fishing reels often do not mix very well. The result is predictably a tangled line that looks like a bird's nest. To little eyes and hands it looks impossible. But an experienced grandfather has found over the years that a little probing and pulling can almost always fix the worst tangles. Just what the doctor ordered for an aging grandfather's ego! "There we are, son. Now let's catch some fish!"

That is the idea here—to repair things so they can be useful. Matthew uses the word to describe fishermen "mending their nets" (Matthew 4:21). Paul uses it in Galatians 6:1 regarding restoring a brother—that is, putting him back in place. It was used in classical Greek for setting a bone.

So the prayer here is a beautiful request that God mend and perfect his children with everything good, thus equipping them to do God's will. We may sense that we are out of joint, or that life is a bird's nest. But this prayer is built on the idea that God can and does equip us with everything good to do his will—and our experience confirms the truth of this.

The relevance of this closing prayer for the church on troubled seas is obvious: God can put you back together so you can do his will, no matter what. Can you hear the prayer as its benediction lingered over the beleaguered congregation with its sweet, healing hope?

His Enabling

The prayer moves very naturally from equipping to enabling: ". . . working in us that which is pleasing in his sight, through Jesus Christ" (v. 21b).

The Scriptures tell us that all creation and all God's works in the world are through Jesus Christ. He not only created everything—he preserves it: "For by him all things were created, in heaven and on earth, visible and invisible, whether thrones or dominions or rulers or authorities—all things were created through him and for him. And he is before all things, and in him all things hold together" (Colossians 1:16, 17). So we should have no trouble believing his statement that "apart from me you can do nothing" (John 15:5). This is ontologically true, for we would not even exist apart from him. But the emphasis of Jesus' word in John is upon bearing spiritual fruit: "I am the vine; you are the branches. Whoever abides *in me* and *I in him*, he it is that bears much fruit, for apart from me you can do nothing."

But gloriously, as believers we are by definition spiritually "in him." According to the famed Greek scholar Adolf Deissman, the term "in Christ" or "in Christ Jesus" occurs some 169 times in Paul's writings.[2] Perhaps the most famous of Paul's "in Christ" statements is 2 Corinthians 5:17—"Therefore, if anyone is in Christ, he is a new creation. The old has passed away; behold, the new has come."

It follows that once we are in Christ, we can do works through him that please him: "For we are his workmanship, created in Christ Jesus for good works, which God prepared beforehand, that we should walk in them" (Ephesians 2:10). So in Christ each of us has an eternally-designed job description that includes the task, ability, and place to serve. And whatever the task to which he has called us, we will be equipped for it as surely as a bird is capable of flight. And in doing the works that he has called us to do, we will be more and more his workmanship and more and more our true self.

Thus the prayer here in Hebrews—"working in us that which is pleasing in his sight, through Jesus Christ"—is eminently doable!

It is an immutable fact that the power to do what is pleasing to God will always be given to us through Jesus Christ—if we want it! But some of us live as if that is not true. The real question is, do we want it? Do we desire it? Do we expect it? Do we desire it! Then pray for it!

The foundation we all share is truly monumental. We have *God's peace*, his own *shalom*. His plans for us are only for our wholeness, our well-being, our completeness. We have *his eternal covenant*, the new covenant in his blood and the promise of a new heart and new relationship. This great promise will never change. We have *his risen Shepherd* who cares for souls with the compassion and power in keeping with his great exaltation at the right hand of God. He is our "great shepherd."

Having, therefore, the foundation of his *peace*, his *eternal covenant*, and his *great Shepherd*, we pray for ourselves and for our churches. We pray for his *equipping* "with everything good that [we] may do his will"—and thus we find him mending us and putting us right so we can do it! We pray for his *enabling*—"working in us that which is pleasing in his sight, through Jesus Christ"—and so find ourselves living under his pleasure and power.

We are, through prayer, equipped and enabled to serve, and our souls soar. Our ship sails well to his glory.

His Glory

There is only one thing left to do, and that is to glorify God—"to whom be glory forever and ever. Amen."

- Glorify him for his peace, for it is his nature and his desire for his people. He has only thoughts of peace for us. Approach him with holy delight!
- Glorify him for his eternal covenant. What an amazing thing that God should enter into a covenant with us! Adore him for his blood, which sealed it. Bless him for our new hearts.
- Glorify him for giving us our "great shepherd," for though we were all going our own way, he sent his Son to save us with his Lamb's blood, and then to shepherd us. Magnify him for his shepherd's compassion and care.
- Glorify him that he has equipped us and enabled us to do his will and to please him—even in the storms!

Glory be to the Father, and to the Son, and to the Holy Spirit. Amen!

Soli Deo gloria!

Notes

Chapter One: The Eloquence of God

1. C. S. Lewis, *Prince Caspian* (London: Fontana Books, 1980), pp. 122–24.

2. F. F. Bruce, *The Epistle to the Hebrews* (Grand Rapids, MI: Eerdmans, 1964), p. lii writes:

> The purpose of our author's exegesis of Old Testament scripture, as of his general argument, is to establish the finality of the gospel by contrast with all that went before it (more particularly, by contrast with the Levitical cultus), as the way of perfection, the way which alone leads men to God without any barrier or interruption of access. He establishes the finality of Christianity by establishing the supremacy of Christ, in His person and in His work.

Also see Philip Edgcumbe Hughes, *A Commentary on the Epistle to the Hebrews* (Grand Rapids, MI: Eerdmans, 1977), p. 36.

3. Bruce, ibid., p. xxx.

4. William L. Lane, *Hebrews: A Call to Commitment* (Peabody, MA: Hendrickson, 1988), pp. 15–26.

5. Ibid., p. 24.

6. William Barclay, *The Letter to the Hebrews* (Philadelphia: Westminster, 1957), p. 1.

7. C. S. Lewis, *Surprised by Joy* (New York: Harcourt, Brace & World, Inc., 1955), p. 227 writes:

> Even if my own philosophy were true, how could the initiative lie on my side? My own analogy, as I now first perceived, suggested the opposite: if Shakespeare and Hamlet could ever meet, it must be Shakespeare's doing. [Note 1:] *I.e.*, Shakespeare could, in principle, make himself appear as Author within the play, and write a dialogue between Hamlet and himself. The "Shakespeare" within the play would of course be at once Shakespeare and one of Shakespeare's creatures. It would bear some analogy to Incarnation.

Chapter Two: The Supremacy of Christ

1. C. H. Spurgeon, *The Metropolitan Tabernacle Pulpit*, vol. 45 (Pasadena, TX: Pilgrim, 1977), p. 385.

2. F. F. Bruce, *The Epistle to the Hebrews* (Grand Rapids, MI: Eerdmans, 1964), p. 4.

3. H. Dermot McDonald, *Commentary on Colossians and Philemon* (Waco, TX: Word, 1980), p. 49.

4. F. F. Bruce, *The Epistles to the Colossians, to Philemon, and to the Ephesians* (Grand Rapids, MI: Eerdmans, 1984), p. 271 writes:

Paul prays here that his readers will appreciate the value which God places on them, his plan to accomplish his eternal purpose through them as the first fruits of the reconciled universe of the future, in order that their lives may be in keeping with the high calling and that they may accept in grateful humility the grace and glory thus lavished on them.

5. Brooke Foss Westcott, *The Epistle to the Hebrews* (Grand Rapids, MI: Eerdmans, 1967), p. 8.

6. Stephen W. Hawking, *A Brief History of Time* (New York: Bantam, 1990), p. 37.

7. Ibid.

8. Ibid., pp. 38, 39.

9. Ibid., p. 50:

The final result was a joint paper by Penrose and myself in 1970, which at last proved that there must have been a big bang singularity provided only that general relativity is correct and the universe contains as much matter as we observe. There was a lot of opposition to our work, partly from the Russians because of their Marxist belief in scientific determinism, and partly from people who felt that the whole idea of singularities was repugnant and spoiled the beauty of Einstein's theory. However, one cannot really argue with a mathematical theorem. So in the end our work became generally accepted and nowadays nearly everyone assumes that the universe started with a big bang singularity. It is perhaps ironic that, having changed my mind, I am now trying to convince other physicists that there was in fact no singularity at the beginning of the universe—as we shall see later, it can disappear once quantum effects are taken into account.

10. Westcott, *The Epistle to the Hebrews*, pp. 13, 14.

11. Hugh Montefiore, *A Commentary on the Epistle to the Hebrews* (London: Adam & Charles Black, 1964), p. 35.

12. Simon J. Kistemaker, *Exposition of the Epistle to the Hebrews* (Grand Rapids, MI: Baker, 1984), p. 29.

Chapter Three: Christ's Superiority to Angels

1. C. S. Lewis, *The Screwtape Letters and Screwtape Proposes a Toast* (New York: Macmillan, 1961), pp. viii, ix.

2. C. S. Lewis, *Perelandra* (New York: Macmillan, 1965), pp. 198, 199.

3. Hugh Montefiore, *A Commentary on the Epistle to the Hebrews* (London: Adam & Charles Black, 1964), pp. 41, 42.

4. F. F. Bruce, *The Epistle to the Hebrews* (Grand Rapids, MI: Eerdmans, 1964), pp. 11, 12.

5. Simon J. Kistemaker, *Exposition of the Epistle to the Hebrews* (Grand Rapids, MI: Baker, 1984), p. 38 where he references F. W. Grosheide, *De Brief aan de Hebreeen en de Brief van Jacobus* (Kampen: Kok, 1955), p. 69.

6. Ibid., p. 39 explains:

The origin of the quotation seems to be a Greek translation of the Hymn of Moses (Deut. 32:43). The translation based on the Hebrew text is rendered:

Rejoice, O nations, with his people,
for he will avenge the blood of his servants;
he will take vengeance on his enemies
and make atonement for his land and people.

The Septuagint and the Dead Sea Scrolls show an addition to the first line of the verse.

Rejoice, O nations, with his people,
and let all the angels worship him,
for he will avenge the blood of his servants.

7. Bruce, *The Epistle to the Hebrews*, pp. 19, 20 who explains:

This is not the only place in the Old Testament where a king, especially of the Davidic line, is addressed in language which could only be described as the characteristic hyperbole of oriental court style if interpreted solely of the individual so addressed. But to Hebrew poets and prophets a prince of the house of David was the vicegerent of Israel's God; he belonged to a dynasty to which God had made special promises bound up with the accomplishment of His purpose in the world. Besides, what was only partially true of any of the historic rulers of David's line, or even of David himself, would be realized in its fulness when that son of David appeared in whom all the promises and ideals associated with that dynasty would be embodied.

8. Ibid., p. 21.
9. Edward Fudge, *Our Man in Heaven* (Grand Rapids, MI: Baker, 1974), p. 23.
10. Montefiore, *A Commentary on the Epistle to the Hebrews*, p. 50:

The present tense of the Greek participle implies that angels are perpetually being sent out on service. Their task is concerned not with the natural order, but with the work of redemption. Their mission is for those who are to inherit salvation, that is, for the people of God.

11. Billy Graham, *Angels: God's Secret Agents* (Waco, TX: Word, 1986), pp. 16, 17.
12. Raymond Brown, *The Message of Hebrews* (Downers Grove, IL: InterVarsity Press, 1982), p. 45 quotes M. Monsen, *A Present Help* (London: Lutterworth Press, 1960), pp. 37, 38.
13. *Pastor's Story File*, March 1987, "Angels," vol. 3, no. 5, p. 1. The story was recounted by Phil Plotts, son of veteran missionary Morris Plotts.
14. Jim Marstaller, in a letter dated December 14, 1990.

Chapter Four: Drifting
1. A. B. Bruce, *Epistle to the Hebrews* (Minneapolis: Klock & Klock, 1988), p. 61.
2. Brooke Foss Westcott, *The Epistles to the Colossians, to Philemon, and to the Ephesians* (Grand Rapids, MI: Eerdmans, 1984), p. 37.

3. Alexander Maclaren, *Expositions of Holy Scripture* (Grand Rapids, MI: Baker, 1974), pp. 206, 207 is the source of the application regarding the tides of years, familiarity, and busyness.

4. C. S. Lewis, *Mere Christianity* (New York: Macmillan, 1976), p. 124.

5. Hudson T. Armerding, *Leadership* (Wheaton, IL: Tyndale, 1978), p. 102.

6. Simon J. Kistemaker, *Exposition of the Epistle to the Hebrews* (Grand Rapids, MI: Baker, 1984), p. 58.

7. William L. Lane, *Hebrews: A Call to Commitment* (Peabody, MA: Hendrickson, 1988), p. 39 says:

The writer's attitude toward the role assigned to the angels in verse 2 is positive. Although it is never said explicitly in the Old Testament that the Law was delivered through angels, this was a common conviction in the Jewish community because of the presence of angels at Sinai. Speaking of that memorable event, Moses said that God came "with myriads of his holy ones" (Deut. 33:2). The Greek translation of the text, which was the Bible the pastor read, added these words: "angels were with him at his right hand." Stephen, who also read his Bible in the Greek translation, makes reference to Moses who was "with the angel who spoke to him on Mount Sinai, and received living words to pass on to us" (Acts 7:38). He reminds his listeners that "you have received the law that was put into effect through angels" (Acts 7:53). The same point of view was asserted by Paul, who affirmed that the Law was "ordained by angels through an intermediary [Moses]" (Gal. 3:19). The same perspective is found in the younger contemporary of Paul and Stephen, Josephus, and in the rabbinic literature.

8. Philip Edgcumbe Hughes, *A Commentary on the Epistle to the Hebrews* (Grand Rapids, MI: Eerdmans, 1977), pp. 77, 78.

9. Ibid., p. 79.

10. *Calvin's Commentaries: The Epistle of Paul the Apostle to the Hebrews and the First and Second Epistles of St. Peter*, trans. William B. Johnston (Grand Rapids, MI: Eerdmans, 1963), p. 19.

11. Hughes, *A Commentary on the Epistle to the Hebrews*, p. 73, says:

Cf. Phillips, "We ought, therefore, to pay the greatest attention." In first-century Greek the superlative form is becoming less common and accordingly the comparative form is often found doing double duty. The adverb (περισσοτέρως) is a good example of this and probably carries an elative sense not only here but whenever it occurs in the New Testament. The elative sense is favored here by Hering and Moffatt, and Moffatt insists that "there is no idea of demanding a closer attention to the gospel than to the Law."

12. Lyle W. Dorsett and Marjorie Lamp Mead, *C. S. Lewis—Letters to Children* (New York: Macmillan, 1985), p. 111.

Chapter Five: The Ultimate Intention

1. F. F. Bruce, *The Epistles to the Colossians, to Philemon, and to the Ephesians* (Grand Rapids, MI: Eerdmans, 1984), p. 34 writes:

The one significant difference between the Septuagint and Hebrew texts comes in the first line of Ps. 8:5; whereas the Hebrew is most naturally translated "thou hast made him but a little lower than God" (ARV), the Septuagint says "thou madest him a little (*or* for a little while) lower than the angels." . . . LXX here translates Heb. *me-elo-hı-m* by (παρ' ἀγγέλους). The question is whether Heb. *'elo-hı-m* here denotes God in the usual OT sense, or is a plural in sense as well as in form, meaning "divine beings" or "angels" (as in Ps. 82:1b, "He judgeth among the gods"). Despite the rendering of Ps. 8:5 in ARV and RSV, the LXX may well be right.

2. William L. Lane, *Hebrews: A Call to Commitment* (Peabody, MA: Hendrickson, 1988), p. 43.

3. Arthur John Gossip, *The Hero in Thy Soul* (New York: Scribner's, 1930), p. 122.

4. Lane, *Hebrews: A Call to Commitment*, p. 44.

5. William Barclay, *The Letter to the Hebrews* (Philadelphia: Westminster, 1957), p. 17.

6. Hugh Montefiore, *A Commentary on the Epistle to the Hebrews* (Grand Rapids, MI: Baker, 1984), p. 58.

7. Ibid.

8. John A. Mackay, *God's Order* (New York: Macmillan, 1953), p. 97.

Chapter Six: A God-Worthy Salvation

1. Paul Johnson, *Intellectuals* (New York: Harper & Row, 1988), pp. 107, 108.

2. Ibid., pp. 130, 131.

3. Leon Morris, *The Expositor's Bible Commentary*, vol. 12 (Grand Rapids, MI: Zondervan, 1981), p. 26.

4. Alexander Maclaren, *Expositions of Holy Scripture* (Grand Rapids, MI: Baker, 1974), pp. 237, 238.

5. Morris, *The Expositor's Bible Commentary*, vol. 12, p. 27.

6. Edward J. Young, *The Book of Isaiah*, vol. 1 (Grand Rapids, MI: Eerdmans, 1965), p. 337.

7. Mike Mason, *The Mystery of Marriage* (Portland: Multnomah, 1978), p. 115.

8. Lewis Bayly, *Practice of Piety: Directing a Christian How to Walk That He May Please God. Amplified by the Author* (London: Printed for Philip Chetwind, 1619), pp. 452–59. The original, which the present author modernized, reads:

Soule. Lord, why, wouldest Thou be taken, when Thou mightest have escaped Thine enemies?
Christ. That thy spiritual enemies should not take thee, and cast thee into the prison of utter darkness.
Soule. Lord, wherefore wouldest Thou be bound?
Christ. That I might loose the cordes of thine iniquities.
Soule. Lord, wherefore wouldest Thou be lift up upon a Crosse?
Christ. That I might lift thee up with Me to heaven.
Soule. Lord, wherefore were Thy hands and feet nayled to the Crosse?

Christ. To enlarge they hands to doe the works of righteousness and to set thy feete at libertie, to walke in the wayes of peace.

Soule. Lord, why wouldest Thou have Thine arms nayled abroad?

Christ. That I might embrace thee more lovingly, My sweet soule.

Soule. Lord, wherefore was Thy side opened with a speare?

Christ. That thou mightest have a way to come near to My heart.

Chapter Seven: Solidarity with the Liberator

1. James Hastings, ed., *The Speaker's Bible*, vol. 17 (Grand Rapids, MI: Baker, 1971), p. 44 quotes Maurice Maeterlinck, *Our Eternity* (London: Methuen, 1913), p. 4.

2. Philip Edgcumbe Hughes, *A Commentary on the Epistle to the Hebrews* (Grand Rapids, MI: Eerdmans, 1977), p. 103, writes:

> Moreover, the attribution to the Son of this work of "sanctifying" accords well with what is taught elsewhere in this epistle. It is by the Father's will that "we have been sanctified through the offering of the body of Jesus Christ once for all" (10:10); by his single offering of himself Christ "has perfected for all time those who are sanctified" (10:14); his blood is the blood of the covenant by which the believer is sanctified (10:29); and Jesus "suffered outside the gate in order to sanctify the people through his own blood" (13:12; similarly 9:13ff.).

3. A. B. Bruce, *Epistle to the Hebrews* (Minneapolis: Klock & Klock, 1988), p. 16.

4. David Gooding, *An Unshakeable Kingdom* (Grand Rapids, MI: Eerdmans, 1989), p. 94.

5. F. F. Bruce, *The Epistle to the Hebrews* (Grand Rapids, MI: Eerdmans, 1964), p. 45.

6. *Calvin's Commentaries, The Epistle of Paul the Apostle to the Hebrews and the First and Second Epistles of St. Peter*, trans. William B. Johnston (Grand Rapids, MI: Eerdmans, 1974), p. 27.

7. Hugh Montefiore, *A Commentary on the Epistle to the Hebrews* (London: Adam & Charles Black, 1964), pp. 63, 64.

8. Mike Mason, *The Mystery of Marriage* (Portland: Multnomah, 1985), p. 70.

9. See J. D. Douglas, ed., *New Bible Dictionary* (Wheaton, IL: Tyndale, 1987), p. 728 which says:

> MAHER-SHALAL-HASH-BAZ. A symbolical name ("speed the spoil, hasten the prey") given to one of the sons of Isaiah to signify the speedy removal of Syria and Israel as enemies of Judah by the Assyrians. This removal was to take place before the child could lisp "my father and my mother" (Is. 8:3–4).

Also see p. 1098, which says:

> SHEAR-JASHUB. A symbolical name ("a remnant will return") given to one of Isaiah's sons to express the truth that out of the judgment God would save a remnant (e.g., Is. 1:9). When Isaiah went to Ahaz, Shear-Jashub

accompanied him as a reminder that the nation, even at that dark time, would not completely perish (Is. 7:3).

10. Somerset Maugham, *A Traveller in Romance* (New York: Crown, 1983), pp. 264, 265.

11. Raymond Brown, *The Message of Hebrews* (Downers Grove, IL: InterVarsity Press, 1982), p. 68 who references B. Russell, *A Free Man's Worship and Other Essays* (London: Unwin, 1976), pp. 18, 19.

12. Philip Schaff, ed., *The Creeds of Christendom* (Grand Rapids, MI: Baker, 1969), pp. 307, 308.

Chapter Eight: Solidarity with the High Priest

1. Henry Chadwick, *The Early Church* (Baltimore: Penguin Books, 1967), pp. 278, 279.

2. Ibid., p. 279.

3. Leon Morris, *The Gospel According to John* (Grand Rapids, MI: Eerdmans, 1971), p. 312.

4. Leon Morris, *The Expositor's Bible Commentary*, vol. 12 (Grand Rapids, MI: Zondervan, 1981), p. 29.

5. Franz Delitzsch, *Commentary on the Epistle to the Hebrews*, vol. 1 (Minneapolis: Klock & Klock, 1978), p. 144.

6. Philip Edgcumbe Hughes, *A Commentary on the Epistle to the Hebrews* (Grand Rapids, MI: Eerdmans, 1977), p. 120.

7. Leon Morris, *The Cross in the New Testament* (Grand Rapids, MI: Eerdmans, 1972), p. 299, where the author says:

Much is often made of the fact that there is an accusative of sin here, εἰς τὸ ἱλάσκεσθαι τὰς ἁμαρτίας τοῦ λαοῦ. Since one does not speak of propitiating a sin the suggestion is made that we should translate "to expiate the sins of the people." This, however, is too simple. It ignores the use of ἱλάσκομαι elsewhere in the Bible and in Greek generally. It is a word which has to do with the averting of the divine wrath, as I have tried to show in chs. iv and v of *The Apostolic Preaching of the Cross* (see pp. 174–77 for a discussion of the present verse). Moreover, it is not usually noticed that in the few examples of an accusative of sin after ἱλάσκομαι or ἐξιλάσκομαι, the meaning "make propitiation with respect to" is usually required rather than "expiate" (see, for example, Sir. 3:30; 5:6; 20:28; 28:5; 34:19; and cf. 16:7 for this author's understanding of ἐξιλάσκομαι). It is in line with the regular use of the verb to take it here in the sense "to make propitiation with respect to the sins of the people." To understand it as "to expiate the sins of the people" is to import a strange, unproven meaning for the verb.

8. Morris, *The Expositors Bible Commentary*, vol. 12, p. 30.

9. J. D. Douglas, ed., *New Bible Dictionary* (Wheaton, IL: Tyndale House, 1987), p. 104 where Leon Morris writes:

The word "atonement" is one of the few theological terms which derive basically from Anglo-Saxon. It means "a making at one," and points to a process of bringing those who are estranged into a unity. The word occurs in the OT to translate words from the *kpr* word group and it is found once in the NT (AV), rendering *katallage* (which is better translated "reconciliation" as RSV). Its use in theology is to denote the work of Christ in dealing with the problem posed by the sin of man, and in bringing sinners into right relation with God.

10. Ibid., p. 362 where Morris writes:

This term does not occur in AV, but it is found in some modern translations in place of "propitiation," *e.g.*, in 4:10, RSV. Objection is made to "propitiation" on the ground that it means the appeasement of an angry God, an idea not found in Scripture. Therefore expiation is substituted for it. But the matter is not so simple. Expiation properly has a thing as its object. We may expiate a crime, or a sin. Propitiation is a personal word. We propitiate a person rather than a sin (though we should not overlook the fact that in the Bible "propitiate" is occasionally found with sin as the object, the meaning being "to make propitiation with respect to sin"). If we are to think of our relationship to God as basically personal we cannot afford to dispense with the concept of propitiation. . . . But if sin affects man's relationship with God, if the relationship with God is the primary thing, then it is difficult to see how expiation is adequate. Once we bring in the category of the personal we need some such term as propitiation.

11. Hughes, *A Commentary on the Epistles to the Hebrews*, p. 122 writes: "To procure our restoration, God himself has met the demands of his own holiness. He has, so to speak, propitiated himself in our place, thereby achieving the reconciliation to himself of mankind."

12. Alexander Maclaren, *Expositions of Holy Scripture* (Grand Rapids, MI: Baker, 1974), p. 255 writes:

Comfort drops but coldly from lips that have never uttered a sigh or a groan; and for our poor human hearts it is not enough to have a merciful God far off in the heavens. We need a Christ who can be touched with the feeling of our infirmities ere we can come boldly to the Throne of Grace, assured of there finding grace in time of need.

Chapter Nine: Superior to Moses

1. F. F. Bruce, *The Epistle to the Hebrews* (Grand Rapids, MI: Eerdmans, 1964), p. 56.

2. William L. Lane, *Hebrews: A Call to Commitment* (Peabody, MA: Hendrickson, 1988), p. 58 writes:

In some strands of the later Jewish tradition the testimony to Moses' faithfulness in Numbers 12:7 was used to prove that Moses had been granted a higher rank and privilege than the ministering angels. One early tradition cites the passage: "If you have a prophet of the Lord, in a vision I will be known to him and in a dream I will speak to him. . . . Not thus have I dealt with my servant Moses, but in all my house he is trusted." The declaration "in all my house he is trusted" is given a striking commentary: "Another interpretation: *In all my house he is trusted:* more than the ministering angels and the sanctuary *he is trusted" (Siphre Zuta Beha alothka* 12:68 [Horowitz, 275–76]). According to this tradition, Moses is honored more than the ministering angels or the sanctuary where God is worshiped!

3. Philip Edgcumbe Hughes, *A Commentary on the Epistle to the Hebrews* (Grand Rapids, MI: Eerdmans, 1972), p. 127.

4. Brooke Foss Westcott, *The Epistle to the Hebrews* (Grand Rapids, MI: Eerdmans, 1967), p. 74.

5. William Barclay, *The Letter to the Hebrews* (Philadelphia: Westminster, 1957), p. 23.

6. Hugh Montefiore, *A Commentary on the Epistle to the Hebrews* (London: Adam & Charles Black, 1964), p. 72 says:

> Moses was part of God's household, but Jesus was its founder; and it was a commonplace of ancient thought that an architect is greater than his construction (cf. Justin, *Apol.* i 20; Philo, *de Plant*, 68). Our writer adds that, of course, God is the universal architect. Jesus' founding of the household of God was done to the glory of God, who is Creator of all things.

7. Leon Morris, *The Expositor's Bible Commentary,* vol. 12 (Grand Rapids, MI: Zondervan, 1981), p. 32.

8. John MacArthur, *Hebrews* (Chicago: Moody Press, 1983), p. 82.

9. Bruce, *The Epistle to the Hebrews*, p. 59.

Chapter Ten: Finishing Well

1. William L. Lane, *Hebrews: A Call to Commitment* (Peabody, MA: Hendrickson, 1988), pp. 61, 62.

2. A. B. Bruce, *Epistle to the Hebrews* (Minneapolis: Klock & Klock, 1988), p. 142.

3. Lane, *Hebrews: A Call to Commitment*, pp. 62, 63 writes:

> As the commentary is developed it becomes clear that the preacher interpreted Psalm 95:7b–11 in terms of the account of Israel at Kadesh-Barnea, as recounted in Numbers 13–14. It is striking that in 3:1–6 there was a quotation from Numbers 12:7 (3:5a); now in 3:12–19 there are several allusions to Numbers 13–14. It seems evident that the preacher had been concentrating his devotional reading on the book of Numbers at the time when he prepared this sermon. He found in Numbers a record of the faithfulness of God to Israel in the wilderness.

4. F. F. Bruce, *The Epistles to the Colossians, to Philemon, and to the Ephesians* (Grand Rapids, MI: Eerdmans, 1984), p. 67.

5. A. B. Bruce, *Epistle to the Hebrews*, p. 143.

Chapter Eleven: Entering the Rest

1. Philip Schaff, ed., *The Nicene and Post-Nicene Fathers*, vol. 1, *The Confessions of St. Augustine*, trans. J. G. Pilkington (Grand Rapids, MI: Eerdmans, 1974), p. 45.

2. Robert Maynard Hutchins, ed., *Great Books of the Western World,* vol. 33, *Pascal*, trans. W. F. Trotter (Chicago: Encyclopedia Britannica, 1952), p. 244.

3. Hugh Montefiore, *A Commentary on the Epistle to the Hebrews* (London: Adam & Charles Black, 1964), p. 82 says:

> (εὐηγγελισμένοι) translated heard the good news, became a technical term for the preaching of the Christian gospel (and the English word *evangel* is transliterated from the same Greek root). In the Old Testament it is used, as here, with its primary meaning of bringing good news (e.g. Is. iii. 7).

4. Leon Morris, *The Expositor's Bible Commentary,* vol. 12 (Grand Rapids, MI: Zondervan, 1981), p. 40.

5. Alexander Maclaren, *Exposition of Holy Scripture* (Grand Rapids, MI: Baker, 1974), p. 305. See pp. 303–8 for an excellent discussion of faith as belief plus trust.

6. Dr. and Mrs. Howard Taylor, *Hudson Taylor's Spiritual Secret* (Philadelphia: China Inland Mission, 1932), p. 147.

7. F. F. Bruce, *The Epistle to the Hebrews* (Grand Rapids, MI: Eerdmans, 1964), p. 73.

8. Montefiore, *A Commentary on the Epistle to the Hebrews*. p. 93.

9. Maclaren, *Exposition of Holy Scripture*, p. 322.

10. Morris, *The Expositor's Bible Commentary,* vol. 12, pp. 41, 42 writes:

> The reason the first group did not enter God's rest was "their disobedience." The word *apeitheia* "disobedience" is always used in the NT of disobeying God often with the thought of the gospel in mind, so it comes close to the meaning disbelief (cf. v. 11, Rom. 11:30).

11. F. F. Bruce, *The Epistle to the Hebrews*, pp. 76, 77 explains:

> Yet it must be recognized that the ordinary reader of the Greek Bible had and still has, where he exists an advantage over the reader of the English Bible because to him "Joshua" and "Jesus" are not two names but one; he could distinguish between our Lord and his most illustrious namesake of Old Testament days, and at the same time appreciate some of the implications of the fact that they are namesakes. The parallel between the Old Testament "Jesus," who led his followers into the earthly Canaan, and Jesus the Son of God, who leads the heirs of the new covenant into their heavenly inheritance, is a prominent theme of early Christian typology.

Chapter Twelve: The Double-Edged Sword

1. William L. Lane, *Hebrews: A Call to Commitment* (Peabody, MA: Hendrickson, 1988), p. 69.

2. Brooke Foss Westcott, *The Epistle to the Hebrews* (Grand Rapids, MI: Eerdmans, 1967), p. 102.

3. J. B. Phillips, *The Ring of Truth* (Wheaton, IL: Harold Shaw, 1967), pp. 76, 77.

4. F. F. Bruce, *The Epistle to the Hebrews* (Grand Rapids, MI: Eerdmans, 1964), p. 80.

5. John Piper, *Desiring God* (Portland: Multnomah, 1986), p. 119, quoting from Sir Norman Anderson, *God's Word for God's World* (London: Hodder and Stoughton, 1981), p. 25.

6. John R. W. Stott, *Between Two Worlds* (Grand Rapids, MI: Eerdmans, 1982), p. 25.

7. John Bunyan, *The Pilgrim's Progress* (New York: Dodd, Mead & Company, 1974), p. 283.

8. C. H. Spurgeon, *The Metropolitan Tabernacle Pulpit*, vol. 34 (Pasadena, TX: Pilgrim Publications, 1974), p. 115.

9. Philip Edgcumbe Hughes, *A Commentary on the Epistle to the Hebrews* (Grand Rapids, MI: Eerdmans, 1977), p. 166.

10. Ibid., p. 166, quoting from *Liber Meditationum* xxvii, in *Augustini Opera*, IX (Lyon, 1664), p. 299.

11. Walter Paxendale, *Dictionary of Illustrations for Pulpit and Platform* (Chicago: Moody Press, 1949), p. 419.

12. A. W. Tozer, *The Knowledge of the Holy* (New York: Harper & Row, 1961), p. 63.

13. Bruce, *The Epistle to the Hebrews*, p. 83.

14. Lane, *Hebrews: A Call to Commitment*, p. 69.

15. William Barclay, *The Letter to the Hebrews* (Philadelphia: Westminster, 1957), pp. 36, 37.

Chapter Thirteen: Our Great High Priest

1. John MacArthur Jr., *The MacArthur New Testament Commentary, Hebrews* (Chicago: Moody Press, 1983), p. 109.

2. Brooke Foss Westcott, *The Epistle to the Hebrews* (Grand Rapids, MI: Eerdmans, 1967), p. 106.

3. Percy A. Scholes, *The Oxford Companion to Music* (New York: Oxford University Press, 1950), p. 14.

If two tuning-forks of the same pitch be placed in position for sounding and one of them be set in vibration, the other will take up the vibrations sympathetically; the first fork is then a generator of sound and the second a resonator. . . .

An instance of true resonance is found in the well-known power of certain singers to break a drinking-glass by loudly singing into it the note to which it happens to be attuned. . . . The French acoustician, Gariel, has called attention to the following very curious passages in the Talmud (the compilation of Jewish civil and religious law completed AD 500):

"When a cock shall stretch forth its neck into the hollow of a glass vessel and sing therein in such a way as to break it, the full loss shall be paid."

"When a horse neighs or an ass brays and so breaks a glass vessel, the half of the loss shall be paid."

This is, of course, academic legalism. We can hardly imagine such incidents occurring. Yet the provision made against them shows knowledge of theoretical possibilities.

4. Raymond Brown, *The Message of Hebrews* (Downers Grove, IL: InterVarsity Press, 1982), pp. 95, 96.

5. C. S. Lewis, *Mere Christianity* (New York: Macmillan, 1952), pp. 124, 125.

6. William L. Lane, *Hebrews: A Call to Commitment* (Peabody, MA: Hendrickson, 1988), p. 75.

7. Hugh Montefiore, *A Commentary on the Epistle to the Hebrews* (London: Adam & Charles Black, 1964), p. 91.

8. Lane, *Hebrews: A Call to Commitment*, p. 77.

9. *Calvin's Commentaries: The Epistle of Paul the Apostle to the Hebrews and the First and Second Epistles of St. Peter*, trans. William B. Johnston (Grand Rapids, MI: Eerdmans, 1963), p. 57.

10. Westcott, *The Epistle to the Hebrews*, p. 109.

11. Leon Morris, *The Expositor's Bible Commentary*, vol. 12 (Grand Rapids, MI: Zondervan, 1981), pp. 46, 47.

Chapter Fourteen: High Priest, High Qualifications

1. Leon Morris, *The Expositor's Bible Commentary*, vol. 12 (Grand Rapids, MI: Zondervan, 1981), p. 47.

2. Ibid.

3. Philip Edgcumbe Hughes, *A Commentary on the Epistle to the Hebrews* (Grand Rapids, MI: Eerdmans, 1977), p. 177.

4. Morris, *The Expositor's Bible Commentary*, p. 47.

5. F. F. Bruce, *The Epistle to the Hebrews* (Grand Rapids, MI: Eerdmans, 1964), p. 94 writes:

> . . . "this day" in our author's mind is the day of Christ's enthronement—the day when the Most High gave public notice that He had exalted the crucified Jesus as "both Lord and Christ" (Acts 2:36). And, says our author, the same God who acclaimed Jesus as His Son has also acclaimed Him as perpetual high priest.

6. William L. Lane, *Hebrews: A Call to Commitment* (Peabody, MA: Hendrickson, 1988), p. 80.

7. Morris, *The Expositor's Bible Commentary*, p. 49.

8. John Calvin, *A Harmony of the Gospels, Matthew, Mark and Luke and the Epistles of James and Jude*, vol. 3, trans. A. W. Morrison (Grand Rapids, MI: Eerdmans, 1975), p. 515.

9. Morris, *The Expositor's Bible Commentary*, p. 50.

Chapter Fifteen: Slow to Learn

1. F. R. Webber, *A History of Preaching in Britain and America*, vol. 1 (Milwaukee: Northwestern Publishing House, 1952), p. 329.

2. J. I. Packer, *A Quest for Godliness* (Wheaton, IL: Crossway Books, 1990), p. 257.

3. Leon Morris, *The Expositor's Bible Commentary*, vol. 12 (Grand Rapids, MI: Zondervan, 1981), p. 52.

4. Philip Edgcumbe Hughes, *Commentary on the Epistle to the Hebrews* (Grand Rapids, MI: Eerdmans, 1977), pp. 191, 192.

5. F. F. Bruce, *The Epistle to the Hebrews* (Grand Rapids, MI: Eerdmans, 1964), p. 109.

6. Philip Schaff, ed., *The Nicene and Post-Nicene Fathers*, vol. III, *St. Augustine: On the Holy Trinity, Doctrinal Treatises, Moral Treatises* (Grand Rapids, MI: Eerdmans, 1956), p. 86 says:

> And if this is understood with difficulty, the mind must be purged by faith, by more and more abstaining from sins, and by doing good works, and by praying with the groaning of holy desires; that by profiting through the divine help, it may both understand and love.

Chapter Sixteen: No Second Genesis

1. Charles Colson, *Who Speaks for God?* (Wheaton, IL: Crossway Books, 1985), p. 153.

2. Hugh Montefiore, *A Commentary on the Epistle to the Hebrews* (London: Adam & Charles Black, 1964), p. 105.

3. F. F. Bruce, *The Epistle to the Hebrews* (Grand Rapids, MI: Eerdmans, 1964), pp. 114, 115 explains:

> This has commonly been regarded as a reference to Christian baptism, but it is very doubtful whether Christian baptism is directly in view here at all. Apart from the fact that the word is in the plural, it may be significant that our author does not use *baptisma*, the Greek noun regularly employed in the New Testament to denote Christian baptism (and the baptism of John), but *baptismos,* which in its two other indubitable New Testament occurrences refers to Jewish ceremonial washings. "Instruction about ablutions" (RSV) or "instruction about cleansing rites" (NEB) expresses the sense more adequately.

4. Ibid., pp. 118, 119.

5. Leon Morris, *The Expositor's Bible Commentary*, vol. 12 (Grand Rapids, MI: Zondervan, 1981), p. 54.

6. Roger Nicole, "Some Comments on Hebrews 6:4–6 and the Doctrine of the Perseverance of God with the Saints," in Gerald F. Hawthorne, ed., *Current Issues in Biblical and Patristic Interpretation* (Grand Rapids, MI: Eerdmans, 1975), pp. 356–59 provides an exact description of the three interpretations of Hebrews 6:4–6.

7. Ibid., p. 358.

8. Bruce, *The Epistle to the Hebrews*, p. 363.

9. John MacArthur Jr., *The MacArthur New Testament Commentary, Hebrews* (Chicago: Moody Press, 1983), pp. 144, 145.

10. Nicole, "Some Comments on Hebrews 6:4–6 and the Doctrine of the Perseverance of God with the Saints," p. 363.

11. Ibid., p. 363.

Chapter Seventeen: Make Your Hope Sure

1. William L. Lane, *Hebrews: A Call to Commitment* (Peabody, MA: Hendrickson, 1988), p. 144.

2. Alexander Maclaren, *Expositions of Holy Scripture* (Grand Rapids, MI: Baker, 1974), p. 379.

3. Henry Fairlie, *The Seven Deadly Sins Today* (Notre Dame, IN: Notre Dame, 1979), p. 128.

4. Commander Eric J. Berryman, "Strange Things Happen at Sea," *Proceedings*, U.S. Naval Institute, June 1989, vol. 115/6/1036, p. 48.

5. Lane, *Hebrews: A Call to Commitment*, p. 105:

The qualification, "through faith and steadfastness" is expanded in reference to include a plurality of figures, perhaps in anticipation of the development in 11:1—12:3. Originally, however, it was conventional terminology in Jewish tradition concerning Abraham (cf. *Jub.* 17:7; 19:1–9), and it is in this restricted sense that these terms are expounded in 6:13–15.

Chapter Eighteen: An Anchor for the Soul

1. Philip Edgcumbe Hughes, *A Commentary on the Epistle to the Hebrews* (Grand Rapids, MI: Eerdmans, 1977), p. 230.

2. Leon Morris, *The Expositor's Bible Commentary*, vol. 12 (Grand Rapids, MI: Zondervan, 1974), p. 60 explains:

Abbot-Smith says that the verb NIV translates "wanted" (*boulomenos*) implies "more strongly than *thelō* . . . the deliberate exercise of volition" (s. v.). The operation of God's will is stressed and is further brought out by the reference to "the unchanging nature of his purpose" (where *boulē*, "purpose," is cognate with the word "wanted").

3. W. E. Sangster, "When Hope Is Dead—Hope on!" in Clyde E. Fant Jr., and William M. Pinson Jr., *20 Centuries of Great Preaching*, vol. 11 (Waco, TX: Word, 1976), p. 364.

4. Ibid., p. 365.

5. William L. Lane, *Hebrews 1–8* (Waco, TX: Word, 1991), p. 153.

6. Hughes, *A Commentary on the Epistle to the Hebrews*, p. 235.

7. William Barclay, *The Letter to the Hebrews* (Philadelphia: Westminster, 1957), p. 64.

Chapter Nineteen: The Greatness of Melchizedek

1. *Facts on File: World News Digest with Index*, vol. 36, no. 1861, July 10, 1976 (New York: Facts on File), pp. 485, 486.

2. F. F. Bruce, *The Epistles to the Colossians, to Philemon, and to the Ephesians* (Grand Rapids, MI: Eerdmans, 1984), pp. 137, 138 explains:

The important consideration was the account given of Melchizedek in holy writ; to him the silences of Scripture were as much due to divine inspiration as were its statements. In the only record which Scripture provides of Melchizedek—Gen. 14:18–20—nothing is said of his parentage, nothing is said of his ancestry or progeny, nothing is said of his birth, nothing is said of his death. He appears as a living man, king of Salem and priest of God Most High; and as such he disappears. In all this—in the silences as well as in the statements—he is a fitting type of Christ; in fact, the record by the things it says of him and by the things it does not say has assimilated him to the Son of God.

3. Simon J. Kistemaker, *Hebrews* (Grand Rapids, MI: Baker, 1984), p. 189 says a priest could assume his priestly duties "as soon as the first signs of manhood made their appearance," but according to rabbinical tradition "he was not actually installed till he was twenty years of age." The period of service for a priest might cover twenty to thirty years, but the end would come. Kistemaker also references Emile Schurer, *History of the Jewish People*, vol. 1, Div. 2, p. 215 and comments:

> Note also that the following passages imply that a priest was installed at age thirty and served until he reached the age of fifty: Num. 4:3, 23, 30, 35, 39, 43, 47; also see I Chron. 23:3. Num. 8:23–26 speaks of Levites twenty-five years of age. And I Chron. 23:24, 27; II Chron. 31:17; and Ezra 3:8 mention the twenty-year old priest.

4. William L. Lane, *Hebrews: A Call to Commitment* (Peabody, MA: Hendrickson, 1988), p. 106.

5. Leon Morris, *The Expositor's Bible Commentary*, vol. 12 (Grand Rapids, MI: Zondervan, 1981), pp. 63, 64 writes,

> And it is the Son of God who is the standard, not the ancient priest-king. The writer says that Melchizedek is "made like" (*aphomoiomenos*) the Son of God, not that the Son of God is like Melchizedek. Thus it is not that Melchizedek sets the pattern and Jesus follows it. Rather, the record about Melchizedek is so arranged that it brings out certain truths that apply far more fully to Jesus than they do to Melchizedek. With the latter, these truths are simply a matter of record; but with Jesus they are not only historically true, they also have significant spiritual dimensions. The writer is, of course, speaking of the Son's eternal nature, not of his appearance in the Incarnation.

6. Bruce, *The Epistles to the Colossians, to Philemon and to the Ephesians*, p. 142, writes:

> Reverting for a moment to the tithe-receiving tribe of Levi, our author points out that Levi, the ancestor of that priestly tribe and the embodiment of its corporate personality, may be said himself to have paid tithes to Melchizedek (thus conceding the superiority of the Melchizedek priesthood) in the person of his ancestor Abraham. Levi was Abraham's great-grandson, and was yet unborn when Abraham met Melchizedek; but an ancestor is regarded in biblical thought as containing within himself all his descendants. That Levi may be thought of thus as paying tithes to Melchizedek is an afterthought to what has already been said about the significance of this particular payment of tithes; lest it should be criticized as far-fetched, our author qualifies it with the phrase "so to say" ("it might even be said," NEB).

Chapter Twenty: The Sufficiency of Melchizedek

1. C. S. Lewis, *Reflections on the Psalms* (New York: Harcourt, Brace, 1958), pp. 50, 51.

2. Gerhard Friedrich, ed., *Theological Dictionary of the New Testament*, vol. 8, trans. Geoffrey W. Bromiley (Grand Rapids, MI: Eerdmans, 1974), pp. 82, 83.

3. F. F. Bruce, *The Epistles to the Colossians, to Philemon, and to the Ephesians* (Grand Rapids, MI: Eerdmans, 1984), p. 149.

4. Philip Edgcumbe Hughes, *A Commentary on the Epistle to the Hebrews* (Grand Rapids, MI: Eerdmans, 1977), p. 259.

5. Hugh Montefiore, *A Commentary on the Epistle to the Hebrews* (London: Adam & Charles Black, 1964), p. 125.

6. William Barclay, *The Letter to the Hebrews* (Philadelphia: Westminster, 1957), p. 83.

7. William L. Lane, *Hebrews: A Call to Commitment* (Peabody, MA: Hendrickson, 1988), p. 109.

8. Donald Grey Barnhouse, *Let Me Illustrate* (Old Tappan, NJ: Fleming H. Revell, 1967), pp. 15, 16.

Chapter Twenty-One: The Superiority of Melchizedek

1. Philip Edgcumbe Hughes, *A Commentary on the Epistle to the Hebrews* (Grand Rapids, MI: Eerdmans, 1977), p. 267.

2. William Barclay, *The Letter to the Hebrews* (Philadelphia: Westminster, 1957), p. 85.

3. Leon Morris, *The Expositor's Bible Commentary*, vol. 12 (Grand Rapids, MI: Zondervan, 1981), p. 71.

4. Hughes, *A Commentary on the Epistle to the Hebrews*, p. 268, note 34 writes:

The adjective (ἀπαράβατος) rendered adverbially in our version as "permanently," is susceptible of a variety of interpretations: "unchangeable" (KJV), "perpetual" (NEB), "indefectible" (F.F. Bruce), "inviolable" (Westcott), "interminable" (Delitzsch) represent one line of exegesis, while "that cannot pass to another" (Erasmus), "that doth not pass from one to another" (Owen), "intransmissible" (Hering, Teodorico), "inalienable" (Spicq, Montefiore), "non-transferable" (Moffatt), "that needs no successor" (Phillips) represent another. Such evidence as the papyri afford seems to favor the former, but this is more than counterbalanced by the preference of the Greek fathers for the latter understanding. In our view, the appropriateness of the term is enhanced by its ambivalence: the priesthood of Christ does not pass to another precisely because it is a perpetual priesthood.

5. Ibid., p. 269.

6. Raymond Brown, *The Message of Hebrews* (Downers Grove, IL: InterVarsity Press, 1982), p. 139.

7. *Tabletalk*, June 1989, vol. 24, no. 5, p. 10.

8. Hughes, *A Commentary on the Epistle to the Hebrews*, p. 80.

9. Ibid., p. 275 writes:

The truth of the transcendental glory of our ever living High Priest guarantees to us the existential reality of his person and work, for it assures us that he is not just a figure of the past, but also of the present and the future, indeed of eternity (Heb. 13:8). The power of his all-sufficient atoning work is available without diminishment to us today as it was to the believers of the first century, and it is so because he who died for us is alive from the dead and enthroned on high. Were he merely a figure of past history, over-taken and held by death, he could be no mediating high priest for us today. But Christ, alive and supremely exalted as he is, is truly our contemporary and our ever present Lord.

Chapter Twenty-Two: Christ's Surpassing Priesthood and Covenant

1. Charles Colson, *Kingdoms in Conflict* (New York/Grand Rapids, MI: William Morrow/Zondervan, 1978), p. 85.

2. F. F. Bruce, *The Epistle to the Hebrews* (Grand Rapids, MI: Eerdmans, 1964), p. 165.

3. Leon Morris, *The Expositor's Bible Commentary*, vol. 12 (Grand Rapids, MI: Zondervan, 1981), p. 76.

4. Edward Fudge, *Our Man in Heaven* (Grand Rapids, MI: 1974), p. 82.

5. *Calvin's Commentaries: The Epistle of Paul the Apostle to the Hebrews and the First and Second Epistles of St. Peter*, trans. William B. Johnston (Grand Rapids, MI: Eerdmans, 1963), p. 107.

6. John Blanchard, *The Truth for Life* (West Sussex, England: H. E. Walter Ltd., 1982), p. 231.

7. Alexander Maclaren, *Exposition of Holy Scripture* (Grand Rapids, MI: Baker, 1974), p. 47.

8. Daniel J. Boorstin, *The Discoverers* (New York: Vintage Books, 1983), p. 482.

9. Bruce, *The Epistles to the Hebrews*, pp. 175, 176:

> But now the assurance of forgiveness of sins is written into the very terms of the covenant in the most unqualified fashion: "I will forgive their iniq-uity, and their sin will I remember no more." For the Hebrew, "remember-ing" was more than a mental effort; it carried with it the thought of doing something to the advantage, or disadvantage, of the person remembered. When Cornelius's prayers and alms ascended as a memorial before God, God took action to Cornelius' advantage and sent His servant to him with a message which brought salvation to him and his household (Acts 10:4, 31; 11:13ff.). When, on the other hand, "Babylon the great was remembered in the sight of God", it was "to give unto her the cup of the wine of the fierce-ness of his wrath" (Rev. 16:19). If men's sins are remembered by God, His holiness must take action against them; if they are not remembered, it is because His grace has determined to forgive them—not in spite of His holiness, but in harmony with it. Under the old sacrificial system, there was "a remembrance made of sins year by year" (Ch. 10:3); if no such remem-brance of sins is made under the new covenant, it is because of a sacrifice offered up once for all (Ch. 7:27).

Chapter Twenty-Three: Covenant and Conscience

1. Leon Morris, *The Expositor's Bible Commentary*, vol. 12 (Grand Rapids, MI: Zondervan, 1981), pp. 81, 82.

2. Hugh Montefiore, *A Commentary on the Epistle to the Hebrews* (London: Adam & Charles Black, 1964), p. 146 explains:

> Cherubim kept watch over the very dwelling place of God himself. They are called Cherubim of the Glory, because Glory here is a synonym for God; an apt periphrasis, since the mystery of this inner sanctuary, together with its gold furnishings suggests the divine glory.

3. Herbert Danby, trans., *The Mishnah* (London: Oxford, 1974), pp. 162–172, which gives the tractate *Yoma* ("The Day of Atonement").

4. Ibid., pp. 200, 201.

5. William Barclay, *The Letter to the Hebrews* (Philadelphia: Westminster, 1957), p. 109.

6. Morris, *The Expositor's Bible Commentary*, vol. 12, p. 83 says:

> The sins "committed in ignorance" point to the truth that there is ignorance that is culpable. Sins of this kind do matter, and we should be on our guard against minimizing their seriousness. In Ecclesiasticus 23:2 the son of Sirach asks not to be spared discipline for these sins of ignorance (he uses the same word that appears here), lest they multiply and bring him low.

Similarly, Montefiore, *A Commentary on the Epistle to the Hebrews*, p. 148: "These sins of ignorance may be very grave both in their nature and in their consequences; but they can be forgiven because they have not been committed with the settled and deliberate intention of disobedience."

7. Charles Colson, *Who Speaks for God?* (Wheaton, IL: Crossway Books, 1985), pp. 76, 77.

8. F. F. Bruce, *The Epistle to the Hebrews* (Grand Rapids, MI: Eerdmans, 1964), p. 194, who cites H. C. G. Moule, *Charles Simeon* (London: Inter-Varsity, 1948), p. 25ff.

Chapter Twenty-Four: Covenant and Blood

1. Simon J. Kistemaker, *Exposition of the Epistle to the Hebrews* (Grand Rapids, MI: Baker, 1984), p. 256, who cites Johannes Behm, *Theological Dictionary of the New Testament*, vol. 2, trans. Geoffrey W. Bromiley (Grand Rapids, MI: Eerdmans, 1974), p. 131.

2. Leon Morris, *The Expositor's Bible Commentary*, vol. 12 (Grand Rapids, MI: Zondervan, 1981), p. 89 comments on the variations:

> But there is no mention of the water, scarlet wool, hyssop, or the sprinkling of the book. Water and scarlet (whether wool or other material is not said) and hyssop were used in the rite of cleansing healed lepers (Lev. 14:4–6; cf. 49–51). Hyssop is mentioned also in connection with the Passover (Exod 12:22) and the cleansing rites associated with the ashes of the red heifer (Num. 19:6, 18). It was the natural thing to use hyssop in cleansing (Ps 51:7). The sprinkling of the scroll is not mentioned in Exodus 24. But the book was written by men, and thus it must be cleansed of any defilement they might have conveyed to it. While we do not know

where this information came from, there is nothing improbable about any of it.

3. The tabernacle, of course, was not in existence when the covenant was confirmed. And when the tabernacle was later consecrated, the Scriptures mention only the use of oil. Josephus, however, evidently knew of a tradition that taught that it was consecrated with oil, water, and blood:

> Then, with the blood of the victims, he sprinkled Aaron's vestments and Aaron himself, together with his sons, purging them with water from the spring and with sweet oil, in order to devote them to God. So for seven days he continued this process, purifying both them and their vestments, as also the tabernacle and its vessels, both with oil that had been previously fumigated, as I have said, and with the blood of bulls and of goats, of which they slaughtered every day one of each sort; then on the eighth day he announced a feast for the people and bade them offer sacrifices, each according to his means. (Josephus *Antiquities* 3.8.6, L.C.L., vol. 4, p. 415)

4. F. F. Bruce, *The Epistle to the Hebrews* (Grand Rapids, MI: Eerdmans, 1964), p. 217:

> "Almost everything" but not absolutely everything; there are certain exceptions. For example, an impoverished Israelite might bring a tenth of an ephah (four pints) of fine flour to the priest as his sin-offering instead of a lamb or even instead of two turtledoves or young pigeons (Lev. 5:11). In Num. 16:46 atonement was made for the congregation of Israel, after the destruction of Korah and his company, by means of incense; in Num. 31:22ff., metal objects captured in war were to be purified by fire and *me niddah*; in Num. 31:50 the Israelite commanders in the fighting against Midian brought the gold objects which they had captured "to make atonement for our souls before Jehovah."

5. I. Epstein, trans., *The Babylonian Talmud, Seder Mo'ed*, vol. 3 (London: Soncino, 1938), p. 17 says, "*For it is the blood that maketh atonement by reason of life!*" Similarly *Seder Kodashim*, vol. I, p. 25.

6. Bruce, *The Epistle to the Hebrews*, pp. 218, 219.

7. John Greenleaf Whittier, *The Eternal Goodness*, Stanza 20.

8. Allan C. Emery, *A Turtle on a Fencepost* (Waco, TX: Word, 1979), p. 86.

9. William L. Lane, *Hebrews: A Call to Commitment* (Peabody, MA: Hendrickson, 1988), pp. 126, 127.

Chapter Twenty-Five: Covenant and Perfection

1. William Barclay, *The Letter to the Hebrews* (Philadelphia: Westminster, 1957), p. 125.

2. F. F. Bruce, *The Epistles to the Colossians, to Philemon, and to the Ephesians* (Grand Rapids, MI: Eerdmans, 1984), p. 230.

3. C. S. Lewis, *Letters to An American Lady* (Grand Rapids, MI: Eerdmans, 1967), p. 38.

4. G. Abbott-Smith, *A Manual Greek Lexicon of the New Testament* (New York: Charles Scribner's, n.d.), p. 427 defines the Greek *suneidesis* of verse 2 as "consciousness"—"In an ethical sense, innate discernment, self-judging consciousness, *conscience.*"

5. Bruce, *The Epistles to the Colossians, to Philemon, and to the Ephesians*, p. 232 explains: "The Greek translator evidently regarded the Hebrew wording as an instance of *pars pro toto*; the 'digging' or hollowing out of the ears is part of the total work of fashioning a human body."

6. Charles Williams, *The Descent of the Dove* (London: The Religious Book Club, 1939), pp. 39, 40.

7. Leon Morris, *The Expositor's Bible Commentary*, vol. 12 (Grand Rapids, MI: Zondervan, 1981), p. 99 explains:

> We should notice a difference between the way the author uses the verb "to sanctify" (NIV, "made holy") and the way Paul uses it. For the apostle, sanctification is a process whereby the believer grows progressively in Christian qualities and character. In Hebrews the same terminology is used of the process by which a person becomes Christian and is therefore "set apart" for God. There is no contradiction between these two; both are necessary for the fully developed Christian life. But we must be on our guard lest we read this epistle with Pauline terminology in mind. The sanctification meant here is one brought about by the death of Christ. It has to do with making people Christian, not with developing Christian character.

8. Bruce, *The Epistles to the Colossians, to Philemon, and to the Ephesians*. p. 241 writes: "Here their character as the people thus set apart is simply indicated in timeless terms, because emphasis is now laid on the fact that by that same sacrifice Christ has eternally 'perfected' His holy people."

9. Donald Grey Barnhouse, *Let Me Illustrate* (Old Tappan, NJ: Revell, 1967), p. 97.

Chapter Twenty-Six: Full Access/Full Living

1. Alan F. Johnson, *The Freedom Letter* (Chicago: Moody Press, 1974), p. 136, who quotes from Henry Hart Milman, *History of Christianity*, vol. 4 (New York: Crowell, 1881), p. 144.

2. Leon Morris, *The Expositor's Bible Commentary*, vol. 12 (Grand Rapids, MI: Zondervan, 1981), p. 104.

3. Bertrand Russell, *A Free Man's Worship*, in *Mysticism and Logic* (New York: W. W. Norton & Company, 1929), pp. 47, 48.

4. James S. Hewitt, *Illustrations Unlimited* (Wheaton, IL: Tyndale House, 1988), p. 291.

5. Ray C. Stedman, *What More Can God Say?* (Glendale, CA: Regal, 1974), p. 171.

6. R. Kent Hughes, "The Discipline of Church," in *Disciplines of a Godly Man* (Wheaton, IL: Crossway, 1991), pp. 151–59.

7. Robert G. Rayburn, *O Come, Let Us Worship* (Grand Rapids, MI: Baker, 1984), pp. 29, 30.

8. Oswald Chambers, *My Utmost for His Highest* (Toronto: McClelland and Stewart, n.d.), p. 192.

9. Elisabeth Elliot, ed., *The Journals of Jim Elliot* (Old Tappan, NJ: Fleming H. Revell, 1978), p. 309.

10. *Dynamic Preaching*, vol. 5, no. 2 (February 1990), p. 8.

Chapter Twenty-Seven: The Perils of Apostasy

1. Sculley Bradley, ed., *The American Tradition in Literature*, 4th edition (New York: Grosset & Dunlap, 1974), p. 46.

2. David Gooding, *An Unshakeable Kingdom* (Grand Rapids, MI: Eerdmans, 1989), p. 201.

3. Leon Morris, *The Expositor's Bible Commentary*, vol. 12 (Grand Rapids, MI: Zondervan, 1981), p. 106.

4. Herbert Lockyer, *Last Words of Saints and Sinners* (Grand Rapids, MI: Kregel, 1969), p. 133.

5. Ibid., p. 132.

6. William B. Johnston, ed., *Calvin's Commentaries: The Epistle of Paul the Apostle to the Hebrews and the First and Second Epistles of St. Peter* (Grand Rapids, MI: Eerdmans, 1977), pp. 77, 78.

7. Simon J. Kistemaker, *Exposition of the Epistle to the Hebrews* (Grand Rapids, MI: Baker, 1984), p. 295.

8. Morris, *The Expositor's Bible Commentary*, vol. 12, p. 107.

9. Kistemaker, *Exposition of the Epistle to the Hebrews*, p. 296, explains:

This song was well known to the readers because they sang it in their worship services. The wording differs somewhat in the original Hebrew and its Greek translation: therefore, scholars have made the suggestion that "the citation in this form may have been stereotyped by apostolic example in the language of the primitive church." The citation occurs in the selfsame wording in Romans 12:19. We may assume that it circulated in the early church as a proverbial saying.

10. Clarence E. Macartney, *Macartney's Illustrations* (New York: Abingdon, 1946), pp. 163, 164.

11. C. S. Lewis, *Surprised by Joy* (New York: Harcourt, Brace, Jovanovich, 1955), p. 232.

Chapter Twenty-Eight: Keep On!

1. C. H. Spurgeon, *The Metropolitan Tabernacle Pulpit*, vol. 10, Sermon 580, "God Is with Us" (London: Passmore & Alabaster, 1973), p. 407.

2. George Abbot-Smith, *A Manual Greek Lexicon of the New Testament* (New York: Scribner's, n.d.), p. 432.

3. F. F. Bruce, *The Epistle to the Hebrews* (Grand Rapids, MI: Eerdmans, 1964), p. 270.

4. "Freeze-dried Pets Article Legitimate," *The Bloomington Indiana Herald-Telephone* (December 26, 1985).

5. Warren Bennis and Burt Nanus, *Leaders, the Strategies for Taking Charge* (New York: Harper & Row, 1986), pp. 69, 70.

6. Bruce, *The Epistle to the Hebrews*, pp. 270, 271 explains:

The word he uses has appeared three times already in this letter; ARV translates it uniformly by "boldness." In Chs. 4:16; 10:19 it is used of the confidence with which Christians may approach the throne of God since Christ is there as their prevailing high priest; in Ch. 3:6 it is used more generally of the courageous confession which Christians should maintain without fail. It is in this last sense that it is used here, with special reference to steadfastness in adverse and disheartening circumstances: "It is, so to say, the content of the Christian attitude in the world, the security of God's salvation and the open confession amidst of opposition." We may think of the "boldness" of Peter and John which made such an impression on the Sanhedrin (Acts 4:13); the forthrightness of their language evinced an inner confidence of heart and life.

7. Simon J. Kistemaker, *Exposition of the Epistle to the Hebrews* (Grand Rapids, MI: Baker, 1984), p. 302.

Chapter Twenty-Nine: Faith Is . . .

1. Brooke Foss Westcott, *The Epistle to the Hebrews* (Grand Rapids, MI: Eerdmans, 1967), p. 350.

2. F. F. Bruce, *The Epistle to the Hebrews* (Grand Rapids, MI: Eerdmans, 1964), p. 278 explains:

This word *hypostaseōs* has appeared twice already in the epistle. In Ch. 1:3 the Son was stated to be the very image of God's *hypostaseōs*; in Ch. 3:14 believers are said to be Christ's associates if they hold fast the beginning of their *hypostaseōs* firm to the end. In the former place it has the objective sense of "substance" or "real essence" (as opposed to what merely seems to be so). In the latter place it has the subjective sense of "confidence" or "assurance." Here it is natural to take it in the same subjective sense as it bears in Ch. 3:14, and so ARV and RSV render it "assurance."

3. William L. Lane, *Hebrews: A Call to Commitment* (Peabody, MA: Hendrickson, 1988), p. 149.

4. William Barclay, *The Letter to the Hebrews* (Philadelphia: Westminster, 1957), p. 145.

5. Daniel J. Boorstin, *The Discoverers* (New York: Vintage Books, 1983), pp. 311, 312.

6. *Leadership Magazine* (Summer 1983), reprinted from the *London Observer*.

7. Bruce, *The Epistle to the Hebrews*, p. 281 explains:

Thus "the visible came forth from the invisible" (NEB). But how do we know this? By faith, says our author. Greek speculation about the formation of the ordered world out of formless matter had influenced Jewish thinkers like Philo and the author of the book of Wisdom; the writer to the Hebrews is more biblical in his reasoning and affirms the doctrine of *creation ex nihilo*, a doctrine uncongenial to Greek thought. The faith by which he accepts it is faith in the divine revelation; the first chapter of

Genesis is probably uppermost in his mind, since he is about to trace seven living examples of faith from the subsequent chapters of that book.

Chapter Thirty: Abel's Faith

1. St. Augustine, *The City of God*, Book 15, Chapter 1, in Philip Schaff, ed., *The Nicene and Post-Nicene Fathers,* vol. 2, trans. Marcus Dods (Grand Rapids, MI: Eerdmans, 1973), p. 284.

2. The deduction that Cain was 129 when he murdered Abel is based on the collation of Genesis 4:25, "And Adam knew his wife again, and she bore a son and called his name Seth, for she said, 'God has appointed for me another offspring instead of Abel, for Cain killed him'" and 5:3, "When Adam had lived 130 years, he fathered a son in his own likeness, after his image, and named him Seth." This deduction, of course, assumes that Seth's birth came soon after Abel's death when God provided a replacement for righteous Abel. But even if there were a decade or two before the advent of Seth, the application still pertains.

3. Franz Delitzsch, *Commentary on the Epistle to the Hebrews*, vol. 2 (St. Paul, MN: Klock & Klock, 1978), p. 225 says:

> Abel's sacrifice was an expression of heartfelt thankfulness, or, as our author says, tracing the disposition of his mind to its root, an expression of his faith. But inasmuch as the relation between God and man had been disturbed by sin, Abel's faith exhibited itself in recognising and laying hold of the divine mercy in the midst of wrath and judgment,—an aspect of his personal standing with regard to sacrifice, which had its correlative in his offering being of a life and of blood. Even Hofmann recognises in Abel's sacrifice the expression of a need of atonement felt by him.

4. Paul Johnson, *Intellectuals* (New York: Harper & Row, 1988), p. 91.

5. Philip Edgcumbe Hughes, *A Commentary on the Epistle to the Hebrews* (Grand Rapids, MI: Eerdmans, 1977), pp. 454, 455.

6. F. W. Boreham, *The Crystal Pointers* (New York: Abingdon Press, 1925), p. 19.

Chapter Thirty-One: Enoch's Faith

1. James Trager, *The People's Chronology* (New York: Henry Holt and Company, 1992), pp. 229, 286, 400, 401, 782. Also helpful are: Jerome Burne, ed., *Chronicles of the World* (Mount Kisco, NY: ECAM Publications, 1988); Bernard Grum, ed., *The Timetable of History*, based on Werner Stein's *Kulturfahrplan* (New York: Simon & Schuster, 1991).

2. Philip Edgcumbe Hughes, *A Commentary on the Epistle to the Hebrews* (Grand Rapids, MI: Eerdmans, 1977), p. 457 explains: "The Septuagint, which our author echoes, has 'he pleased God' instead of 'he walked with God'; but this is not to say something different, since only he who pleases God walks with God, that is, enjoys a relationship of harmonious fellowship with him."

3. Warren W. Wiersbe, *Run with the Winners, A Study of the Champions of Hebrews 11* (Wheaton, IL: Tyndale House, 1985), p. 44.

4. Annie Dillard, *Teaching a Stone to Talk* (New York: Harper & Row, 1982), p. 69.

5. H. Dermot McDonald, *Commentary on Colossians and Philemon* (Waco, TX: Word, 1990), p. 49.

Chapter Thirty-Two: Noah's Faith

1. Lance Morrow, "Evil," in *Time* (June 10, 1991), vol. 137, no. 23, p. 48.

2. Derek Kidner, *Genesis* (Downers Grove, IL: InterVarsity Press, 1975), p. 85 says, "The term for *imagination* (*ye-s.er*) is closer to action than the English suggests: it is derived from the potter's verb 'to form' (*cf.* 2:7), and implies design or purpose."

3. Henry M. Morris, *The Genesis Record* (Grand Rapids, MI: Baker, 1976), p. 191 postulates:

> A worldwide rain lasting forty days would be quite impossible under present atmospheric conditions; so this phenomenon required an utterly different source of atmospheric waters than now obtains. This we have already seen to be the "waters above the firmament," the vast thermal blanket of invisible water vapor that maintained the greenhouse effect in the antediluvian world. These waters somehow were to condense and fall on the earth.

4. Brooke Foss Westcott, *The Epistles to the Colossians, to Philemon, and to the Ephesians* (Grand Rapids, MI: Eerdmans, 1984), p. 356 says: "The faith of Noah was directed to a special revelation which was made known to others also."

5. Leon Morris, *The Expositor's Bible Commentary*, vol. 12 (Grand Rapids, MI: Baker, 1974), p. 116 says:

> In the expression "holy fear" (*eulabe-theis*), some put the emphasis on "holy" and some on "fear." While it is true that this verb may convey the notion of fear, it is not easy to see it in this context. The author is not telling us that Noah was a timid type but that he was a man of faith. He acted out of reverence for God and God's command.

6. Philip Edgcumbe Hughes, *A Commentary on the Epistle to the Hebrews* (Grand Rapids, MI: Eerdmans, 1977), p. 464, quoting from *Sibylline Oracles* 1.125ff.

7. Francois Mauriac, *Viper's Tangle* (Garden City, NY: Image Books, 1957), p. 98.

8. The Kingston Trio, "The Merry Melody":

> They're rioting in Africa, they're starving in Spain.
> There are hurricanes in Florida, and Texas needs rain
> The whole world is seething with unhappy souls.
> The French hate the Germans, the Germans hate the Poles.
> The Poles hate the Yugoslavs, South Africans hate the Dutch.
> And I don't like anybody very much.
> But we all should be grateful and thankful and proud,
> That man's been endowed with a mushroom shaped cloud.
> And we know for certain that some lucky day,
> Someone will set the spark off and we'll all be blown away.

Chapter Thirty-Three: Abraham's Faith

1. Merrill C. Tenney, ed., *The Zondervan Pictorial Encyclopedia of the Bible*, vol. 5 (Grand Rapids, MI: Zondervan, 1975), pp. 847, 848.

2. Philo, *The Migration of Abraham*, 43, 44, vol. 4, trans. F. H. Colson and G. H. Whitaker, The Loeb Classical Library (Cambridge, MA: Harvard, 1985), p. 157:

> There is a deliberate intention when his words take the form of a promise and define the time of fulfillment not as present but future. He says not "which I am shewing" but "which I will shew thee" (Gen. xiii.1). Thus he testifies to the trust which the soul reposed in God, exhibiting its thankfulness not as called out by accomplished facts, but by expectation of what was to be. For the soul, clinging in utter dependence on a good hope, and deeming that things not present are beyond question already present by reason of the sure steadfastness of Him that promised them, has won as it [exercised] faith, a perfect good; for we read a little later "Abraham believed God" (Gen. xv.6).

3. Hugh Montefiore, *A Commentary on the Epistle to the Hebrews* (Grand Rapids, MI: Baker, 1984), p. 58.

4. F. F. Bruce, *The Epistle to the Hebrews* (Grand Rapids, MI: Eerdmans, 1984), p. 296 explains:

> Our author points out that Abraham did not receive the promise of the inheritance at the time of his first call; the land to which he was directed to go was the "place which he was to receive for an inheritance"; the promise of the inheritance was not given until he had returned from Egypt and Lot had chosen the well-watered circuit of Jordan to settle in (Gen. 13:14ff.); it was reaffirmed to him along with the promise of an heir (Gen. 15:18ff.), and again after the bestowal of the covenant of circumcision (Gen. 17:8). The divine bidding was sufficient for him at his first call, "and he went out, not knowing whither he went." The promise of the inheritance was not in the first instance an incentive to obedience; it was the reward of his obedience.

5. Jaroslav Pelikan, ed., *Luther's Works*, vol. 29 (Saint Louis: Concordia, 1987), p. 238.

6. Bruce, *The Epistle to the Hebrews*, p. 297, n. 85.

7. Leon Morris, *The Expositor's Bible Commentary*, vol. 12 (Grand Rapids, MI: Zondervan, 1981), p. 119.

8. Brooke Foss Westcott, *The Epistle to the Hebrews* (Grand Rapids, MI: Eerdmans, 1967), p. 360.

9. Bruce, *The Epistle to the Hebrews*, pp. 301, 302.

Chapter Thirty-Four: Abraham's and the Patriarchs' Faith

1. E. A. Speiser, *Genesis* (New York: Doubleday, 1964), pp. 161, 162.

2. Brooke Foss Westcott, *The Epistle to the Hebrews* (Grand Rapids, MI: Eerdmans, 1967), p. 365 explains: "The time . . . marks the immediate coincidence of the act of obedience with the call for it."

3. Ibid., p. 365 explains: "The first verb expresses the permanent result of the offering completed by Abraham in will; the second his actual readiness in preparing the sacrifice which was not literally carried into effect."

4. G. Abbott-Smith, *A Manual Greek Lexicon of the New Testament* (New York: Scribner's, n.d.), p. 270 indicates that the root idea of *logizomai* is numerical calculation that, of course, came to be used metaphorically without reference to numbers for a reckoning of characteristics or reasons.

5. Paul Hendrickson, *Seminary, a Search* (New York: Summit Books, 1983), p. 313.

Chapter Thirty-Five: Moses' Faith

1. William L. Lane, *Hebrews: A Call to Commitment* (Peabody, MA: Hendrickson, 1988), p. 58.

2. H. St. J. Thackeray, trans., *Josephus Jewish Antiquities* 2.9. 4, vol. 4 (Cambridge, MA: Harvard, 1978), p. 259.

3. John Brown, *Hebrews* (Edinburgh: Banner of Truth, 1972), p. 539 explains:

We know that, at the time this Epistle was written, it was the common faith of the Jews that such a revelation had been made. Josephus, in his "Antiquities of the Jews," Book ii. chap. v., expressly states, that a divine communication was made to Amram during the pregnancy of Jochebed, that the child about to be born was to be the deliverer of his nation from Egyptian tyranny. There is nothing in Scripture inconsistent with this. Though we have no account in Scripture of an express revelation made as to sacrifice, we conclude, from its being said that it was "by faith Abel offered a more excellent sacrifice than Cain," that such a revelation was made; and on the same principle, I cannot help considering the Apostle as here giving sanction to the commonly received belief of the Jews on this subject and stating that it was the faith of Moses' parents in this revelation that led them to act as they did, in preserving their infant's life at the risk of their own.

See also Warren Wiersbe, *Run with the Winners, A Study of the Champions of Hebrews 11* (Wheaton, IL: Tyndale House, 1985), p. 100.

4. W. B. Johnston, trans., *Calvin's Commentaries: The Epistle of Paul the Apostle to the Hebrews and the First and Second Epistle of St. Peter* (Grand Rapids, MI: Eerdmans, 1963), pp. 175, 176.

5. Simon J. Kistemaker, *Exposition of the Epistle to the Hebrews* (Grand Rapids, MI: 1984), p. 345.

6. Boris Pasternak, *Dr. Zhivago* (London: Collins and Harvill Press, 1958), p. 160.

7. F. F. Bruce, *The Epistle to the Hebrews* (Grand Rapids, MI: Eerdmans, 1964), p. 320.

8. Ibid., pp. 131, 132.

9. Brown, *Hebrews*, p. 218.

Chapter Thirty-Six: Joshua's and His People's Faith

1. C. F. Keil and F. Delitzsch, *Joshua, Judges, Ruth* (Grand Rapids, MI: Eerdmans, 1963), p. 62.

2. John Calvin, *Commentaries on the Book of Joshua*, ed. Henry Beveredge (Grand Rapids, MI: Baker, 1984), p. 88.

Chapter Thirty-Seven: Rahab's Faith

1. John J. Davis, *Conquest and Crises, Studies in Joshua, Judges and Ruth* (Grand Rapids, MI: Baker, 1976), n.p.

2. Brooke Foss Westcott, *The Epistle to the Hebrews* (Grand Rapids, MI: Eerdmans, 1967), p. 375.

3. Norman L. Geisler, *The Christian Love Ethic* (Grand Rapids, MI: Zondervan, 1979), pp. 78–80.

4. John Calvin, *Commentaries on the Book of Joshua* (Grand Rapids, MI: Baker, 1984), p. 47.

5. W. Robertson Nicoll, *The Expositor's Bible* (New York: A. C. Armstrong and Son, 1903), p. 89.

6. Geoffrey W. Bromiley, ed., *The International Standard Bible Encyclopedia*, vol. 4 (Grand Rapids, MI: Eerdmans, 1991), p. 34 explains:

> The detail about the scarlet cord (*tiqwat hût. haššanî*, v. 18) is intriguing. Elsewhere this item seems to have erotic connotations. In Cant. 4:3 the bride is said to have lips like a "scarlet thread" (*hût. haššanî*); Jeremiah associated scarlet with Israel's vain beautification (Jer. 4:30); the midwife of Tamar (who had conceived while pretending to be a prostitute; cf. Gen. 28:12–26) used a scarlet thread (*[haš]šanî*, 38:28, 30) to distinguish the newborn twins; and Isaiah linked the color with sin (Isa. 1:18). S. D. Walters has suggested that the scarlet rope may have been the mark of a prostitute—i.e., that she lived in the "red rope" district! Also since *tiqwâh* more commonly means "hope" than "rope," there may be a conscious pun here: the "rope" is the prostitute's "hope" (i.e., for customers); but now, having confessed Yahweh as God, her "rope" betokens a new kind of "hope."

7. Martin H. Woudstra, *The Book of Joshua* (Grand Rapids, MI: Eerdmans, 1983), p. 75.

8. Francis A. Schaeffer, *Joshua and the Flow of Biblical History* (Downers Grove, IL: InterVarsity Press, 1975), p. 78.

9. Abraham Kuyper, *Women of the Old Testament* (Grand Rapids, MI: Zondervan, 1961), p. 69.

10. Trent C. Butler, *Word Biblical Commentary: Joshua* (Waco, TX: Word, 1983), p. 32.

Chapter Thirty-Eight: Triumphant Faith

1. "The Gay Baby Boom," *Chicago Tribune* (September 13, 1992), Section 5, pp. 1, 2.

2. William B. Johnston, trans., *Calvin's Commentaries: The Epistle of Paul the Apostle to the Hebrews and the First and Second Epistles of St. Peter* (Grand Rapids, MI: Eerdmans, 1963), p. 182.

3. Brooke Foss Westcott, *The Epistle to the Hebrews* (Grand Rapids, MI: Eerdmans, 1967), p. 377.

4. R. H. Charles, *The Apocrypha and Pseudepigrapha of the Old Testament*, vol. 2 (London: Oxford, 1968), p. 162; cf. also TB *Sanhedrin* 103b.

5. Simon J. Kistemaker, *Exposition of the Epistle to the Hebrews* (Grand Rapids, MI: Baker, 1984), pp. 357, 358. See also Leon Morris, *The Expositor's Bible Commentary*, vol. 12 (Grand Rapids, MI: Baker, 1981), p. 132 who succinctly explains:

> But here it is not a question of "the promises" but of "the promise." God made many promises to his people and kept them. So there were many blessings that they received along the way. But the ultimate blessing (which the author characteristically sees in terms of promise) was not given under the old dispensation. God kept that until Jesus came.

6. Morris, *The Expositor's Bible Commentary*, vol. 12, pp. 132, 133.

Chapter Thirty-Nine: Consider Him

1. F. F. Bruce, *The Epistle to the Hebrews* (Grand Rapids, MI: Eerdmans, 1965), p. 346 writes:

> But in what sense are they "witnesses"? Not, probably, in the sense of spectators, watching their successors as they in their turn run the race for which they have entered; but rather in the sense that by their loyalty and endurance they have borne witness to the possibilities of the life of faith. It is not so much they who look at us as we look to them—for encouragement.

2. *Webster's 11th New Collegiate Dictionary* (Springfield, MA: G & C Merriam Co., 1971), p. 881:

> sundew: any of a genus (*Drosera* of the family Droseraceae, the sundew family) of bog-inhabiting insectivorous herbs having leaves covered with gland-tipped adhesive hairs.

3. William Barclay, *The Letter to the Hebrews* (Philadelphia: Westminster, 1957), p. 196.

4. John H. Gerstner, *The Rational Biblical Theology of Jonathan Edwards*, vol. 1 (Powhatan, VA: Berea Publications, 1991), p. 418.

5. Bruce, *The Epistle to the Hebrews*, p. 352.

6. Brooke Foss Westcott, *The Epistle to the Hebrews* (Grand Rapids, MI: Eerdmans, 1967), pp. 394, 395.

7. John Henry Cardinal Newman, *The Kingdom Within (Discourses Addressed to Mixed Congregations)* (Denville, NJ: Dimension Books, 1984), pp. 328, 329.

8. Hugh Montefiore, *A Commentary on the Epistle to the Hebrews* (London: Adam & Charles Black, 1964), p. 35.

Chapter Forty: Divine Discipline

1. R. Kent Hughes, *The Eschatological Use of 'ΟΡΓΗ in the New Testament*, a thesis presented to Talbot Theological Seminary, June 1972, pp. 31–60.

2. Theodore Laetsch, *Bible Commentary Jeremiah* (St. Louis: Concordia, 1965), pp. 234, 235.

3. John MacArthur Jr., *Hebrews* (Chicago: Moody Press, 1983), pp. 385–89. The author explains and amplifies the three types of discipline in greater detail.

4. James Moffatt, *Epistle to the Hebrews* (Edinburgh: T & T Clark, 1963), p. 201.

5. John Perkins, *Let Justice Roll Down* (Ventura, CA: Regal, 1976), p. 31.

6. John H. Gerstner, *The Rational Biblical Theology of Jonathan Edwards*, vol. 1 (Powhatan, VA: Berea Publications, 1991), p. 423, quoting from *Works* (Worcester reprint), IV, p. 174.

7. Richard John Neuhaus, *Freedom for Ministry* (Grand Rapids, MI: Eerdmans, 1979), p. 72.

Chapter Forty-One: Failing Grace

1. Art Carey, "Beating Agony and the Marathon," *Philadelphia Inquirer* (April 12, 1978).

2. Leon Morris, *The Expositor's Bible Commentary,* vol. 12 (Grand Rapids, MI: Zondervan, 1981), p. 139.

3. F. F. Bruce, *The Epistle to the Hebrews* (Grand Rapids, MI: Eerdmans, 1964), pp. 364, 365 explains:

> The verb translated "be . . . turned out of the way" should rather be rendered "be put out of joint" (ARV margin, RSV, NEB); it is dislocation and not deviation that is suggested by the following words, "but rather be healed." Sprains and similar injuries must be bound up, so that the whole community may complete the course without loss.

4. Brooke Foss Westcott, *The Epistle to the Hebrews* (Grand Rapids, MI: Eerdmans, 1967), p. 405.

5. J. R. R. Tolkien, *The Fellowship of the Ring* (New York: Ballantine, 1969), pp. 450, 451.

6. G. Abbott-Smith, *A Manual Greek Lexicon of the New Testament* (New York: Scribner's, n.d.), p. 119.

7. Westcott, *The Epistle to the Hebrews*, p. 406.

8. John Blanchard, *Truth for Life* (West Sussex, UK: H. E. Walter, Ltd., 1982), p. 254.

9. Westcott, *The Epistle to the Hebrews,* p. 406.

10. Morris, *The Expositor's Bible Commentary*, vol. 12, p. 139.

11. Westcott, *The Epistle to the Hebrews*, p. 407.

12. Philo, *Question and Answers on Genesis*, trans. Ralph Marcus, The Loeb Classical Library (Cambridge, MA: Harvard, 1979), p. 494.

13. Bruce, *The Epistle to the Hebrews*, p. 367.

14. Dietrich Bonhoeffer, *Temptation* (London: SCM Press, 1961), p. 33, writes:

> It makes no difference whether it is sexual desire, or ambition, or vanity, or desire for revenge, or love of fame and power, or greed for money, or, finally, that strange desire for the beauty of the world, of nature. Joy in God is in the course of being extinguished in us and we seek all our joy in the creature. At this moment God is quite unreal to us, he loses all reality, and only desire for the creature is real; the only reality is the devil. Satan

does not here fill us with hatred of God, but with forgetfulness of God. And now his falsehood is added to this proof of strength. The lust thus aroused envelops the mind and will of man in deepest darkness. The powers of clear discrimination and of decision are taken from us. The questions present themselves: "Is what the flesh desires really sin in this case?" "Is it really not permitted to me, yes—expected of me, now, here, in my particular situation, to appease desire?" The tempter puts me in a privileged position as he tried to put the hungry Son of God in a privileged position. I boast of my privilege against God. It is here that everything within me rises up against the Word of God.

15. William B. Johnston, trans., *Calvin's Commentaries: The Epistle of Paul the Apostle to the Hebrews and the First and Second Epistles of St. Peter* (Grand Rapids, MI: Eerdmans, 1963), p. 197.

Chapter Forty-Two: Marching to Zion

1. F. F. Bruce, *The Epistle to the Hebrews* (Grand Rapids, MI: Eerdmans, 1964), p. 371.
2. John Bunyan, *The Pilgrim's Progress* (Old Tappan, NJ: Revell, 1987), p. 23.
3. See Chapter 3 for bibliographical information on angel stories.
4. Olive Fleming Liefeld, *Unfolding Destinies* (Grand Rapids, MI: Zondervan, 1990), p. 236.
5. Bruce, *The Epistle to the Hebrews*, p. 377.
6. Brooke Foss Westcott, *The Epistle to the Hebrews* (Grand Rapids, MI: Eerdmans, 1967), p. 415.
7. Raymond Brown, *The Message of Hebrews* (Downers Grove, IL: InterVarsity Press, 1982), p. 245.

Chapter Forty-Three: A Consuming Fire

1. *Aesthetic* is used here in the original Greek idea of *aisthetikos*—sense perception.
2. Charles Colson, *Kingdoms in Conflict* (New York/Grand Rapids, MI: William Morrow/Zondervan, 1987), pp. 222, 223.

Chapter Forty-Four: Ecclesial Ethics

1. Marvin Olasky, *Abortion Rites* (Wheaton, IL: Crossway Books, 1992), p. 140, which quotes from John McDowall, *Magdalen Facts Number 1* (New York: Magdalen Society, 1832), p. 33.
2. Olasky, *Abortion Rites.*, pp. 140–142.
3. Brooke Foss Westcott, *The Epistle to the Hebrews* (Grand Rapids, MI: Eerdmans, 1967), p. 429 says: "The use of (μενέτω) suggests that the bond had been in danger of being severed."
4. Reported by George Cowan to Campus Crusade at the U.S. Division Meeting Devotions, Thursday, March 22, 1990.
5. William Barclay, *The Letter to the Hebrews* (Philadelphia: Westminster, 1957), p. 218.

6. A. M. Harmon, trans., *Lucian*, vol. 5, The Loeb Classical Library (Cambridge, MA: Harvard, 1972), p. 19.

7. Kirsopp Lake, trans., *The Apostolic Fathers*, vol. 1, The Loeb Classical Library (Cambridge, MA: Harvard, 1970), p. 327.

8. Westcott, *The Epistle to the Hebrews*, p. 430.

9. Eugene H. Peterson, *Working the Angles* (Grand Rapids, MI: Eerdmans, 1989), p. 74.

10. Harmon, *Lucian,* p. 13.

11. J. Rendel Harris, ed., *The Apology of Aristides*, "Texts and Studies," vol. 1, ed. J. Armitage Robinson (Cambridge: The University Press, 1891), pp. 48, 49.

Chapter Forty-Five: Personal Ethics

1. Philip Edgcumbe Hughes, *A Commentary on the Epistle to the Hebrews* (Grand Rapids, MI: Eerdmans, 1977), p. 556.

2. Paul Johnson, *Intellectuals* (New York: Harper & Row, 1988), p. 121 where he quotes Henri Troyat, *Tolstoy* (London, 1968), pp. 525, 526.

3. Hugh Montefiore, *A Commentary on the Epistle to the Hebrews* (London: Adam & Charles Black, 1964), p. 240.

4. William Barclay, *The Letter to the Hebrews* (Philadelphia: Westminster, 1957), p. 221.

5. C. H. Spurgeon, *The Metropolitan Tabernacle Pulpit*, vol. 24 (Pasadena, TX: Pilgrim, 1972), p. 699.

6. Henry Hart Milman, *History of Christianity*, vol. 4 (New York: Crowell, 1881), p. 144.

Chapter Forty-Six: Sustaining Wisdom

1. Paul Johnson, *Modern Times* (New York: Harper Collins, 1991), pp. 1–4.

2. F. F. Bruce, *The Epistle to the Hebrews* (Grand Rapids, MI: Eerdmans, 1964), p. 395, 396.

3. Katherine Tynan, *The Flying Wheel*.

4. Leon Morris, *The Expositor's Bible Commentary*, vol. 12 (Grand Rapids, MI: Zondervan, 1981), p. 150, and Bruce, *The Epistle to the Hebrews*, pp. 399–401.

Chapter Forty-Seven: Responsibility toward Leadership

1. Brooke Foss Westcott, *The Epistle to the Hebrews* (Grand Rapids, MI: Eerdmans, 1967), p. 444.

2. F. F. Bruce, *The Epistle to the Hebrews* (Grand Rapids, MI: Eerdmans, 1964), p. 407.

3. Philip Edgcumbe Hughes, *A Commentary on the Epistle to the Hebrews* (Grand Rapids, MI: Eerdmans, 1977), p. 586.

4. Bruce, *The Epistle to the Hebrews*, p. 408.

5. Phillips Brooks, *The Influence of Jesus* (London: H. R. Allenson, 1895), p. 91.

6. Bruce, *The Epistle to the Hebrews*, p. 408.

7. J. E. Rosscup, "The Priority of Prayer in Preaching," Richard L. Mayhue, ed., *The Master's Seminary Journal* (Spring 1991), vol. 2, no. 1, p. 42.

8. Ibid., p. 42.

9. C. H. Spurgeon, *The New Park Street Pulpit*, vol. 1 (Pasadena, TX: Pilgrim, 1975), p. 204.

Chapter Forty-Eight: Soaring Benedictions

1. Hugh Montefiore, *A Commentary on the Epistle to the Hebrews* (London: Adam & Charles Black, 1964), pp. 250, 251.
2. John A Mackay, *God's Order* (New York: Macmillan, 1953), p. 99.

Scripture Index

General Index

Index of Sermon Illustrations

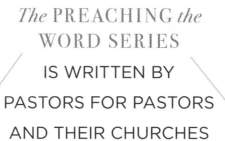

The PREACHING *the*
WORD SERIES
IS WRITTEN BY
PASTORS FOR PASTORS
AND THEIR CHURCHES